NAMING-CONSTRUCTIONS

PHILOLOGICAL MONOGRAPHS
OF THE
AMERICAN PHILOLOGICAL ASSOCIATION

NUMBER 27

Accepted for publication by the Committee on the Publication of Monographs
of the American Philological Association

Edited by John Arthur Hanson, Princeton University

NAMING-CONSTRUCTIONS

IN SOME INDO-EUROPEAN LANGUAGES

By

E. ADELAIDE HAHN

Hunter College

PUBLISHED FOR

THE AMERICAN PHILOLOGICAL ASSOCIATION

BY THE PRESS OF

CASE WESTERN RESERVE UNIVERSITY

1969

© The American Philological Association 1969

Library of Congress Catalog Number: 69–11126

SBN: 8295–0162–2

Composed by William Clowes and Sons Ltd
London and Beccles, England

Photolithographed by Cushing-Malloy, Inc.
Ann Arbor, Michigan, U.S.A.

This book, in gratitude for assistance in its composition, is dedicated to the eminent colleagues who in the true spirit of scholarship and fellowship placed their specialized knowledge at the author's disposal.

PREFACE

One whose research lies in the field of syntax can hardly hope to attain results characterized by the same degree of objectivity and certainty as those achieved by his colleagues who work in the field of phonology or of morphology. In syntax as in phonology and morphology, studies of origins must rest on a firm basis of historical and comparative investigation. This ideally demands an intensive and extensive acquaintance with many different languages which the worker in syntax—or at all events *this* worker in syntax—can hardly hope to acquire. A study of sounds and forms is to a certain extent static; one investigates individual words. But a study of the relationship of one word to another in the sentence is dynamic; one must go to the living moving language, whether embodied in speech or—our sole recourse in the many languages no longer in contemporary use—in writing. It is the author's firm conviction that no quotation should ever be made for syntactic purposes unless the passage quoted has been examined in context, as an archaeologist would fain examine his artifacts *in situ*; one should know the situation and the circumstances in connection with which the passage is used, and the characteristic style and idiom of the person who uses it. In short, the linguist must be also a philologist.

I must in this connection apologize for a defect in my equipment which has perforce given this study a lack of proportion and of personal authority. In the fields of Hittite, Old Persian, Greek, Latin, Gothic, and (to a lesser degree) Old English, I have been able to carry on personal and reasonably extended investigations, such as ought to be made by any one working in linguistic research, whether historic or descriptive. But to some extent in Sanskrit and Gaelic, and completely in Avestan, Britannic, and Tocharian, I have been obliged to depend on the examples and/or explanations most graciously and generously provided for me by specialists in these fields—though I have of course endeavored to make independent interpretations of all quotations given to me. Armenian, Balto–Slavic, and Albanian I have made no attempt to treat at all. This is a lack which, as I have said, must confront the worker in the comparative field, particularly the worker in syntax. For it I can only express my regret.

To the scholars who have helped me, either by supplying illustrative passages or by answering questions on special points which I have addressed to them, I extend sincere and heartfelt thanks; and as a slight earnest of my indebtedness, I am dedicating this book to them. In my expressions of gratitude to them for specific aid, I have left standing the present and present perfect tenses that I originally used, although, alas, in some instances these no longer apply.

EDITOR'S NOTE

The Monograph Committee of the American Philological Association enthusiastically accepted *Naming-Constructions* for publication early in July 1967. Before they could communicate that decision to Professor Hahn, they learned of her death on July 8, 1967. No changes have been made in the text, except for the correction of a handful of typographical errors. To this editor, her manuscript was characteristic of its author: well-written, accurate, marked by meticulous attention to detail. We might have argued over details of style and punctuation, but she felt strongly about such matters and had a reason for every comma—or lack of one—and she would have won most of the arguments, as I know from previous experience. So I have not tampered.

The manuscript was retyped—she had an ancient typewriter and a *horror vacui*—and Professor James Poultney read and checked the entire typescript. For his generous contribution of time and labor I am extremely grateful. It was felt that the value of the work would be enhanced by an index of passages cited; and Mr. Hunter Rawlings, a graduate student in Classics at Princeton University, prepared it. His labor in tracking down and systematizing references to Hittite and

Sanskrit texts extended far beyond the mere mechanical preparation of index cards.

Neither the index of passages nor the Table of Contents—a bare list of languages—adequately suggests the variety of material treated by Miss Hahn, especially in the notes. Despite its "monographic" subject and its rather formidable format, it is also a book for browsing, for the author's *obiter dicta* on morphology, semantics, and style, as well as on syntax. The editing of it has been a pleasure.

TABLE OF CONTENTS

BIBLIOGRAPHY

References to the works cited in the Bibliography are to pages unless there is indication to the contrary.

Documents and literary works are cited by common or self-evident abbreviations. Quotations from them are sufficient to show sense and syntax, but are not necessarily complete; there is no indication of omissions. On methods of transliteration (which are observed even in quotations from scholars who use a different system), see the following footnotes: 58, on Hittite; 158, on Sanskrit; 198, on Iranian (Avestan and Old Persian); 296 and 486, on Greek; 503, on Gothic; 584, on Old English; 707, on Old and Middle Irish; 827, on Tocharian.

AAA	*Annals of Archaeology and Anthropology.*
ACD	*The Ancient Cornish Drama*, edited and translated by Edwin Norris. 2 vols. Oxford, 1859.
AJP	*American Journal of Philology.*
Akademie	*Akademie der Wissenschaften, Philosophisch-historische Klasse* (or *Abteilung*).
Akten	*Akten des vierundzwanzigsten internationalen Orientalisten-Kongresses, München*, edited by Herbert Franke. Wiesbaden, 1959.
Alex.	*Die Geschichte von Philipp und Alexander von Macedonien aus dem Lebar Brecc*, edited and translated by Kuno Meyer. Leipzig, 1887. (*IT* 2.2.1–93.)
Ameis	*Homers Odyssee*, edited by Karl Friedrich Ameis. 2 vols. Leipzig, 1856–58.
ANET	*Ancient Near Eastern Texts Relating to the Old Testament*, edited by James B. Pritchard. Princeton, 1950.
AOF	*Archiv für Orientforschung.*
AOr.	*Archiv Orientální.*
Arndt and Gingrich	William F. Arndt and F. Wilbur Gingrich, *A Greek-English Lexicon of the New Testament and*

xiii

Other Early Christian Literature, 4th revised edition. Cambridge, 1952.

Ayres   *Beowulf*, translated by Harry Morgan Ayres. Williamsport, Pa., 1933.

Barbe   *Buhez Sante Barba, Le mystère de Sainte Barbe*, edited and translated by Émile Ernault. Nantes, 1885. (*Archives de Bretagne* 3.)

Bartholomae, *AiW*   Christian Bartholomae, *Altiranisches Wörterbuch*. Strassburg, 1904.

Bartholomae, *Ar. Forsch.*   Christian Bartholomae, *Arische Forschungen*. 3 vols. Halle, 1882–87.

Bartholomae, *Grund.*   Chr. Bartholomae, *Awestasprache und Altpersisch*. Strassburg, 1895. (*Grundriss der iranischen Philologie*, edited by Wilh. Geiger and Ernst Kuhn, vol. 1, section 1, pp. 152–248.)

Bauer   D. Walter Bauer, *Griechisch-Deutsches Wörterbuch zu den Schriften des Neuen Testaments*, 2nd edition. Giessen, 1928.

BB   *Beiträge zur Kunde der indogermanischen Sprachen*.

BBal.   *Excerpten aus dem Book of Ballymote*, edited by Kuno Meyer. Leipzig, 1887. (*IT* 2.2.94–108.)

BDD   *Togail Bruidne Da Derga*, edited by Eleanor Knott. Dublin, 1936. (*IS* 8.)

BDe.   *Buchedd Dewi o Lawysgrif Llanstephan 27*, edited by D. Simon Evans. Cardiff, 1959.

Bekker   *Carmina Homerica*, edited by Immanuel Bekker. 2 vols. Bonn, 1858.

Bell.   *Belleten*.

Benveniste, *GrVP²*   A. Meillet, *Grammaire du Vieux-Perse*, 2nd edition, corrected and enlarged by E. Benveniste. Paris, 1931.

Bernhardt, *Got. Gr.*   Ernst Bernhardt, *Kurzgefasste gotische Grammatik*. Halle, 1885.

Berry   George Ricker Berry, *A New Greek-English Lexicon to the New Testament*. New York, 1897.

BL   *The Odyssey of Homer*, translated by S. H. Butcher and A. Lang. London, 1917.

Blass   Friedrich Blass, *Grammatik des neutestamentlichen Griechisch*. Göttingen, 1896.

Blass-Debrunner   Friedrich Blass, *Grammatik des neutestamentlichen Griechisch*, revised by Albert Debrunner, 10th edition. Göttingen, 1959.

Blass–Funk	*A Greek Grammar of the New Testament and Other Early Christian Literature*, F. Blass and A. Debrunner, translated and revised from 9th–10th German edition by Robert W. Funk. Chicago, 1961.
Bloomfield, *Language*	Leonard Bloomfield, *Language*. New York, 1933.
BMer.	*Beunans Meriasek: The Life of Saint Meriasek*, edited and translated by Whitley Stokes. London, 1872.
Bolling	*Ilias Atheniensium*, edited by George Melville Bolling. Lancaster, Pa., 1950.
Bolling, *Athetized Lines*	George Melville Bolling, *The Athetized Lines of the Iliad*. Baltimore, 1944.
BoSt.	*Boghazköi-Studien*, edited by Otto Weber. 10 parts. Leipzig, 1917–24.
Bothe	M. *Atti Plauti Comoediae*, edited by Fridericus Henricus Bothe. Berlin, 1809–11.
Botkine	*Beowulf*, translated by L. Botkine. Havre, 1877.
Branwen	*Branwen Uerch Lyr*, edited by Derick S. Thomson. Dublin, 1961.
Brugmann, *Grund.*	Karl Brugmann, *Grundriss der vergleichenden Grammatik der indogermanischen Sprachen* 1–2, 2nd edition. 2 vols. Strassburg, 1897–1916.
Brugmann–Thumb	Karl Brugmann, *Griechische Grammatik*, 4th edition, revised by Albert Thumb. Munich, 1913.
BSL	*Bulletin de la Société de linguistique de Paris.*
Buck, *Comp. Gr.*	Carl Darling Buck, *Comparative Grammar of Greek and Latin*. Chicago, 1933, 4th impression 1948.
Buck, *OU*	Carl Darling Buck, *A Grammar of Oscan and Umbrian*. Boston, 1904, new printing with corrections and additions 1928.
Buck, *Syn.*	Carl Darling Buck, *A Dictionary of Selected Synonyms in the Principal Indo-European Languages*. Chicago, 1949.
Buttmann	Alexander Buttmann, *A Grammar of the New Testament Greek*, translated by J. H. Thayer. Andover, 1873.
Camerarius	*Comoediae M. Accii Plauti viginti*, edited by Joach. Camerarius and Ioan. Sambucus. Frankfort, 1593.
Child	*Beowulf*, translated by Clarence Griffin Child. Boston, 1904.

Christct
: *Homeri Iliadis Carmina*, edited by Wilhelm von Christ. Leipzig, 1884.

CJ
: *The Classical Journal.*

Clapp
: *Homer's Iliad, Books XIX–XXIV*, edited by Edward Bull Clapp. Boston, 1899.

Clark
: *The Peterborough Chronicle*, edited by Cecily Clark. London, 1958.

CO
: *The Classical Outlook.*

Conington
: *P. Vergili Maronis Opera*, edited by John Conington, 4th edition, revised by Henry Nettleship. 3 vols. London, 1881–84.

Conington, translation
: *The Poems of Virgil*, translated by John Conington. London, 1893.

Corson
: Henry Corson, *Hand-Book of Anglo-Saxon and Early English*. New York, 1871.

Couvreur, *Toch.*
: Walter Couvreur, *Hoofdzaken van de Tochaarse Klank- en Vormleer*. Leuven, 1947. (Katholicke Universiteit te Leuven, *Philologische Studien*, 2nd series, no. 4.)

Crawford
: *Beowulf*, translated by D. H. Crawford. London, 1926.

Cremer
: Hermann Cremer, *Biblio-Theological Lexicon of New Testament Greek*, translated by D. W. Simon and William Urwich. Edinburgh, 1872.

Cruickshank
: *Euripidis Bacchae*, edited by A. H. Cruickshank. Oxford, 1894.

Curme Vol.
: *Curme Volume of Linguistic Studies*, edited by James Taft Hatfield, Werner Leopold, and A. J. Friedrich Zieglschmid. Baltimore, preface dated 1930. (*Language Monograph 7.*)

CW
: *The Classical Weekly*, later *The Classical World.*

Darmestetter, *Ét. ir.*
: James Darmestetter, *Études iraniennes*. 2 vols. Paris, 1883.

Delbrück, *AS*
: B. Delbrück, *Altindische Syntax*. Halle, 1888. (*SF 5.*)

Delbrück, *AW*
: B. Delbrück, *Die altindische Wortfolge aus dem Çatapathabrāhmaṇa*. Halle, 1878. (*SF 3.*)

Delbrück, *Grund.*
: B. Delbrück, *Vergleichende Syntax der indogermanischen Sprachen*. 3 vols. Strassburg, 1893–1900. (*Grundriss der vergleichenden Grammatik der indogermanischen Sprachen 3–5.*)

Dobbie — *Beowulf and Judith*, edited by Elliott Van Kirk Dobbie. New York, 1953.

Doederlein — *Homeri Ilias*, edited by D. Ludovicus Doederlein. 2 parts. Leipzig, 1863–64.

Edgerton, *VV* — Maurice Bloomfield, Franklin Edgerton, and (vol. 3) Murray Barnson Emeneau, *Vedic Variants*. 3 vols. Philadelphia, 1930–34.

Em. — *Tochmarc Emire* = *Compert Con Culainn and Other Stories* 16–68, edited by A. G. Van Hamel. Dublin, 1933. (*IS* 3.)

Ernout and Meillet — A. Ernout and A. Meillet, *Dictionnaire étymologique de la langue latine*, new edition. Paris, 1939.

Ernout and Thomas — Alfred Ernout and François Thomas, *Syntaxe latine*. Paris, 1951.

Et. — *Tochmarc Etáine*, edited by Ernst Windisch. Leipzig, 1880. (*IT* 1.113–33.)

Ettmüller — *Beowulf*, translated by Ludwig Ettmüller. Zurich, 1840.

EtymMag. — *Etymologicon Magnum*, edited by Fridericus Sylburgius. Leipzig, 1816.

Fairclough and Brown — *Virgil's Aeneid Books I–VI*, edited by H. R. Fairclough and Seldon L. Brown. Boston, 1908.

Festgruss Roth — *Festgruss an Rudolf von Roth zum Doktor-Jubiläum*, editor not named, preface signed by Ernst Kuhn. Stuttgart, 1893.

Forbiger — *P. Vergili Maronis Opera*, edited by Albertus Forbiger, 4th edition. 4 vols. Leipzig, 1872–75.

Friedrich *El.* — Johannes Friedrich, *Hethitisches Elementarbuch*. 2 parts. Heidelberg, 1940–46.

Friedrich, *Ges.* — *Die Hethitischen Gesetze*, edited by Johannes Friedrich. Leiden, 1959.

Friedrich, *Vert.* — *Staatsverträge des Ḫatti-Reiches in hethitischer Sprache*, edited by Johannes Friedrich. 2 parts. Leipzig, 1926–30. (*MVAG* 31 and 34.)

Friedrich, *Wört.* — Johannes Friedrich, *Hethitisches Wörterbuch*. Heidelberg, 1952.

Gaedicke — Carl Gaedicke, *Der Accusativ im Veda*. Breslau, 1880.

Garnett — *Beowulf*, translated by James M. Garnett, 4th edition. Boston, 1906.

Gauthiot — R. Gauthiot, *Le fin de mot en indo-européen*. Paris, 1913.

Gehring — Augustus Gehring, *Index Homericus*. Leipzig, 1891.

Genzmer — *Beowulf*, translated by Felix Genzmer. Stuttgart, 1953.

Gering — *Beowulf nebst dem Finnsburg-Bruchstücke*, translated by Hugo Gering, 2nd edition. Heidelberg, 1929.

Gildersleeve-Lodge — B. L. Gildersleeve and Gonzalez Lodge, *Gildersleeve's Latin Grammar*, 3rd edition. Boston, 1894.

Gl. — *Glotta.*

Goetz and Schoell — T. *Macci Plauti Comoediae*, edited by Georgius Goetz and Fridericus Schoell. 3 vols. Leipzig, 1893–96.

Goetze, *Kizz.* — Albrecht Goetze, *Kizzuwatna and the Problem of Hittite Geography*. New Haven, 1940.

Goodwin, *GMT* — William Watson Goodwin, *Syntax of the Moods and Tenses of the Greek Verb*, revised edition. Boston, 1900.

Götze, *AM* — *Die Annalen des Muršiliš*, edited by Albrecht Götze. Leipzig, 1933. (*MVAG* 38.)

Götze, *Hatt.* — *Ḫattušiliš*, edited by Albrecht Götze. Leipzig, 1925. (*MVAG* 29.)

Götze, *Kleinasien* — Albrecht Götze, *Kleinasien zur Hethiterzeit*. Heidelberg, 1924. (*Orient und Antike* 1.)

Götze, *Madd.* — *Madduwattaš*, edited by Albrecht Götze. Leipzig, 1928. (*MVAG* 32.)

Götze, *MS* — *Muršilis Sprachlähmung*, edited by Albrecht Götze and Holger Pedersen. Copenhagen, 1934. (*Selskab* 21.1.)

Grandgent — C. H. Grandgent, *An Introduction to Vulgar Latin*. Boston, 1907.

Grein — C. W. M. Grein, *Sprachschatz der angelsächsischen Dichter*. 2 vols. Cassel and Göttingen, 1861–64. (*Bibliothek der angelsächsischen Poesie* 3–4.)

Gummere — *Beowulf, The Oldest English Epic*, translated by Francis B. Gummere. New York, 1923.

Güterbock, *Kum.* — *Kumarbi*, edited by Hans Gustave Güterbock. Zürich and New York, 1946.

Hahn, *Coordination* — E. Adelaide Hahn, *Coordination of Non-Coordinate Elements in Vergil*. Geneva, N.Y., 1930.

Hall   *Beowulf,* translated by Jno. Leslie Hall. Boston,
                        1898.
Hall-Wrenn   *Beowulf,* translated by John R. Clark Hall,
                        revised by C. L. Wrenn. London, 1950.
Harpers'   *A New Latin Dictionary,* edited by E. A. Andrews,
                        revised by Charlton T. Lewis and Charles
                        Short. New York, 1879.
Harrison and Sharp   *Beowulf,* edited by James A. Harrison and Robert
                        Sharp, 4th edition. Boston, 1894.
Henry   James Henry, *Aeneidea.* 4 vols. Dublin, 1889.
Herzfeld, *ApI*   Ernst Herzfeld, *Altpersische Inschriften.* Berlin,
                        1938.
Heyne   *Homeri Carmina,* edited by C. G. Heyne. 9 vols.
                        Leipzig, 1802–22.
Heyne-Schücking   *Beowulf,* edited by Moritz Heyne, revised by
                        Levin L. Schücking, 14th edition. Paderborn,
                        1931.
Hofmann, *Lat. Gr.*   Manu Leumann and Joh. Bapt. Hofmann,
                        Stolz-Schmalz Lateinische Grammatik, 5th edi-
                        tion. Munich, 1928.
Holder   *Beowulf,* edited by Alfred Holder, 3rd edition.
                        2 vols. Freiburg, 1895–99.
Holthausen   *Beowulf,* edited by F. Holthausen, 7th edition.
                        2 vols. Heidelberg, 1938.
Hoopes   Johannes Hoopes, *Kommentar zum Beowulf.* Hei-
                        delberg, 1932.
Hrozný, *CH*   Frédéric Hrozný, *Code hittite provenant de l'Asie
                        Mineure.* Paris, 1922.
Hrozný, *SH*   Friedrich Hrozný, *Die Sprache der Hethiter.*
                        Leipzig, 1917. (*BoSt.* 1.)
Humbert   Jean Humbert, *Syntaxe grecque.* Paris, 1945.
Huyshe   *Beowulf,* translated by Wentworth Huyshe.
                        London, no date.
IF   *Indogermanische Forschungen.*
IJ   *Indogermanisches Jahrbuch.*
IS   *Mediaeval and Modern Irish Series.*
IT   *Irische Texte,* edited by Wh. Stokes (vol. 2) and
                        E. Windisch.
JA   *Journal Asiatique.*
Jackson, *Av. Gr.*   A. V. Williams Jackson, *An Avesta Grammar in
                        Comparison with Sanskrit.* Boston, 1892.
JAOS   *Journal of the American Oriental Society.*

JCS — Journal of Cuneiform Studies.

JNES — Journal of Near Eastern Studies.

Johnson, GrAP — Edwin Lee Johnson, Historical Grammar of the Ancient Persian Language. New York, 1917.

Kent, OP — Roland G. Kent, Old Persian. OP¹ = 1st edition, New Haven, 1950. OP² = 2nd edition, New Haven, 1953. References not specially designated apply to either edition.

Kirtlan — The Story of Beowulf, translated by Ernest J. B. Kirtlan. London, 1913.

Klaeber — Beowulf and the Fight at Finnsburg, edited by Fr. Klaeber. Boston, 1922.

KlF — Kleinasiatische Forschungen.

Knapp — The Aeneid of Vergil, Books I–VI, Selections VII–XII, edited by Charles Knapp, revised edition. Chicago, 1928.

Körös — Analecta Orientalia Memoriae Alexandri Csoma de Körös Dicata. Budapest, 1942. (Bibliotheca Orientalis Hungarica 5.)

Kraeling — Emil G. Kraeling, The Brooklyn Museum Aramaic Papyri. New Haven, 1953.

Kramer — Mythologies of the Ancient World, edited by Samuel Noah Kramer. Garden City, N.Y., 1961.

Krebs-Schmalz, Antibarbarus — J. Ph. Krebs, Antibarbarus der lateinischen Sprache, 7th edition, revised by J. H. Schmalz. 2 vols. Basel, 1905–7.

KZ — Zeitschrift für vergleichende Sprachforschung auf dem Gebiete der indogermanischen Sprachen.

Lane, SKG — George S. Lane, Studies in Kuchean Grammar I. Baltimore, 1952. (Supplement to JAOS 13.)

Lang, Myth — Andrew Lang, Myth, Ritual and Religion. 2 vols. London, 1906.

Laroche, Onom. — Emmanuel Laroche, Recueil d'onomastique hittite. Paris, 1952.

LC — Literarisches Centralblatt.

Leaf, LLM: see LLM.

Leo — Plauti Comoediae, edited by Fridericus Leo. 2 vols. Berlin, 1895–96.

Leonard — Beowulf, translated by William Ellery Leonard. New York, 1923.

Leskien — A. Leskien, Handbuch der altbulgarischen (altkirchenslavischen) Sprache. Heidelberg, 1955.

Leumann, *Lat. Gr.*: see Hofmann, *Lat. Gr.*

Lg.   *Language.*

Lindsay   *The Captivi of Plautus*, edited by W. M. Lindsay.
                           London, 1900.

LL   Book of Leinster (excerpt "The Power of
                           Women"), edited by Julius Pokorny. Halle,
                           1923. (*Historical Reader* 12–15.)

LLM   *The Iliad of Homer*, translated by Andrew Lang,
                           Walter Leaf, and Ernest Myers, revised edition.
                           New York, 1915.

Lodge   Gonzalez Lodge, *Lexicon Plautinum.* 2 vols.
                           Leipzig, 1904–33.

LSJM   Henry George Liddell and Robert Scott, *A
                           Greek-English Lexicon*, revised by Henry Stuart
                           Jones and Roderick McKenzie. 2 vols. Oxford,
                           1925–40.

Mackail, *Lat. Lit*   J. W. Mackail, *Latin Literature.* New York, 1895.

Mackail, translation   *The Aeneid of Virgil*, translated by J. W. Mackail.
                           London, 1931.

Martin   *Buchedd Sant Martin*, edited by Evan John Jones.
                           Cardiff, 1945.

Meillet, *Altarm. El.*   A. Meillet, *Altarmenisches Elementarbuch.* Heidel-
                           berg, 1913.

Meillet, *Arm. cl.*   A. Meillet, *Esquisse d'une grammaire comparée de
                           l'arménien classique*, 2nd edition. Vienne, 1936.

Meillet, *GrVP*   A. Meillet, *Grammaire du vieux perse.* Paris, 1915.

Meillet, *Introd.*   A. Meillet, *Introduction à l'étude comparative des
                           langues indo-européennes*, 7th edition. Paris, 1934.

Mélanges Navarre   *Mélanges offerts a* [sic] *M. Octave Navarre par ses
                           élèves et ses amis.* Toulouse, 1935.

Merry   *Homer's Odyssey, Books I–XII*, edited by Walter
                           Merry and James Riddell, 2nd edition. Oxford,
                           1886.

Mer. Uil.   *Merugud Uilix Maic Leirtis*, edited by Robert T.
                           Meyer. Dublin, 1958. (*IS* 17.)

Miklosich   Franz Miklosich, *Vergleichende Grammatik der
                           slavischen Sprachen*, 2nd edition. 4 vols. Vienna,
                           1875–83.

Monro   *Homer's Odyssey, Books XIII–XXIV*, edited by
                           D. B. Monro. Oxford, 1901.

Morgan   *Beowulf*, translated by Edwin Morgan. Aldington,
                           1952.

Morris and Wyatt   *Beowulf*, translated by William Morris and A. J. Wyatt. London, 1898.
MSL   *Mémoires de la Société de linguistique de Paris.*
MSS   *Münchener Studien zur Sprachwissenschaft.*
MVAG   *Mitteilungen der Vorderasiatisch-Aegyptischen Gesellschaft (E. V.).*
Myers, *LLM*: see *LLM*.
Nonne   *Buez Santes Nonn, Vie de Sainte Nonne*, edited and translated by E. Ernault. Paris, 1887. (*RC* 8.230–301, 405–91.)
O   *Ordinale de Origine Mundi*, edited and translated by Edwin Norris. Oxford, 1859. (*ACD* 1.1–219.)
Oppert, *Mèdes*   Jules Oppert, *Le peuple et la langue des Mèdes.* Paris, 1879.
Otten, *MGK*   Heinrich Otten, *Mythen vom Gotte Kumarbi.* Berlin, 1950. (Deutsche Akademie der Wissenschaften zu Berlin, Institut für Orientforschung 3.)
Otten, *Pud.*   *Das Gelübde der Königin Puduḫepa an die Göttin Lelwani*, edited by Heinrich Otten and Vladimir Souček. Wiesbaden, 1965.
Page   *The Aeneid of Virgil, Books I–VI*, edited by T. E. Page. London, 1894.
Paley   *The Iliad of Homer*, edited by F. A. Paley. 2 vols. London, 1866–71.
Paley, *Hesiod*   *The Epics of Hesiod*, edited by F. A. Paley, 2nd edition. London, 1883.
Pascon   *Pascon agan Arluth*, edited and translated by Whitley Stokes. London, 1862. (*TPS* for 1860–61, Appendix 1–100.)
Patrice   *Buez Sant Patrice, La Vie de Saint Patrice*, edited and translated by Joseph Dunn. Paris, 1909.
Patrick   *The Tripartite Life of Patrick*, edited and translated by Whitley Stokes. 2 vols. London, 1887.
Peck, *Classical Philology* Harry Thurston Peck, *A History of Classical Philology.* New York, 1911.
Pedersen, *KG*   Holger Pedersen, *Vergleichende Grammatik der keltischen Sprachen.* 2 vols. Göttingen, 1909–13.
Pedersen, *Toch.*   Holger Pedersen, *Tocharisch vom Gesichtspunkt der indoeuropäischen Sprachvergleichung.* Copenhagen, 1941. (*Selskab* 28.1.)

Peerlkamp	*P. Virgili Maronis Aeneidos Libri*, edited by P. Hofman Peerlkamp. 2 vols. Leiden, 1843–45.
Pierquin	*Le poème anglo-saxon de Beowulf*, translated by Humbert Pierquin. Paris, 1912.
Plummer, *Bede*	*Venerabilis Baedae Historia Ecclesiae*, edited by Carolus Plummer. Oxford, no date, preface dated 1895.
Plummer, *Chronicles*	*Two of the Saxon Chronicles*, edited by Charles Plummer, on the basis of an edition by John Earle. 2 vols. Oxford, 1892–99.
Pokorny, *Historical Reader*	*A Historical Reader of Old Irish*, edited by Julius Pokorny. Halle, 1923.
Prokosch, *Comp. Germ. Gram.*	E. Prokosch, *A Comparative Germanic Grammar.* Philadelphia, 1939.
Pwyll	*Pwyll Pendeuic Dyuet*, edited by R. L. Thomson. Dublin, 1957.
R	*Ordinale de Resurrexione Domini Nostri Jhesu Christi*, edited and translated by Edwin Norris. Oxford, 1859. (*ACD* 2.1–200.)
RA	*Revue d'assyriologie*, later *Revue d'assyriologie et d'archéologie orientale.*
RBH	*The Red Book of Hergest*, edited by John Rhys and J. Gwenogvryn Egans. 2 vols. Oxford, 1887–90. References are to vol. 2, *The Bruts.*
RC	*Revue celtique.*
Renou	Louis Renou, *Grammaire sanscrite.* 2 vols. Paris, 1930.
RHA	*Revue hittite et asianique.*
RhM	*Rheinisches Museum für Philologie.*
Ribbeck	*P. Vergili Maronis Opera*, edited by Otto Ribbeck. Leipzig, 1898.
Robertson	A. T. Robertson, *A Grammar of the Greek New Testament in the Light of Historical Research.* New York, 1914.
Robinson	Edward Robinson, *A Greek and English Lexicon of the New Testament*, new edition. New York, 1850.
Schaeder, *Ariaramnes*	Hans Heinrich Schaeder, *Über die Inschrift des Ariaramnes.* Berlin, 1931. (*Sitzungsberichte der Preussischen Akademie*, 1931, 635–45.)
Schipper	*König Alfreds Übersetzung von Bedas Kirchengeschichte*, edited by Jacob Schipper. Leipzig, 1899. (*Bibliothek der angelsächsischen Prosa* 4.)

Schirlitz   S. Ch. Schirlitz, *Griechisch-Deutsches Wörterbuch zum Neuen Testamente*. Giessen, 1858.

Schmidt, *Plur.*   Johannes Schmidt, *Die Pluralbildungen der indogermanischen Neutra*. Weimar, 1889.

Schulze, *Kl. Schr.*   Wilhelm Schulze, *Kleine Schriften*. Göttingen, 1933.

Schwyzer, *Gr. Gr.*   Eduard Schwyzer, *Griechische Grammatik*. 2 vols. 2nd vol. completed and edited by Albert Debrunner. Munich, 1934–50.

Schwyzer, *Parenth.*   Eduard Schwyzer, *Die Parenthese im engern und im weitern Sinne*. Berlin, 1939. (*Abhandlungen der Preussischen Akademie 1939.6.*)

ScM (Thurneysen)   *Scéla Mucce Maic Dáthó, Die Geschichte vom Schweine des Mác Dáthó*, edited by Rudolf Thurneysen. Dublin, 1935. (*IS* 6.)

ScM (Windisch)   *Scél mucci Mic Dáthó*, edited by Ernst Windisch. Leipzig, 1880. (*IT* 1.93–112.)

Sedgefield   *Beowulf*, edited by W. J. Sedgefield, 2nd edition. Manchester, 1913.

Selskab   *Det Kgl. Danske Videnskabernes Selskab, Historisk-filologiske Meddelelser.*

Seymour   *The First Six Books of Homer's Iliad*, edited by Thomas D. Seymour, revised edition. Boston, 1901.

SF   *Syntaktische Forschungen*, edited by B. Delbrück and (vols. 1–3) E. Windisch. 5 vols. 1871–88.

Sievers, *OEGr.*   Eduard Sievers, *An Old English Grammar*, translated by Albert S. Cook. Boston, 1899.

Skeat, *Dialects*   Walter W. Skeat, *English Dialects from the Eighth Century to the Present Day*. Cambridge, 1911.

Skeat, *Gospels*   *The Holy Gospels in Anglo-Saxon, Northumbrian, and Old Mercian Versions, Synoptically Arranged*, edited by Rev. Walter W. Skeat. 4 vols. Cambridge, 1871–87.

Sommer, *AU*   *Die Aḫḫijavā-Urkunden*, edited by Ferdinand Sommer. Munich, 1932. (*Abhandlungen der Bayerischen Akademie*, NS 6.)

Sommer, *Heth.*   Ferdinand Sommer, *Hethitisches* [1]. Leipzig, 1920. (*BoSt.* 4.)

Sommer, *HAB*   *Die hethitisch-akkadische Bilingue des Ḫattušili I. (Labarna II.)*, edited by Ferdinand Sommer and

Adam Falkenstein. Munich, 1938. (*Abhandlungen der Bayerischen Akademie*, NS 16.)

Sommer, *Hdb.* — Ferdinand Sommer, *Handbuch der lateinischen Laut- und Formenlehre*, 2nd and 3rd edition. Heidelberg, 1914, reprinted 1948.

Sommer and Ehelolf, *Pap.* — *Das hethitische Ritual des Pāpanikri von Komana*, edited by Ferdinand Sommer and Hans Ehelolf. Leipzig, 1924. (*BoSt.* 10.)

Souter, *NT* — *Novum Testamentum Graece*, edited by Alexander Souter. Oxford, 1910.

Speijer, *SS* — J. S. Speijer, *Sanskrit Syntax*. Leyden, 1886.

Speyer, *VSS* — S. Speyer, *Vedische und Sanskrit-Syntax*. Strassburg, 1890. (*Grundriss der Indo-Arischen Philologie und Altertumskunde*, edited by George Bühler, 1.6.)

Spiegel, *GrAS* — Fr. Spiegel, *Vergleichende Grammatik der altiranischen Sprachen*. Leipzig, 1882.

Spiegel, *Keil.* — Fr. Spiegel, *Die altpersischen Keilinschriften*, 2nd edition. Leipzig, 1881.

SS — E. Sieg and W. Siegling, *Tocharische Sprachreste*. Berlin and Leipzig, 1921.

SS, *B* — E. Sieg and W. Siegling, *Tocharische Sprachreste, Sprache B*. 2 vols. Göttingen, 1949–53.

SSS — Emil Sieg and Wilhelm Siegling, with Wilhelm Schulze, *Tocharische Grammatik*. Göttingen, 1931.

Steineck — *Beowulf*, translated by H. Steineck. Leipzig, 1898.

Streitberg, *GotB* — *Die gotische Bibel*, edited by Wilhelm Streitberg. 2 parts. Heidelberg, 1908–10.

Streitberg, *Got. El.* — Wilhelm Streitberg, *Gotisches Elementarbuch*. Heidelberg, 1910.

Strong — *Beowulf*, translated by Archibald Strong. London, 1925.

Sturtevant, *Chr.* — Edgar H. Sturtevant and George Bechtel, *A Hittite Chrestomathy*. Philadelphia, 1935, 2nd printing 1952.

Sturtevant, *Gl.* — Edgar H. Sturtevant, *A Hittite Glossary*, 2nd edition. Philadelphia, 1936.

Sturtevant, *HG* — Edgar H. Sturtevant, *A Comparative Grammar of the Hittite Language*. HG^1 = 1st edition, Philadelphia, 1933. HG^2 = 2nd edition, New Haven, 1951.

Sweet, *Dict.* Henry Sweet, *The Student's Dictionary of Anglo-Saxon.* New York. 1911.

Szantyr J. B. Hofmann, *Lateinische Syntax und Stilistik,* revised by Anton Szantyr. Munich, 1965.

Tain (St.) Stories from the *Táin,* edited by John Strachan, 3rd edition, revised by Osborn Bergin. Dublin, 1944.

Tain (YBL) *The Táin Bó Cuailnge from the Yellow Book of Lecan,* edited by John Strachan and J. G. O'Keeffe. Dublin, 1912.

TAPA *Transactions of the American Philological Association.*

Thayer Joseph Henry Thayer, *A Greek-English Lexicon of the New Testament,* being Grimm's Wilke's *Clavis Novi Testamenti,* translated and revised, corrected edition. New York, 1889.

Thes. *Thesaurus Palaeohibernicus,* edited by Whitley Stokes and John Strachan. 2 vols. Cambridge, 1901–3.

Thieme, P. Thieme, *Untersuchungen zur Wortkunde und* *Untersuchungnen* *Auslegung des Rigveda.* Halle, 1949. (*Hallische Monographien,* edited by Otto Eissfeldt, 7.)

Thilo *Servii Grammatici qui feruntur in Vergilii Carmina Commentarii,* edited by Georgius Thilo and Hermannus Hagen. 3 vols. Leipzig, 1923–27.

Thorpe *Beowulf,* translated by Benjamin Thorpe, 3rd edition. London, 1889.

Thurneysen Rudolf Thurneysen, *A Grammar of Old Irish,* revised and enlarged edition, translated by D. A. Binchy and Osborn Bergin. Dublin, 1946.

Tinker *Beowulf,* translated by Chauncey Brewster Tinker. New York, 1902.

Tolman, *Lex.* Herbert Cushing Tolman, *Ancient Persian Lexicon and the Texts of the Achaemenidan Inscriptions.* New York, 1908.

TPS *Transactions of the Philological Society.*

Trautmann *Die altpreussischen Sprachdenkmäler,* edited by Reinhold Trautmann. Göttingen, 1910.

Troi *Togail Troi, The Destruction of Troy,* edited and translated by Wh. Stokes. Leipzig, 1884. (*IT* 2.1.1–142.)

Uisl.   *Longes Mac n-Uislenn, The Exile of the Sons of Uisliu,* edited by Vernam Hull. New York, 1949.

Uisn.   *Oided mac nUisnig, The Death of the Sons of Uisnech,* edited and translated by Whitley Stokes. Leipzig, 1887. (*IT* 2.2.109–84.)

Usn.   *Longes mac n-Usnig, Die Verbannung der Söhne Usnech's,* edited by Ernst Windisch. Leipzig, 1880. (*IT* 1.59–92.)

Ventris and Chadwick, *Doc.*   Michael Ventris and John Chadwick, *Documents in Mycenaean Greek.* Cambridge, 1959.

Wackernagel, *AiG*   Jacob Wackernagel, *Altindische Grammatik.* 3 vols., vol. 2.2 by Albert Debrunner, vol. 3 by Albert Debrunner and Jacob Wackernagel. 1896–1954.

Wackernagel, *Vorlesungen*   Jacob Wackernagel, *Vorlesungen über Syntax,* 2nd edition. 2 vols. Basel, 1926–28, reprinted 1950–57.

Wb.   *The Old Irish Glosses at Würzburg and Carlsruhe,* edited and translated by Whitley Stokes. Hertford, 1887.

Wd.   *Word.*

Whitney   William Dwight Whitney, *Sanskrit Grammar,* 2nd edition, 5th issue. Cambridge, 1923.

Winer   Georg Benedict Winer, *Grammatik des neutestamentlichen Sprachidioms als sichere Grundlage der neutestamentlichen Exegese,* 5th edition. Leipzig, 1844.

Winer-Lünemann   Georg Benedict Winer, *A Grammar of the Idiom of the New Testament,* 7th edition, revised and translated by Gottlieb Lünemann. Andover, 1872.

Winer-Moulton   G. B. Winer, *A Treatise on the Grammar of New Testament Greek,* translated by W. F. Moulton. Edinburgh, 1870.

Winer-Schmiedel   Georg Benedict Winer's *Grammatik des neutestamentlichen Sprachidioms,* 8th edition, revised by Paul Wilh. Schmiedel. Göttingen, 1894.

Winkler, *Germ. Casussyntax*   Heinrich Winkler, *Germanische Casussyntax.* Berlin, 1896.

Wolf   *Theogonia Hesiodi,* edited by Frid. Aug. Wolf. Halle, 1783.

WP   Alois Walde, *Vergleichendes Wörterbuch der indo-germanischen Sprachen*, edited and revised by Julius Pokorny. 2 vols. Berlin and Leipzig, 1927–30.

Wrede   *Ulfilas, Stamm-Heyne's* [i.e. edition by Friedrich Ludwig Stamm and Moritz Heyne], *oder die uns erhaltenen Denkmäler der gotischen Sprache*, edited by Ferdinand Wrede, 13th and 14th edition. Paderborn, 1920.

Wrenn   *Beowulf with the Finnesburg Fragment*, edited by C. L. Wrenn. Boston, no date (preface dated 1953).

Wright, *Gr. Goth.*   Joseph Wright, *Grammar of the Gothic Language*. Oxford, 1917.

Wright, *OEGr.*   Joseph Wright and Elizabeth Mary Wright, *Old English Grammar*. London, 1908.

WS   *Wörter und Sachen.*

Wyatt-Chambers   *Beowulf with the Finnsburg Fragment*, edited by A. J. Wyatt, revised by R. W. Chambers. Cambridge, 1914, reprinted 1952.

WZKM   *Wiener Zeitschrift für die Kunde des Morgenlandes.*

ZA   *Zeitschrift für Assyriologie.*

ZCP   *Zeitschrift für celtische Philologie.*

ZDMG   *Zeitschrift der Deutschen morgenländischen Gesellschaft.*

PRELIMINARY REMARKS

1. In a paper published in 1954 (*TAPA* 85.197–289), in which I dealt, on the basis of a study of Homer, with two syntactic phenomena, partitive apposition and the so-called Greek accusative, I endeavored to prove that the second is derived from the first. In the paper in question I confined myself to those manifestations of the supposed accusative of specification which truly merit the name of *accusativus graecus*, being practically restricted to that language (or its artificial imitations by Hellenizing Roman writers). One particular type of accusative of specification, which must be due at least indirectly to an inherited usage, I merely touched upon in passing, promising further treatment elsewhere (288 fn. 298). This promise is being fulfilled in the present study, which, as new by-paths opened up to be explored, has grown from the anticipated paper to a full-sized monograph.

2. The usage is that involved in the so-called accusative of specification *onoma* 'in name'. Like the word for 'name' itself,[1] a peculiar use involving the word is strikingly widespread among Indo–European languages,[2] but I question whether its source has been correctly identified. Constructions that are more or less like those of Greek in one way or another, or that at least merit study in this connection, occur in all

---

[1] Apparently all the Indo–European languages, certainly all the important Indo–European languages, except Lithuanian and Lettish, use words for 'name' derived, though with considerable variation, from the same root (see Buck, *Syn.* 1263–64; also WP 1.132). Thus the words for 'name' surpass even those for 'father' in their uniformity. (It should be noted here that for the sake of convenience and uniformity, I am using *Indo–European* to include Hittite, though I am not at all sure that this is really desirable; cf. Lane, *Lg.* 37.472 and fn. 12a; Goetze apud Lane, ib.; and Sturtevant, *Lg.* 38.105–10. However, for my purposes it does not make any appreciable difference whether we call the *Ursprache* Indo–Hittite or Indo–European, and whether we assume Hittite to be derived from Indo–Hittite or from an early form of Indo–European.)

[2] Blümel (*IF* 33.27) holds that the construction is an independent development in each of the languages exhibiting it, but he is alone, I believe, in denying its inheritance from Indo–European.

the principal Indo–European groups[3] except Germanic, although those in Latin are in my opinion borrowings from Greek, and those in Tocharian may, I am told, be similar borrowings from Sanskrit.[4] Armenian uses *anun* just as Greek does *onoma*.[5] The accusative of specification *nomen* does not, so far as I know, exist in Celtic or in Slavic,[6] but the stuff out of which I believe it to have developed is present at least in Old Irish.[7] However, the principal illustrations come from Hittite, Indo–Iranian (notably Old Persian), and Greek; and it is to

[3] Also in Semitic. See fn. 62 on Akkadian, and fn. 208 on Aramaic. For an attempt, unsuccessful in my opinion, to connect the Semitic and Indo–European words for 'name', see fn. 59.

[4] The Latin examples that might perhaps be cited, e.g. Vergil, *Aen.* 3.614, 3.693, and 12.515 (on which see below, §§148, 156, and 148 respectively), do not constitute evidence for Italic, since, as I have just pointed out (§1), they are clearly literary imitations of Greek. On the origin and development of the Greek accusative in Latin, see my paper in *TAPA* 91.221–38. As for the relation of Tocharian to Sanskrit, see below, §264 and fn. 828.

[5] Meillet, *Altarm. El.* 78 and *Arm. cl.* 94; Blümel, *IF* 53.108. Meillet quotes a particularly interesting example from the Bible, *Lk.* 1.5, in which a Greek dative of specification *onomati* 'in name' is rendered by an Armenian "accusative of specification" *anun*: khananay omn anun Zakharia (for the Greek version and for the Latin, Gothic, and Old English translations of the same passage, see below, §§177, 180, 181, and 197).

[6] Slavic does occasionally, though rarely, employ an accusative of specification, but apparently the usage is restricted to parts of the body. See Miklosich 4.392.

[7] Celtic and Slavic also illustrate the quite different stuff out of which many scholars believe the accusative of specification to have developed. This is the interpolated parenthetical "Nominalsatz". Osthoff (*LC* 1880 col. 1469–70) and Brugmann (*IF* 27.143–46) trace the supposed accusative of specification 'in name' to a misunderstood nominative in such a clause (see below, §6 and fn. 15). I believe, in opposition to them, that positive examples of this construction are not met in Indo–Iranian or in Greek (similarly Schmidt, *ZCP* 28.230); but I admit that they *are* met in Celtic and in Slavic. Though I would not so class all the Old Irish passages that are thought to exemplify this construction, there assuredly are some, e.g. *Scala Mucc* 1 (this will be treated below, in §238).

As for Slavic, Hermann, *IF* 48.25, cites an example from Old Church Slavonic that has often been quoted from him (e.g. by Blümel, *IF* 53.108; Humbach, *MSS* 5.91; Schmidt, *ZCP* 28.233). This is from the story of Isaac in the Codex Suprasliensie (given in Leskien 238) Césarъ prizъva dъva boljarina, imę jedъ nomu Saternikъ a druguumu Uiktor 'the emperor called two noblemen—the name to one (was) Satornik, to the other Victor'. Professor Roman Jakobson tells me that there are other instances in Old Church Slavonic.

An attempt has been made to recognize a similar instance in Germanic (Old English): see Foy, *IF* 12.178; Brugmann, *IF* 27.144; Hermann, *IF* 48.25 (he incorrectly refers to the language involved as "altnordisch"); Humbach, *MSS* 5.91; Schmidt, *ZCP* 28.230. All these scholars quote the same passage, *Beowulf* 1457; all of them, I regret to say, are in serious error, since they all misinterpret a misinterpretation of a different sort made by Gray, *IF* 11.309. See below, §§207–23; also my article in *Lg.* 37.479–83.

occurrences in these languages that I shall pay particular attention, although I shall also study certain germane, though different, features of these languages and of Italic (Latin), Celtic (mainly Old and Middle Irish, with a little attention to Britannic), and Germanic (Gothic and Old English). I shall likewise cite some examples of the usage from Tocharian, without committing myself as to whether they are due to inheritance or to borrowing. Unfortunately I am not competent to deal with Armenian or Balto–Slavic.

3. However, before presenting the evidence furnished by individual languages, I believe it will be convenient to provide at the outset the hypothesis that I base upon this evidence. In the interest of brevity and clarity, I offer translations and paraphrases in Latin,[8] although these perforce frequently do violence to Latin grammar and idiom. The use of parentheses in these pseudo-Latin passages indicates that the word or words within them may be either present or absent.

4. I assume that the construction started with a clause of the type (*est*) *homo nomen Iulius*. To the English-speaking reader, it is possible, and perhaps necessary, to choose out of several a particular interpretation and translation, or at least to indicate that grounds for such a choice exist. The native speaker was doubtless unaware of the existence of various variant analyses,[9] although he may have altered his use of pauses and intonation in a way that implied them (just as we of today, without thinking about it, can pronounce the words *all out* in such a way that they constitute a command, a question, or a statement).

5. In the first place, there is room for doubt about the force of the verb *est* if present.

6. (1) If the *homo* has not been spoken of before, it is probably used with predicative force, 'there is a man'; in that case it is particularly likely to stand in initial position in its clause, where I have placed it,[10]

---

[8] The fact that Latin is, as already noted (fn. 4), one of the few ancient languages lacking the construction under consideration, of course makes my Latin sentences particularly objectionable; yet it perhaps assists in obtaining objectivity, since the renderings are not slanted in favor of an already familiar interpretation.

[9] As Brugmann well says in the same connection (*IF* 27.146): "die Grenzen, die wir Grammatiker durch Gebrauchseinteilungen und Anwendung verschiedener Benennung anbringen, bestehen ja für den Sprecher selbst niemals in der Schärfe, in der wie sie ziehen."

[10] A typical example is the well-known beginning of the Nala story, *MBh* 3.50 āsīd rājā Nalo nāma. In English too *there is* (the phrase which we employ to distinguish the

and it is particularly unlikely to be omitted, at least in more polished writing.[11] Clauses of this type are especially common at the outset of a narrative.[12] At a comparatively late period, we would call *Iulius*

---

predicative use from the copulative) regularly appears at the beginning; Kipling's "a fool there was" is both emphatic and artificial.

[11] It does get omitted possibly in Hittite (but see fn. 74) and certainly in Old Persian (see §90).

[12] The type occurs particularly often in popular literature, especially narrative: it seems natural for the story-teller to start out with a statement which, in some form or other (syntactic constructions vary), conveys the idea 'there was a man named so-and-so'. We shall meet examples in Hittite Märchen (§23), in Sanskrit and Greek epic (§§44 and 117), in the narrative portions of the New Testament (§177), and abundantly in Old and Middle Irish tales (§§224, 233). It is also extremely frequent in the historical documents of Old Persian, which are composed in what impresses us as a naive and informal style more suitable for a folk-tale (see §90 in particular) and perhaps to be accounted for at least in part by the fact that this really was oral literature, since the composers were dictating and not writing.

It does not seem a feature of Latin, perhaps because Latin literature, so far as we have it, is already more or less sophisticated; and when it does occur, it does not usually take the form 'there was a man named so-and-so'. Even the far from elegant Plautus, though his dramas often include expository passages in the form of narratives, has only one instance, *Truc.* 12 hic habitat mulier nomen quoi est Phronesium 'here lives a woman whose name is Phronesium'. There are a few passages in the *Aeneid* in which Vergil seems to be deliberately imitating the style of the folk-tale: notably four that are perhaps artificially simple in their structure, 1.530 = 3.163 est locus, Hesperiam Grai cognomine dicunt 'there is a place, the Greeks call (it) Hesperia by name', 7.607 sunt geminae Belli portae, sic nomine dicunt 'there are twin gates of war, so (people) call (them) by name', 6.440-41 monstrantur lugentes campi, sic illos nomine dicunt 'there show themselves the mourning fields, so (people) call them by name' (all cited below in §146), and 3.693-95 Sicanio praetenta sinu iacet insula, nomen dixere priores Ortygiam 'stretched out in the Sicanio Bay there lies an island, the ancients called (it) Ortygia by name' or 'the ancients called (its) name Ortygia' (cited below in §156); also three rather odd ones in which Vergil introduces not very successful variations of construction, 6.106-7 hic inferni ianua regis dicitur 'here (is) the gate, (it) is called (the gate) of the nether king' (cited in fn. 407), 12.845 dicuntur geminae postes cognomine Dirae '(there are) twin pests, (they) are called Furies by name' (cited in §146 and fn. 407), and 3.210-11 Strophades Graio stant nomine dictae insulae Ionio in magno 'they stand (there) called Strophades [or simply they are called Strophades?] by a Greek name, islands in the great Ionian' (cited in §146). But in general such tournures seem out of keeping with Vergil's highly artistic and stately narrative style. Neither are they characteristic of the realistic and down-to-earth narrative style of Petronius, whose prose conveys somewhat of the "dead-pan" effect of the *New Yorker*; in the *Satyricon* people are usually referred to directly by their name, either by the author or by some speaker—'Julius', not 'a man called Julius'; of the latter construction I find only two instances, 20.2 ancilla quae Psyche vocabatur and 140.1 matrona inter primas honesta, Philomela nomine. I expected to meet many instances in Apuleius' tale of Cupid and Psyche, but I do not, possibly because Apuleius in his story-telling is archaistic rather than archaic, or perhaps more because he is romantic rather than classic. He begins in what has come to seem to us the

a nominative in apposition with *homo*, and *nomen* an accusative of specification modifying *Iulius*; but many (including myself) believe that at the outset in a locution of this sort *nomen* was a nominative,[13] its shift to the accusative being due to a subsequent misinterpretation facilitated by the fact that the two cases are identical in form.[14] This

---

traditional fairy-tale way, 4.28 erant in quadam civitate rex et regina, but we never learn the name of the country or of the king and queen, or of Psyche's two older sisters and their husbands, or of their countries; when Psyche visits them, we learn only that she 'went to a certain country' (5.26 accedit quandam civitatem) and later that she 'went to another country' (5.27 pervenit ad civitatem aliam). Even our heroine's name is introduced late, and rather casually: 4.30 Psychen (hoc enim nomine puella nuncupabatur) coram ostendit 'Psyche (for it was by this name that the girl was called) she personally pointed out'. (This reminds me somewhat of *Aen*. 3.210–11 and 12.845.) The only other personages in the tale whose names we learn are relatively unimportant ones, Venus' three handmaids (6.8 una de famulitione Veneris, nomine Consuetudo, and 6.9).

[13] On the other hand some scholars have thought the accusative use of *nomen* was the original one. Gaedicke (216) explains that Sanskrit *nāma* (*nomen*) began as the direct object of a verb of 'having' or 'giving', and that the accusative proper name (*Iulium*) which might accompany it in the construction was attracted into the same case as the word designating its bearer (*homo*), so that instead of (*homo*) *Iulium nomen habet* we find (*homo*) *Iulius nomen habet*; then (217) "das Prädicat wird zur Apposition", and *Iulius*, still accompanied by *nomen*, may become subject of the sentence. Delbrück expresses tentative accord with Gaedicke in *AS* 185; but in *Grund*. 3.388, while he still agrees that the construction began with an accusative use of *nomen*, he assumes that this use was as an appositive of *Iulium* (he translates an Avestan passage "welchen die Menschen *Dužaka* als Namen nennen") and that the development of the appositive into an accusative of specification came with the shift to the passive, as when the Homeric ἥν ἅμαξαν ἐπίκλησιν καλέουσιν (*Il*. 18.487 = *Od*. 5.273) became ἥ ἅμαξα ἐπίκλησιν καλεῖται. This seems to me a complete begging of the question: why *epiklêsin* and not *epiklêsis*, if *nomen* is an appositive? Kieckers (*IF* 30.361–66) also starts with *nomen* as an accusative with a verb of naming, but prefers to call it an inner object rather than an appositive (cf. below, fn. 37); it could be associated with two "outer accusatives", *hominem* and *Iulium*, and eventually it got separated from the verb and combined with the predicate accusative *Iulium* (see especially 362). Fundamentally Gaedicke, Delbrück, and Kieckers are all in agreement in their method, and Brugmann's objection (*IF* 27.146) to Delbrück's explanation applies equally to Gaedicke's and Kieckers': it makes of *nomen* a special case distinct from the Avestan and Greek words meaning 'size', 'length', 'breadth', etc., as well as from Greek 'race', all of which are similarly used as accusatives of specification and all of which similarly alternate with instrumentals of specification (cf. below, fn. 378 on the dimension words in Avestan and Greek, and §§125–32 on 'race' in Greek). Brugmann finds Delbrück's interpretation "unannehmbar"; Blümel, less positively, terms the views of Delbrück and Kieckers not "unmöglich" but certainly not "gesichert" (*IF* 33.26), although he finally accepts them in part (see below, fn. 15).

[14] This is true of the word everywhere except in West Germanic and Old Prussian, in which it became masculine. This shift in gender is common to all *mn̥* forms in West Germanic and Baltic; but so far as Baltic goes, our particular root, as we have seen (fn. 1), does not occur in Lithuanian and Lettish. I know of no re'evant examples in

was the explanation of the development of the "Beziehungsakkusativ" given by Brugmann,[15] who held that originally *Iulius nomen*—i.e. *Iulius (est) nomen*—constituted an independent parenthetical clause, of course of the type called by the Germans a *Nominalsatz*, a term which, though usually rendered into English as 'nominal sentence', I prefer to

---

West Germanic, despite the misguided efforts of a number of scholars who went astray in following one another in regard to a line in *Beowulf* (see fn. 7); and certainly the scanty remains of Old Prussian (as revealed in Trautmann) have no help to offer us, for their use of *emmens* 'name' is confined to religious formulas such as "hallowed be thy name", "in the name of the Father and the Son and the Holy Ghost", "thou shalt not take the name of the Lord thy God in vain", and do not illustrate "naming-constructions". A change of gender occurs in Tocharian, but there the nominative and accusative remain the same in words that were originally neuter. The change of gender from neuter to masculine in the Romance Languages and in Middle Irish is of course far too late to have a bearing on our problem.

[15] Something of the sort had been suggested thirty years earlier by Osthoff, *LC* 1880 col. 1469–70; but for the first elaborate treatment of the theory we must turn to Brugmann, *IF* 27.143–46 (1910). This view was repeated, of course in much briefer form, in Brugmann, *Grund.* 2.2.641 (1911) and in Brugmann-Thumb 437 (1913); it was accepted by Schwyzer, *Parenth.* 43 and *Gr. Gr.* 2.86, and, apparently, by Humbert 251 (but cf. fn. 19). A disadvantage of this view is the extreme choppiness of the expression: one wants a genitive or a possessive to render the idea 'Julius (is) *his* name' or a dative to render the idea 'Julius (is) the name *to him*', not just 'Julius (is) *the* name' (cf. below, fnn. 305 and 579 on Homer, §137 on Xenophon, and §190 on the *NT*). Another objection lies in the date of some of the passages cited by Brugmann as evidence for his supposed parenthetical "Nominalsatz"; in Sanskrit, to be sure, these are as early as the *RV*, but in Greek they are as late as the *Anabasis* (cf. below, §137 and fn. 379). Blümel (*IF* 33.17) takes cognizance of this difficulty; yet he follows Brugmann in believing that at first the only instances of the usage were interpolated clauses of the type posited by him with *Iulius* as subject and *nomen* as predicate. He recognizes the fact (15–16) that the existence of a passage in which this supposed clause was combined with e.g. *hominis* instead of *homo* would be favorable to Brugmann's hypothesis, and he offers as such support one passage from Avestan (16), to which in a later article (*IF* 44.260) he adds one from Greek; but actually the first is probably spurious and the second extremely late (see below, §§57 and 139, respectively). The lack of such evidence is as favorable to my view—to be presented directly below, in §10—as it is unfavorable to Brugmann's. Blümel disagrees with Brugmann's positing a shift of *nomen* from nominative to accusative; this he considers "ganz unwahrscheinlich" (19). And so he ends up straddling: while he agrees (18 and 19) that in *homo nomen Iulius*, *nomen* is a predicate nominative as Brugmann believes, yet he holds (23) that in *hominem nomen Iulium nominant*, it is an inner object as Kieckers believes (see above, fn. 13, and below, fn. 37). He insists (26 and 84) that in neither instance did it generate an accusative of specification, but finally concludes (77–78) that beside the nominative *nomen* of Brugmann and the accusative *nomen* of Delbrück and Kieckers there developed the use of *nomen* as accusative of specification under the influence of *genos* and *geneên* (I think the development was in the other direction; see below, §12). It seems to me that a single theory which accounts for all three usages is definitely to be preferred; cf. below, fn. 177.

represent by 'nominal clause', since the type of predication involved can of course occur in a dependent clause as well as in a main clause. In the combination *Iulius nomen*, one noun is the subject and the other the predicate nominative; it does not particularly matter which we say is which.

7. (2) If on the other hand the *homo* has been spoken of before, then the verb *est* if present is copulative rather than predicative, and may occupy any place in the clause, but it is very likely to be absent;[16] in that case not merely *Iulius nomen*, but the entire entity, *homo Iulius nomen*, is a nominal clause. If we find *homo (est) Iulius nomen* in this sense, it is natural to translate 'the man is Julius by name', or, more idiomatically, "the man is called Julius', and there may seem nothing for it but to view *nomen* as the accusative of specification.[17]

8. There are of course passages in which *homo* is the subject of some other verb, e.g. *homo Iulius nomen in Italia incolit*; or in which instead of a subject *homo* there occurs some other case-form playing a quite different part in the sentence, e.g. *hominem Iulium nomen cognosco*. Brugmann's explanation of *Iulius nomen* as an interpolated clause is less natural in the first case, and utterly impossible in the second; but obviously both may be viewed as later developments from the original construction,[18] and certainly *nomen* in both instances would be classed as an accusative of specification.

[16] If there is some point in stressing the fact that past time is involved, then *erat* is likely to be used; nominal predication cannot indicate time as verbal predication can, and so is usually employed only when the general implication is present (but this may include the "historical present") or timeless (i.e. always true). However, Celtic seems not to adhere to this rule; see below, fn. 725.

[17] A possible variant, if the individual concerned has already been mentioned, is one not involving the repetition of such a noun as *homo*. In that case, there being no nominative substantive to constitute the subject of a nominal clause, the only kind of predication possible is the verbal type: if we do not say *homo Iulius nomen* 'the man (is) Julius by name', we must say *est Iulius nomen*' (he) is Julius by name'. This at once becomes ambiguous: *est* may mean not '(he) is' but simply 'is', with either *Iulius* or *nomen* as subject and the other as predicate nominative: 'Julius is (his) name' or '(his) name is Julius'. This ambiguous type occurs several times in Hittite (see §24), in Sanskrit (see §52), and in Greek (see §117 and fn. 305). I myself question the second interpretation, because of the extreme choppiness involved; cf. above, fn. 15.

[18] So Brugmann, *IF* 27.144, in citing two Sanskrit examples, *RV* 1.53.7 and 10.49.2 (discussed below, §47): "In der Zeit, aus der uns solche indische Sätze überliefert sind, wäre aber *nåma* jedenfalls, nach Analogie seines sonstigen Gebrauchs, unempfunden, also als abhängig vom Eigennamen empfunden gewesen."

9. However, I would propose a different explanation for *nomen* in (*est*) *homo nomen Iulius* which will also account directly for its use in *hominem nomen Iulium cognosco*.

10. I suggest that originally *nomen* was in partitive apposition[19] with *homo*.[20] I have already published several discussions of the phenomenon of partitive apposition,[21] which I believe was very prevalent at an early stage of the language, but subsequently declined, leaving behind it, however, a number of vestiges, both direct and indirect. The shift that thus took place in noun usage, by which the combination of two sub-

[19] The suggestion that *nomen* is an appositive, but with *Iulius*, not (as I think) with *homo*, was made, mainly though not exclusively on the basis of Indo–Iranian evidence, as long ago as 1900, in an article by Gray (*IF* 11.307–13). This article in my opinion, despite one shocking error (on which see below, §§207–23), deserves more attention and more commendation than it has received. In the year after its appearance, it was bitterly attacked by Foy (*IF* 12.172–78), in a polemic which Brugmann (*IF* 27.145) terms "in great part thoroughly justified". Foy pounced upon the great weakness of Gray's presentation, a confusion of the historical and the descriptive approach, especially as embodied in his conclusion (313): "dass bei der indogermanischen Verbindung *nāman [sic! this is Gray's way of representing the form normally written today *nōmn̥*] + Eigenname, *nāman ursprünglich bloss in Apposition zum Nom. proprium est, und dass es also keineswegs notwendig ist, *nāman als Akkusativ der Beziehung aufzufassen." While I agree with Gray that in Indo–European the word for 'name' was an appositive (though not necessarily confined to the nominative case, as we shall see), I also agree with Foy that in some of Gray's examples (though perhaps not so many as Foy thinks) such is no longer the case, for its development into an accusative of specification has probably already taken place. Yet I do not think this justifies Foy's final thrust (178), by which he manages to throw doubt on the validity of Gray's entire investigation, to the effect that he can see no benefit that "Sprachwissenschaft" would derive from a definite decision as to what the original construction was: "Begnügen wir uns damit, die Verhältnisse der Einzelsprachen genau kennen zu lernen!"

It appears at first sight as if Meillet shared my view, for he calls *nomen* as used in Sanskrit, Old Persian, and Greek a "nominatif apposé" (*Introd.* 345); but his use elsewhere (e.g. 359 and 360) of the terms *apposé* and *apposition* shows that he used them in a much broader sense than one would expect. Humbert, who quotes his phrase "un nominatif apposé" (251), indicates by his translation (of Hesiod, *Theog.* 144) "Des Cyclopes—c'est là leur nom—ils étaient", and by his reference to Brugmann-Thumb (437), that he is really taking *nomen* (*onoma*) as a predicate noun as did Brugmann (see above, fn. 15), *not* as an appositive.

[20] Probably in that case the original form was rather *homo nomen Iulius* (as I have written it so far); but with the misinterpretation of *nomen*, the shift in order to the perhaps commoner *homo Iulius nomen* was doubtless natural. Variations in word order of various kinds are noted below: fnn. 73 and 95, on Hittite; 160, 173, and 176, on Sanskrit; 257, on Old Persian; 374 and 377, on Greek. But what is significant is that *homo*, the "whole" noun, almost invariably precedes (whether directly or not) *nomen*, the "part" noun; cf. *TAPA* 84.95 fn. 10, and 85.213 fn. 49, together with the cross-references given in each place.

[21] *TAPA* 84.92–123 (1953), 85.197–289 (1954); *Lg.* 29.246–51 (1953).

stantives standing side by side in the same case was replaced by a phrase consisting of a single noun modified by a second one, normally in the genitive, may be compared to the shift that took place in usage involving clauses, with parataxis changing to hypotaxis.

11. The appositional use with the word denoting the *homo* and the word denoting his *nomen* is particularly natural because, according to widespread ways of thinking, the *nomen* constitutes a particularly important and integral part of the *homo*; indeed, it may almost be viewed as equivalent to, or representative of, the entire *homo*. We find repeated evidence of this in folklore as well as in language. The Max Müller allegorizing school of intepreting myths, whose followers believed that the province of gods and the behavior of heroes could be explained if one but knew the etymological origin (usually a purely fanciful one) of their names, is properly discredited today;[22] yet their slogan of "*nomen-numen*" may have some applications that they did not suggest. The most obvious instance is the use, particularly in folk-tales and drama, of "redende Namen"; the classicist thinks first of Roman comedy, but there are of course plenty of examples in English literature, from Bunyan to Sheridan; and, though the modern novelist normally eschews anything of the sort, I think I have noted a recurrence of the practice in the Jalna novels, thoroughly realistic though they are, by Mazo de la Roche. That genuine significance attached to the name is shown by the puns on names which we find in ancient drama, not only in the quips of such comic writers as Aristophanes and Plautus, which might be discounted because these writers, like Shakespeare after them, delight in plays-on-words of any kind, but even in serious passages in tragedy (e.g. Euripides, *Bacchae* 367 and 526; also 286–97, and the parallels cited by Cruickshank in his note on 286, where he defends the genuineness of the passage against those who reject it as spurious). Darmestetter, in an article on words for 'name' otherwise of scant value for us of today,[23] has some interesting comments on superstitions attesting the power of the name; he tells for instance (125) of a Jewish

---

[22] For a good brief résumé, with bibliography, see Lang, *Myth* 1.24–28.

[23] *Ét. ir.* 2.123–26 (1883). Here Darmestetter (123) explains the Indo–Iranian word for 'name' as presenting the fusion of two roots, which he writes **gnā-* 'name' and **gan-* 'race'. Probably no linguist of today would attribute an original palatal to the Indo–European root for 'name'; Latin *cognomen* must be due to a false analogy based on *cognosco* beside *nosco* (Buck, *Comp. Gr.* 147) or (less probably in my opinion) to a confusion with the quite different stem seen in Greek *gnôma* (WP 1.132).

custom of changing the names of a desperately ill person. Bloomfield (*Language* 155) refers to taboos involving names, specifically that of the male Cree Indian who may not utter the names of his sisters and some other female relatives; presumably such an act was viewed as tantamount to incest.[24] The widespread existence of secret names must be due to the intimate connection of the name with its bearer's survival or safety: Rome had a secret name, and still more famous is the Hebrew tetragram embodying the "unpronounceable" (or rather incommunicable) name of the Lord; to descend from the sublime to the ridiculous, we may recall the story of the dwarf Rumpelstilzchen included in Grimm's collection of fairy-tales.

12. In a sense, then, the *nomen* was more than a part of the *homo*; it *was* the *homo*. But when the paratactic type *homo nomen* came to be replaced by the hypotactic type *hominis nomen*, difficulties began! If the original statement was simply *homo nomen* (*est*) *Iulius* 'the man (his) name is Julius', this could easily change to *hominis nomen* (*est*) *Iulius* 'the man's name is Julius';[25] one might even change *hominem nomen Iulium cognosco* 'I know (i.e. am acquainted with) a man (his) name Julius' to *hominis nomen Iulium cognosco* 'I know (i.e. am acquainted with) the man's name Julius', though this involves a change in sense. But if the original statement was *homo nomen Iulius in Italia incolit* or *hominem nomen Iulium video*, the employment of the genitive construction— *hominis nomen Iulius in Italia incolit* or *hominis nomen Iulium video*— produced nonsense. Thus one simply had to retain the original paratactic version; but since parataxis was now no longer normal, a new interpretation arose for the old form, to wit 'a man Julius in name',

---

[24] Bloomfield's friends used to gain amusement from his query in this connection, so typical of the wry, dry humor that characterized him, as to whether little Cree boys used to write their sisters' names on back fences.

[25] There is also a quite different construction in which the verb has a more vivid force —in English, 'belongs (to)' rather than the colorless 'is'—and is therefore not likely to be omitted. Here instead of the genitive of possession *hominis*, closely combined with the noun *nomen*, we have the "dative of possession" (or, better, "dative of possessor") *homini*, closely combined with the verb *est*. The exact difference in shade of meaning conveyed that exists between *hominis nomen est Iulius* and *homini nomen est Iulius* is easier to perceive than to define (I endeavored to discuss it briefly in *CO* 26.27); but this need not concern us here. The construction is widespread: it occurs in Hittite (see §24); in Greek (see §123); in Latin, with a special "illogical" variety, *homini nomen est Iulio* (see §§142 and 149–50); and in Old English (see §§199–200 for Northumbrian, §220 and fnn. 694 and 695 for West Saxon).

and thus was generated a new construction, the accusative of specification. But this accusative had a rival in what was doubtless the case originally used in expressions of specification, to wit the instrumental. This *Urkasus*, in the form of its descendants, the instrumental in Indo-Iranian, the dative in Greek and Gothic, and the ablative in Latin, continued to be used to express specification, the last-named almost exclusively so.[26] In Sanskrit the accusative of specification was confined to *nāma*,[27] but in Avestan it occurs also in the case of words of magnitude and dimension; this use too is presumably inherited, since we meet it in Greek as well (however, see fn. 378 below). The construction's extension in Greek to words denoting 'ancestry' or 'race' is doubtless a natural outgrowth of its use in words denoting 'name'; among a people whose members bore only a single name, it was necessary, in order completely to identify the *homo*, to know his *genus* as well as his *nomen*.[28] But the widespread development of the *accusativus graecus* to denote parts of the body has, I believe, no connection whatsoever with its use to denote the name, apart from the fact that I attribute both to a common origin, partitive apposition.[29] Yet even in Greek the dative of specification existed side by side with the accusative;[30] and eventually,

[26] Gaedicke (218) speaks as if the original construction for specification was the accusative, which was supplanted in Latin and Germanic by the instrumental; but surely the actual development was just the reverse.

[27] Cf. Gaedicke 216; Kieckers, *IF* 30.365–66. The latter (365) uses this as an argument against Brugmann: "so sieht man, falls man nicht mit einem blinden Zufall rechnen will, nicht recht ein, weshalb im Altindischen nur *nāma* 'mit Namen' als Akkusativ der Beziehung vorkommt." The other accusatives listed by Delbrück, *AS* 165–66, are of a quite different type. However, note the widespread use of the adverbial accusative (cf. below, §43).

[28] Cr. Delbrück's reflection (*Grund.* 3.390) "dass *genos* seine natürliche Stelle hinter dem Geschlechtsnamen hatte wie *onoma* hinter dem Personennamen". For examples of Greek *genos*, and of its synonym *geneê*, used in parallel or similar ways to *onoma*, see below, §§125–32. In *koine* Greek too, we find references to a man's *genos* (in this case his nationality rather than his family) as well as his *nomen*; see fn. 529. Similarly in Old Persian, a man is often identified by family and/or nationality as well as by name; see fn. 257. Even in Latin, where the use of the triple name made the indication of a man's ancestry less necessary, there is a tendency to associate *nomen* and *genus*; see §§157 and 159. Thus Darmesteter's attempt to connect *nomen* etymologically with *genus* (referred to above in fn. 23), while certainly wrong linguistically, is understandable sociologically.

[29] The evolution of the accusative of the body-part from partitive apposition I try to trace in *TAPA* 85.254–89.

[30] Perhaps some instances of this, however, are also to be classed rather as instances of partitive apposition; see *TAPA* 85.214–19. These would of course have to be explained as genuine datives rather than as inherited instrumentals.

as not infrequently happens, it was the older construction that won out.[31]

13. The fact that all the words normally involved—'name' and 'race', also 'size', 'weight', 'length', 'breadth', and 'depth'—were regularly neuter, doubtless has something to do with the growth of the construction.[32] Yet I think it is in favor of my theory that it does not have to rest completely on the assumption of a nominative misunderstood as an accusative, as does that of Brugmann,[33] or on the assumption of an accusative misunderstood as a nominative, as do those of Gaedicke, Delbrück, and Kieckers.[34] Beside the very common nominative type (*est*) *homo nomen Iulius*, there must have existed an accusative type, *hominem*—or, more naturally, *puerum*—*nomen Iulium nominant* 'they name the boy (his) name Julius'.[35] Here *nomen* is again, according to my view, in partitive apposition, this time with the accusative, *puerum*. As for *Iulium*, that, like *Iulius* in (*est*) *homo nomen Iulius*, may be either in appositional relationship with the two nouns (*puerum nomen*) or in predicative relationship with the verb; *puerum Iulium nominant* (I am simplifying by leaving out for the moment the apposi-

[31] The dative was rare in comparison with the accusative in early Greek, but was preferred in Hellenistic times (cf. Schwyzer, *Gr. Gr.* 2.86 and 168), and was indeed so far as 'in name' goes almost the sole survivor in the *NT* (see below, §176).

[32] According to Havers' article, "Eine syntaktische Sonderstellung griechischer und lateinischer Neutra" (*Gl.* 13.171–89), it had everything to do with it! (However, I would not go so far as he does; see *TAPA* 85.246–47.) Havers believes that the nominative-accusative neuter once served as a general oblique case equivalent to any case of a masculine or feminine noun; see especially 178–80. Wackernagel, *Vorlesungen* 1.293–94, concurs; but he admits that one type of expression which he cites as the result of this early usage, and therefore as apparently ancient, namely, the neuter accusative absolute, is met in early times only in Greek, and there not before the fifth century.

[33] See above, §6 and fn. 15.

[34] See above, fn. 13.

[35] This form with the triple accusative, with *Iulium* a predicate accusative (which must of course be distinguished from the type *hominem nomen Iulium cognosco*, with *Iulium* an appositive), is preserved mainly in Avestan (§55) and Greek (§118); I have suggested a possible instance in Hittite (§28), and there is a very late example in Latin (§156). By the time of *koine* Greek, the construction has apparently disappeared; in the *NT* we meet only two accusatives, either *puerum Iulium* (*nomine*) *nominant* or *pueri nomen Iulium nominant*, never three (see §§169, 170, and 173 for the Greek original, and §§171, 172, and 173 for its renderings in Latin and Gothic). Even the construction with two accusatives is not common in classical Latin; for *nomen Iulium nominant*, I know of no example in Plautus, and only one—a doubtful one—in Vergil (see §156); and for *puerum* (*nomine*) *Iulium nominant*, I know of only one example—in the passive—in Plautus (see §141), and not very many in Vergil (see §146).

tive *nomen*) in the first case means 'they name the boy, Julius', i.e. 'they bestow a name upon the boy Julius', and in the second case means 'they name the boy Julius', i.e. 'they bestow the name, Julius, upon the boy', which seems more likely, since the boy might hardly be spoken of as *puer Iulius* before the act of naming him *Julius* had taken place.[36] In such a combination, Kieckers (*IF* 30.361–62) calls *nomen* an "inner object"[37] and *puerum* and *Iulium* "outer objects", the latter used predicatively; but if I am right in viewing *nomen* as in apposition with *puerum*, they are both presumably "outer objects" (what I prefer to call "accusatives of affect"), whereas the predicative accusative *Iulium* is closer to an "inner object" (or "accusative of effect").[38]

14. A common alternative to the construction *puerum nomen Iulium nominant* is *puero nomen Iulium indunt* (or *faciunt*).[39] Here *Iulium* is

[36] For some passages from Vergil exemplifying this ambiguity, see below, fn. 407.

[37] Delbrück, *Grund.* 3.388, does not try to decide whether in Greek the word for *nomen* is an inner object or an appositive with the word corresponding to *Iulium*, but in Avestan (as already noted above in fn. 13) he definitely pronounces for the second alternative ("welchen die Menschen *Dužaka* als Namen nennen"). Kieckers (*IF* 30.361) rejects the latter view—rightly, according to Blümel, *IF* 33.21 fn. 1. Obviously I agree that *nomen* is not in apposition with *Iulium*, since it is my fundamental thesis that it is in apposition with *puerum*; I have indicated that *Iulium* might be in apposition with *puerum nomen*, but probably is rather in predicative relation with these words. It is necessary to seek for precision in the analysis, although I admit with regret that some of my attempts in this direction may seem unduly reminiscent of Lewis Carroll's fooling in Chapter 8 of *Through the Looking Glass*: the song is called "Ways and Means", but the name of the song is called "Haddocks' Eyes", and the name really is "The Aged Aged Man".

[38] In the construction to be taken up next (§14), *puero nomen Iulium indunt*, probably both *nomen* and *Iulium* would have to be called outer objects, though in its common variant *puero nomen Iulium faciunt* they might rather be viewed as inner objects; but here the distinction is hardly worth making.

[39] Examples are cited below for Hittite (§§27 and 28), Greek (§124), Latin (§§143 and 149), *koine* Greek and its translations into Latin and Gothic (§175), Old English (§§195 and 209), and Britannic (§257). The verbs used in this construction are mainly those meaning fundamentally 'put, place, set'. Most of them come from the root *dhē-* (WP 1.826–27): Hittite *dai-* (Sturtevant, *HG* 62 and 135–36), Greek *tithēmi*, Latin *indo*, possibly Welsh *dodi* (Buck, *Syn.* 832–33; cf. below, fn. 818). We also find, mostly at a later period, similar verbs from other roots meaning 'place' or 'set', including Latin *pono* (§149) and *impono* (§§175 and 195), and several from the root *sed-* in Germanic, namely, Gothic *satjan* (§175) and Old English *settan* with prefixes (§195); with these we may compare Latin *addo* (§150). One common verb meaning 'make', namely Latin *facio*, which is used interchangeably with *indo* (§143 and fn. 399), is also from the stem *dhē-*. Later verbs with much the same meaning include Old English *scyppan* 'shape' or 'make' (§209) and Breton *ober* (§257 and fn. 818); with these we may perhaps compare Latin *paro* (§143). In most instances it is convenient to translate these verbs by English

manifestly in apposition with *nomen*,[40] and there is of course no partitive apposition; but we shall need to consider the construction later for other reasons.

15. We must take cognizance of a few more difficulties. I have set forth the view that (in the pre-Beziehungsakkusativ days) *nomen* in *homo nomen Iulius est* is an appositive of *homo*. If the noun *homo* is replaced by the pronoun *ille*, *nomen* must similarly be an appositive of *ille*. But if, in a parallel instance, we have no expressed subject but simply *nomen Iulius est*, then *nomen* is still to be viewed as an appositive of the subject of *est* and not as itself its subject. What applies to the third person must apply to the other persons as well: *ego nomen Iulius sum* and *nomen Iulius sum*[41] must be precisely parallel to *ille nomen Iulius est* and *nomen Iulius est*. The meaning doubtless once was 'I (my) name am Julius'.[42] But because with a nominative *nomen* we would expect the verb *est* rather than *sum*,[43] the explanation of *nomen* here as an accusative of specification must have arisen at a particularly early stage. Also, the problem is avoided by the common substitution for *nomen Iulius sum* of an altogether different construction, *mihi nomen Iulius est*; here, obviously, *nomen* really is the subject of *est*.

16. A similar problem arises if one wishes to ask a person's name. Shall we make the interrogative predicate nominative agree with the

---

'give', but verbs meaning 'give' are not common in this usage, except in Britannic, namely Welsh *rodi* and Cornish *ry* (§257 and fn. 818); I can also cite one example with Latin *do*, Vergil, *Aen*. 10.200 (fn. 417).

[40] The fact that it is clearly better to view *Iulium* as in apposition with *nomen* rather than to view *nomen* as in apposition with *Iulium* is probably an argument against Delbrück's adoption of the latter view in regard to *puerum nomen Iulium nominant*; see fn. 37. It is also definitely in opposition to Gray's view in regard to both *homini nomen Iulium indunt* and *est homo nomen Iulius*; see fn. 19 and §§208–10.

[41] If we had *sum homo nomen Iulius*, *homo*, and consequently its appositive *nomen*, would probably need to be classed as predicate nominatives.

[42] For examples from Indo–Iranian, see below, §§45 and 52 for Sanskrit, §54 for Avestan. For some similar Greek examples, see §126 with fn. 341, and §133.

[43] Actually a noun lacks person, and may therefore be subject of a verb in any person. The construction abounds in Hittite, which says *rex scribo* as freely as *rex scribit*; because we perforce translate the first 'I, the king, write', we are tempted to explain *rex* as in apposition with the subject of *scribo*, but surely it is itself the subject of *scribo*, just as of *scribit*. Examples in Greek and Latin are rare, but they exist: Thucydides 1.137.4 Θεμιστοκλῆς ἥκω; Nepos, *Them*. 2.9.2 Themistocles veni (an obvious imitation of the Greek); Suetonius, *Nero* 49.1 qualis artifex pereo. Cf. Ernout and Thomas 108, and my review of it, *Lg*. 30.272 and fn. 157.

"whole" substantive, *homo* or its equivalent, and say *quis (homo) nomen est?, quis (ille) nomen est?, quis (tu) nomen es?*; or shall we make it agree with the "part" substantive, *nomen*, and in each case use *quid* instead of *quis*? Manifestly, the former.[44] This is perhaps rendered doubly natural because of the fact that the answer, giving the *nomen*, is in the masculine form *Iulius*; but in any case I could hardly imagine saying *quid nomen es?*[45] But once more the doubtless original form, *quis nomen es?*, must seem anomalous; and once more it must lead to the interpretation of *nomen* as an accusative. However, with the third person verb *est* if no subject is expressed, *nomen* would be likely to be interpreted as subject; and then in this case too the original subject, whether *homo* or *ille* or zero, would probably be represented by a noun in an oblique case: *quid eius nomen est?* or *quid ei nomen est?*[46]

17. One more point remains to be noted in regard to usages involving *homo* and *nomen*. Because the *nomen* is so essential a part of the *homo* that it is often employed as a substitute for the *homo*, and also because *Iulius* in one sense is an equivalent for *homo* and in another is an equivalent for *nomen*[47] (it may serve as an answer to the question *quis est homo?* or to the question *quid est nomen?*), it is not surprising that the three types of substantive may get interchanged and confused. Thus arise peculiar variants of the logical constructions. In a sentence in which *homo* and *nomen* are in different cases, *Iulius* may be made to agree in case with *homo* instead of with *nomen*: *homo nomen Iulius habet*[48] instead of *homo nomen Iulium habet*,[49] *homini nomen Iulio est*

[44] Thus the Sanskrit *ko nāmāsi? = ko nāma asi?* (*Br.* 11.5.4.1), discussed below, §45 and fn. 171.

[45] Presumably on the analogy of *quis nomen es?*, Latin can even say *quis vocare?* (Plautus, *Mil.* 436), discussed below, §§142 and 144, and *quem vellet vocari eum* (*Lk.* 1.62), discussed below, fnn. 500 and 596.

[46] This formula is particularly common in Latin comedy. (On the use of *quid* rather than *quod*, see Gildersleeve-Lodge 60.)

[47] Cf. §23.

[48] Here it may be possible to explain that *nomen habet* is equivalent in sense to *nominatur* or *vocatur*, and that *Iulius* therefore is in normal predicate relationship to the subject, in other words is a predicate nominative (cf. below, §48). Still another explanation is that *Iulius* is simply the so-called *nominativus tituli* (on which see fn. 205); but in view of the undoubted attraction of *nomen* to the case of *homo* in *homini nomen Iulio est* and in *puero nomen Iulio induut*, treated directly below, I think it is better to recognize the same attraction in *homo nomen Iulius habet*.

[49] The construction with *Iulius* (already referred to in fn. 13) is the regular one in Sanskrit; see below §§48-50. I can also cite a few isolated instances, possible though not

instead of *homini nomen Iulius est*,[50] *puero nomen Iulio indunt* instead of *puero nomen Iulium indunt*.[51] On the other hand, in all these constructions the relation of *Iulius* or *Iulium* to *nomen* may lead to its replacement by an adjective *Iulium*[52] agreeing in gender and case with *nomen*.[53] Still more oddly, *nomen* itself, in (*est*) *homo nomen Iulius* or (*est*) *provincia nomen Gallia*, may be replaced by an apparently adjectival form agreeing in gender, and, I feel sure, in case, with *homo* or *provincia*; this I simply cannot render in Latin, no matter how barbarous![54]

18. That the identification or confusion of a *homo* with his *nomen* is a fundamental one seems to be evidenced by its frequent occurrence even in late literary works. This is undoubtedly likely to be found at all times in all languages, from Hittite[55] to English;[56] but it seems to

---

positive, from classical Greek (fnn. 186 and 328) and classical Latin (§162 and fn. 186), and from *NT* Greek and Latin (fn. 519). See also fn. 205.

[50] The construction with *Iulio* is very common in Latin, and interchanges with *Iulius* apparently without distinction of meaning; see below, §§142 and 150.

[51] This too is common in Latin; see below, §§143 and 150.

[52] Gellius actually declares that the form *Iulium* could be so used in Old Latin; see 15.29, quoted and discussed below (§163).

[53] Since *Iulium* has a termination, it is not a typical example. In a number of instances in a number of languages, the neuter nominative-accusative of an adjective, unlike *Iulium*, is identical with the bare stem of the corresponding noun, and accordingly the question will frequently arise as to which we have. Possibly there are also passages in which this bare stem is a quoted vocative, but that seems less likely. (For possible instances in Hittite, see below, §§30, 34–36; for a possible instance in Sanskrit, §51.)

[54] This is the regular construction in Old Persian; see below, §§58–115 passim, and especially §§64 and 74–76.

[55] Cf. in the Hymn to the Sun Goddess of Arinna, *KUB* 24.3.1.30 *nu-ut-tak-kan SUM-an lam-na-as is-tar-na na-ak-ki-i* 'your name (is) revered among names', i.e. 'you are revered among *the gods*'. So too doubtless the mutilated *KUB* 24.1.2.21.

[56] Note how often in English we speak of *great men* as *great names*, of *new books* as *new titles*, etc., making the substitution in illogical as well as logical ways. Examples of the confusion of a man and his name are legion; here are a few from the writings of classicists. Conington 2.96, in his note on *Aen.* 2.77–104: "He says his name is Sinon, a relation of Palamedes". Mackail, *Lat. Lit.* 53: "Gaius Valerius Catullus of Verona, one of the greatest names of Latin poetry, belonged, like most of this group, to a wealthy and distinguished family". Peck, *Classical Philology* 275: "One name in the history of this period is, however, so closely linked with the recovery of priceless manuscripts, as to justify at least a passing mention, because of the services which he rendered in the revival of learning". A not dissimilar confusion is that which arises between the title of a book in the form of a noun, and the person to whom this noun applies; I cite just two instances, one involving a common noun and the other a proper noun. From the *Times Book Review*, Dec. 21, 1919, p. 776 (anonymous review of books for young people):

be especially favored by Vergil, in whose works words strictly applicable only to the *homo* are applied to the *nomen*, and vice versa.[57] While this confusion may be more a matter of style than of syntax, it does not detract from the illumination that it throws on the original development of the construction here under study.

"'The Guardsman,' by Homer Greene, is another young hero of the war." From the *New York Herald Tribune Book Review*, Mar. 8, 1953, p. 3 (review headed "The Catholic Bookshelf" and signed by George N. Shuster): "More scholarly in tone, though still readable, is Father James Brodrick's 'St. Francis Xavier,' that great pioneer missionary to the Orient whose exploits leave one quite breathless."

[57] Cf. §§151–55.

I. HITTITE

19. The Hittite[58] word for 'name', *laman* (originally recognized by Friedrich, *Vert.* 2.92 and *AOF* 6.114), is unquestionably cognate with Sanskrit *nāma*, Latin *nōmen*. The initial *l* in place of *n* is explained as due to dissimilation of the nasal.[59]

[58] To simplify the copy for the printer and to clarify the text for the reader, I am in quoting Hittite texts omitting all accents (e.g. I write LU for LÚ) and other diacritics (e.g. I write *h* and *s* for *ḫ* and *š*) and also all determinatives. Were the latter included, a paper dealing with proper names would simply bristle with them, for the Hittite scribe regularly preceded every proper name with a sign that served as a determinative (not pronounced) to indicate a person, a man, or a woman. These signs respectively we regularly transcribe by I, LÚ or SAL, all superscript; but I think that in a paper of the present type, they are adequately represented by *our* corresponding determinative, the capital letter with which we begin a proper name. (I do, however, keep the determinatives in fn. 115, where there is a reason for so doing.)

[59] So Hrozný, *JA* 218.316–17; Sturtevant, *HG*[1] 94 and *HG*[2] 32 and 43; Duchesne-Guillemin, *TPS* for 1946, 85; Ernout and Meillet 676. Cuny, *Mélanges Navarre* 105–7, objects to this explanation because such dissimilation is unparalleled in the Indo–European languages, and offers a very daring alternative explanation of his own. Writing in 1935, he adopted a belief then prevalent (but now, so far as I know, universally abandoned) in a particularly close connection between Hittite and Tocharian, the two jointly being supposed to constitute a Hittite-Tocharian group parallel to Indo–European (105); and he assumed that Hittite *l* in *laman* and Tocharian *ñ* in *ñom* (on which see below, §260) represented an original *n'* ("n mouillé") which these languages kept distinct from original *n*, although the two had fallen together in Indo–European (106). Going still further in his daring hypothesis, he assumes an ultimate common origin of his postulated Hittite-Tocharian "*n* mouillé", Finno–Ugrian and Indo–European n-, and Semitic *š*- as seen e.g. in Akkadian *šumu*, Hebrew *šēm*, etc. (106–7), asserting that "la parenté de *l* et de *s* est bien connu par l'akkadien" (107 fn. 4). Cuny's hypothesis so far as Hittite *l*- goes seems to have been deprived of its force by the disproving of any close connection between Hittite and Tocharian (the latter language will be treated below, in §§260–64). Nor do I think his insistence on a parallel for the dissimilation seen in *laman* is necessary; dissimilation is not always uniform or predictable, but if we must have a reason for it here rather than elsewhere, it may be thought to lie in a tendency to avoid the occurrence of *three* nasals in a row. Whatever the explanation, Hittite has one other well-known example of initial *l* where we would expect a nasal; this is in the negative particle *le*, in which the *l*- presumably corresponds to the *m*- of Sanskrit *mā* Greek *mê*, though it might have the same origin—whatever that is thought to be—as the *n*- in Latin *nē* Gothic *ni*. In the very early *Bilingue* of Hattusilis I, we find *leman* appearing twice in the

20. The use of *laman* in Hittite, which is presumably the closest to the original state of affairs, seems to me to provide the strongest evidence that the construction began as partitive apposition; indeed, I think that in Hittite at least, whatever we may say about other languages, it never went beyond that stage. I know of no certain evidence for the existence of an accusative of specification in Hittite,[60] which

---

same line (3.65), first as *li-e-ma-* (-*ma* for -*man*, as elsewhere) and then as *li-e-ma-an-*; this combination of the negative particle *le* and the potential particle -*man* Sommer (*HAB* 237, 238; see also 189) interprets as equivalent to Latin *utinam ne*. Now if this collocation was at all common at an early period, it might be thought to be a dissimilated form resulting from an earlier *meman or even *neman, and in that case it would provide an excellent parallel for *laman* as a dissimilated form resulting from *naman*. However, we must not ignore the possibility that the *l-* in *le* was a borrowing from the corresponding Akkadian negative particle *la*.

[60] A possible example, not of a name but of a body-part, occurs in *Ull.* 2.2.11–13 (=*Bo* 2527.2.11–13) LU-*is-wa du-ud-du-ud-mi-ya-an-za nu-wa* U-UL *is-ta-ma-as-zi* [IG]I.HI.A-*wa-ma-wa-ra-as da-su-wa-an-za nu-wa* U-UL *a-us-zi* 'the man (is) deaf and hears not, and he (is) blind in (his) eyes and sees not'. Ehelolf supplies IGI (*KlF* 1.395) and explains it as a Greek accusative (ib. fn. 6). This is apparently accepted by Otten and Güterbock, who translate respectively "er ist blind auf den [Augen]" (*MGK* 22) and "in his eyes he is blind" (*JCS* 6.15); and it certainly seems extremely plausible, indeed almost inevitable. On the other hand it is dangerous to build a syntactic rule on a suppletion, no matter how probable. As for the supposed parallels which Ehelolf cites (*KlF* 1.395 fn. 6) from Friedrich (*Vert.* 1.31 fn. 5), namely, *KUB* 8.36.2.12 SAG.DU-*ZU* 'his head', 3.16 KA×U-*SU* 'his mouth', 8.38.2.8 IGI.HI.A 'eyes', these exemplify not the accusative of specification but the stuff out of which the accusative of specification is made, being combined in partitive apposition (as Friedrich realizes) with the accusative of the person as direct object of the verb 'afflict with illness', which in Hittite governs the accusative of the person affected. It is even possible that in our example IGI-*wa* (i.e. Hittite *sakuwa*, a neuter plural) is similarly in partitive apposition with the subject -*as* 'he'. One would expect the substantive denoting the whole (-*as*) to precede the one denoting the part (IGI), but in this passage if -*as* 'he' and *da-su-wa-an-za* 'blind' are to correspond in order to their counterparts LU-*is* 'the man' and *du-ud-du-ud-mi-ya-an-za* 'deaf' in the preceding clause, the prior position of IGI is mandatory, since -*as* is an enclitic. Partitive apposition is very common in relation to a body-part (cf. *TAPA* 84.101 and 85.199 and 211). In Greek expressions involving a person and a part of his body, partitive apposition is not met in the nominative; either the body-part noun appears as a dative or accusative of specification, or the person noun appears as a genitive of possession (change of 'he the eyes' to 'his eyes') or a dative of reference (see *TAPA* 85.210–11). But of course the fact that in such expressions partitive apposition does not appear in Greek does not prove that it never existed (actually there are two possible examples in Mycenaean Greek; see below, fn. 852); and if it did once exist, sporadic examples of it might have survived in Hittite, in which partitive apposition in general is both more widespread and more varied than in the later languages (cf. e.g. *TAPA* 84.95, and 101 fnn. 44 and 46). Indeed, an instance of it has been recognized by Götze (*AM* 214–15) in *KUB* 14.15.2.6 *na-as gi-nu-us-si du-ud-du-wa-ri-es-ta*, which according to his interpretation means 'and he the knee to him gave way'. But this seems to me dubious because of

indeed uses the accusative in a rather restricted way, mainly as direct
object of the verb; in the expression 'call (upon) by name', it employs
the instrumental, as in *KBo* 5.11.1.6–7 NI.DU-*ma-as-kan ha-at-ti-li
lam-ni-it hal-zi-is-sa-i* 'the porter calls them by name in Hattic',
KUB 14.34.3.49–50 *na-as-ta* HUR.SAG.MES *lam-ni-it hal-za-a-i*
'then he calls the mountains by name'.[61] On the other hand, partitive
apposition, as has already been said (fn. 60), is extremely common in
Hittite, and the manner in which *laman* is used is in complete conformity with the regular pattern. In the first place, the usage alternates
with the genitive construction which ultimately supplanted it in most
languages (*homo nomen* vs. *hominis nomen*), the two being practically
interchangeable; we meet them in close proximity in a given text, or
even in variant versions of a given passage. In the second place, with
both constructions the Hittite frequently inserts a possessive adjective which from our point of view is tautological[62] (*homo nomen suum*

---

the position of the enclitic dative -*si*, which normally is joined to the first word of the
clause; and, as I have already said (*TAPA* 85.199 fn. 10), there is an alternative explanation
which I prefer. This problem I treat in *JAOS* 85.295–307.

[61] In the passages cited the verb (*halzai*- or its durative *halzessa*-) means 'rufen' not
'nennen'; for another example (*KUB* 24.8.3.14) cf. §28 and fn. 99. But this verb, like
many others (e.g. Latin *appello* and *voco*, English *call*) combines both meanings (on its
double use in the sense of both 'rufen' and 'nennen', see Sommer, *Heth.* 1.10–11), and
the two uses overlap to a considerable extent. See further below on distinctions of
meaning in verbs of calling: in Greek, fn. 297; Latin, fnn. 391, 404, 406, 435; Breton,
fn. 813. On the various verbs of calling used in the *NT*, see fnn. 493 and 516 on Greek,
Latin, and Gothic, and fn. 593 on Latin and Old English.

[62] Is there a possibility that the Hittite is influenced by the parallel Akkadian *šum-šu*?
However, the possessive reappears in Indo–European in Celtic (see below, §232), and I
do not agree with Pokorny (*ZCP* 16.390) in his view that the Old Irish usage is non-
Indo–European (cf. fn. 747). In any event, the relation between Hittite *laman-set* and
Akkadian *šum-šu* is indeed baffling. The Hittite construction, apart from the use of the
possessive, is indubitably Indo–European, since something like it appears in Indo–
Iranian and Greek (cf. §2); the Akkadian construction is apparently not common
Semitic, although something like it reappears centuries later in Aramaic (see fn. 208).
The Akkadian use probably antedates our Hittite records, being attested as early as
2000 B.C.; and in any event Akkadian would hardly have borrowed from Hittite.
Professor E. A. Speiser of the University of Pennsylvania tells me by letter of a special
development within Akkadian, which certainly has no parallel in Hittite: *šum-šu* and the
longer form *mimma šum-šu* 'whatever his name may be' become indefinites, meaning
respectively 'any, a, a certain' and 'any at all' (I would suggest as Latin equivalents
'quidam' and 'quivis'). On this usage see Landsberger and Balkan, *Bell.* 14.248–50.
Furthermore—as Professor Speiser adds—the entire phrase *mimma šum-šu* becomes
practically a compound noun and as such can take a possessive suffix, *mimmašumšu-ya*
'my what-you-may-call-it'. We are of course reminded of jocular English *Mr. What's-*

or *hominis nomen suum*[63]), the use apparently being purely optional.

21. As instances of these variations, all absolutely equivalent in meaning, I cite a few passages from the Law-Code as given by Friedrich, *Ges.* The standard text of the Code, *KBo* 6.3 (Friedrich's B), uses the rarer genitive construction in §15,[64] LU.ULU^LU-*as EL-LAM is-ta-ma-na-as-sa-an is-kal-la-a-ri* 'hominis liberi aurem suam divellit', but the appositional construction directly after it in §16, IR-*an* GESTUG-*as-sa-an is-kal-la-ri* 'servum aurem suam divellit'; the latter construction appears in the duplicate text *KBo* 6.5 (Friedrich's C) in its version of §15, UKU-*an IL-LAM* GESTUG-*an is-kal-la-a-ri* 'hominem liberum aurem divellit'. Furthermore, in *KBo* 6.3, *is-ta-ma-na-as-sa-an* and its partially Sumerian equivalent GESTUG-*as-sa-an* evidently represent *is-ta-ma-na-an* 'aurem' plus *-san* 'suam'; but in *KBo* 6.5, GESTUG-*an* probably stands merely for *is-ta-ma-na-an* 'aurem' with no possessive. In the later version of the Code (*KBo* 6.4),[65] the paragraphs corresponding to §§15 and 16 (respectively xiv and xv) both agree with *KBo* 6.5 in having only GESTUG-*an* with no possessive, but this probably does not betoken a growing tendency to omit the unnecessary possessive.[66] The possessive appears alike in §§11, 12, 13,

---

His-Name; but for the general indefinite use I know of no parallel in Indo–European, though Foy may have had something of the sort in mind in his suggestion (*IF* 12.174) that Old Persian *nāma* means 'ein gewisser'; on this see fn. 227.

According to Professor Speiser, still another language, neither Semitic nor Indo–European, may come into the picture, namely Sumerian. In a letter of October 18, 1955, he writes as follows concerning the Akkadian locutions: "The chances are, moreover, that their meaning was influenced by Sumerian. For Sumerian m u . š è 'for its name' comes to mean 'on account of.' This is translated into Akkadian *aššum < ana šumi* 'on account of', which is in turn copied in Aramaic *miš-šum* and *ᶜal-šum* 'on account of/with reference to.' In all of these forms the basic element is the word for 'name.' And in all of them Sumerian played either a direct or an indirect part. Orthodox Semitic was not involved." This is extremely interesting, but probably has no bearing on my particular problem, except in so far as it suggests a direct connection between Akkadian and Aramaic, widely separated in time though they are.

[63] The Hittite possessive of the third person may be either reflexive or non-reflexive; hence my use of Latin *suus* to translate or represent it is not always accurate so far as Hittite goes, or idiomatic so far as Latin goes.

[64] But in §9 it has an ambiguous form LU.ULU^LU with no phonetic complement at all—where the duplicate *KBo* 6.2 (Friedrich's A) has the genitive LU.ULU^LU -*as.* Cf. fn. 67.

[65] It is customary, as a matter of convenience, to use Roman numerals in citing paragraphs of this version, and Arabic ones in citing those of the earlier version.

[66] This version occasionally introduces textual modifications which are undoubtedly

and 14 of the earlier version, and in their counterparts, §§x, xi, xii, and xiii of the later version. It is true that in 9 we have LU.ULU^{LU} SAG.DU-*ZU hu-u-ni-ik-zi* 'hominem caput suum laedit',[67] replaced in §viii by LU-*an* SAG.DU-*an hu-u-ni-ik-zi* 'hominem caput laedit' with no possessive; but right after this, the possessive reappears in §ix (in a passage which has no precise parallel in the earlier version) LU *EL-LUM* SAG.DU-*ZU ha-pal-la-sa-iz-zi* 'hominem liberum caput suum frangit'. Certainly on the whole in the Law-Code, the tendency is to use the appositional construction rather than the genitive, and to insert the seemingly redundant possessive rather than to omit it.[68]

22. We find much the same state of affairs in expressions involving *laman*. Both the appositional construction *homo nomen Iulius* and the genitive construction *hominis nomen Iulius* occur, the latter of course being possible only if the *homo* has been previously mentioned. And in both instances the possessive adjective may appear: *homo nomen suum Iulius* or *hominis nomen suum Iulius*. Were *laman* in these constructions an accusative of specification, the use with it of the possessive would seem to me a little odd: 'a man Julius in name' strikes me as more natural than 'a man Julius in *his* name'. But 'a man his name Julius' or 'a man's his name Julius', no matter what effect it has in English, was perfectly good Hittite and, I believe, was perfectly good Indo-European.[69]

---

modernizations of the archaic language of the earlier version. (See my study of its substitutions of *man* for *takku*, *Lg.* 20.91-107.) But such changes are usually in new material representing additions in content to the earlier form of the laws; and varieties of the sort that I have cited here are doubtless without linguistic significance.

[67] Here the Sumerian LU.ULU^{LU} with no phonetic complement probably represents the Hittite accusative in -*an* (which we have in the form LU-*an* in the corresponding §VIII); but the duplicate, *KBo* 6.2, has the genitive LU.ULU^{LU} -*as* (as already noted above, fn. 64).

[68] In classical Hittite, I think the genitive increases in frequency, and the possessive when accompanying it gives the effect of reinforcing it and thus adds emphasis, being no longer otiose. (I discussed this at the 24th International Congress of Orientalists at Munich in 1957; see the volume of *Akten* 159.)

[69] However, it cannot be denied that the possessive is also accounted for by Brugmann's theory as to the forerunner of the accusative of specification: certainly, *homo nomen suum Iulius* might mean 'there (is) a man—his name *Julius*' (indeed, I have already indicated the need of precisely this; cf. fn. 15). But the appositional form is in keeping with the style of the rest of the stories. Cf. (if we accept Friedrich's extremely plausible suppletion) the redundant apposition in *Appus* 1.29-30 *pa-a-i-ta-as* [SAL-] *za* 'she went, the woman', and the partitive apposition in 8-9 *a-ru-ni* ZAG-*si* 'by the sea (its) border'.

23. We find these constructions in two folk-tales or Märchen,[70] the story of Appus and his two sons, and the story of the hunter Kessis. The tale of Appus, after a short generalization which provides in advance the moral of the tale, starts off as follows: 1.7–10 URU-*as*[71] *SUM-an-se-it Su-du-ul Lu-ul-lu-wa-ya-as-sa-an* KUR-*e -a-ru-ni* ZAG-*si e-es-zi nu-kan se-ir* LU-*as Ap-pu SUM-an-se-it* KUR-*e-kan is-tar-na a-pa-a-as ha-ap-pi-na-an-za* 'there is a city its name Sudul in the country of the Lulluwans by the seashore,[72] and (there is) up (there) a man Appus his name.[73] In the midst of the country he (is) rich.' This is the first time in the story that we hear of either Sudul or Appus, and the verb *eszi*, despite its position at the end of the clause, is certainly used predicatively,[74] not copulatively. The beginning of the tale of Kessis is almost entirely lost; the hero Kessis has undoubtedly been heard of already, and evidently another man named Udubsarris. There follows a mutilated line (*KUB* 33.121.2.4) which is plausibly restored by Friedrich as meaning 'Kessis took Udubsarris' sister to be his wife'. The text continues (5–6) SAL-*as SUM-se-it Si-in-ta-li-me-ni mi-is-ri-*

Friedrich's translation (*ZA* 15.215) 'seitwärts am Meere', somewhat obscures the apposition, I think; but this is surely just as much an example of partitive apposition as the accusative phrase in the Law-Code, A. SA-*an* ZAG-*an* (Friedrich, *Ges.* 2 §53 = Hrozný, *CH* §168), which he himself cites in his discussion of partitive apposition (*Vert.* 1.44), translating it 'des Ackers Grenze' (similarly in *Ges.* 77 "die Grenze eines Feldes").

[70] Respectively *KUB* 24.8, *Bo* 2595, and *ABoT* 48; and *KUB* 17.1 and 33.121, and *Bo* 4473, 8143, and 8206. Published by Friedrich, *ZA* 15.214–25 and 234–43.

[71] URU-*as*, here as elsewhere, is unquestionably nominative, though the word sometimes behaves like an -*i* stem (genitive URU-*yas*, ablative URU-*riaz*); see Sturtevant, *Gl.* 43, Götze, *MS* 72, Friedrich, *Wört.* 299. Götze (*Kleinasien* 1.31 fn. 2, *MS* 72; less positively *AOr.* 5.17 fn. 1) equates the dative (URU-*ri*) with *happiri*, and, presumably on the strength of this, Sturtevant in his *Glossary* gives the Hittite nominative as **hap(p)iris* (43) or simply *happiris* (170); but in his personal copy of the *Glossary*, now in my possession, he changed the second *i* to *a* in the margin, thus giving *happiras*, the form accepted by Friedrich in his *Wörterbuch* (55 and 299). This form is surely preferable, in view of the indubitable examples of the nominative URU-*as* (*Kup.* §10 C 36, *Hukk.* 2.25, *KBo* 2.5.3.54, *KUB* 14.17.3.21, 24.7.4.46).

[72] Cf. fn. 69.

[73] It is worth noting that, while as usual *homo* precedes *nomen* (cf. fn. 20), the position here of *Iulius* is, also as usual, free: in 7 we have *homo nomen suum Iulius* (or, rather, *urbs nomen suum Roma*), and in 9–10 *homo Iulius nomen suum*. However, in one Hittite document, *Pud.*, the order is invariable, *homo Iulius nomen suum*; see fn. 135.

[74] It doubtless serves as predicate not only to URU-*as* 'city' in its own clause but to LU-*as* 'man' in the following clause. Friedrich's rendering in the latter ('wohnte') is rather free. Thus the construction is *urbs nomen Roma est, homo Iulius nomen (est)*, like that seen in the Sanskrit passage cited in fn. 10; cf. too §6 and fn. 12.

wa-an-za hu-u-ma-an-da-az-za as-sa-nu-wa-an-za 'the woman's her name (is) Sintalimenis—beautiful (and) endowed with everything'. Presumably here we have the genitive construction[75]—*mulieris nomen suum Iulia*, the later development that replaced *mulier nomen suum Iulia—SUM-set* (= *nomen suum*) the subject of a nominal clause, and *Sintalimeni* (= *Iulia*) the predicate. This is perfectly normal and natural, since we have already heard of the woman as being taken in marriage by Kessis. But in view of this, the following construction is exceedingly loose. In the Appus passage, the sentence clearly ends with the second *SUM-an-set*; *-kan* in the following *KUR-e-kan* marks the beginning of a new clause, which has its own subject *apas* 'he', and its own predicate *happinanz* 'rich'. In the Kessis story, Friedrich treats *misriwanz* and *humandaz assanuwanz* as predicates also, but he is compelled to supply a subject for them, which is completely irregular: note his translation (*ZA* 15.235), "(sie war) schön (und) mit allem ausgestattet". There is nothing at all to suggest that these two nominative adjectives are in a new clause; I think that much more probably they are in very loose agreement with *SUM-set*, since for the moment the writer was treating SAL-*as SUM-set* 'mulieris nomen suum' as if it had had the form of the phrase which was so often its equivalent, SAL-*za SUM-set* 'mulier nomen suum'.[76] The insertion of the name *Sintalimeni* (or *Iulia*),[77] which might have been used as predicate to either SAL-*za* (*mulier*) or *SUM-set* (*nomen suum*), would facilitate the inconcinnity.

24. We find in Hittite not only the type *hominis nomen Iulius* (*est*) but also the type *homini nomen Iulius* (*est*).[78] A certain example[79] in the Appus story is 3.10 *nu-us-si-[is-sa-an* HUL-*l]u SUM-an e-es-du*,

[75] I am assuming that SAL-*as* is a genitive, for SAL is normally an -*n*- stem, with nominative SAL-*za* (Friedrich, *El.* 1.107). However, instances of a nominative SAL-*as* are citable (Friedrich, *Wört.* 290, lists *KBo* 4.6.1.15, *KDB* 7.6.9); if that is what we have in *KUB* 33.121.2.5 (which, however, Friedrich does not list in his *Wörterbuch*), then SAL-*as* is in the same case as URU-*as* and LU-*as* in the Appus Story. But it is not used just as they are: the meaning is not '(there is) a woman, her name Sintalimenis, beautiful and endowed with everything', but 'the woman, her name Sintalimenis, (is) beautiful and endowed with everything'.

[76] Cf. §§12 and 21.

[77] Cf. §17.

[78] See fn. 25.

[79] The reading HUL-*lu* is assured by 3.7 (to be quoted later, §27). The reading -*san* is perhaps not assured (see §28), but is not pertinent.

literally 'the name Bad shall be to him', i.e. 'his name shall be Bad', 'he shall be called Bad'. But when Bad's younger brother,[80] Right or Just, is to be christened[81] in his turn, a different construction is used: 3.16 NIG.SI.SA-*an* SUM-*an* e-es-du. This is the ambiguous type, *Iulius nomen esto*.[82] Friedrich (*ZA* 15.221) translates "(sein) Name soll Recht sein!", presumably making SUM-*an* (*nomen*) the subject and NIG.SI.SA-*an* (*Iulius*) the predicate. Güterbock (*JAOS* 65.250) translates "Just be the name!", apparently making NIG.SI.SA-*an* the subject and SUM-*an* the predicate. But I would propose that here we have our familiar partitive apposition, 'he his name shall be Just.'[83]

25. My reason is as follows. The whole passage runs (following a lacuna): pa-id-du NIG.SI.SA-*an* SUM-*an* e-es-du. Güterbock begins his quotation and translation with NIG.SI.SA-*an*; *paiddu* plays no part in the point that he is making. Friedrich's translation of the entire line is as follows: "[nun] mag er gehen, (und) (sein) Name soll Recht sein!" As Friedrich indicates by enclosing *und* in parentheses, this word has no counterpart in the Hittite. And that is very significant. The absence of a connective to join *paiddu* and *esdu* shows clearly that they are in the same clause, with *paiddu* serving as a quasi-auxiliary to introduce *esdu*,[84] or, in other words, as an example of what Friedrich himself elsewhere (*Vert.* 1.162) calls a "phraseologisches Verbum".[85] The

---

[80] They are probably not twins, as Güterbock calls them (*Kum.* 120); note Friedrich's very plausible suppletion, 3.11–12.

[81] I hope I may be pardoned the anachronism!

[82] See fn. 17.

[83] This is of course the type that ultimately, in Sanskrit probably and in Greek certainly, became 'he shall be good in name' with *nomen* an accusative of specification. But, as I have already said (§20), I do not believe this step has been taken in Hittite.

[84] The construction reminds us somewhat of our English *go and see him* for *go to see him*, although the English usage differs in two ways: (1) a connective is used (in the also possible *go see him*, *see* must be an infinitive, for we cannot say *he goes sees him*); (2) the meaning of *go* (like that of *try* in *try and do it* instead of *try to do it*), is always present, I think, even though at times it may be very faintly adumbrated (note that there is no difference in meaning between the alternative names for the childhood game, *hide-and-seek* and *hide-and-go-seek*).

[85] Sommer and Ehelolf (*Pap.* 72) have a different explanation of such collocations, regarding the first verb as impersonal, 'it happens (that)'; but I think Friedrich is surely right in his opposition to this view (*Vert.* 1.162 fn. 2) on the basis of passages—such as *KBo* 3.3.1.7–8—in which both verbs are plural. Sommer (*HAB* 55, on 2.24) cites Friedrich's discussion (*Vert.* 1.162–63) apparently with approval, and even echoes his characterization of the first verb as "phraseologisch"; yet in the same breath he calls the second verb the predicate of the first (I would rather say its subject if I agreed with Sommer's

verbs *i-* 'go', *pai-* 'go', and *uwa-* 'come', are all used in this way.[86] At times the idea of motion is, or at least may be, strong, as in *KBo* 6.29.2.25 *pa-a-i-u-e-ni-wa-ra-an-kan ku-en-nu-um-mi-e-ni* 'we will go (and) kill him';[87] but at other times, especially when the second (or main) verb is static in sense, it is, or at least may be, weak or practically non-existent, as in *Tel.* 2.13 *nu-us-ma-as* E.MES *tag-ga-as-ta pa-a-an-du-wa-az a-sa-an-du* 'he built houses for them (with the words), "let them go (and) stay (there)"', and, still more, *Kup.* §4 D26–27 *nu-wa-ra-as-mu* DUMU-*as e-es-zi nu-wa u-iz-zi zi-la-ti-ya* A-NA KUR-*TI* [*e-es-zi*[88]] EN-*as* 'he is my son and henceforth he will go (and) be lord in the land'. The imperative[89] is particularly common in this use, as in *Tel.* 2.13 (just quoted) as well as in our own example *KUB* 24.8.3.16.[90] The close connection between the two verbs, and the fact that they belong to one and the same clause, is shown by another circumstance: the enclitics such as *-wa*, the unemphatic personal pronouns,[91] the adverbial particles *kan* and *san*, etc., which are always attached to the *first* word of the clause in which they belong, are added to the sentence-connective *nu* if it precedes the auxiliary verb (we have already noted that there is no connective between this verb and the main verb), or to the auxiliary verb itself if *it* stands first in the clause

---

interpretation), and he shows by his translation (*HAB* 4) of the passage in question ("Und *so* wird *es* kommen: [Er wird] sie vernichten") that he still retains the opinion expressed in *Pap.*

[86] For examples, see Friedrich, *Vert.* 1.162–63.

[87] The would-be murderers had been with their intended victim (23), who had taken refuge in the city of Samuhas (20), and whom Hattusilis was apparently pursuing (21); but it was in the city of Sulappas (22) that they met Hattusilis to make their treasonous offer, so presumably some physical 'going' would be necessary before the killing could take effect.

[88] This is my conjecture in place of Friedrich's [*a-pa-a-as*] (*Vert.* 1.110). Friedrich's suppletion, which he himself terms "unsicher" (ib., fn. 1), assumes a nominal type of expression 'he (will be) lord', but I prefer the verbal type, '(he) will be lord', for I think that after *uizzi* a second verb is in order. Besides, after the subject *-as* a second subject *apas* referring to the same person seems scarcely likely, though I admit it is possible.

[89] The imperative of verbs meaning 'go' in any case easily loses its full force. Sometimes it becomes almost an interjection, as in German *geh'!*, English *go on!*

[90] Cf., from *i-*, *KBo* 5.6.3.22, *Yuzg.* 1.21; from *uwa-*, *KBo* 6.34.3.27–28. So too in Latin, e.g. Plautus, *Aul.* 829 i redde aurum (see Hofmann, *Lat. Gr.* 654 and 824; and Szantyr 339, 471, and 783); similarly *age*.

[91] Even before the construction was fully understood, Götze (*Hatt.* 109) noted this use of a "proleptic object" in *KBo* 6.29.2.25.

(as I believe it always does unless the sentence-connective *nu* introduces it, in which case it stands second). Finally, it is, or should be, obvious that this type of construction is possible *only* when the two verbs involved have a common subject.

26. This brings me back to our passage *KUB* 24.8.3.16 and to Friedrich's translation of it, "[nun] mag er gehen, (und) (sein) Name soll Recht sein!" I do not believe it is possible to make the *puer* ('er') subject of *paiddu*, and the *nomen* ('Name') subject of *esdu*. Since I doubt whether an inanimate like a name would be directed to 'go and be Just', I believe we must conclude that this order is directed to the baby; unless we view *SUM-an* as an accusative of specification[92] ('he shall be Just in name'), we must explain it as in partitive apposition with the subject of the two verbs, the meaning being 'he (his) name shall be Just'.

27. The ten lines (3.7–16) in the tale of Appus devoted to the naming of the two children constitute a veritable *locus classicus* for naming constructions, of which they provide a considerable number and a considerable variety. We have already noted two examples of completely different types with the verb 'be', *(ille) Iulius nomen esto* (16) with a representative of *puer* as subject, and *illi Iulius nomen esto* (10) with the word representing *puer* in the dative. We also find two examples of the construction *puero nomen Iulium* (or *Iulium nomen*) *indunt*,[93] both with the word representing *puer* in the dative: *nu-us-si-is-sa-an sa-ni-iz-zi*[94] *lam-an* HUL-*lu da-a-is* (7) 'he set upon him the sweet name Bad', and *nu-us-si-kan* NIG.SI.SA-*an SUM-an da-is* (13) 'he set on him the name Just'.[95]

---

[92] I have already recorded my objection to this. See §20 and fn. 83.

[93] Cf. §14 and fn. 39.

[94] The locution *sanezzi laman* 'sweet name', which almost reminds us of our English *pet-name*, and which certainly does not seem appropriate as the description of an appellation meaning 'Bad', is apparently a technical expression of some sort, or perhaps *sanezzi* is a stock epithet. We meet the phrase also in *Kum.* (33.93.3.14), where Güterbock (*Kum.* 15) originally translated it "den süssen Namen" (as did Friedrich in the Appus passage, *ZA* 15.221), but later changed this to "dear name" (*JCS* 5.153), whereas Goetze (*ANET* 122) rendered it "a propitious name". The effect of 'sweet name' or 'dear name' here is somewhat like that of 'dear child' in the comparable naming passage in Greek, Homer, *Od.* 19.403–4; on this see below, fnn. 326 and 331.

[95] Here once more (cf. above, fn. 73) we note the free variation in order: *nomen Iulium* in 7, *Iulium nomen* in 13. But the variation between -*san*, which suggests motion up, and -*kan*, which suggests motion down, is rather odd (still cf. English *drink up* and

28. Finally, we find the construction *nomen Iulium nominant*[96] in 14 [...]*-sa-an* NIG.SI.SA-*an* SUM-*an hal-zi-es-sa-an-du*. Güterbock (*JAOS* 65.250) so reads, and translates "let them call his name Just!", though '*the* name', which he there used, as we have already noted, for 16 (also for 33.93.3.29), would better fit his text. Friedrich (*ZA* 15.221) gives a similar rendering, "[Nun] soll man [seinen] Namen Recht rufen!", but he accounts for his "[seinen]" by his suppletion at the beginning of the line, which he prints as follows: [*nu-us-si-is*]-*sa-an* NIG.SI.SA-*an* SUM-*an hal-zi-es-sa-an-du*. Now the only one of the five passages that actually begins *nu-us-si-is-sa-an* (i.e. *nu* 'et' + *-si* 'ei' + particle *-san*) is 7 *nu-us-si-*[*i*]*s-sa-an sa-ni-iz-zi lam-an* HUL-*lu da-a-is* 'et ei (*-san*) dulce nomen Malum indidit'. The parallel passage, 13, has *-kan* instead of *-san*:[97] *nu-us-si-kan* NIG.SI.SA-*an* SUM-*an da-is* 'et ei (*-kan*) Iustum nomen indidit'. In 10 *-san* is supplied by Friedrich: *nu-us-si-*[*is-sa-an* HUL-*l*]*u* SUM-*an e-es-du* 'et ei (*-san*) Malum nomen esto'. I am not sure that this suppletion is well-advised; the presence of *-san* with the verb *dai-* 'put, set' by no means justifies its insertion with *es-* 'be'. In the corresponding passage where *es-* occurs (though, as we have seen, with a quite different construction), 16 NIG.SI.SA-*an* SUM-*an e-es-du* '(is) Iustum nomen esto', there is again a lacuna at the opening of the clause.[98] Finally, in 14, as we have seen, *-san* stands in the text, *halziessa-* 'call'[99] evidently requiring a particle of the sort just as *dai-* does; but in this instance it is the suppletion of the dative *-si* 'ei' that I would question. This cannot be a dative of indirect object, as with *dai-*, or a dative of possession, as with *es-*; and I question whether a dative of reference (as implied by Friedrich's "[seinen]") is in order here. I would suggest instead, if it will fill the space, [*na-an*]-*sa-an* NIG.SI.SA-*an* SUM-*an hal-zi-es-sa-an-du*. Neither for Friedrich's version, 'et ei (*-san*) Iustum nomen nominanto', nor for mine, 'et eum (*-san*) Iustum nomen nominanto', can I cite a

---

drink down, burn up and burn down, without very much difference in meaning); I have tried to suggest the shift by using 'upon' in the first passage, 'on' in the second.

[96] Cf. above, §13 and fn. 35.

[97] As we already observed in fn. 95.

[98] But if we are to supply either *-san* or *-kan* in the similar passage from *Ullikummi* (on which see below, fn. 108), we should perhaps do so here too, perhaps reading [*na-as-sa-an*] or [*na-as-kan*].

[99] We have already observed in fn. 61 the use of this verb in this sense.

positive parallel from Hittite:[100] but mine is at least better suited to the usual behavior of the language, and conforms to the regular Indo–European pattern, at least as seen in Avestan and Greek (cf. fn. 35). Incidentally, the general dearth of examples of this type in Hittite would seem to militate against the view of Delbrück and Kieckers (discussed above in fn. 13) that it was with it that the *nomen* construction began.

29. To turn from folk-tale to epic, we find an excellent parallel to *KUB* 24.8.3.16 (treated in detail above) in the Kumarbis myth, 33.93.3.29 in Güterbock's original edition (1940) *nu-wa-ra Ul-li-kum-mi SUM-an e-es-du* (12). Güterbock in *JAOS* 65.250 translates the two passages in the same way: "Just be the name!", "Ullikummi be the name!";[101] and Otten, in his notes on the Kumarbis passage (*MGK* 15 note 5), specifically compares the same Appus passage. Laroche in *RHA* 8.21–23 (1948) ingeniously shows that a different alignment of fragments necessitates a new arrangement of the passage; and the designation of the name now appears in 33.93.3.18 *pa-id-d[u ...*] *Ul-li-kum-mi SUM-an e-es-du*, which Laroche restores *pa-id-d[u-wa nu-ka]n Ul-li-kum-mi SUM-an e-es-du*, and translates "Qu'il marche, et que son nom soit Ullikummi!" Laroche's general treatment is brilliant, but I am sure this particular bit of restoration is wrong.[102] If we supply *nu*, thus putting *paiddu* and *esdu* into separate clauses, we certainly must supply *-wa* also[103] (this particle is freely omitted in the

---

[100] We do find somewhat similar passages (though without *laman*) in the sense 'they (or you) called me a child', *KBo* 3.4.1.23–24 and 2.12; so far as form goes, the pronoun *-mu* might also be a dative (it is only in the third person that the enclitic personal pronouns distinguish the two cases), but the sense surely demands an accusative.

[101] In his original edition (16) he had translated "Und [...] Ullikummi soll *sein* Name sein!", which would rather have provided a parallel for 24.8.3.10, which he renders (*JAOS* 250), "Evil be *his* name!" (italics mine in both instances). This looks as if he was supplying a dative in the lacuna before *Ul-li-kum-mi* (like *-si-* in 24.8.3.7). Since his text began the clause with *nu-wa-ra-*, which presupposes a following enclitic beginning with *a-*, like *-as*, I do not see how the suppletion of a dative could be justified. However, in the light of the new arrangement of the passage, which places *nu-wa-ra-* eleven lines after the *Ul-li-kum-mi* clause, the question becomes purely academic.

[102] I also question another small detail in Laroche's treatment of the passage. He, and after him Otten (*MGK* 15) and Güterbock (*JCS* 5.153), to judge by their translations, refer *ku-in* DUMU-*an* in 17 back to *-si* in 16; but it is much more in keeping with Hittite word order to put a stop after the supplied verb in 16, and refer *ku-in* DUMU-*an* to the subject (probably *-as* to be restored in 17) of the verb *wa-at-ku-ut* in 18 (I gather from Goetze's translation, *ANET* 122, that he shares this view).

[103] I am not sure whether we need *-kan*; cf. below, fn. 108.

informally written folk-tales like the one about Appus, but the story of Kumarbis, being a myth or even an epic, is written in a more careful and dignified style, of which the regular use of -wa is a feature). Güterbock's restoration in *JCS* 5.152 (1951) is vastly superior; it runs as follows, *pa-id-d*[*u-wa-as*(-*si?*)-*sa-a*]*n Ul-li-kum-mi* SUM-*an e-es-du*. He bases this suppletion (ib. note 8) on 24.8.3.10, 14, 16, as published by Friedrich; he evidently gets his questionable -*si* [104] from 10 *nu-us-si-*[*is-sa-an*], -*san* from 14 [*nu-us-si-is*]-*sa-an*, and—admirably—the combination of *paiddu* and *esdu* in a single clause from 16. Yet in his translation (153) he separates the two verbs just as Laroche did: "He shall go! Ullikummi be his name!" [105] In other words, he errs, in my opinion, just as Friedrich erred when he translated *paiddu* in 24.8.3.16 "[nun] mag er gehen".[106] Also, since, as I insist, *paiddu* and *esdu* must have the same subject, the -*si* which he inserts doubtfully is in my opinion quite impossible.[107] As for -*san*, which he gets from 24.8.3.14, I have already expressed doubt about transferring a particle used with *halzessa-* 'call' to *es-* 'be'; but if the traces of a character (presumably just a verticle wedge) which Laroche records as [-*ka*]*n* and Güterbock as [-*a*]*n* are indubitable, then I suppose we must read -*kan* with Laroche or -*sa-an*—i.e. -*san*—with Güterbock.[108] I would accordingly restore

---

[104] There would of course be no such objection on phonetic grounds to the occurrence of -*si* here as I have raised in connection with his earlier reading (see fn. 101). But I believe there is an objection on syntactic grounds, as I shall show just below.

[105] See Goetze in his translation (*ANET* 122): "let him go and [his] name be Ullikummis!" Otten, however, seems to be interpreting *pa-id-du* as I do (both here and in 24.8.3.16, which he specifically compares), to judge by his translation (*MGK* 15): "Wohlan [,   ] Ullikummi soll ⟨sein⟩ Name sein!", for his "wohlan" may correspond roughly to the Hittite auxiliary; but I cannot agree with the remainder of his translation. See below, fn. 107.

[106] It may be that he is influenced by the next line, 19 *nu-wa-ra-as-kan ne-pi-si* [LUGAL-*iz-na-*] *an-ni* UGU *pa-id-du*, which he renders "Up to Heaven to kingship he shall go!" By his double "he shall go", involving a repetition not introduced by any of the other translators, he may seem to indicate a belief that *pa-id-du* in 18 anticipates *pa-id-du* in 19. Then *Ul-li-kum-mi* SUM-*an e-es-du* in 18 might be viewed as more or less parenthetical. This would justify the omission of *nu* with this clause, but hardly the omission of -*wa*, and still less the transfer of (-*si?*)-*sa-an* from *e-es-du* to *pa-id-du*. Besides, the giving of the names is seemingly too important an act to be relegated casually to a parenthesis.

[107] So, too, Otten's "⟨sein⟩" and Goetze's "[his]" (see fn. 105).

[108] I do not know which is preferable. Our passage is less close in construction to 24.8.3.14, which has -*san*, than it is to one which perhaps has -*kan*, namely 24.8.1.9-10 *nu-k*[*an*] *se-ir* LU-*as Ap-pu* SUM-*an-se-it*; but here the *kan*, if it is the correct reading,

pa-id-d[u-wa-as], *pa-id-d[u-wa-as-sa-an]*, or *pa-id-d[u-wa-as-kan]*; and I would translate 'he (his) name shall go (and) be Ullikummi', i.e. 'let him go and be named Ullikummi'.

30. One more detail remains to be noted about the use of the *laman* construction in Hittite, and that is the form that corresponds to *Iulius*. This is uniform, whether a nominative or an accusative is called for: *i-* stems, *Sintalemini* (nominative), *Ullikummi* (nominative); *u-* stems, *Appu* (nominative), HUL-*lu*, i.e. *Idalu* (nominative and accusative); consonant stems, NIG.SI.SA-*an*, i.e. *Handan*[109] (nominative and accusative), *Sudul* (nominative). These are explained by Güterbock (*JAOS* 65.250) and Laroche (*RA* 43.75–76) as bare stem-forms, used, to quote Güterbock "as a kind of 'absolute' form (for names introduced into the story or bestowed on a child)"—in other words when the name is spoken of as a name.[110]

31. But there is a complication which Güterbock himself recognizes (ib.). HUL-*lu* (i.e. *Idalu*) is the stem-form of HUL-*lus* (i.e. *Idalus*), and NIG.SI.SA-*an* (i.e. *Handan*) may (as was noted in fn. 109) be said to be the stem-form of NIG.SI.SA-*anza* (i.e. *Handanza*, doubtless pronounced *Handanz*). But were the brothers named HUL-*lus* and NIG.SI.SA-*anza*? The older one is always called HUL-*as*[111] (*KUB* 24.8.4.4, 8, 21, 24, 28); and the younger one, when he is given a phonetic complement at all,[112] is called both NIG.SI.SA-*za* (4.6) and

does *not* seem to have anything to do with the naming construction, in view of its absence in the previous, and parallel, sentence 1.7 URU-*as* SUM-*an-se-it Su-du-ul*. Whatever we do here, we should probably also do in the very similar passage 24.8.3.16 (cf. fn. 98).

[109] According to the ingenious conjecture of Güterbock, *JAOS* 65.250. Actually, the stem is *handant-* (the nominative *handanz* represents *handant-* + -*s*). But final *t* disappears after *n* (see Sturtevant, *HG* 60); and so if the stem *handant-* really appears as a separate entity, presumably it would have to take the form *handan*.

[110] Both these scholars, in opposition to Goetze (*Kizz.* V), believe that this is an argument for using the stem-form when we cite Hittite names in English; so too Laroche, *Onom.* 5. I cannot follow them here at all. If they are right, perhaps we ought to say, "There was a man called Appu", but I see no relevant reason for saying anything but "*Appus* got up"—which is what the story says, 1.38. I discuss this question in some detail in a review of Laroche, *Onom.*, in *Wd.* 11.455–58. However, I agree with Güterbock (*JAOS* 65.250 fn. 17) that Goetze for the sake of consistency should use the inflected form in geographical as well as personal names.

[111] HUL-*lu-us* in the second fragment (*ABoT* 48.6) is a conjecture of Friedrich's, and should doubtless be HUL-*as* in view of all the earlier passages.

[112] Three times his name appears simply as NIG.SI.SA with no phonetic complement.

NIG.SI.SA-*as* (4.21).[113] Of HUL-*as* and NIG.SI.SA-*as* Güterbock says (*JAOS* 65.250), "Apparently the two brothers here bear names in -*a*-stems different from those in the earlier part of the text."[114] If the brothers really had *a*-stem names, HUL-*lu* in 3.7 and (probably) 10, and NIG.SI.SA-*an* in 3.13, 14, and 16, cannot be the stem-forms of these names.

32. But what were these names? It is certain that they meant something more or less like 'Bad' and 'Good, Right, Just'; the reasons for choosing them are said by Appus to lie in the phrases HUL-*pa-an*[115] KASKAL-*an* 'bad way' (3.9) and NIG.SI.SA-*an* KASKAL-*an* 'right way' or 'good way' (3.15; cf. 8–9),[116] but the connection may be merely one of semantics, not necessarily of actual etymology.

33. It seems to me that there can be little doubt that the name of the older one was *Huwappas*. In the *Hatt.* text, where *KUB* 1.1.1.49 (Götze's A) has HUL-*lu*, i.e. *idalu*, *KUB* 1.4.1.41 (Götze's B) has -*an*, which cannot come from *idalus* but can come from *huwappas*, and *KUB* 1.5.1.21 (Götze's D) has *hu-u-wa-ap-p[a]* (see Götze, *Hatt.* 11 note *n*). Similarly in the Appus text (as has just been noted in fn. 115)

In the first two instances none is needed, since the case is clearly indicated by a following appositive, SES-*si* in 4.4 and SES-*ni* in 4.8; and probably the same thing is true of the occurrence in 4.29, which is followed by a lacuna. (In SES-*si*, -*si* is the dative of the enclitic possessive, and in SES-*ni*, -*i* is the dative case-ending, and *n* must be the root of the unknown Hittite word for 'brother', which is obviously an *a*-stem in -*nas* like *arunas*, since it appears in the nominative as SES-*as* in 4.4, 6, 8, and 24.)

[113] The accusative form NIG.SI.SA-*an* in *ABoT* 48.5 is ambiguous; it might correspond to a nominative in -*as* or in -*anz*(*a*).

[114] However, he later reversed himself so far as NIG.SI.SA-*as* goes. See below, fn. 122.

[115] The main text, *KUB* 24.8.3.9, has LUHUL-*lu* KASKAL-*an*, which does not seem possible to me. In the first place, HUL-*lu* is preceded by the determinative LU 'man', which certainly does not belong here; and in the second place, HUL-*lu* is neuter and KASKAL-*an* is masculine (the nominative appears as KASKAL-*as* and KASKAL-*is*; see Friedrich, *Wört.* 280). I suggest that LUHUL-*lu* here is a scribal error, the writer's eye having been caught by the form LUHUL-*lu* two lines above in almost the same position in the line, and that we should rather adopt the variant HUL-*pa-an* (even though the HUL here is not certain), which occurs in the duplicate, *Bo* 2595.2.7 (see Friedrich, *ZA* 15.220 fn. 4).

[116] Friedrich suggests that these phrases refer to Appus' life: he had ill fortune in the beginning (*ZA* 15.245) so long as he was young (ib. 221 fn. 2). But I have wondered whether 'the bad way' and 'the right way' may have something to do with the manner of birth of the children; cf. the reference in *KUB* 33.120.2.23–38 to the possible birth of Kumarbis' son the Storm-God from 'the good place' (Goetze, *ANET* 121).

where the main text *KUB* 24.8.3.9 has HUL-*lu*, the duplicate *Bo* 2595.2.7 (Friedrich's D) has HUL(?)-*pa-an*, which like HUL-*an* in *Hatt.* cannot come from *idalus* but can come from *huwappas*. The word *huwappas* is sometimes preceded by the sign called the Glossenkeil, which is supposed to be used to designate the following word as Luwian; [117] for instance the dative *huwappi* is so marked in *Hatt.* 1.40 (though not so in 4.12). To be sure, there is a Luwian word corresponding to *idalus* which appears as *adduwala* and *adduwalin* (so Sommer, *AU* 50 and fn. 5, and Rosenkranz, *IF* 56.282–83); but certainly a language can have more than one word for 'bad'.[118] As for the younger brother, if he really had an *a*-stem name I have wondered whether it might have been *Handas* 'true, right'.[119] Güterbock (*JAOS*

[117] It has been suggested (by Rosenkranz, *IF* 56.282) that Luwian was the "Umgangssprache" of Hatti, and if so it is particularly in place in a folk-tale. Furthermore, the story of Appus is Hurrian in its origin, and the presence of "Luwian loanwords in Hittite texts dealing with Hurrian myths" is commented on by Güterbock (Kramer 143); cf. also Goetze (*JAOS* 69.178) on the "almost indissolvable mixture from Hattic, Luwian, Hittite and Hurrian elements", and Otten (*MGK* 33) on the large number of words in the Kumarbis myths that are shown by the Glossenkeil to be Luwian.

[118] Cf. English *bad, evil, ill, naughty*; French *mauvais, méchant*; Italian *cattivo, malo*; etc. Roots meaning 'bad' in Indo–European languages, and words meaning 'bad' within a single language, show much more variety than those meaning 'good'; cf. Buck, *Syn.* 1175 and 1177, and note e.g. that his listing for New High German includes only a single word for 'good' (1175) but five different ones for 'bad' (1177).

[119] This meaning was proposed by Götze, *Hatt.* 91–93 (1925), and accepted by Sommer, *AU* 70, 81, 126, 160 (1932). Later, however, in *AM* 222 (1933), Götze gave up his earlier view in favor of the suggestion by Friedrich, *IF* 49.226 (1931), that *handas* is merely a by-form of the postposition *handa* meaning "gemäss, entsprechend, um ... willen". Szemerényi (*Körös* 1.13), although he accepts the view that *handas* is a "Nebenform" of *handa*, pronounces it "morphologisch nicht deutlich", and I quite agree with him. Hittite has several pairs of adverbs (classed also as postpositions or preverbs) ending in *-a* and *-an*, as *anda andan, appa appan, katta kattan*; but the only pair in *-a -as* that I can cite is *istarna istarnas* (as in the almost identical passage *KUB* 24.3.1.30 and 24.1.2.21), which, being derived from a "frozen" noun form, is hardly a parallel for what would appear to be a genuine postposition. (One may think of Greek *houtō houtôs, ek ex*, Latin *ab abs*; but Hittite, though it has evidence of *s* movable, apparently does not use it in this way.) It is true that *handa* and *handas* in the examples cited by Götze, *AM* 222, seem used in a parallel way (cf. too *handas* in *Tav.* 1.38 and 59); it is likewise true that in all the examples known to me, *handas* follows a dative and therefore may well be a postposition; but on the other hand it is also true that in all these examples the verb is in the singular, and therefore *handas* may well be an adjective in agreement with the subject. If *handas* is indeed an adverb or postposition, I would suggest—and here we have a way of accounting for it morphologically—that it may be a "frozen" form of a nominative singular adjective. The transition may have come about precisely in such a phrase as Hattusilis' oft-repeated *SA SES-YA na-ak-ki-ya-an-ni ha-an-da-as*

65.250) equates *NIG.SI.SA-* with *handant-*, the stem of *handanza* (cf. fn. 109), because *handandatar* of the main *Hatt.* text (1.45) appears as *NIG.SI.SA-tar* in the duplicate *ABoT* 62.1.38. But *handandatar* of *Hatt.* 4.18 appears as *handatar* in another duplicate (*KUB* 1.4.3.60, Götze's B; see Götze, *Hatt.* 53). Hence *NIG.SI.SA-tar* must represent *handatar* as well as *handandatar*,[120] and *NIG.SI.SA-* should be equal to

---

U-UL ma-an-ka i-ya-nu-un (*Hatt.* 3.38–39, 4.29–30, 4.61; cf. *KBo* 6.29.1.35–36, 2.37–38), reappearing in the shorter form in the *Tawagalawas* letter, *A-NA ŠEŠ-YA ha-an-da-aš* etc. (*Tav.* 2.56). Note that the adjectival meaning 'true' fits in both varieties: 'true to respect for my brother, I did nothing' and 'true to my brother, I did nothing'. Presumably the same postposition can be used after the abstract noun 'respect' and the personal noun 'brother'; yet it does look as if Friedrich had chosen his translations of his postposition *handaš* with a special eye to these possibilities—'in accordance with respect for my brother' (*gemäss, entsprechend*), or 'for the sake of my brother' (*um ... willen*). The development of a masculine adjective (or participle) into an adverb or even a preposition, though less common than that of a neuter adjective, is not unexampled in the ancient languages: cf. Latin *comminus, eminus, versus, adversus, trans.* An adjective meaning 'true' would seem particularly susceptible to such a development; cf. such an English expression as *to run true to form*, where it is quite possible to regard *true*, normally an adjective, as an adverb, or *true to* as a preposition. The shift from adjective to preposition is complete in the common use, whether purists approve in every case or not, of *according to*, which is very close in sense to *true to*, and in the somewhat less similar *respecting* and *regarding*, as well as the quite different *owing to* and *due to*—not to mention, in German, Friedrich's own *gemäss* and *entsprechend*! Furthermore, even if this explanation of the origin of *handaš* in all the passages cited is not accepted, I think the existence of an adjective *handaš* is still strongly supported by the adverbial accusative *handan* 'truly, really' (as in *Hatt.* 3.78) and also by the denominative verb *hantiya-* 'be true to, support, worship', German 'betreuen', as in *KBo* 6.29.1.16, *KUB* 14.3.3.58). The adverb *handan*, to be sure, might come from the participle *handanz*, but it seems to me to fit much better an adjective *handaš* 'true'—whereas contrariwise *handan* in *KUB* 13.2.3.28 *ku-it ha-an-da-an a-pa-a-at i-iš-ša* 'do that which (is) ordained' (on which see Sommer, *HAB* 98 fn. 4, and Gurney, *AAA* 27.75) seems to me to fit much better the participle *handanz* 'ordained (by moral law), just, right' (as in *KUB* 24.3.1.34). The verb *hantiya-* bears the same relationship to *handaš* as *irmalaya-* 'be ill' bears to *irmalaš* (cited below, fn. 121); to be sure, *hantiya-* is transitive (cf. Sommer, *AU* 160), but that may be a secondary development in meaning. Götze when he believed in the existence of an adjective *handaš* associated *hantiya-* with it (*Hatt.* 93; also *KlF* 1.128, though he offered a different explanation in *KlF* 1.232); so too Sommer, *AU* 160 (who agrees with *KlF* 1.128, not 232).

[120] On the interchangeability of *para handatar* and *para handandatar*, see Hrozný, *SH* 73; Sommer and Ehelolf, *Pap.* 30; Götze, *Hatt.* 53 and 118, *Madd.* 136; Sturtevant, *Chr.* 229 (where *handatar*, fourth line from the end, should be changed to *handandatar*), *Gl.* 42; Sommer, *HAB* 98; Gurney, *AAA* 27.76; Friedrich, *Wört.* 53. (We may note in passing that *handatar* is in the same relation to *handaš* as *marsatar* is to *marsaš*, cited in fn. 121.) To discuss the precise meaning and interrelationship of the two nouns and of the corresponding verbs *para handa-* and *para handanda-* (Sturtevant, *Gl.* 41; Gurney, *AAA* 27.77; Friedrich, *Wört.* 52) would take us too far afield; but I cannot help wondering whether *handaš* (stem *handa-*) and *handanz* (stem *handant-*) come into the picture.

handa- as well as to *handant-*; and so while NIG.SI.SA-*za* stands for *Handanz(a)* in *Appus* 4.6, NIG.SI.SA-*as* can stand for *Handas* in *Appus* 4.21.[121] However, it is not absolutely necessary to assume that NIG.SI.SA-*as* represents an *a*-stem.[122] The whole form is NIG.SI.SA-*as-s[a]*, and this can stand not only for *Handas-a* but also for *Handanz-a*, since an adjective in -*anz*(a) before the enclitic -*a* can be written -*an-za-as-sa* as well as -*an-za-sa*.[123]

34. Finally, how are we to explain *lam-an* HUL-*lu* and the probable [HUL-*l*]*u* SUM-*an* in 3.7 and 10, and NIG.SI.SA-*an* SUM-*an* in 3.14 and 16? As has been said in fn. 121, NIG.SI.SA-*an* can be the stem-form of *Handanz(a)* (though not of the perhaps possible variant *Handas*), but HUL-*lu* cannot possibly be the stem-form of *Huwappas* or of any other *a*-stem. However, both HUL-*lu* and NIG.SI.SA-*an* can be nominative-accusative neuters of the adjectives HUL-*lus* or *idalus* and NIG.SI.SA-*anz(a)* or *handanz(a)* (as well as of NIG.SI.SA-*as* or *handas* if we accept this possibility), both these adjectives being in agreement with SUM-*an* or *laman* (cf. above, §17). Then these names might be described as 'a bad name' and 'a right or good name', even though at least one of the adjectives used is not identical with the actual name; such a shift seems to me much easier if HUL-*lu* and NIG.SI.SA-*an* are adjectives modifying the word *laman*[124] than if they are stem-forms actually representing the true names.

[121] Cf. e.g. *marsas* and *marsanz(a)* 'bad', *irmalas* and *irmalanz(a)* 'ill', *dapiyas* and *dapiyanz(a)* 'whole'; and see Friedrich, *Vert.* 1.80 and *El.* 1.13, and Sturtevant, *HG* 79. Perhaps we may add to these doublets *masiyas* and *masiyanz(a)* 'quantus'; see Hahn, *Lg.* 18.96. The fact that in some instances, e.g. *irmalanz(a)* and *dapiyanz(a)*, the form in -*anz*(a) is evidently a direct derivative from the form in -*as*, while in others, e.g. *marsanz(a)* (on which see Friedrich, *Vert.* 1.80–81) and our own *handanz(a)* (on which see Gurney, *AAA* 27.77), it is probably rather to be classed as the participle of a verb, need not affect the mutual relationship of the doublets in actual practice. The interchangeability of these doublets may have been facilitated by the fact that they are identical in the nominative-accusative neuter in -*an*. This is the form that is presumably represented in our text not only by NIG.SI.SA-*an* in *ABoT* 48.5 (on which see fn. 113), but also perhaps by NIG.SI.SA-*an* with *SUM-an* in *KUB* 24.8.3.14, which thus can fit equally well with either of the younger brothers' names (if he really has two) if it is a neuter adjective as I think, but not if it is a stem-form as Güterbock thinks.

[122] Güterbock made this comment orally at a meeting of the American Oriental Society in March 1963.

[123] See Friedrich, *Vert.* 1.33 fn. 1 and 166 fn. 2; Sturtevant, *HG* 15–16; Friedrich, *El.* 1.7.

[124] Güterbock, who considers only to dismiss it the possibility that the words are neuter adjectives modifying *laman* (*JAOS* 65.250 fn. 15), feels that under this hypothesis

35. In general in the naming constructions (as already pointed out in fn. 53), it is impossible to decide whether the word denoting the proper name (*Iulius* of our type example) is a stem-form or a neuter adjective, since the two are identical in form. The only declension that has an inflectional ending for the nominative-accusative neuter is that of the *a*- stems (Indo-European *o*- stems), where we find -*an* corresponding to Greek -*on*, Latin -*um*; but even here in the adjectives (though apparently not in the nouns) -*an* alternates with zero.[125]

36. Most Hittite personal names are "masculine" (i.e. animate) vowel-stems,[126] and thus in the naming construction we usually find forms in -*a*, -*i*, and -*u*, as we have already noted.[127] Güterbock's rejected suggestion (*JAOS* 65.250 note 15) that HUL-*lu* and NIG.SI.SA-*an* might be neuter adjectives used as attributes of *laman* is not intended to apply to such a form as *Ullikummi* in 23.93.3.29 (indeed, one of his reasons for rejecting the suggestion is precisely that the latter form is against this assumption); but I cannot help wondering whether such forms as *Ullikummi* and *Appu* might not be adjectives quite as much as HUL-*lu*, even though the words themselves are in origin nouns.[128] It may seem fantastic to suggest that in *homo nomen Iulius* the noun *Iulius* can turn into an adjective *Iulium* in agreement with *nomen*,[129] but it is no more fantastic than what certainly happens in Old Persian, in which the noun *nomen* turns into an adjective in agreement with

---

too the difference between the words used in bestowing the names, and the names used later in the text, remains unexplained; to me, the explanation appears much simpler. His principal objection to the use of "two attributes, one preceding the noun and one following it", in the phrase *sa-ni-iz-zi lam-an* HUL-*lu* 'the sweet name Bad', does not seem to me valid, since 'sweet name' is certainly a stereotyped phrase (cf. above, fn. 94).

[125] Thus in absolutely parallel passages in two of the Treaties we find ZAG-*an*, i.e. *kunnan*, in the one (*Targ.* 1.21), and Zag-*na*, i.e. *kunna*, in the other (*Kup.* §19.D.3). See Friedrich, *Vert.* 1.77–78 (a note on *Targ.* 1.21 which involves other examples of the same type of variation) and *El.* 1.14 and 16; Sommer, *AU* 164.

[126] Cf. Laroche, *Onom.* 130: "Sauf de très rares exceptions, les noms de personnes hittites ... se fléchissent avec l'appui d'une des trois voyelles, *a*, *i* et *u*".

[127] The only consonantal stems that I have noted in this construction are two in the Story of Appus (*KUB* 24.8), namely: the adjectival NIG.SI.SA-*za* in 4.6 (which, as I have already said, §31, alternates with the -*a* stem NIG.SI.SA-*as*); and the place-name *Sudul* in 1.7, which, being presumably a neuter like other -*l* stems, might be a normal nominative, but is doubtless to be explained like its neighbor the masculine *Appu* (in 10).

[128] The same problem arises in connection with Sanskrit *dhenu* in *RV* 6.66.1. See below, §51; also above, §17 and fn. 53.

[129] However, Gellius (15.29) suggests precisely that. Cf. above, §17 and fn. 52, and below, §163 and fn. 466.

homo.[130] It is true that Hittite frequently uses what seem to be stem-forms of personal names in other places too,[131] especially in the formulaic introductions to the historical texts, and as genitives and datives with Akkadian prepositions (such as *SA* 'of' and *A-NA* 'to') everywhere;[132] but in all such instances it is probable that the proper noun is to be regarded as written in Akkadian, not in Hittite,[133] and quite possibly we should print it in capitals.

37. There is one rather remarkable document[134] containing a long

[130] See above, §17 and fn. 54, and below, §§74–76.

[131] I am not including their use as vocatives (see Güterbock, *JAOS* 65.248–49, and Hahn, *JAOS* 70.237), for here the bare stem is the regular inherited case-form through the Indo–European languages; cf. Brugmann, *Grund.* 2.2.118 and 132–33.

[132] Thus the regular declension of Hattusilis' name (with uninflected forms possibly to be interpreted as Akkadian) is as follows: nominative, *Hattusilis* (*KBo* 4.12.2.5) or, in introductions, *Hattusili* (*KUB* 1.1.1.1, *KBo* 4.12.1.1., *KBo* 6.29.1.1); accusative, regularly the inflected form, *Hattusilin* (*KUB* 1.1.1.10); genitive, *SA Hattusili* (ib. 4.87), or, without the preposition, in introductions, *Hattusili* (*KBo* 4.12.1.4), and occasionally elsewhere (*KUB* 1.1.4.81; on this see further below); dative, *A-NA Hattusili* (*KUB* 1.1.1.14, 4.22). The Märchen and the epics may follow this pattern, but, as might be expected, they show greater freedom: we find inflected forms not only in the nominative and the accusative, as *Kessis* (Story of Kessis *passim*) and *Kessin* (*KUB* 33.121.2.16 and 18), but also in the genitive and the dative, as *Kessiyas* (*KUB* 17.1.2.7) and *Kessiya* (*KUB* 33.121.2.12), in addition to the stem-forms with prepositions, as *SA Anu* (*KUB* 33.120.1.26), *A-NA Kessi* (*KUB* 33.121.2.9), and *IT-TI Apu* (24.8.1.30). Furthermore we find stem-forms in these cases even without a preposition, but only, I think, when the context makes the sense perfectly clear, especially with words of relation in the genitive, as AMA *Kessi* 'Kessis' mother' (*Bo* 4473.2.2), DAM *Appu* 'Appus' wife' (*KUB* 24.8.3.3), DUMU *Kumarbi* 'Kumarbis' son' (*KUB* 17.7.3.9). (Compare with these the examples from the *Puduhepas* document quoted in fn. 153; and note too that the genitive *Hattusili*, which, as already remarked above, can be accounted for as occurring in an introduction in *KBo* 4.12.1.4 but not in *KUB* 1.1.4.81, is in both these instances similarly combined with NUMUN 'descendant'.) In *KUB* 24.8.3.4 *Appu* is almost assuredly a dative of reference; when Güterbock pronounced it a nominative (*JAOS* 65.255) he did not have all the facts later available in regard both to the Appus text, and to the Kumarbis text with which he compared it. In general, the stem-form is not used in the Märchen as a nominative (for some possible but not positive uses in the myths or epics, see Güterbock, *JAOS* 65.255–57); and so its use in the naming construction becomes all the more striking.

[133] This is the view of Sturtevant, *Chr.* 84–85; cf. too Güterbock, *JAOS* 65.255, 256. Sommer, *HAB* 114, points out in opposition to Sturtevant that the names are not necessarily Akkadian; but that need not prevent the scribe from giving them an Akkadian form in writing, just as he did with many words that were either genuine Hittite or borrowings from some other foreign language. However, the question is a difficult and complicated one; doubtless the scribes themselves could hardly have answered it, so how can we? (See my comments in my review of Laroche's *Onom.*, *Wd.* 11.456.)

[134] Published in 1949 by Laroche (*RA* 43.55–78) under the title *Le voeu de Puduhepa*; and again, in considerably augmented form, in 1965, by Otten and Souček (referred to here jointly as Otten) under the title *Das Gelübde der Königin Puduhepa an die Göttin*

list of families or households consecrated to the cult of Lelwanis (Ishtar?) by Queen Puduhepas, wife of Hattusilis III. The document is totally devoid of art or skill, and is syntactically a hodge-podge; for that very reason, its almost complete consistency in using stem-forms in the naming-construction, and inflected forms elsewhere, is all the more noteworthy.[135] Numerous names occur simply as items in a list, and take the inflected nominative form;[136] but when, as frequently happens, some additional information is given as to age and sex, or kinship to a previously mentioned person, *SUM-SU* is regularly used,[137] and the name appears in the stem-form.[138] This supposed

---

Lelwani. I refer to the document simply as *Pud*. In citations I of course quote the text as given by Otten, and employ the convenient numbering of lines used in his translation, except where there is special reason to follow Laroche.

[135] Cf. Laroche, *RA* 43.76: "L'opposition du nominatif syntactiquement construit au thème non fléchi est remarquable tout au long du texte." He recognizes one exception to the general rule, 2.1–2 (76 fn. 2), quoted and discussed below in §40. But actually there are two others according to his recension. These he prints as follows, 4.3 1 DUMU.NITA.GAB *SUM-SU A-x-x-na-as-wi-is*, and 4.8 *ISTAR-at-ti-is* 1 SAL-*TUM SUM-SU me-ir-ta-as-ma*; and they are to be interpreted according to him as '1 boy nursing, his name A--naswis' and '1 woman, Ishtarattis her name—but she has disappeared'. When I read this article, I was troubled by the word-order (unparalleled in *Pud*.) in both passages, respectively *homo nomen Iulius* and *Iulius homo nomen*, in place of the regular *homo Iulius nomen* invariably used elsewhere in this document, which lacks the freedom in this respect met in many Hittite texts (cf. fn. 73). Also, in the second passage the employment after *ISTARattis* of 1 SAL-*TUM* (not '*a* woman' but '*one* woman') led me to think that this woman must be a different one from Ishtarattis, and to wonder whether *merta* 'disappeared' might not rather (despite Laroche's -*as*) refer to the name than to the woman. Otten's improved and enlarged edition clears up these difficulties completely—and, incidentally, gratifyingly confirms my views. He reads—with new numbers—4.10 1 DUMU.NITA.GAB *SUM-SU* [(*m*)*e-ir-ta-at*] and 4.15 1 SAL-*TUM SUM-SU* [*me-ir-ta-at*]. In neither instance is the name given, for it 'has disappeared', it 'is lost'. Otten's conjectural *me-ir-ta-at* 'it has disappeared', in both places with a neuter subject -*at* (seemingly redundant after *SUM-SU*), is justified by its actual occurrence in the later part of 4.15 (before SU.NIGIN). It must be this *me-ir-ta-at* that Laroche reads as *me-ir-ta-as-ma* in his 4.8 (his -*as-ma* lacks one horizontal at the beginning as compared with Otten's -*at*). The nominative form following *SUM-SU m*[*e-ir-ta-at*] in 4.10, which Otten reads *x-x-wa-wi-is* (his reading -*wa*- before -*wi*- lacks one horizontal as compared with Laroche's -*na-as*), and the one preceding 1 SAL-*TUM SUM-SU* [*me-ir-ta-at*] in 4.15, *ISTAR-at-ti-is*, refer to persons distinct from the nameless ones, and are not to be combined with *SUM-SU*.

[136] The only exception is *Su-na*-DINGIR-*LIM* in 2.7, 2.8, and 2.10. On these see below, §41.

[137] There are four exceptions. Of these, three are much alike: 1.13–14 2 DUMU.MES-*SU Ti-es-ma-ra-as Ya-ar-ra-LU-is-sa* '2 sons of her, Tesmaras and Yarrazitis; 17–18 [2 DUMU.MES-*SU* ...] *Pi-en-ni-zu-us-s*[*a*]' [2 sons of her, X] [and] Pennizus' (Otten's

stem-form may perhaps be explained in one of two ways. It may be an Akkadian form, since invariably in *Pud.*, as regularly elsewhere also, 'his (or her) name' is written in Akkadian *SUM-SU*, and this may attract the writing of the juxtaposed name into Akkadian too, as an Akkadian preposition attracts the writing of its dependent noun (cf. just above, §36 and fn. 132). Or it may be a neuter adjective in agreement with *SUM*, i.e. *laman*, in accordance with my previous suggestion (§§34–36).

38. The first family group is described as follows: 1.10–11 *A-ab-ba-a-as* 1 DUMU.SAL-*ZU Ni-wa SUM-SU* 1 DUMU.SAL-*ma* BA.UG DUMU.NITA *Du-du SUM-SU* 'Abbas, 1 daughter of her, Niwa her name, 1 daughter, however, died, a boy, Dudu his name'. *Abbas*, 1 DUMU.SAL-*ZU* '1 daughter of her', and DUMU.NITA 'a boy' are simply items in a list; but the second 1 DUMU.SAL '1 daughter' is the subject of the verb BA.UG 'died'. The interpolated *Ni-wa SUM-SU*, i.e. *Iulia* (or, rather, *Iulium*, according to my interpretation) *nomen suum*, can as usual be explained in Brugmann's manner as a parenthetical clause, but I think it is much more in keeping with the structure of the list to say that *SUM-SU* 'nomen suum' is in partitive apposition with DUMU.SAL-*ZU* 'filia sua', and that *Ni-wa* if a stem-form used as a nominative is in apposition with both, and if

---

suppletion here seems practically certain; see 17 fn. 19); 2.19–20 2 DUMU.SAL.MES-*SU* ...-*as* GE-*wi-ya-as-sa* '2 daughters of her, Xxxas and Armawiyas'. Does the fact that in each of these three passages *two* persons are named have any bearing on the omission of *SUM-SU*, or, rather, *SUM-MES-SU-NU*? *SUM-SU* would be inaccurate, and *SUM-Mes-SU-NU* is uncommon. However, note that we do have *SUM-MES*, quite possibly *SUM-MES* [-*SU-NU*], in 2.2, and *SUM-MES-SU-NU* in 2.12 (quoted and discussed in §§40 and 41 respectively). The fourth example is 1.52 1 DUMU.NITA *Ta-ti-li-is* SES *Ti-ta-i* '1 boy, Tatilis, brother of Titais'. This is exceptional also in that the noun denoting kinship follows the proper noun instead of preceding it as it regularly does (typical examples 1.13 and 2.3–4, are quoted in fnn. 139 and 138 respectively). The change from the usual order may perhaps be due to the fact that in the present passage— again exceptionally—the related person is identified by a genitive noun and not by a possessive pronominal adjective: *Ti-ta-i* instead of -*SU*. Can SES *Ti-ta-i* have edged out *SUM-SU*? However, note 2.31 1 DUMU.SAL *U-da-ti SUM-SU* DUMU.SAL *As-du-wa-ri* '1 girl, Udatis her name, daughter of Asduwaris', where DUMU.SAL *As-du-wa-ri* almost positively refers to the same person as *U-da-ti* (cf. Otten 52 and 54).

[138] As typical examples, I cite 1.32 1 DUMU.NITA *Tu-ut-tu SUM-SU* '1 boy, Tuttus his name', 1.65 1 DUMU.SAL.GAB *Ma-am-ma SUM-SU* '1 girl nursing, Mammas her name'. 2.3–4 1 DUMU-*SU Pi-it-ta-at-ta SUM-SU* '1 son of her, Pittattas his name'.

a neuter adjective is in agreement with *SUM-SU* = *laman-set*. The same treatment of course applies to *Dudu SUM-SU*.

39. Somewhat later[139] we read 1.51–57[140] (51) 1 DUMU.SAL *Ti-ta-i SUM-SU A-NA A-pal-lu-u* E.GE.A-*an-ni pi-ih-hu-un* (52) 1 DUMU.NITA *Ta-ti-li-is* SES *Ti-ta-i A-NA A-pal-lu-u sal-la-nu-ma-an-zi* (53) AD-DIN EGIR-*an-ma-an-si-kan* U-UL *tar-na-ah-hu-u-un* (54) 1 DUMU.SAL.GAB *Pi-ta-ti SUM-SU* 1 DUMU.NITA *Te-me-it-ti SUM-SU* (55) A-NA SUM-*ya sal-la-nu-ma-an-zi pi-an-za* (56) 1 DUMU.NITA *Tu-ut-tu SUM-SU A-NA* Xxx *sal-la-nu-um-ma-an-zi* AD-DIN (57) U-UL-*as-si-ya-as pi-an-za* '(51) 1 woman, Titais her name, to Apallus in marriage I gave. (52) 1 boy, Tatilis brother of Titais, to Apallus to rear (53) I gave, but I did not turn him over (permanently) to him. (54) 1 girl nursing, Pitatis her name, 1 boy, Temettis his name, (55) to SUM-yas (was [sic]) given to rear. (56) 1 boy, Tuttus his name, to X to rear I gave; (57) he (was) not given to him.' Here DUMU.SAL 'girl' (51) and the first and third DUMU-NITA 'boy' (52 and 56) are—or should be!—accusatives, objects of the verb meaning 'I gave', written as *pihhun* (51) or as its Akkadian representative *AD-DIN* (53 and 56). In contrast to this, with DUMU.SAL.GAB 'nursing girl' ('infant') and the second DUMU.NITA (54) we find the participle *pianza* 'given' (55),[141] used either as an attribute of the nouns 'datus' or as a predicate 'datus (est)'; the latter seems more likely, since it is the only possibility for *pianza* just below (57). Thus unless *Titai*, *Pitati*, *Temetti*, and *Tuttu* are subjects of a clause à la Brugmann, the first and last must be accusatives and the other two nominatives. At least in the historical documents (on which see fn. 132), the use of the stem-form as a nominative is found, but I know of no instance of its use as an accusative—which is perhaps an added reason for viewing all

---

[139] I shall skip isolated items which, like *Abbas* and 1 DUMU.SAL-ZU in the passage just quoted, stand alone with no verb, such as 1.13 *Ma-am-ma-as* DUMU.SAL-ZU ISTAR-*at-ti SUM-SU* 'Mammas, daughter of her, Ishtarattis her name'. There are many of these, and all follow the same pattern: see e.g. 1.58–2.4 and 2.10–12, including respectively fifteen and eight items of the sort.

[140] Since I am quoting here a particularly lengthy passage, I am for convenience numbering the separate lines.

[141] The use of the singular verb with a compound subject is not a serious solecism in Hittite. (It is possible that *pianza* belongs with DUMU.NITA alone, which would leave DUMU.SAL.GAB as an isolated item; but this seems less likely, since the queen throughout 51–56 is telling how she disposed of various young people.)

these forms in *-a*, *-i*, and *-u*, just as much as the more obviously adjectival forms HUL-*lu* and NIG.SI.SA-*an* in 24.8.3.7 and 13 (which, as we have seen in §27, also must be accusatives), as neuter adjectives. But meanwhile what of *Tatilis* (52)? This is part of a really amazing passage. In it we have already noted (fn. 137) two exceptions to the regular form, that the expression of kinship (SES *Ti-ta-i* 'the brother of Titais') follows the proper noun (*Ta-ti-li-is*) instead of preceding it, and that with this expression of kinship no *SUM-SU* follows the proper noun; and we shall note later (fn. 153) that *Ti-ta-i* seems to be used as a genitive though it does not look like one. But there is something stranger still (concerning which I am surprised to find no comment in Laroche and Otten) about *Ta-ti-li-is*: it is clearly used as the object of *AD-DIN* (53), yet it is just as clearly a nominative in form![142] Puduhepas (if it was really she who composed the document, as I feel it was) *could* use an accusative in due form; note her employment of the pronoun *-an* as object of *tarnahhun* in the very next line. The only way I can account, if accounting it be, for the anomalous use of the nominative of the proper noun is that in this document all the other proper nouns when not used in the stem-form because of the following *SUM-SU* are in the nominative as items in a list, and this case may have come to seem natural. After all, Puduhepas was not a native speaker of Hittite!

40. The next eight lines (1.58–65) need no special comment: they contain eight names in list form, with no verbs (cf. fn. 139), plus two names used as objects of verbs. But then we come to another surprising passage, 2.1–2 1 SAL-*TUM U-da-ti Za-kap-pa-u-te-ni SUM-SU* 2 DUMU.MES-*SU Ha-ap-pa-nu-us Sar-ra-du-wa-as-sa SUM*-MES '1 woman, the Widow[143] of Zakappautis her name, 2 sons of her,

---

[142] We also meet objects of 'I gave' in 1.60, 63–64, and 2.5 (see §41 on this last), as well as here in 51 and 56; but in all these instances it is impossible to judge of their case-forms, since they are all written as Sumerian ideograms (DUMU.NITA and DUMU. SAL), and the names in apposition with them, being, as is regular, accompanied by *SUM-SU*, all alike, as is also regular, at least in this document, appear in the stem-form.

[143] The form which I am rendering by 'widow' is met frequently in our document: 1.58, 61 (the first occurrence in the line), 63, 65, 2.1 (the present passage), 2a, 3, 11. In my translation, I am following Laroche, who endeavors to prove that *udatis* means 'widow' (70), and provides additional support for this demonstration by offering an excellent etymology (ib. fn. 2), comparing the Hittite word with Sanskrit *vidhava*, Latin *vidua*, Gothic *widuwo*, and Irish *fedb*. Laroche does not account for the use of the word in our

document in the stem-form *udati*. I suggest that it is regarded as part of the woman's name, and accordingly (unlike Laroche) I spell it with a capital; note that in six of the passages just listed, it occurs in conjunction with *SUM-SU* (which is plausibly restored in a seventh, 1.58). Hence my translation as given above, '1 woman, the Widow of Zakappautis her name', rather than Laroche's version (64), "une femme veuve, Zakap-pauteni son nom". The form with nominative case-ending occurs in 2.11, no *SUM-SU* being present (on this see §41 and fn. 148). Otten does not accept Laroche's interpretation 'widow'. He points out (42 fn. 1) that in some of the new fragments *Udati(s)* is a proper name. So it is undoubtedly in 1.61 (the second occurrence in the line) and 2.31 (the latter partially restored) 1 DUMU.SAL *U-da-ti SUM-SU* '1 girl, Udatis her name'; also in 4.11, where it appears as *U-da-ti-is* (no *SUM-SU*). Elsewhere in our text, continues Otten (loc. cit.), "wird *utati* in einem Sinne benutzt, der die Möglichkeit eines Appella-tivums einschliesst". In these passages Otten (like Laroche) certainly treats *udati(s)* as a common noun; he spells it with a lower-case initial, and he transcribes the feminine determinative SAL, whereas in the other three passages he uses a capital and transcribes the feminine determinative f (just as he transcribes the determinative with proper names of men m). In the passages where it is not a genuine name, *Udati(s)* regularly precedes what seems to be a masculine name with the ending -*eni* (surely, I think, to be restored in 2.11), which Otten (49) plausibly suggests is a "Zugehörigkeitssuffix". Another peculiarity of the usage is that this masculine noun, except in one instance (1.61), always lacks the determinative denoting a male; perhaps it is practically an adjective; perhaps if *Udati(s)*—which always has the determinative denoting a female—really means 'widow', this sufficiently indicates the sex of the person designated by the -*eni* form. In the only instances in our document of such a form in -*eni* with a noun other than *Udati(s)*, namely 1.59 1 SAL-*TUM Kat-ti-it-ta-hi Ta-ti-li-e-ni* and 2.34 DUMU.SAL *Par-zu-u-e-ni* (which last example, however, Otten would not class with the others; see 49 fn. 5), the noun in -*eni* does have a masculine determinative. In the first of these passages, the female noun is surely a proper name (we hear in the next line of another female of the same name, who happens to be the first one's niece); and if the woman so called *belongs* to Tatilis, the latter is *probably* her father or her husband (her father rather than her husband if in *U-ta-ti Ta-ti-li-e-ni* of another woman in 1.63 the same Tatilis is referred to), but this does not seem to be made explicit. In the second passage, the female noun is a kinship term ('daughter'), as I think *Udati(s)* is, but one that does not show the other relative's sex as *Udati(s)* does. Thus in neither case is there clear indication of the sex of the person designated by the -*eni* form, and accordingly the determinative is necessary as it is not after *Udati(s)* if the latter really means 'widow'. Indeed, everything seems to me to point to this meaning for *udatis* when it is not used as a proper name, and Otten gives no reason that I can see for declining to follow Laroche's interpretation. However, Goetze in his review of Otten expresses approval of this rejection by Otten (*JCS* 20.52, 1966), and adds (ib. fn. 10) that "the Hitt. word for 'widow' is *wannumi(ya)*-". This he had himself asserted with considerable certainty much earlier (*JAOS* 74.189, 1954). But the meaning of *wannum(m)iyas* is a moot point. Laroche (*RHA* 9 fascicle 49.14–15, 1948–49) and Güterbock (*IF* 60.205 fn. 1, 1949–50) both expressed the view that *wannumiyas* might have a more extensive denotation than the roughly corresponding modern terms: Laroche compared Greek *orphanos* and Latin *orbus* (both of which can mean either 'childless' or 'orphan'), and Güterbock offered as a modern equivalent German *alleinstehend*. Laroche, in part because of his belief that the word for 'widow' in Hittite is *udatis*, naturally ruled out this meaning for *wannumiyas* (loc. cit. 14), but Güterbock later (*JAOS* 78.240 fn. 19, 1958) suggested that *wannummiyas* could "include the notions" of all three states, 'widow', 'childless', and 'orphan'. It is significant that, while he

Happanus and Sarraduwas (their) names'.[144] Here we have the two sons' names given with the nominative case-ending.[145] This example also departs from the typical pattern in that it has the plural *SUM-MES* (presumably *lamna*, though I believe the form is not attested) 'nomina'. Could this second anomaly have any connection with the first one? There seems no reason why the normal forms *Happanu* and *Sarraduwa* could not have been used with *lamna* if they are stem-forms; but if, as I believe, they are in this usage adjectives in agreement with the word for 'names', they might as singulars not seem to accord well with the plural *SUM-MES* or *lamna*, yet they certainly could not go into plural forms themselves, so the regular masculine nominative noun form might seem more in order than the neuter adjective.[146] Still a third anomaly may be the omission with *SUM-MES* of the usual possessive, but possibly this has been lost in the space at the end of the line after *SUM-MES*.

41. There follow several routine items in 2.2a–5: five stem-form names with *SUM-SU*, the last, in 5, serving as the object of *AD-DIN* 'I gave' (cf. §39 and fn. 142). Then come two passages that merit observation. The first of these is 7–8 *Su-na-DINGIR-LIM U-ul-te-du-uk-ki-is* 1 DUMU-*SU Su-na-DINGIR-LIM SUM-SU Su-na-DINGIR-LIM*. Here are four names, of which the second, in the nominative without *SUM-SU*, and the third, in the stem-form with *SUM-SU*, are perfectly regular, whereas the first and fourth, perhaps influenced by the third, lack the termination that we would expect, as does also their recurrence in 10 (cf. above, fn. 136); however, in all three places there is a variant reading with an added -*is*, the nominative ending (see Otten 23 fn. 10), which form also appears twice in 4.14. The second noteworthy passage is 2.10–12 *Si-mi-ti-li-is Sar-ra-du-wa-as*

---

tentatively offered the meaning 'Witwe' for *wannummiyas* in both *KUB* 34.30.4.20 (*IF* 60.205) and 31.134.9 (ib. fn. 1), he ultimately shifted these respectively to "solitary" (*JCS* 10.98, 1956) and "bereaved" (*JAOS* 78.240, 1958; see also his note, ib. 19, already referred to). I have discussed the meaning of *udatis* and *wannumiyas* at greater length in *Studies in Historical Linguistics in Honor of George Sherman Lane* (Chapel Hill 1967) 154–70.

[144] Laroche's translation (64) "leur nom" seems to me inaccurate; I would expect "(leurs) noms" (cf. below, fn. 149). Otten's rendering "mit Namen" is non-committal.

[145] This is the exception recognized by Laroche to the regular rule. See fn. 135.

[146] However, we do find the stem-form *Mamma* with *SUM-MES-SU-NU* below (2.12). See §41 and fn. 152.

As-du-wa-ri-is Su-na-DINGIR-*LIM* I IR-*ZU* Si-mi-ti-li *SUM-SU* U-da-ti-is Pi-iz-zu-ur- 2 DUMU.SAL-*SU* Ma-am-ma *SUM-MES-SU-NU* 'Simitilis, Saraduwas, Asduwaris, Sunailis, I servant of him, Simitilis his name, the Widow of Pizzur-xx, 2 daughters of her, Mamma their names'. Here we have in succession three nominative case-forms, no *SUM-SU*; a form without *SUM-SU* for which variant readings offer either an anomalous bare stem or a nominative (cf. just above); a typical phrase of relationship 'I servant of him' etc., with bare stem and *SUM-SU*; a nominative *Udatis*, followed by the mutilated form Pi-iz-zu-ur- (which I assume must have originally ended in -e-ni [147]) and no *SUM-SU*; [148] and finally a stem-form again, Ma-am-ma, to denote the name held in common by the two sisters, *SUM-MES-SU-NU* 'their names'.[149] Since the two sisters share the same name, the usual singular *SUM* instead of the plural *SUM-MES*, though with *SU-NU* 'their' instead of *SU* 'his' or 'her',[150] would probably be more logical;[151] and perhaps Mamma here, if I am right in viewing it as a neuter adjective, agrees with it according to sense.[152]

42. After 2.12 there is nothing especially interesting or illuminating

[147] It might be suggested that *Udatis* is a proper noun standing alone here, as in 1.61 and 2.31, and that Pizzur- represents a second proper noun, coordinate with *Udatis*. But there are two cogent reasons against this: (1) Pizzur- can hardly be an independent item, since it lacks a determinative, as do all the nouns but one that depend on *Udati(s)* (see fn. 143); (2) if Pizzur- were a separate person, there would be nine members of the household of Simitilis, and we are told twice that there are eight (2.12 and 3.40).

[148] Laroche supplies *SUM-SU* at the end of the line, which is broken off, but the nominative form *Udatis* militates against this; see fn. 143.

[149] Hence Laroche's translation "leur nom", while again inaccurate (cf. above, fn. 144), is perhaps more logical than would be a literal rendering of what the Hittite actually says, namely, 'leurs noms' (cf. below, fn. 151). Otten preserves the plural by his translation, "ihre Namen sind Mamma"; the insertion of *sind* is a complete departure from the structure of the Hittite, but of course his usual "mit Namen" would have been ambiguous (cf. fn. 144).

[150] In Akkadian *SU* is only 'his', but the Hittite scribes used it incorrectly for 'her' as well, undoubtedly because their own possessive -*sis*, like Latin *suus*, could refer to a possessor of either sex.

[151] I am not sure of this, since *each* sister has a separate name *Mammas*. The situation is not quite the same as that which we meet in *koine* Greek (§175) and in Middle Irish (fn. 720), where the term 'names' is certainly applied inaccurately to the plural surname *Boanerges* bestowed jointly on both brothers, and to the plural ethnicon *Itcifai* shared in common by the whole people.

[152] This may be why we do not have *Mammas* here, as we might expect if I am right in my tentative explanation of the case-forms with *SUM-MES* in 2.1-2. Cf. above, §40 and fn. 146.

in the way of naming-constructions; the patterns already set (as summarized above in §37) continue to be followed. But there is one point perhaps worthy of mention. The list of dedications for the first four years closes with a summary of nine 'households' consecrated to the cult, 3.26–52. Each begins with the Sumerian word E (= Hittite *pir*) 'house', followed by the name of the person seemingly serving as the head of the familial group (and a feminist is pleased to note that three of the nine are women). All nine names are in what looks like the stem-form: from *a*-stems, *A-ab-ba-a* (3.26), *Ma-am-ma* (29), *XXX-wi-ya*, i.e. *Armawiya* (33); *i*-stems, GAL-*li* (35), *Su-na-*DINGIR-*LIM*, i.e. *Sunaili* (37), *Si-mi-ti-li* (40), *Wa-si-li* (46), *Hi-mu-*DINGIR-*LIM*, i.e. *Himuili* (51); *u*-stem, *Ku-uk-ku* (49). Otten translates them as genitives ('"Haus" der Alba' etc.), but does not comment on the form. It seems to me that they involve the same question as the name-forms with *SUM-SU* (cf. §37). Are they indeclinable Akkadian forms written because of their juxtaposition with a non-Hittite form (here the Sumerian E, exerting the same influence as the Akkadian *SUM-SU*)?[153] Or are they possibly neuter adjectives, in agreement with the neuter noun *pir* (represented by E), just as I have suggested concerning names with *laman* (represented by *SUM*)?

[153] The same explanation might apply to the stem-form used after kinship terms (also left without comment by the editors), 1.52 SES *Ti-ta-i* (quoted in fn. 137 and §39), 1.55 DUMU *Pi-ta-u-x-x-ya*, 2.31 DUMU.SAL *As-du-wa-ri* (quoted in fn. 137), 2.34 DUMU.SAL *Par-zu-u-e-ni* (quoted in fn. 143), and the -*eni* forms following *Udati* (quoted in fn. 143). Or is a perhaps simpler explanation possible instead: that the stem-form suffices because the genitival relationship of the dependent noun is made clear by the use of E or (as already suggested in fn. 132) of a kinship term? Incidentally, the stem-forms in -*eni* raise still another question: do they represent the nominative of an adjective (in accord with Otten's suggestion that -*eni* is a Zugehörigkeitssuffix) or the genitive of a noun?

II. INDO-IRANIAN

A. INDIC

43. The situation in Sanskrit[154] is quite different from that in Hittite. In this language, including the early Vedic, the use of an adverbial accusative, or accusatival adverb, is very widespread;[155] according to Renou 1.155, "en principe tout nom à l'accusatif sg. . . . peut figurer comme adverbe", and *nāma* is included in all the lists of such accusatives.[156] If we class *nāma* as an accusative anywhere, I suppose it must be so classed everywhere; but there are many instances where what I believe was its original use, as appositive to a nominative or accusative designating the bearer of the name, is strongly pointed to, and *could* be viewed as still in force. If we ever found it with a noun for

[154] I have not undertaken any independent search for examples in Sanskrit literature; my control of Sanskrit is not adequate for that. But there are good illustrative lists of the use of *nāma* in Gaedicke 216–18 (1880), Gray, *IF* 11.307–13 (1900), and Brugmann, *IF* 27.144–45 (1910); and these I think I am competent to interpret. Gaedicke's study, dealing as it does specifically with the accusative in Vedic, is particularly valuable; most later writers have obviously drawn on him just as I am doing. Also, Professor Franklin Edgerton has given me some exceedingly valuable information by letter.

[155] Cf. fn. 27.

[156] See also Delbrück, *AS* 184–88; Speijer (or Speyer), *SS* 41–42, and *VSS* 10, 70–71; and Whitney 92–93 and 408–9. Translations offered for adverbial *nāma* are: 'by name' (Whitney 408), 'en apparence' (Renou 155), 'namely, of name' (Speijer, *SS* 42), 'freilich, allerdings' (Speyer, *VSS* 71), 'in der That, wirklich' (Gray, *IF* 11.308, following Grassmann); but its use in other senses is noted as well. However, Professor Paul Thieme does not agree with this classification of *nāma*. He wrote to me, September 2, 1958: "The 'adverbial accusatives' of Sanskrit are all *real* adverbs in that they qualify the action of the verb; *nāma* is something quite different, as it always goes with a noun (name) or a pronoun standing for a name. The *prōton pseudos* seems to me that everybody includes *nāma* in the list of the real adverbs. The 'adverbial' accusatives are *none* of them 'accusatives of specification', but accusatives of time or inner accusatives or other types of accusative known to Sanskrit, amongst which there certainly is no 'accusative of specification', which is a purely Greek idiom." So far as I have a right to have an opinion in the matter at all, I completely agree with Professor Thieme; and I am happy to say that he has expressed himself as in agreement with my explanation of the original use of *nāma*.

the name-bearer in some case other than the nominative or accusative, that—and that alone—would furnish convincing proof that *nāma* had surely become an accusative of specification; but apparently no such passage can be cited in Sanskrit, at least so far as competent Sanskrit scholars know.[157] Accordingly in citing the following examples[158] I shall analyze them in terms of what their prototypes might have been, without in any way committing myself to a belief that the original syntactic pattern still remains unchanged.[159]

44. For the type (*est*) *homo Iulius nomen*[160] with *est* used predicatively,[161] probably the most familiar Sanskrit example is the one in the opening line of the story of Nala,[162] *MBh.* 3.50.1 āsīd rājā Nalo nāma 'there was a king Nala (his) name'.[163]

[157] So Jolly in a communication to Blümel (cited *IF* 33.16 fn. 1), and so Edgerton in one to me. According to Blümel *IF* 33.16), one such example is citable for Avestan; but this is doubtful (see §57).

[158] I hope I may be pardoned by Sanskritists for my simplification of citations from the Vedas by the omission of accents.

[159] I do not wish to risk such a criticism as that directed, not without reason, by Foy against Gray, on the ground that he confused historical and descriptive data; see above, fn. 19.

[160] As I have indicated (fn. 20), I believe the order must have been originally *est homo nomen Iulius*; but, as I have also indicated (ib.), we find both varieties.

[161] See above, §6.

[162] We may compare our Hittite example from the opening of the story of Appus, LU-*as Ap-pu* SUM-*an-se-it* '(there is) a man Appus his name'. The Hittite example has two characteristic differences: it does not use the copula, since the opening of the story is told in the present tense; and the possessive adjective 'his' is used with 'name' (as already noted in §20).

[163] Blümel specifically discusses this passage in *IF* 44.260. Here, and also in 253, he shows willingness to agree with Brugmann that *nāma* is a predicate nominative in an independent clause, although he had earlier (*IF* 33.19) pronounced "unwahrscheinlich" Brugmann's next step (*IF* 27.144) in assuming a shift of *nāma* to the accusative "durch Kasusassimilation" when the proper name is in the accusative (cf. above, fn. 15, and below, fn. 177). Blümel also in connection with the Nala passage (*IF* 44.260) discusses the relationship to it, and the difference from it, of the "bahuvrihi" compound. This type of compound, while it had a particularly extensive development in Sanskrit, is common to many languages (cf. our own Greatheart, Bluebeard, Red Ridinghood, etc.); and it resembles the use that I am positing for *nāma* in that it too involved a sort of partitive apposition: a special feature or article of apparel was so striking or so characteristic of the person to whom it belonged that it stood for that person as a whole and so became his name. But apart from this common origin I do not think the bahuvrihi compound has any direct connection with the naming construction; see my earlier discussion, *TAPA* 85.247–50. In addition to the points made there, another difference between the bahuvrihi compound and partitive apposition (or its wider use in the figure called synecdoche) is that the former requires an adjective and the latter does not. A man can be called only

45. An interesting example involving the verb 'be' used copulatively [164] is *RV* 10.97.9 Iṣkṛtir nāma vo mātātho yūyaṃ stha Niṣkṛtīḥ 'your mother (her) name (is) Healer, hence you too are Removers (of illness)'. Here *nāma* appears only in the first clause, in combination with a third person singular *vo mātā* 'your mother'; it is probably implied, though not repeated, in the second clause with a second person plural subject *yūyam* 'you'. I think in both instances it represents an original appositive, 'your mother (her) name', 'you (your) name'. In the first clause the verb if present would have been a third singular, and could be viewed as agreeing with either 'mother' or 'name'; [165] in the second clause the verb *stha* ('estis') agrees with *yūyam* ('vos'), and would, I am sure, have done so even had *nāma* been present. [166] Parallels [167] for this are, in the first person singular, [168] *RV* 3.26.7 Havir asmi nāma '(I) (my) name am Havi', [169] i.e. 'I am called Havi' or 'my name is Havi', and *Mn.* 2.122 asāu nāmāham [= *nāma + aham*] asmi 'I (my) name am So-and-So'; and, in the second person singular [170] (the question which would elicit as a reply such a sentence as either of the fore-

---

Greatheart or Bluebeard, not just Heart or Beard; not only would we of course in that case not have a compound at all, but the use is just not idiomatic. On the other hand no adjective is necessary (though of course one can be used) if he is identified with one of his members in partitive apposition, or in the usage that developed from it, such as the employment of *head, hand, body, soul* as synonyms for *person*. I have made a special study of Vergil's very common use of *corpus* or *anima* in apposition with a word designating the whole *homo*, or as a substitute for it (*TAPA* 92.193–219). Similarly in English, a pitiful old woman can be called either "a poor old *body*" or "a poor old *soul*". Cf. further our characterization of a very attentive person as being "all eyes" or "all ears", and Catullus' amusing quip (13.13–14) that when Fabullus smells Lesbia's perfume he will pray to be made 'all nose'.

[164] See above, §7.
[165] On this ambiguous type, see fn. 17.
[166] Cf. above, §15 and fn. 42.
[167] The incidental detail that in these three instances the second, like the passage cited directly before them, has an expressed subject pronoun (*aham* 'ego'), while the other two do not, of course has no bearing on the case.
[168] Another example, R 3.56.9, is cited in §52 in another connection.
[169] In my opinion, Gray's interpretation of this passage, "'Havi' bin ich, mein Name" (*IF* 11.308), while I do not agree with it completely (since he views *nāma* as in apposition with the proper noun, and I with the subject of the verb), none the less does not deserve Foy's characterization of it as "absolut unmöglich" (*IF* 12.173). Foy believes even Gray himself would not see apposition in *asāu nāmāham asmi* or *ko nāmāsi*: I do not see why Gray would not; I do! See directly below.
[170] A possible example, KS 92, is also cited in §52 (cf. fn. 168).

going), *Br.* 11.5.4.1 ko nāmāsi (= *nāma* + *asi*)? 'who are you (your) name?', i.e. 'what is your name?'[171]

46. Of course the nominative appositional phrase *homo nomen* can be subject of a verb other than 'be',[172] as in *RV* 10.86.23 Parśur ha nāma Mānavī[173] sākam sasūva viṃśatim 'the daughter-of-Manu (her) name Parsu has borne twenty at once',[174] and *RV* 5.37.4 kṣeti kṣitīḥ subhago nāma Subhago Puṣyan 'he dwells being prosperous in dwellings, he (his) name Of Good Share'.

47. We also find the appositional phrase in the accusative,[175] as in *RV* 1.53.7 yad nibarhayo Namucim nāma māyinam[176] 'when you struck down the demon (his) name Namuci',[177] and 10.49.2[178] mām dhur Indram nāma devatā divas ca gmas cāpām ca jantavaḥ 'the creatures of the sky and the earth and the waters established me (my) name Indra in a state of divinity'.[179]

[171] Hence it is not necessary to explain this as Gaedicke does (217) as a sort of contamination of an imaginary *ko nāma patyase* grotesquely translated "wer Namen hast du?", and *ko asi* "wer bist du?" On this supposed development see below, fn. 185. The type has already been discussed above; see §16 and fn. 44.

[172] This is the type *homo nomen Iulius in Italia incolit*. See above, §8.

[173] Here we again have a different order, *Iulia nomen mulier* (cf. above, fn. 160), but this time a distinctly unusual one (see fnn. 20 and 153).

[174] Gaedicke (217) explains that here "das Prädicat wird zur Apposition". My explanation, that we have original apposition in every case, seems much simpler.

[175] This is the type *hominem nomen Iulium cognosco*. See above, §8.

[176] Again, as in *RV* 10.86.23 (see fn. 173), we have unusual order, *Iulium nomen hominem*.

[177] Gaedicke (217) has an excruciatingly complicated explanation which I find implausible and well-nigh incomprehensible (cf. fn. 185). He assumes as usual that 'name' was originally the object of a verb meaning 'have', *Namucim nāma patyamānam* 'a demon possessing the name Namuci', and that 'Namuci' was attracted to the case of 'demon', which involved changing *nāma patyamānam* 'having a name' to *santam* 'being' but still keeping *nāma*, the result being *Namucim nāma santam* 'a demon being Namuci' (but what at this stage is *nāma*?), which ultimately became the simple *Namucim nāma*. Brugmann's explanation (*IF* 27.144) is much simpler and more plausible (though Blümel, *IF* 33.19, as already noted above in fnn. 15 and 163, deems it "unwahrscheinlich"); he derives the accusative *Namucim nāma* from an original nominative *Namucir nāma* 'Namuci (ist) der Name' by "Kasusassimilation". But surely my method is simpler and more plausible still, since according to it *Namucim nāma* (accusative) is just as primitive as *Nalo nāma* (nominative).

[178] This is another passage concerning which Foy pronounces Gray's interpretation "absolut unmöglich" (*IF* 12.173); cf. above, fn. 166.

[179] Gaedicke (217) has a different interpretation which at first sight seems not unattractive. He treats *nāma dhā-* as a phrase meaning 'nennen'; and in view of the similar use of Hittite *laman dai-* (see §27), Greek *onoma tithêmi* (see §124), and Latin *nomen facio*

48. There are instances in which *homo* and *nomen* cannot be in apposition, since the one serves as subject, and the other as object, of the verb, which is usually *patya-* 'possess'. Their peculiarity lies in the fact that the name itself is put into the case of *homo*, not that of *nomen*; in other words, we have not *homo nomen Iulium habet* but *homo nomen Iulius habet*.[180] This seemingly anomalous construction is the regular one in Sanskrit, and I think is due primarily to the attraction exercised by the case of *homo* over that of *Iulius*,[181] though some additional influence may perhaps be exercised by the fact that *nomen habet* can be felt as similar to *nominatur*,[182] or even to *est*, so that *Iulius* in combination with it can be looked upon as resembling a predicate nominative.

and *indo* (see §143), all using verbs from the same root *dhē* (see fn. 39), one might be tempted to concur. It is true that in such cases, as Gaedicke himself recognizes (218), the other languages use the dative to denote the person who receives the name (cf. above, §14 and fn. 39) and not the accusative as Gaedicke's interpretation would assume; but Greek has an alternative construction with the accusative after *kaleô* (see §118), and Sanskrit, like Greek, is freer than Hittite and Latin in its use of double accusatives (cf. Delbrück, *AS* 180–81 and *Grund.* 3.381–85; Brugmann, *Grund.* 2.2.634–37; also Kieckers, *IF* 30.362–63, on both Greek and Avestan, referred to again below in fn. 204), so we might be inclined to view this passage as an instance of the construction in question. But alas, Gaedicke is guilty of a serious sin of omission, for he quotes the Sanskrit sentence only as far as *devatā*, which he evidently takes as a nominative plural (sandhi form of *devatas*) to judge by his translation (217), "mich haben die Götter Indra genannt". But the subject of *dhur* cannot be *devatā*, because it is *jantavah*! As for *devatā*, I think it must be an -*ā*- stem instrumental singular of a type common in Vedic (see Whitney 134; this special form occurs twelve times according to Wackernagel, *AiG* 3.117) used "adverbially" (see Whitney 409) and meaning 'in a state of divinity' or something of the sort. Delbrück (*Grund.* 3.388–89) expresses doubt concerning Gaedicke's interpretation of *dhur nāma*, but he evidently copies Gaedicke's quotation without verifying it, since he too takes *devatā* as subject, translating "mich, den Indra mit Namen, haben die Götter geschaffen" (389). Just as Delbrück copies from Gaedicke, so Gray copies from Delbrück (*IF* 11.308), repeating his erroneous translation verbatim. Brugmann (*IF* 27.144) quotes the passage complete, and correctly translates "mich, den Indra mit Namen (mit den Namen Indra), haben als Gott eingesetzt die Geschöpfe des Himmels, der Erde und der Wasser".

[180] Cf. §17 and fn. 49.

[181] As I have already said (fn. 48), I am led to this conclusion in great part by the fact that the similarly anomalous construction *homini nomen Iulio est* rather than the logical *homini nomen Iulius est* is the regular one in Latin. For examples see below, §§143 and 150.

[182] Perhaps this usage is fostered by the common employment of a predicate noun with middle verbs meaning 'call oneself' (cf. the French *s'appeler*), which is almost a synonym for 'have a name'. On this see Delbrück, *AS* 104, Whitney 89. In many instances of a middle (i.e. reflexive) verb, words relating to the object are readily transferred to the subject, since both subject and object denote the same entity. For an example of this in Homer, see *Il.* 16.230 and my discussion of it in my paper on partitive apposition, *TAPA* 85.264 fn. 216.

49. This doubtless is the reason why Gaedicke (216) took this construction as his starting-point for his explanation of the entire situation involving *nāma*.[183] He apparently assumes that once the word denoting the name was transferred from its original case[184] to the case of the noun denoting the name's bearer, the copula 'be' could be substituted for the original transitive verb, and (217) later could itself be replaced by some other verb (as *sru-*) or even by no verb at all (in which case the predicate noun becomes an appositive); yet somehow the accusative *nāma* would dangle on, and develop into the accusative of specification. In other words, the development would be: *homo Iulius nomen habet*; *homo Iulius (nomen) est*; *homo, Iulius nomen, aliquid facit*.[185] But if *nāma patyate* 'nomen habet' is a single unit, justifying the use of what to all intents and purposes is a predicate nominative, then it is not *habet* alone that is replaced by *est* but *nomen habet*, and so Gaedicke's explanation leaves no real place for *nomen* in the picture. Besides, there is the much more serious objection that both Hittite and Greek have the construction *homo Iulius nomen*, but so far as I know the construction *homo Iulius nomen habet* is lacking in Hittite and is late and rare in Greek.[186]

50. A typical example of the construction *homo Iulius nomen habet*, and the one which Gaedicke began with (216), is *RV* 2.37.2 Dadir yo nāma patyate 'who possesses the name Giver', *Dadir* 'giver' being nominative.[187]

[183] See above, fn. 13.

[184] I assume that the original case would have been the accusative, but Gaedicke (216) assumes that the form would have been the bare stem or the genitive. The bare stem cannot be ruled out; see below, §51. But the genitive I think would have been impossible; the appositional genitive, which we meet in Latin (cf. fn. 467), needs explaining there (I offer a tentative attempt *TAPA* 84.97–98), and apparently does not exist in Sanskrit (cf. Whitney 98–99).

[185] See the earlier summaries of his views on the development of *ko nāma asi?* and *Namucim nāma*, fn. 171 and fn. 179, respectively.

[186] Two possible examples from classical Greek are quoted in fn. 328, namely, Euripides, *Tro.* 1233 and Plato, *Leg.* 956B–C. They are not certain, and in any event these passages are too late to throw light on the genesis of the accusative of specification; but even had their type been early and common, I again fail to see how it could have involved a misunderstanding of *nomen* and thus have fostered the development of the construction *homo Iulius nomen*. In this connection it may be noted that Gaedicke (217) cites an example from Latin (Ovid, *Met.* 1.169, on which see above, fn. 49, and below, §162), also too late to be of real significance, and in any event wholly irrelevant, since Latin never developed the construction *homo Iulius nomen*.

[187] This Gray (*IF* 11.308) cavalierly dismisses from consideration on the ground that *nāma* is "bloss Objectsakk.". So it is, and not in apposition with any other noun, either with the proper noun as *nāma* regularly is in Gray's theory, or with *homo* as it is in mine;

51. Finally, I want to offer an example in which the word *dhenu*
(occurring instead of the nominative feminine *dhenuḥ*, which we would
expect[188]) presents the same problem as *Appu* and HUL-*lu* in Hittite.[189]
This is *RV* 6.66.1 vapur nu tac cikituṣe cid astu samenaṃ nāma dhenu
patyamānam 'now that (thing) [i.e. creature] possessing[190] the same
name cow [or the same milk-giving name?] shall be a wonder to the
wise'. Gaedicke (19 note **) pronounces *dhenu* a unique example
"des reinen, nicht als Vocativ gebrauchten Stammes"; the objection
to this is the lack of parallels. Others view it—preferably, in my
opinion—as a neuter. Dr. Andrew Yarrow has suggested to me by
letter that perhaps *dhenu* is neuter under the influence of the neuter
pronoun *tat* 'id' used as subject; the objection to this is, in my opinion,
that a subject pronoun of the sort is more likely to be attracted than
to attract (cf. Vergil, *Aen.* 6.129 hoc opus, hic labor est). It seems to me
far preferable to explain *dhenu* as getting its gender from the preceding
nāma. Gray proposed this long ago (*IF* 11.310), calling *dhenu* a neuter
singular adjective; the objection to this, as he realizes, is the unusual
(for Sanskrit) position of the adjective after its noun, but Gray defends
this by a reference to Delbrück's statement (*AW* 36) that an adjective
may follow its noun if it is used like a substantive in the sense of an
appositive to that noun, thus acquiring an independent position.[191]

---

but none the less the sentence involves a very real difficulty which Gray ignores. His
translation, "welcher, 'der Geber', einen Namen besitzt", while literal, does not really
render the idea of the sentence; the point is not that the person involved 'possesses a
name' (practically every one does that!), but that he possesses a name (being) Julius'.
This I think shows clearly the flaw in Gray's assumption that *nomen* is in apposition with
Iulius: the significant thing is not the inherent relationship between *Iulius* and *nomen*, but
that between *homo* and *nomen*; and when the two get interchanged, with the proper
noun agreeing with the first instead of with the second, a certain degree of anomaly
results.

[188] After the pattern of the nominative *Dadir* in the preceding example.

[189] See above, §17 and fn. 53.

[190] I assume that *patya*- here, as regularly, is middle. Gray seems to view it as passive,
to judge by his translation (*IF* 11.310), "ein Wunder nun sei dies auch dem Verständigen,
derselbe Name Kuh besessen", and his explanation, "d. h., dass dieser Name besessen
wird". That would, if I understand him aright, make *nāma dhenu* nominative instead of
accusative. Certainly Bradke (*Festgruss Roth* 121), whom he cites in agreement, does not
so take it; note his translation, "dass sie denselben Namen Milchkuh besitzen" (query:
why the plural verb?). But this has no bearing on the form of *dhenu*.

[191] Gray does not seem to realize that this explanation of *dhenu* as a modifier of *nāma*
used like an appositive to it is completely out of line with his regular view (*IF* 11.307)
that the word for 'name' is an appositive of the proper noun denoting the name.

Professor Paul Thieme has indicated to me that in his opinion *dhenu* actually is an appositive to *nāma* and gets its gender from it, in accordance with the rule which he gives in his *Untersuchungen* (32) to the effect that a noun used as an appositive (or a predicate) may assume the gender of the noun that it qualifies. However, Wackernagel (*AiG* 2.1.3) calls *dhenu* a substantive that has become an attribute, and sees in such instances "Ansätze zu adjectivischer Bedeutung". It does not seem to me to make any essential difference whether we view *dhenu* (and *Appu*) as an adjective agreeing in gender with the word for 'name', or as an appositive to it borrowing its gender from it; in either case I believe the construction lends support to my general view as to the close connection between *nomen* and *Iulium*.

52. There remains to be noted a peculiar construction in which we meet both the nominative-accusative form *nāma*, and another of the same word, either the instrumental *nāmnā* or the so-called adverb (practically an ablative) nāmatas.[192] Either one of these may be used alone interchangeably with *nāma* in the sense 'in name';[193] but what is odd is that they may also be used in combination with *nāma*. If in such instances *nāma* was always an accusative of specification, its employment with an instrumental or an ablative of specification seems tautological to an amazing extent; but if *nāma* was originally in apposition with a nominative (or accusative) denoting the bearer of the name, and if the latter noun plays the leading part in the thought, the pleonasm, though certainly still existent, is not quite so marked. The sense would then be *homo nomen Iulius nomine* (*est*), 'the man [that part of him constituting his name] is Julius by name', rather than 'the man is Julius in name [accusative] in name [instrumental or adverb]'.[194] Examples for

---

[192] I owe my knowledge of this construction, and of the passages chosen to illustrate it (which come from BR), to Professor Franklin Edgerton. He holds that they militate against my theory, but I think they perhaps support it.

[193] Exactly like the Latin ablative *nomine*.

[194] The date of these passages has a bearing on the validity or invalidity of my argument. As Professor Edgerton reminds me, they are all post-Vedic: the first five are from the Epics, and the last is from *KS*, which, while perhaps pre-Epic, is not strictly Vedic. This fact is open to two interpretations. *Either* it indicates that the passages have no bearing on the genesis of the *nāma* construction; in other words, this constitutes a point against me. *Or* it indicates that, despite the use of *nāma* as an adverb, i.e. an accusative, none the less when used in conjunction with the substantive denoting the bearer of the name, *nāma* was still an appositive, nominative or accusative as the case might be, not only as it had been in proto-Indo-Iranian (as I assume) but even in Sanskrit, and not only

nāmnā include: *R* 1.35.7 = 6.2.27 nāmnā Satyavatī nāma 'nomine Iulia (est) nomen' 'she—(her) name—(is) Satyavati by name'; *R* 3.56.9 Jatāyur nāma nāmnāham (= *nāmnā* + *aham* 'ego') 'Iulius nomen nomine ego (sum)', 'I—(my) name—am Jatayu by name'; *MBh.* 13.1392 kanyām Suprabhām nāma vai nāmnā 'virginem Iuliam nomen nomine' 'the maiden Suprabha—(her) name—by name'. It may be noted that the first of these is of the ambiguous type,[195] which might also be interpreted as '(her) name (is) Julia by name'; but in the second there can be no doubt that the subject is 'I',[196] and I believe in the first it is similarly 'she'. In the third *Suprabhām* is an accusative in apposition with *kanyām* (direct object of the verb), and I believe *nāma* is in apposition with it too. Examples for *nāmatas* include: *MBh.* 3.68.5 Bāhuko nāma nāmataḥ 'he—(his) name—is Bāhuka by name'; *R* 1.1.47 nāmato Rāvaṇo nāma 'in name he—(his) name—is Rāvana'; and *KS* 92 Jyeṣṭham yan nāma nāmataḥ 'since thou—thy name—(art) Jyestha [Eldest] by name'. The first two examples again are of the ambiguous type. The last one is more complicated: it occurs in a direct address, and perhaps therefore we should supply the verb *asi* 'thou art';[197] on the other hand it is normal in a nominal clause to assume that the verb if present would be third singular *asti*, and in that case the meaning would be '(thy) name is Jyestha by name'. There is also perhaps a possibility that *yat* (appearing here as *yan*) is a relative pronoun, 'what— (its) name—(is) eldest by name', which would give us the same general structure as if the verb were *asi*. But the passage is very obscure.

B. IRANIAN

53. When we turn to Iranian,[198] we find a very interesting situation. Avestan is possibly further developed than Sanskrit; Old Persian, far less so.

---

in the earliest Sanskrit but even in post-Vedic Sanskrit; in other words this constitutes a point in my favor.

[195] Cf. fn. 17.

[196] Cf. §15 and fn. 42.

[197] So BR; Professor Edgerton tells me he is in doubt.

[198] In citing Iranian (both Avestan and Old Persian) I omit all diacritics except macrons, even in quotations from scholars using them.

1. AVESTAN

54. Avestan[199] evidently behaves much as Sanskrit does. Absolutely parallel to the Sanskrit passage *RV* 3.26.7 havir asmi nāma 'I (my) name am Havi' is the Avestan passage *Yt.* 15.46 Taxmō nama ahmi taxmōtəma nama ahmi[200] '(I) (my) name am Taxma [i.e. Fortis], (I) (my) name am Fortissimus'. Just as in Sanskrit so in Avestan, we find the word for 'name' used in combination with a substantive in the nominative not only as subject of the verb 'be' (as in the example just given), but also as subject in a nominal clause, or as subject of a verb other than 'be'. As examples of these, respectively, I cite *Yt.* 19.56 vairis yo Haosrava nama 'the sea which (its) name (is) H.';[201] *Vd.* 7.16 Arədvī nama āpa hā mē āpō yaozdaδaiti 'the water (its) name A., this my water effects cleansing'.[202]

55. Avestan also has many instances of the construction *puerum nomen Iulium nominant.*[203] I cite as a typical example *Vd.* 13.2 spānəm yim masyāka Duzakəm nama aojaiti 'the dog whom (his) name men call D.'[204] This construction occurs very frequently in Avestan, but there is one odd variant of it: *Vd.* 18.15 mərəyō yō parō-dars nama yim masyāka kahrhkatās nama aojaite 'the bird which (its) name (is) parodarsh, which (its) name men call kahrkatāt'. As Gray points out

[199] Unfortunately I have no first-hand knowledge of Avestan, and I am therefore compelled simply to accept uncritically what I have found in books and articles, and in helpful letters from kindly scholars.

[200] For the Sanskrit example, see §45; for the construction in general, see §15 and fn. 42. In the Avestan passage as in the Sanskrit one, Foy (*IF* 12.173) objects to Gray's interpretation. See above, fn. 166.

[201] This is the type *homo Iulius nomen (est)*; see §7. Cf. in Sanskrit *RV* 10.97.9 (quoted in §45).

[202] This is the type *homo Iulius nomen in Italia incolit*; see §8. Cf. in Sanskrit *RV* 10.86.23 (quoted in §46).

[203] See §13 and fn. 35. The construction usually appears in the form *quem* (rather than *puerum*) *nomen Iulium nominant*; this is true of Greek too (see fnn. 306 and 308).

[204] This is the passage which Delbrück (*Grund.* 3.388) takes as a starting-point for his hypothesis on the genesis of the accusative of specification (see above, fnn. 13 and 37). He explains it as having originally meant 'welchen die Menschen *Duzaka* als Namen nennen'. Thus *nomen* in *puerum Iulium nomen nominant* he considers an appositive to *Iulium*, as Gray does (see above, fn. 19), and not to *puerum*, as I do. The construction, as I have said, is exceedingly common in Avestan; for other examples, see Gray, *IF* 11.512. Kieckers, who (*IF* 30.362–63) cites several examples of this triple accusative from Avestan and Greek, calls *hominem* an outer object (361), *Iulium* a second outer object used predicatively (362), and *nomen* originally an inner object (361).

(*IF* 11.312), *kahrkatās* is certainly a nominative singular of a stem in -*tāt*-, although we would of course expect an accusative like *Duzakəm* in the preceding example. Is there some sort of confusion with the (normal) nominative *parō-dars* in the preceding clause? Or is the nominative a quoted form which is the equivalent in force of a vocative? Or does the name here simply exist as an invariable form independent of syntax?[205]

56. In addition, if Blümel is right, we find in Avestan something that we do *not* find in Sanskrit[206]—the word for 'name' used in combination with a substantive in the genitive. But *is* Blümel right? I doubt it.

57. He cites (*IF* 33.16) what he considers "ein sicheres Beispiel", *Yt.* 13.120 Asəm-yeŋhe-raocā nama asaonō fravasīm, which he renders "das Unsterbliche des A. genannten rechtgläubigen". Here it is quite true that *asaonō* (Blümel's "des . . . rechtgläubigen") is the genitive of the substantively used adjective (meaning 'devout, orthodox'), its sense being 'of the holy one, of the true believer'. It modifies the accusative *fravasīm*, which denotes the immortal element of the believer, compared by Bartholomae (*AiW* col. 992) to the Roman *manes* (I would rather suggest the Roman *genius*). But what is *Asəm-yeŋhe-raocā*? In form it seems to be a neuter nominative-accusative

---

[205] This is the so-called *nominativus tituli*, of which isolated instances can be cited from both Greek and Latin. For a perhaps possible, but to my mind highly dubious, example from Homeric Greek, *Il.* 1.403, and for a positive example from classical Greek, *Oec.* 6.14, see fnn. 314 and 328 respectively. For classical Latin, I know of one positive example, Ovid, *Met.* 15.96 (see §162 and fnn. 314 and 417), and four possible ones, Vergil, *Aen.* 8.332 and 10.200 (fnn. 417 and 460), Horace, *Epis.* 1.7.37–38 (fn. 461), and Propertius 1.18.31 (fn. 461), in all four of which, however, the supposed *nominativus tituli* can be otherwise accounted for. As examples from *koine* Greek, we may cite from the OT 1 *Sam.* 9.9 (fnn. 497 and 519), and from the *NT Jn.* 13.13 (fnn. 497 and 519) and possibly *Mt.* 10.25 (fn. 494) and *Lk.* 19.29 and 21.37 (fn. 498). Examples of the type *homo nomen Iulius habet* (see §17 and fn. 49) may also be classed here, although I think it is preferable to regard them as instances of attraction (see fnn. 48 and 181). I cite elsewhere examples from Sanskrit, *RV* 2.37.2 (§50); classical Greek, Euripides, *Tro.* 1233 and Plato, *Leg.* 956B–C (fnn. 186 and 328), and *koine* Greek, *Rev.* 9.11 (fn. 519); classical Latin, Ovid, *Met.* 1.169 (§162 and fnn. 186 and 417), and the Vulgate, *Rev.* 9.11 (fn. 519). It may be noted that there are examples of other constructions as well in both the Greek and Latin versions of *Rev.* 9.11, but the instances that I have in mind are respectively ὄνομα ἔχει Ἀπολλύων and habens nomen Exterminans.

[206] Blümel declares (*IF* 33.16) that there is nothing of the sort in Sanskrit (cf. above, §43 and fn. 157) or in Greek (however, this he modified later; cf. below, §139 and fn. 383).

plural. It is one of three triple compounds serving as proper nouns, which occur in the same passage, all preceding *nama asaonō*; the other two (which Blümel ignores) are *Asəm-yahmāi-usta* and *Asəm-yeŋhe-varəza*. All three are made up of quotations from elsewhere. Bartholomae (*AiW* col. 258) calls all of them indeclinable nouns used as genitives —which to me seems practically a counsel of despair.[207] He himself is evidently not without his doubts concerning them: he says of *Asəm-yeŋhe-raocā* that as a quotation (from *Y.* 12.1) it does not make much sense, since the first element does not belong with the other two; similarly of *Asəm-yahmāi-usta* that the first element comes from *Asəm-yeŋhe-raocā* and the other two from *Y.* 43.1; and of *Asəm-yeŋhe-varəza* (which resembles *Asəm-yeŋhe-raoca* in its first two elements) that the form of the last member is uncertain. Professor Bernhard Geiger of the Center of Iranian Studies has written to me that he considers the passage very suspicious not only because the three personal names "are artificial and inaccurate formations out of words which occur in other parts of the Avesta", and are not case-forms but "awkward quotations from different contexts" which are "taken over mechanically", but also because here and only here, in the oft-repeated formula 'we worship the *fravasi* of the righteous [*asaonō*] So-and So', is the word for 'name' added; indeed in the very same paragraph after these three made-up names there follow two genuine personal names, without *nama*. In short, he believes that *nama* represents a later addition to the text, and that therefore the passage is of no value as evidence for the syntactical use of *nama*. Hence there is no reason to assume a different state of affairs for Avestan from that which prevailed in Sanskrit.

2. Old Persian

58. In striking contrast to Avestan, Old Persian behaves in so aberrant a manner[208] that it requires special intensive consideration.

---

[207] I do not mean that such proper names are utterly impossible: Jackson (*Av. Gr.* 245), in connection with his citation of this particular appellative, which he translates "Bright-in-Righteousness", as an example of a compound, compares our own Puritan names. But once an agglomeration of this sort becomes established as a name, one would expect it to fit into the morphological pattern of the language; note that in modern English and German, the nouns *forget-me-not* and *Vergissmeinnicht* have inflected forms for the genitive and the plural.

[208] The employment of the naming construction is extremely common in Old Persian. To quote Kent (*OP* 97), "It is a feature of OP style, that at the first mention of

I have therefore made an exhaustive study of the remains, which—
whether fortunately or unfortunately—are scanty enough to make
such a procedure possible.[209]

59. The problem involved, both formal and syntactic, Bartholomae
described in 1904 as "noch nicht gelöst" (*AiW* col. 1064 note 6); that
little progress has been made in this direction is indicated by the fact
that Bartholomae's own proposed solution of the problem was retained by Kent in 1950 and 1953, almost half a century later (see below,

---

a person (other than of the ruling king) or of a place (other than of a governmental
province) the name of that person or place should be followed by *nāma* or *nāmā*". There
is very similar usage in Aramaic involving the word *šmh*; this, to quote Kutscher (*JAOS*
74.241) "appears at the first mention of a proper name which is supposed to be unknown
to the reader". Kent sees in this feature of Old Persian as in some others the result of
Aramaic influence (*OP* 9 and 98); on the other hand Kutscher (loc. cit.) believes that more
probably Aramaic borrowed from Persian, since it does not use the construction either
before or after the Persian period. But Old Babylonian did have the construction (cf.
Kraeling 145 on Aramaic); and so, as Kutscher succinctly puts it, "you are back where
you started". The situation is rendered even more baffling than Kutscher indicates by
the fact that the mutual relation of Akkadian (i.e. Old Babylonian) *šum-šu* and Hittite
laman-set presents much the same problem (see above, fn. 62) as that between Aramaic
šmh and Old Persian *nāmā*. Quite apart from the question of naming constructions in
particular, there has been considerable discussion as to whether Old Persian shows
Semitic influence. Benveniste sees Aramaic influence in the "nominative absolute" in
general (*MSL* 23.180–82 and *GrVP²* 14) and Akkadian influence in the recurring 'says
Darius the king' (*GrVP²* 14); Gray (*AJP* 72.325) calls the latter Aramaic, and Kent in
OP² (217) adds it as an Aramaicism to those already listed in *OP¹* (9). On the other hand
Aramaic influence so far as the naming construction goes is denied by Schaeder (*Aria-
ramnes* 638 fn. 2—this part printed on 639) and by Schwyzer (*Parenth.* 14); and as proof
that the construction is Indo–European, indeed is Indo–Iranian, parallels are cited from
Vedic by Hoffmann (*MSS* 9.81), from Buddhistic Sanskrit by Wüst (*WS* 20.252–53),
and from Pali by Thieme (*KZ* 68.216–17), while Printz (*IJ* 15.151) mentions that similar
constructions occur in Old Irish. It is interesting to note that, with the exception of
Schaeder, who thinks the Old Persian construction is the nominative absolute, and of
Printz and Kutscher, who respectively quote Benveniste and Kent on the nominative
absolute in Old Persian but do not commit themselves, all the scholars who deny
Aramaic influence as the basis of the Old Persian construction also deny that this
construction is a nominative absolute (see below, fn. 252).

[209] All the examples are from *DB*, the great inscription of Darius the Great at Bisitun,
unless otherwise stated. Also quoted from Darius are two passages from *DSf*, at Susa, on
the building of the palace there (cf. §§103 and 104); and one from *DZc*, at Suez, on the
opening of his canal from the Red Sea to the Nile (cf. §101). There are also two quotations from Xerxes, son of Darius, *XPf*, at Persepolis, on his accession to the throne; these
are different from those of Darius as they occur in a genealogy (cf. §94). The remaining
quotations, also genealogies, are considerably later, being those of Artaxerxes II (*A²Hc*)
and Artaxerxes III (*A³Pa*), respectively great-grandson and great-great-grandson of
Xerxes (cf. §§112–14).

§§71 and 72). The difficulties raised are so great that in their consideration of the name construction both Gray in 1900 (*IF* 11.311 fn. 2) and Brugmann in 1910 (*IF* 27.143 fn. 2) specifically declined to deal with them. Yet the Old Persian usage has, I think, a very important bearing on the case, and a consideration of the issue raised by it must not be dodged because of the difficulties inherent in it.

60. In the first place, there is the problem of the Old Persian script. The Persians themselves were doubtless illiterate;[210] and their records do not begin until, presumably at the direction of one of the kings, probably Cyrus the Great or Darius the Great,[211] a cuneiform syllabary[212] was adopted and adapted to serve as a medium for writing Old Persian. The scribes who did the job (a difficult one even for linguistic scholars today) of providing a non-written language with a system of writing originally developed by a completely alien language, were presumably foreigners;[213] and how accurate they were in representing the pronunciation of Persian, and how consistent in adhering to their own plan, we can hardly hope to know.[214] At all events, however successful they were in first devising, and then applying, their system, modern scholars perhaps are not wholly successful in interpreting it today.[215] To add to the confusion which confronts the non-initiate

[210] Sturtevant, *JAOS* 48.73.

[211] See Kent, *OP* 12 with notes.

[212] But what was this syllabary? According to Kent (*OP* 11–12) it "quite obviously goes back to the cuneiform syllabary of Akkadian"; but, as Paper points out (*JCS* 4.196), the Akkadian and Old Persian systems of writing resemble each other only in that both are cuneiform and that both are syllabic. The Old Persian syllabary, happily, has only 36 characters; these characters, as Kent himself indicates (12), are not like those of Akkadian, and there have been changes in sound values as well as in shape. Furthermore, the two systems of writing are completely different in principles and structure. According to Paper (*JAOS* 76.25), "scholars are generally agreed that the OP syllabary is merely a transmogrification of that used for Aramaic", and the Aramaic writing system doubtless served "as the primary model for the inventing scribe or scribes" who devised the system used for Old Persian.

[213] They were probably Babylonian; see Sturtevant, *JAOS* 48.73. But this does not mean that they were using the Old Babylonian writing system; see fn. 212.

[214] On some apparent flaws, see Kent, *OP* 20–23. The bafflingly haphazard and unsystematic character of the whole syllabary is made very clear in Paper's illuminating diagram (*JAOS* 76.26) and in the comments that accompany it.

[215] Cf. Paper's statement in his review of Kent's *OP*[1] (*JCS* 4.196), quoted with approval by Hamp (*JNES* 13.115): "The whole problem of interpretation of the OP syllabary requires further study and re-examination." Hamp does study it from the viewpoint of a phonemicist (*JNES* 13.115–17).

who attempts to penetrate into the inner sanctum of Persian mysteries, as a rule Iranian scholars do not transliterate the cuneiform script syllable by syllable (as Assyriologists and Hittitologists regularly do), but provide a broad transcription involving a system of "normalization" which, though now reasonably standardized, does unfortunately lack complete uniformity in various details.[216] A particularly dangerous feature of it in my opinion is the almost universal dependence upon etymology;[217] this it seems to me is bound to result in inconsistency, since we do not always know the etymology, and in inaccuracy, since there is no guaranty that comparative or historical considerations will tell us what the Persian sounds actually were at the time the inscriptions were made.[218]

61. Kent tells us that "OP final *ă* was written with the sign of length; that is, with addition of the separate character for *a*" (*OP* 17); and that

[216] Cf. Kent, *OP* 12–13 and 19–20. Kent defends the practice (19 fn. 2) on the ground "that it works, enabling us to make cogent comparisons with cognates in other IE languages and with borrowed words in non-IE languages". I think we could make the comparisons without the normalization, and I am afraid that actually preconceived views about the comparisons have been not the result but the cause of the normalization. Benveniste (*BSL* 47.90) in his review of *OP* warns against undue dependence on Kent's system of normalization: "L'étudiant devra donc constamment rectifier et compléter les graphies qui lui sont données" (Benveniste himself, and his master and predecessor Meillet, are among the few scholars who do usually give transliterations as well as transcriptions of cited forms, and in so doing seem to me to be following a much sounder method than the majority of Iranists). But in his preface to *OP²* (vi) Kent lists the use of a "close transcription" as one of "some suggestions made in the reviews" which he "found it impossible or undesirable to adopt".

[217] This seems to be the regular approach used by Iranian scholars in general, from Spiegel (*Keil.* 156) in 1881, to Kent (*OP* 13 and 15) in 1950 and again in 1953. Exceptions are Meillet and Benveniste; see in particular their treatment of final *a* (*GrVP* 80–81 and *GrVP²* 92–93 respectively). I quote Benveniste (92): "La transcription par *-ā* de tous les *-a* finaux, *même étymologiquement brefs*, répond sans doute à une réalité" (italics mine). See further fn. 219. In this connection I am happy to have complete confirmation of my perhaps presumptuous assumptions from a scholar who, unlike me, *is* qualified to have an opinion on the matter, Professor Herbert H. Paper, who has written to me as follows: "You can be stronger in criticizing OP transcription practices than 'occasional dependence upon etymology'. Etymology and dependence upon Sanskrit are present at every step. It is dependence on etymology and on the surface closeness to Sanskrit that has proved so seductive to OP scholars that they have not realized that many problems exist, but rather take a great deal too much for granted." Similarly Benveniste protests (*BSL* 47.89) against Kent's preference in *OP* for starting from Indo–European instead of from Old Persian itself.

[218] A similar line of reasoning would force us to conclude that the Greek aspirates are voiced rather than voiceless.

"when final in the word, pIE * n̥* and *m̥* became pAr. *a*, which of course was written *ā* in OP" (27). I really do not see how we can be sure that the final *a* representing original Indo–Iranian or Aryan ("pAr.") *ă*—whether descended from original Indo–Iranian final vocalic *n* or from some other source—was at the time the Old Persian inscriptions were written still pronounced *ă*; all that we know about it is that it was written *a-a*, which suggests *-ā* rather than *-ă*.[219] And all that we know about the form which represented Indo–European *nōmn̥*, Indo–Iranian *nāma*, is that it was written in Old Persian *na-a-ma-a*, which is normalized as *nāmā* (and it may be, as we shall see later, that we do not positively know even this!).

62. But the history of *a* before a final consonant was different. Kent talks about "an unwritten *minimal final consonant*" (*OP* 17), and says of such consonants (*t, d, n,* and *h̥*) that "they were still pronounced, *though with a minimal value*, at least after short *ă*" (18; italics mine in both cases).[220] I cannot follow him here; it seems to me that either a consonant is pronounced or it is not. In this instance all that we know is that a form that historically must have once had one of these final consonants after the *a* is written without this consonant; that if the *a* was historically long, it was written with "Pleneschreibung" like final

---

[219] Cf. the statement of Benveniste, *GrVP²* 92, already quoted above in fn. 217. He goes on to say (93): "l'*a* expressément noté [i.e. written *-a-a*] entraînait la prononciation *ā*". Consequently, in instances "de graphie défective [i.e. writing of *-a* not *-a-a*], il y a lieu de supposer qu'on prononçait en effet *-ă*". On this see further fn. 222.

[220] This seems to be the view of Gauthiot too (100), who says that in Old Persian there appears "un degré intermédiaire entre l'articulation implosive des consonnes finales postvocaliques et leur disparition totale". These consonants he considers "phonèmes de transition", which he describes as "essentiellement fugitifs, ondoyants et malaisés à fixer", and "rarement attestés", for in general languages are not attested "sous les formes instables qu'elles revêtent en leurs périodes critiques". But, since linguistic change is unending (even though admittedly more rapid and more radical at some periods than at others), it would seem to me that for some feature or other, every period is a "période critique", and such instability is revealed not by "intermediate" forms but by sporadic fluctuation between the old form and the new, until one or the other ultimately wins out. Gauthiot admits (102) that the "implosions finales" which he posits for Old Persian "ne sont pas même attestées directement" and that of them "il ne subsiste, dans certains cas, aucune trace écrite"; the *indirect* traces of them which *are* exhibited seem to me to prove only that they existed once, not that they still existed at the time the language was committed to writing (just as Homeric prosody reveals the earlier presence of a digamma no longer pronounced and therefore no longer written in the dialect of those who recorded the standard text).

a, i.e. -*Ca-a* (C representing any consonant); but if it was historically short, it was written simply -*Ca*, with no extra final -*a*.

63. Would not the simplest explanation be that at a period before the inscriptions were written, final *a* had become long,[221] but *a* before a final consonant remained short; that later a final consonant following *a* was lost;[222] but that by this time the law that final *a* became *ā* had ceased to operate?[223] At all events what we do know apparently is that *na-a-ma-a*, i.e. *nāmā*, might represent an earlier *nāmān* as well as *nāmā* (or *nāmă*), but *na-a-ma*, i.e. *nāmă*, could represent only an earlier *nāmăn*.

64. Now the reason for concerning ourselves about the difference between *nāmă*[224] and *nāmā* is an amazing one (cf. above, §17 and fn. 54). Whenever Old Persian uses the construction *homo Iulius nomen* (or *provincia Gallia nomen*, or *oppidum Noviodunum nomen*)—and (as already noted in fn. 208) it uses it very often indeed—the word representing *nomen* varies in form according to the gender of the word representing *homo* (or *provincia*, or *oppidum*). If this word is masculine or neuter, we have the form *nāmă*; if it is feminine, we have the form *nāmā*.[225] Of course *nāmā* is the form to be expected, the nominative-accusative

---

[221] Professor Paper by letter partially confirms the plausibility of this conjecture of mine by telling me that in Avestan final short vowels regularly developed into long ones. Of this he writes: "Was this merely a graphic practice, or was it a metrical lengthening, or did the change actually take place in the phonology of Avestan?" (On metrical lengthening in Vedic Sanskrit, cf. below, fn. 232.)

[222] This would not be correct if these final consonants persisted in a later language that can be definitely proved to have been descended from the dialect of the inscriptions, which was the official language of the Achaemenian kings; but I believe there is no certain evidence that any such language exists (cf. Kent, *OP* 6–7).

[223] I am happy to find that this is more nearly in line with the view of Benveniste. Meillet evidently agreed with Gauthiot (on whom see above, fn. 220), for he spoke of "la présence ancienne d'une consonne qui n'est pas notée et qui sans doute ne se pronçait plus proprement, mais qui laissait sa trace dans un arrêt net de la voyelle ..., excluant tout son trainé", and in this connection cited Gauthiot (*GrVP* 85). Benveniste, however, in revising Meillet, omitted the word *proprement*, thus changing the sense significantly; yet he retained Meillet's reference to Gauthiot (*GrVP*² 98).

[224] In this portion of my monograph I am regularly writing *nāmă* to point up the contrast with *nāmā*. But when I come to the transcription of texts, I shall conform to usual practice and omit the breve.

[225] I believe Spiegel was the first to point this out, in *Keil.*¹ 152 (1862)—repeated in *Keil.*² 171 (1881). Received rather dubiously by Bartholomae (*Ar. Forsch.* 1.59 fn. 1), it was later accepted unquestioningly by him (*Grund.* 1.226) as by other scholars. (I owe to Bartholomae the reference to *Keil.*¹; I myself have seen only *Keil.*²)

neuter representing IE *nōmṇ*; but what is *nāmă*? And why do we have two different forms?

65. Schmidt, *Plur.* 82 (1889), though he does not go in detail into the particular problem of *nāmă* vs. *nāmā*, explains *nāmā*—e.g. as seen in *Yautiyā nāmā* [which he writes *yutiyā-nāmā*] *dahyāuš* 'a district by name Yautiya' in 3.23—as an adjective *n*-stem in the nominative singular feminine, comparable to Greek *hê hêgemôn*. Tolman (*Lex.* 105) refers to this statement of Schmidt's as indicating that he regarded *nāmā* here as a feminine formation (from an original *-ōn* ending) constituting the second member of a bahuvrihi compound[226] with the meaning 'possessing the name of Yutiyā'; this interpretation may be based on a correct inference, but it certainly involves putting several extra words into Schmidt's mouth—or pen.

66. Thumb, *KZ* 32.131 (1893), objected that this did not account for the masculine forms with *nāmă*; he suggested that the forms involving *nāmă* and *nāmā* were not genuine bahuvrihi compounds, but that they became "für das sprachgefühl eine art bahuvríhi-compositum". I question whether even this is true. It is typical of a bahuvrihi compound that it has but a single main stress, in other words that it is a single word. The scribes who wrote the inscriptions, whatever their failings, were generally meticulous about separating words (note that personal pronouns which are regularly enclitic in Indo-European languages are written as such); and *nāmă* is always marked off as an independent member. Furthermore, the word denoting the name has (as Thumb himself notes, loc. cit.) its full inflectional ending, thus showing that it too is a separate word.

67. Foy, *IF* 12.172 fn. 1 (1901), approves Thumb's opposition to Schmidt's idea of a bahuvrihi compound, and does not go so far as Thumb does in speaking of "eine art bahuvríhi-compositum"; but his explanation, *IF* 12.174, amounts to much the same thing without the use of the objectionable word.[227] He repeats what he had already said

---

[226] On other attempts to find a connection between the bahuvrihi type of compound and the accusative of specification, see Hahn, *TAPA* 85.247–50 (cf. above, fn. 162).

[227] Foy seems to think he has adequately explained the use of *nāma* by saying it means 'ein gewisser' (*IF* 12.174); he says the same applies to *nama* in Avestan (*IF* 12.177) and queries what the situation is with regard to Greek. But the introduction of 'ein gewisser' provides merely a convenient idiomatic translation into a given language, *not* a syntactic explanation! To render a particular notion, English and German use adjec-

two years earlier, in *KZ* 35.55 (1899), that *Arsāma nāma puça* (*A³Pa* 20) 'Arsames (nominative) nomen filius', is "ein Kompositum", and adds that that is why *Arsāma* (which is nominative) is not in the genitive.[228] He does not explain why, directly above (18–19) in the same inscription, we have *Vistāspahyā nāma puça* 'Histaspis nomen filius', with *Vistāspahyā* in the genitive! The truth is that in *A³Pa*, which is the latest of all the royal inscriptions, the whole case system of Old Persian seems to have completely collapsed, at least so far as its written representation goes (cf. below, fn. 294).

68. As for the origin of the two forms *nāmă* and *nāmā*, Thumb traced the commoner *nāmă* to **nōmn̥*, and the rarer *nāmā* to **nōmn̥*, a less common lengthened form; *KZ* 32.132–33 (1893). He thus equates *nāmă* (not *nāmā*) with Sanskrit *nāma* and Greek *onoma*, maintaining that final *a* in Old Persian from Indo–European vocalic *n* may have maintained "eine leichte nasale färbung", and therefore like final *a* from earlier *-an*, might be written *-ă*; the writing *-ā* was necessary only when "ein reiner vocal" appeared at the end of the Indo–European primitive. How a scholar of Thumb's standing could say anything of the sort puzzles me. Let us grant that the "pure vowels" of Indo–European differed inherently from vocalic *n*. Yet I know of no indication that the Indo–Iranian *a* which developed from the "pure vowels" *a*, *e*, and *o* of Indo–European could be distinguished in any respect from the Indo–Iranian *a* which developed from the vocalic *n* (or *m*) of Indo–European; and to suggest that in Darius' time in the sixth century the natives who spoke Old Persian or the foreigners who wrote it could possibly have differentiated one of these *a*'s from the other is actually grotesque. Bartholomae (*Grund.* 1.226) and Foy (*KZ* 35.11 fn. 2) are perfectly right in categorically rejecting Thumb's explanation on the ground that Indo–European *n̥* became *a* and only *a* in Aryan.

---

tives meaning 'definitely known' (though not specified), respectively *certain* and *gewiss*; on the other hand, Greek and Latin use indefinite pronominal forms, respectively *tis* and *quidam*; but what has any of this to do with the syntax of Old Persian or Avestan? (That Akkadian *šum-šu* really did develop into an indefinite, as noted above, fn. 62, is certainly irrelevant.)

[228] He had also (in *KZ* 35.32 and 55 fn. 4) explained the troublesome *Pirāva nāma* in *DZc* 9 hacā Pirāva nāma rauta 'from the river called Nile' as a compound, evidently taking *Pirāva* as a nominative; but this he later retracted (in *IF* 12.176), suggesting instead that *Pirāva* may be an ablative. See below, fn. 273.

69. Foy in opposition to Thumb traced *nāmā* to either *nōmņ̄* or *nōmņ̄* in Indo–European,[229] while he derived *nāmă* from an earlier Old Persian **nāman*, to be explained either as an inheritance from an Indo–European sandhi variant **nōmņn*, or as an Old Persian development in which the *n* of the oblique cases had intruded into the nominative-accusative; *KZ* 35.11 (1899), reiterated *KZ* 37.505 and 506. Meillet adopts the second alternative, citing a Slavic parallel for the "restitution de la nasale du thème" in the nominative *nāman*, *GrVP* 161 (1915), repeated by Benveniste in slightly different terms, *GrVP²* 179 (1931).

70. All these scholars without question assume that the two Old Persian forms *nāmă* and *nāmā* must go back to nominative-accusative doublets of an earlier period. It seems to me rather unlikely that two nominative-accusative forms (even if ultimately put to different uses) should have survived on equal terms side by side, one with an *n* (whether inherited from Indo–European or added in Old Persian) and the other without it. It should be noted that in the nominative of masculine-feminine *n*-stems, which under certain conditions lost the final nasal (in their case a consonant) in Indo–European, an *n* is *uniformly* present in Greek (*poimên, termôn*, etc.), and *uniformly* absent in Sanskrit (*ātmā, rājā*, etc.) and in Latin (*sermō, homō*, etc.).

71. Bartholomae eventually introduced a quite different type of explanation. He too had originally viewed *nāmā* and *nāmă* as nominative-accusative doublets, tracing them respectively to Indo–European *nōmņ̄* and Old Persian *nāman*, and explaining the *-n* of *nāman* as introduced into the nominative by the analogy of the other cases, just as Meillet was to do a generation later, only Bartholomae compared Greek[230] instead of Slavic; *Ar. Forsch.* 1.58–59 (1882). Thumb (*KZ*

---

[229] See *KZ* 35.11, where *nāma* is a misprint for *nāmā* (as Foy himself states in *IF* 12.1 fn. 1), and *nōmņ̄* is surely intended, although the macron is very faint (the form is clear in *KZ* 37.506, though printed only *nōmņ̄* just above, p. 505).

[230] I am not sure the comparison is justified. Bartholomae obviously has in mind Greek masculine nouns with nominative in *-n* such as those cited in the previous paragraph; but scholars in general are agreed that these are inherited just as are the Sanskrit and Latin forms without *-n*. Buck for instance (*Comp. Gram.* 187) explains that Indo–European had sentence doublets with and without *-n* (as also with and without *-r*) "of which one type or the other might come to prevail in a given language". Cf. further Brugmann, *Grund.* 1.346 (with some reservations) and 883, 2.2.125–26; Sommer, *Hdb.* 365–66; Leumann, *Lat. Gr.* 264. But of course this difference of opinion does not vitiate Bartholomae's general argument; he might have safely cited as a parallel the intrusion of an *-r* from the oblique cases into the nominative of Latin *s*-stems, which e.g. changed *honos* to *honor*

32.132) calls this derivation possible, though he prefers his own explanation; and Foy (*KZ* 35.11) quotes it with approval, though he also offers as a possible alternative a different explanation for the presence of the *n*. But later Bartholomae suggested that *nāmǎ* and *nāmā* represent different cases, the former a locative, *nāman*, and the latter an accusative, *nāmā*; *Grund.* 1.226 (1895). Gray, though (as already noted, §59) he refuses to treat "das dunkle Problem", expresses general agreement with this view (*IF* 11.311 fn. 2); and Foy, though he advocates a different explanation, says that Bartholomae's is not ruled out (*IF* 12.172 fn. 1). According to Tolman (*Lex.* 105), Bartholomae "later shifted his position", taking both forms as locatives representing respectively *nāman* and *nāmān*. Unfortunately Tolman does not document his quotation, and I have been unable to locate its source.

72. Kent wavers between Bartholomae's two explanations, *OP¹* 193 (1950) and again *OP²* 193 (1953). He is sure that *nāmǎ* represents *nāman*, a suffixless locative; *nāmā* he views as representing either *nāmā* an accusative, or *nāmān* a suffixless locative with lengthened grade.[231]

---

and *rōbus* to *rōbur*. (The fact that a few sporadic instances of *honos* persisted beside *honor* would not justify the assumption that *nāmā* and *nāmǎ* endured on equal terms side by side; cf. §68).

[231] It is rather odd that Kent made no comment concerning the bearing on this problem of Cameron's new reading (*JCS* 5.52) *carmā* (*ca-ra-ma-a*) in 4.90, coordinate with *pavastāy[ā]* in 89–90. This bit of the text was determined too late to be made available by Cameron—as many of his other readings most generously were—to Kent in time for the publication of *OP¹* in 1950; but Kent commented on it in *JCS* 5.56 (1951) and in *JAOS* 72.14 and 19 (1952), and made the necessary corrections in *OP²* (1953), without, however, any reference to the implication of this discovery on his view that *nāmǎ* must be a locative and *nāmā* may be. Obviously, the quantity of the final *a* in *carmā* would suggest just the reverse, if *carmā* is a locative. Kent at first (*JCS* 5.56) took *pavastāyā* and *carmā* as instrumentals, but later (*JAOS* 72.14) he wrote, "*pavastāy[ā]* and *carmā* are in the same case, as the *utā* 'and' shows; therefore in the locative", and he classes them as locatives in *OP²* (184 and 196). As a matter of fact, formally *pavastāyā* can be an instrumental quite as well as a locative; and it seems to me that in the phrase in which it occurs, referring to the materials used for the inscriptions, though we would normally translate in a manner suggesting a locative, an instrumental is quite as much in order. The meaning and use of the phrase *pavastāyā utā carmā*, which has some bearing on the case, has been the subject of discussion. The two words have been explained in terms of the Modern Persian *pōst* 'hide' and *carm* 'leather' (this seems plausible, though it cannot be denied that tracing meanings backward from descendants in the modern form of the ancient language may be as dangerous as assuming them on the basis of supposed, or even assured, cognates in other ancient languages). Kent at first (1951) adopts a suggestion of Cameron's (which he reports *JCS* 5.56) and translates "on papyrus and parchment" (ib. 55–56); later (1952) he accepts Benveniste's proposal (made in 1951, *BSL* 47.41–46)

Since these two forms are used absolutely as parallels apart from the matter of gender, I cannot believe that one is an accusative and the other a locative; but neither do I believe that they are both locatives. It does not seem to me likely that a given noun should have two different ablaut grades existing side by side in the same case. Nor does it seem likely that the locative should be used to express specification; no parallels are cited by Kent in *OP* for this supposed use of *nāmǎ* other than two doubtful and disputed instances, *karsayā* and *stūnāyā* (81).

---

that *pavastā-* "means the thin clay envelope used to protect unbaked clay tablets" (*JAOS* 72.14) and translates "on clay tablets and on parchment" (ib. 13 and *OP²* 132). However, even though the envelope contained the same inscription as the tablet which it protected, if *pavastā-* means the envelope I do not think we should translate it as if it stood for the tablet proper. Hinz (1952) disagrees with practically all the previous statements: he objects to Kent's earlier interpretation "papyrus and parchment" because in Modern Persian *pōst* is 'skin' (i.e. 'parchment') and *carm* is 'leather' (*ZDMG* 102.34); and he objects to Benveniste's interpretation of *pavastā-* because it is inconsistent with the wording of both the Old Persian and the Elamite versions (ib. fn. 1). He is convinced that there must be a specific reference to the clay tablets in the Old Persian as well as in the Elamite; and consequently he proposes (35) that Cameron's *ga-ra-* in 4.90 (*JCS* 5.52), which Kent took as the beginning of *gra[thitā āha]* 'was written' (ib. 55, also *JAOS* 72.13 and *OP²* 130), was a misreading for *ut[ā]*, after which he supplies (*h*)*istā*. This I suppose is intended as an instrumental or possibly a locative, though I should rather have expected (*h*)*istiyā*, for the word for 'sun-dried brick', which occurs in *DSf* 29, is certainly *istis*, an *-i-* stem; Hinz himself (35) cites it in the form (*h*)*istis* (see also Kent, *OP* 61 and 175). If the reading *ut-* instead of *gra-* is justified by the traces, Hinz' suppletion seems to me very plausible; *grathitā āha* is not needed, for all the words denoting materials can go back to *āha* in 89. The whole passage would then run: 89–91 patisam ariyā āha utā pavastāyā utā carmā utā (h)istā 'besides, it was (written) in Aryan and [or both?] on sun-dried brick and on parchment and leather'; though the *utā* before *pavastāyā* may be correlative with the following *uta*'s, it may also be a genuine connective uniting *ariyā* 'in Aryan' with the subsequent words denoting materials, and in that case the fact that *ariyā* is unquestionably an instrumental may favor the view that *pavastāyā*, *carmā*, and the assumed (*h*)*istā* are instrumentals too. On the other hand, if *carmā* is an instrumental it must be an *-a-* stem (i.e. an Indo-European *-o-* stem), whereas the etymological evidence, which in this instance is so striking as to seem compelling, certainly favors the view that the word is an *-n-* stem, cognate with Sanskrit *carman-*, Avestan *carəman-* 'hide, skin' (so Kent, *JAOS* 72.14 and *OP²* 184, and Benveniste, *BSL* 47.41; cf. WP 2.573). In that case *carmā* must be a locative, as it is taken by Benveniste (loc. cit.), who adds the comment that it is the first locative of an *-n-* stem attested, and, eventually, by Kent (loc. cit.). Since I myself consider both *nāmā* and *nāmǎ* nominatives (as I shall show below, §§88–111), I am not at all disturbed by the discovery of an *-n-* stem locative in *-ā*; but I certainly would find it hard to justify an assumed locative *nāmǎ* in the face of this fairly certain locative *carmā*, though Kent contents himself by calling it a "strong-grade" or "long-grade" form (*JAOS* 72.14 and *OP²* 65 respectively). It is a pity that we have no occurrence of the word in the nominative; it would be interesting to know whether it resembled *casmǎ* or the (supposed) neuter *taumā* (see §§77–79).

73. I question whether it is necessary to account for the two forms in terms of two prehistoric ancestors.[232] I certainly would not go so far in minimizing the difference between them as did Tolman, *Lex.* 105 (1908), approved by Johnson, *GrAP* 128 (1917): Tolman suggested, though to be sure only tentatively, that the distinction might be merely one of writing, the *scriptio plena* in *nāmā* being influenced by the feminine noun that it accompanied. Presumably the scribes wrote at dictation, and put down what they heard; besides, were the differentiation between *nāmă* and *nāmā* merely an orthographical one, we might well expect an occasional deviation, but none ever occurs. However, it seems to me that the explanation which Debrunner, *IF* 52.153 (1934), offers in opposition to Meillet-Benveniste and to Bartholomae is an eminently sensible one. He views the development of the doublets (masculine and neuter *nāmă* and feminine *nāmā*) as "nichts altes" but purely a Persian matter.

74. I agree with Debrunner—indeed, I had come to the same conclusion as he does before I had ever read his article—that the word for 'name' was misinterpreted as an adjective 'named'. Debrunner starts with *nāmă*, equating it with Sanskrit *nāma* as Thumb had done, but for a different reason. He does not discuss how Indo–Iranian -*ă* could give Old Persian -*ă*; he simply contents himself with citing a parallel, *ca-sa-ma*, and referring to the discussion of it by Wackernagel (*KZ* 61.205–8), who identifies it (or, as he spells it, *c s m = casma*), with Avestan *casman-* (on this see below, §86). Debrunner then assumes that *Kabūjiya nāmă* 'Cambyses nomen' was interpreted as 'Cambyses nominatus', and that thus was generated, with the feminine word for

---

[232] If we must do so, there are various expedients that we might use. After all there must have been considerable opportunity for confusion of *ā* and *ă* in *ā*-stem and *n*-stem nouns, in which *ā* and *ņ* developed into *ā* and *ă*; and the complications would extend in Indo–Iranian to the *ŏ*-stem nouns, since here *ŏ* developed into *ă*. Note the discussion in Schmidt, *Plur.* 82–83 and 95–97, of the similarities and interchanges of forms (of different genders) belonging to *ā*-, *ă*-, and *n*-stems; also the particular reference (89) to the coming together in "Old Bactrian" (i.e. Avestan) of neuter *man*-stems in the nominative-accusative plural and neuter *ma*-stems in the nominative-accusative singular. With this we may compare the existence of such Latin doublets as *columna* and *columen*, referred to below in §82. Furthermore, there is in Vedic an interchange between *ă* and *ā* which has nothing to do with the history of the forms: it is what is called "metrische Auslautdehnung" or "rhythmische Auslautdehnung" by Wackernagel (see *AiG* 1.310–16, 3.272–73), "rhythmic lengthening" by Edgerton (see *VV* 2.216–48, especially 226–27 on neuters in *mă*:*mā*).

'fortress', *Arsādā nāmā* 'Arsada nominata';[233] he does not specifically discuss the development of *nāmă* with a neuter word as 'nominatum', although I think he should (see below §87).

75. Twenty years later, Humbach, *MSS* 5.95 (1954), offers an explanation rather similar to Debrunner's, which he seems not to know; at all events he does not mention it. He, too, starts with *nāmă*, but with *nāmă* as met with a neuter noun, not with a masculine. He declares that on the testimony of Avestan and Sanskrit we may "mit Sicherheit" assume that *nāmă* is the nominative-accusative singular of the stem *nāman-*; but he, unlike Debrunner, does recognize the problem why the usual Old Persian lengthening in Auslaut has not in this instance produced *nāmā*. The answer he finds in the fact which he has noticed that the word denoting the possessor of the name, if neuter, always follows the word for 'name' (on this correct observation, cf. further fn. 257 below), and he maintains that the absence of lengthening is due to the close phonetic connection with the following word, as in *DB* 3.4–5 Patigrabanā nāma vardanam. Thus is produced "Kongruenz" between the two words, as in Greek **Ilion onoma ptoliethron*; and as a result with a feminine noun the word for 'name' takes a feminine form as if we had pseudo-Greek **Ilion onymê polis*. With a masculine noun, no matter what the order, we everywhere find *nāmă* from **nāmah*, as

---

[233] K. H. Schmidt, *ZCP* 28.227 (1961), declares that Debrunner's explanation "versagt in Fällen wie DB III, 4f. *Patrigrabanā nāma vardanam*, wo trotz des eindeutigen Femininums *Patrigrabanā nāma* statt des nach Debrunner zu erwartenden *nāmā* steht." It seems unthinkable that a scholar like Debrunner could have been guilty of such a lapse as Schmidt attributes to him. I believe that Schmidt misunderstands Debrunner's use (perhaps not altogether clear) of *Cambyses nominatus* and *Arsadā nominata*, where it seems certain that *Cambyses* and *Arsadā* are predicate nouns with *nominatus* and *nominata* (cf. below, fn. 257, near the beginning), and the nouns with which the adjectives agree are not given—in other words *Cambyses nominatus* means '(some one) named Cambyses', not 'Cambyses named', which really would hardly make sense. Indeed, Debrunner shows that this is the meaning he intends by quoting the Meillet-Benveniste rendering (*GrVP²* 179), "un nommé Cambyse". Schmidt himself offers an explanation which starts like the one that I suggest in §77 (written before I read his article), but which continues quite differently. He too begins with *nāmā*, which he considers an accusative (I take it as an original nominative), preserved only "bei den in der Endung formal passenden Feminina" (227). Masculine *nāmă* was then assimilated to the masculine nominative form, which he says was written -*a* but was probably to be read (by which I think he means to be pronounced) -*ah* (this I question, but at all events it appears irrelevant), and the neuter adopted the masculine form by analogy (this I doubt, for second declension masculine and neuter adjectives are *not* alike in the nominative; cf. below, §87).

if we had Greek *magos Gômatês onymos. (I do not know why he spells his made-up forms onymê and onymos, after starting with the usual Homeric and Attic onoma.)

76. Humbach's explanation is somewhat more complicated than Debrunner's, and in my opinion somewhat less attractive. The shortening of final a that he posits, while regular only before an enclitic (see Kent, OP 47), is possible also before a separate word, especially if the two are closely connected syntactically (ib. 17); but there is a serious objection to Humbach's assumption that we have an example of it in the case of nāmă vardanam, for if it occurs before a neuter, why not also before a feminine? (On this see below, fn. 257, close.) Furthermore, masculine nāmă is so much more common than neuter nāmă, and is used with so many more different nouns, that it seems to me a much better starting-point than neuter nāmă.

77. However, we can equally well start with what is usually assumed to be the normal form, nāmā. This when employed in connection with a feminine noun might, though actually the nominative-accusative of a neuter n-stem noun, have been wrongly interpreted as the nominative of a feminine ā-stem adjective, just like kartā.[234] The -a of nāmā (from Indo–European -n̥) was historically short, and the -a of kartā (from Indo–European -ā) was historically long; but in Old Persian they were written alike, and I assume they were pronounced alike. Then from nāmā with a feminine noun would have been generated nāmă with a masculine noun, just like kartă, the masculine nominative adjective form which corresponded to the feminine kartā. The -a of kartă is from proto-Iranian -ah (from Indo–Iranian -as, from Indo–European -os), and Kent (OP 18) believes, as I have already said (§62), that a final ḥ was pronounced in kartă and a final n in nāmă; but they were written alike, and again I assume that they were pronounced alike.[235]

<hr>

[234] Such transfers of declension are by no means unexampled in Old Persian. Thus the Persian name of Ahuramazda, which Kent (OP 64) classifies as an ēs-stem, has an ambiguous nominative Auramazdā, an s-stem genitive Auramazdāha (h representing s, and a representing the genitive ending -es or -os) as well as two variant forms, and an ā-stem accusative Auramazdām. The Persian name of Xerxes, which Kent (OP 65) classes as an n-stem, and Benveniste (GrVP² 180–81) as an s-stem, has a similar ambiguous nominative Xsayārsā, and follows the forms of Auramazdā in general.

[235] Although I am not seriously suggesting it, I should like to point out that if kartă really was pronounced kartaḥ, we have no way of knowing that nāmă, if created to balance a supposedly feminine nāmā, was not similarly pronounced nāmaḥ! Indeed,

78. Of course if one starts with *nāmă*, the process would be reversed: *nāmă* is misinterpreted as a masculine adjective, and generates a feminine one *nāmā*, as Debrunner thought.

79. I do not see how we can choose positively between *nāmă* and *nāmā* as the original form that generated the adjective. Certainly, the early inherited form was Indo–Iranian *nāma*, which in the ordinary development would have become Old Persian *nāmā*; but I am willing to believe that the ordinary development might have been checked by the intrusion into the nominative-accusative of the *n* that was present in all the other cases, so that Indo–Iranian and very early Persian *nāmă* was supplanted by *nāman* before it had a chance to turn into *nāmā*. Thus I am in agreement with Foy, Meillet, and Benveniste (cited above, §69) as to a possible origin for *nāmă*; but I am not in agreement with them that, if and when the form *nāman* which was ultimately to produce *nāmă* thus came into being, the form *nāma* which *nāman* supplanted would have continued in existence and thus could ultimately produce *nāmā*.

80. Recorded forms of *n*-stems are too few to permit us to come to a positive decision between *nāmă* and *nāmā*. A nominative masculine in *-ā* is adequately attested; there are two occurrences that seem certain, both plausibly classed by Kent (*OP* 52 and 64) as *-van* formations, a noun, *xsaçapāvā* 'satrap' (3.14 and 56), and an adjective, *artāvā* 'blessed' (*XPh* 48 and 55); and there is a third example according to Kent (*OP* 65), *Xsayārsā* 'Xerxes' (Xerxes inscriptions *passim*), which, however, is disputed (cf. above, fn. 234). But what we need are nominative-accusative neuters. Of these two instances have been cited, both possible, neither positive; one, *taumā* 'strength' (4.74, 78), favors *nāmā*; and the other, *casmă* 'eye' (2.89 and probably 2.75), favors *nāmă*!

Bartholomae (*Ar. Forsch.* 1.59 fn. 1) seems to assume that if Spiegel was right (which he doubts; cf. fn. 225), this must have been the case. He then correctly points out the logical corollary to this: that if *nāmă* with masculine nouns represents *nāmah*, with neuter nouns analogy would demand *nāmam*. So far as I know, no scholar except Bartholomae has raised this objection, and no scholar except Thumb has tried to obviate it. The latter (*KZ* 32.133) explains the lack of a neuter form *nāmam* (and also of a masculine form *nāmah*) as a sign "dass *nāma* seinen ursprung noch nicht ganz verleugnet hatte, so zwar, dass jene verschiebung des sprachgefühls in *nāmā* sich vollziehen konnte, wo die fertige äussere form darauf hindrängte, dass aber diese association keineswegs die kraft hatte, lautlich widersprechende formen in ihren bereich zu ziehen und umzugestalten".

81. There are said to be two Old Persian nouns which in the nominative are written *taumā*. The need to distinguish them is stressed by Oppert, *Mèdes* 100 (1879), who, however, misprints one of them as *tautā*; Bang, *ZDMG* 43.533 (1889); Foy, *KZ* 35.47 (1899); Bartholomae, *AiW* col. 623–24 (1904); Tolman, *Lex.* 91 (1908); Kent, *JAOS* 35.329–31 (1915).

82. One of these nouns means 'family', and is derived from a stem *teuk-* (according to Kent, *OP* 37, Indo–European velar *k* before *m* > Iranian *x* > Persian *h*, which was not written). The word is well attested: we meet the nominative singular seven times; the accusative singular, *taumām*, once; the genitive singular, *taumāyā*, eleven times; and the ablative singular, also *taumāyā*, once. Obviously, this is a feminine *ā*-stem; but it is akin so far as its root goes to *n*-stem nouns in the related languages, Sanskrit *tokman-* (which Kent, *JAOS* 35.329, seems wrong in calling masculine) 'young shoot of grain (especially barley)', Avestan *taoxman-* 'seed, shoot'[236] (WP 1.713). On the basis of Avestan *taoxman-*, Thumb (*KZ* 32.133) assumes that *taumā* was originally an *n*-stem which shifted to the *ā*-declension; and he holds that Avestan *taoxman-* and Old Persian *taumā* (also Latin *columen* and *columna*) correspond to each other as do *nāma* and *nāmā*; i.e., they are derived respectively from forms in -*mn̥* and *mn̄*. But I have already expressed lack of faith in Thumb's theory (above, §68), and I know of no one else who has thus used *taumā* 'family' to explain *nāmā*.

83. However, Kent (*OP* 52) so uses the (supposed) other *taumā*,[237]

---

[236] Also to a Sanskrit masculine *a*-stem *tokma-* 'young shoot of grain' and a Sanskrit neuter *a*-stem *toka-* 'offspring'. The existence side by side in Sanskrit of two words of similar meaning, the neuter *n*-stem *tokman-* and the masculine *a*-stem *tokma-*, might be thought to justify Kent's assumption (see below, §86) that the Old Persian cognate of the Avestan *n*-stem *casman-* 'eye' is an *a*-stem *casam* (he also assumes that this is neuter, but if it is an *a*-stem it might just as well be masculine, for it is an accusative form and therefore ambiguous in gender).

[237] He associates with this noun an adjective **taumā-*, assumed by him as the positive corresponding to the comparative *tauvīyā* (*JAOS* 58.324, *OP* 66 and 185). The latter occurs in *DSe* 39–41 hya tauvīyā tyam skauthim naiy jatiy naiy vimardatiy, translated by Kent (142) 'the stronger does not smite nor destroy the weak'. There is nothing in the context to force us to render hya tauvīyā 'the stronger' rather than 'the strong', but it certainly does exemplify the regular Indo–European comparative formation with -*yes* -*yos* frequently seen in Indo–Iranian (Kent, *OP* 66; Brugmann, *Grund.* 2.1.547–48, 555–56). If the combination of the noun *taumā* and the adjective *taumā* forms part of a fairly extensive pattern in Old Persian, and if the noun *taumā* is a neuter *n*-stem, and if the original neuter *n*-stem meaning 'name' appeared in Old Persian as *nāmā*, then we

which means 'strength, power', and occurs, both times in the nominative, in 4.74 and 78. According to WP 1.706, this word comes from a stem *tēu-tǝu-tǔ-*, and the only Indo-Iranian nouns classed with it are the neuter Avestan *tavah-* and a Sanskrit adjective used as a noun which, being found in the accusative *tavasam* and in the (Vedic) instrumental *tavasā*, is presumably a neuter *tavasam*. Both these nouns mean 'strength' as does *taumā*, but their structure is not sufficiently similar to justify any conclusion as to the stem of the Old Persian word. WP (1.706), Bartholomae (*AiW* col. 623), and Reichelt (*KZ* 39.74) all, like Kent, list it as a neuter *n*-stem; but none of them gives any reason for so doing. Meillet (*GrVP* 142 and 146) and Benveniste (*GrVP*² 156 and 161) both comment on the ambiguity of the form: Meillet (142) says it may be a masculine or neuter with the suffix -*man*-, or a feminine with the suffix -*mā*-; Benveniste (without indicating why) in his revision of Meillet (156) omits precisely the possibility which is the only one accepted by Kent, that it is a neuter with -*man*-.

84. But subsequently we find Benveniste proposing what I believe was a wholly new idea in *BSL* 47.37–38 (1951), namely, that there was only a single *taumā* meaning not only 'race, famille, descendance' but also, in the physical sense, 'semence', in other words 'le pouvoir générateur'. He cites Herodotus 1.136 to prove the particular virtue ascribed by the Persians to an abundance of offspring; and I am reminded also of our own use in English of *potent, potency*, and above all *impotent* with special reference to procreation.[238] The only occur-

---

might suggest that the formation of an adjective *nāmǎ* 'having a name, named' beside the noun *nāmā* 'name' was furthered by the analogy of the adjective *taumǎ* 'having strength, strong' beside the noun *taumā* 'strength'. But that involves a great many *if*'s! Also, in that case we would expect *nāmǎ nāmā nāmam* corresponding to **taumǎ *taumā *taumam*; and that is just what we do not have. Cf. above, fn. 235, and below, §87.

[238] Kent, *OP*² 218, opposes Benveniste's suggestion on the ground that the word meaning 'family' is an *ā*- stem, whereas the word meaning 'strength' is an *n*- stem. The only evidence for this is *anuv taumanisaiy* 'according to his (natural) power' in *DNb* 25–26; this seems to me far too dubious a form to build upon in explaining *taumā*. The part of it preceding the enclitic -*saiy* can be interpreted as either *taumani* or *taumanis* (on the latter see Kent, *OP* 18 and 47). Herzfeld, *ApI* 327, who discusses it at some length, has no doubt that it belongs to *taumā* 'strength'; as for its case, he considers the possibilities that it is genitive, locative, or accusative, but does not seem happy about any of these explanations (and neither am I!). Kent (*Lg.* 15.175–77 and *OP* 65) asserts that *taumanis* (as also *arasanis* in *DSf* 26) is an instrumental plural; I have no opinion about *arasanis*, but I consider the suggestion out of the question so far as *taumanis* goes. He

rences of this supposed separate *taumā* certainly bear Benveniste out. Kent's use of it in *OP¹* in suppletion in 5.19 and 35 was abandoned by him in *OP²* on the basis of Cameron's discoveries (see *JCS* 5.56–57 and *JAOS* 72.16–18), and we have left only 4.74 and 78, where the alternation of this word with the common *taumā* in 75 and 79 makes a distinction particularly unlikely. The meaning of the passages then is: 72–76 'If you see this inscription or these sculptures (and) you do not destroy them but [literally, and] protect²³⁹ them as long as there is

---

justifies the case (*Lg.* 15.176) by 1.92 anuv Ufrātuvā 'beside the Euphrates'. Even if *Ufrātuvā* really is an instrumental, as he holds (*Lg.* 15.176 and *OP* 176), which is by no means certain (Herzfeld, *ApI* 71–72, takes it as genitive), the meaning of the preposition is too different to permit the use of 1.92 as a parallel for *DNb* 25–26. I have not the least doubt that in the latter passage we must interpret *taumanis* as a genitive, for it is almost perfectly parallel to two other phrases occurring *in the same document* and almost directly preceding it, namely *DNb* 16–17 martiya hya hataxsataiy anudim hakartahyā avathādim paribarāmiy 'the man who cooperates, him according to (his) cooperativeness him then I protect', and *DNb* 17–19 hya vināthayatiy anudim vinastahyā avathā parsāmiy 'who does harm, him according to (his) harmfulness then I punish', while our passage runs, 24–26 martiya tya kunautiy yadivā ābaratiy anuv taumanisaiy xsnuta amiy 'what a man does or if he performs according to his power I am satisfied'. Note that the other two genitives with anu(v), hakartahyā (16–17) and vinastahyā (18), are neuter adjectives (really participles) used as nouns, and I think the same may be said of *taumanis* (25–26). In the same document we find a nominative adjective *yāumainis* 'trained, skilled' (40) and also its negative *ayāumainis* (59). Kent explains *yāumainis* as a form with epenthesis (*Lg.* 15.173 and *OP* 204) from an adjective stem *yāumani-*, which he calls "adj. to *yau-man-*". I would suggest that similarly our *taumanis* is from an adjective stem *taumani-*, adjective to **tauman-* (later, of course after the formation of the adjective, changed to *taumā-*, if we accept Benveniste's view, as I am inclined to do; obviously my proposal about the derivation of *taumanis* still holds good if we do *not* accept Benveniste's view). Kent (*Lg.* 15.172) objects to the interpretation of the form as a genitive on the ground that we "hardly find -man- stems extended by -i-", but if we take *taumanis* as an adjective his opinion is refuted by his own findings in regard to *yāumainis*. If *taumanis* is, as I have already indicated I feel sure it must be, parallel to the two adjectives *hakartahyā* and *vinastahyā*, it must be a neuter genitive. There is no difficulty about the case: the genitive ending of *i*-stems is interpreted as -ais (*OP* 61), but it is not always differentiated in the Persian script from -is (see *OP* 14), and I am not sure whether when it is not we are justified in differentiating it in print (note that both Herzfeld, *ApI* 327, and Kent himself, *Lg.* 15.171, say taumani before -saiy may represent taumanis or taumanais). I do not think the gender need present any difficulty either: it is true that no neuter nominal-adjectival *i*-stems are cited in Old Persian, but they exist in Sanskrit and Avestan (see Brugmann, *Grund.* 2.1.173–74 and 577), and there is no reason why they could not have existed in Old Persian. (An interpretation similar to mine is among those envisaged by Herzfeld, *ApI* 327, but he does not defend it and seems highly doubtful about it; see also ib. 72).

²³⁹ I cannot go along with Benveniste (*BSL* 47.37) in his objection to 'protect' as the meaning of *paribarāh(y)* in 74 and 78. He asks how one could 'protect' the inscriptions, and whether they were not 'protected' by their inaccessible site. But he does not ques-

taumā to you, may Ahuramazda be a friend to you and may there be *taumā* in abundance to you'; 76–80 'If you see this inscription or these sculptures (and) you destroy them and do not protect them as long as there is *taumā* to you, may Ahuramazda be a smiter to you and may there not be *taumā* to you'. In other words, on the good or bad use that the viewer makes of his *taumā* as long as he has it will depend whether or not the great god will (continue to) grant him *taumā*. This certainly involves a fitting manifestation of divine justice such as the Persians cherished.

85. But doing away with an *n*-stem *taumā* does not necessarily rule out all connection with *nāmā*. If a cognate of Sanskrit *tokman-* and Avestan *taoxman-* could in Old Persian shift from a neuter *n*-stem to a feminine *ā*-stem, why could not likewise a cognate of Sanskrit *nāman-* and Avestan *nāman-*? If *nāmā* had already become a feminine *ā*-stem in Old Persian, its development into a feminine adjective would become most natural. This development of course could be posited even if we accept the existence of a neuter *n*-stem *taumā*, since the feminine *ā*-stem *taumā* is still there as proof of what *could* happen to a neuter *n*-stem. On the other hand the nominative-accusative *casma* (if this is the correct interpretation of *ca-sa-ma*) and the locative *carmā* are also there to show that neuter *n*-stems *could* survive; on them see §86 and fn. 231 respectively.

86. Foy (*KZ* 35.11), Meillet (*GrVP* 146 and 161), Benveniste (*GrVP*² 161–62 and 180), and Debrunner (*IF* 52.153) all offer *casmă*[240]

---

tion the meaning 'destroy' for *vikanāh(y)* in 73 and 77, and surely the power to destroy implies the contrary power to protect.

[240] This used to be thought to be *ucasma*, and a great deal of learning and ingenuity were expended in accounting for it: scholars were troubled by the singular ending, for they thought the word must mean 'the eyes' or 'the two eyes'; and still more by the beginning, for the *u* was quite unexampled and practically inexplicable. Thus Meillet in 1915 characterized both the value of the *u* and the character of the form as obscure (*GrVP* 146; cf. 161); and attempts by himself and others to clarify them did not introduce much light. It was suggested that the word was a singular used as a dual (Foy, *KZ* 35.39; Johnson, *GrAP* 199) or as a collective (Benveniste, *GrVP*² 162), or even that the form was a neuter plural (Benveniste, ib.). As for the *u*, Weissbach, *ZDMG* 61.726 (1907)—quoted by Tolman, *Lex.* 75, and accepted by Meillet, *MSL* 19.348, and by Benveniste, *GrVP*² 162 and 179—proposed that it was a prefix meaning 'good', which certainly would not suit the sense; and Wackernagel (*KZ* 61.206–8), accepted by Debrunner (*IF* 52.153), that it was the preverb *ud* meaning 'up', separated from the verb by "tmesis", which, as Wackernagel himself admits, is not found in Old Persian.

(in 2.89) as a parallel for *nāmă*. The word is in this form a perfect cognate for the Avestan *casman-* 'eye', a neuter *n*-stem, as is pointed out by Foy (*KZ* 35.39), Meillet (*GrVP* 146), and Benveniste (*GrVP²* 162). Kent, refusing to admit the possibility, declares (*Lg.* 19.225–26 and *OP* 184) that *ca-sa-ma* must be interpreted as *casam*, neuter accusative of an *ă*-stem. (It is varieties in interpretation of this sort on the part of editors that make me desiderate a syllabic transcription of all texts.) Kent's assumption of an *ă*-stem (Indo–European *o*-stem) variant for an *n*-stem, though less satisfactory, is certainly not unparalleled; cf. fnn. 232 and 236. Yet I am troubled by his inflexibility, and am by no means convinced that the last word has been said upon the subject.²⁴¹ Kent is clinging to the rule that seems to forbid the existence of a nominative-accusative *n*-stem in *-ă* like *nāmă* or *casmă*; therefore he calls *nāmă* a locative and *ca-sa-ma* an a-stem. But *nāmă*, as Thumb points out (*KZ* 32.132), is commoner than *nāmā* (in the existing remains *nāmă* occurs 56 times, *nāmā* 14 times); perhaps that may suggest that *nāmă* rather than *nāmā* generated the double construction. If *nāmă* is the form representing Indo–European *nōmn̥*, it is both a nominative-accusative (Bartholomae and Kent are most unconvincing in calling it a locative) and an *n*-stem. And *ca-sa-ma* is certainly an accusative (it is direct object of the verb *avajam* 'I put out') and very probably a neuter *n*-stem (this is favored, even though not proved, by the parallel from the closely related Avestan). Here then we have two words which the evidence strongly suggests are nominative-accusative neuter *n*-stems ending in *-ă*; is it not possible that the rule forbidding the existence of such forms may be wrong? May it not be *nāmă* and not *nāmā* that brought the alternative form into being?

However, the double problem has been settled by a single correction: Cameron (*JCS* 5.49–50), on the basis of a fresh examination of the inscription, declares the correct reading to be *1 ca-sa-ma*, not *u-ca-sa-ma* as had been believed, though it seems hard to see how the character for the numeral '1' could ever have been misread as part of the character for *u*; the vertical, according to Cameron, *JCS* 5.50, "could never have been a part of *u*; it is too tall." At all events, now we know that *casma* is indubitably singular: Darius was not quite so monstrous as he has been thought, for he put out only '1 eye', not 'the two eyes'. (I do not see why, even without the numeral '1', *casma* could not have been interpreted from the start as a singular, but, so far as I know, only Gray so took it; cf. his translation, 'I put out his eye', *JAOS* 21 2nd half, 128 fn. 1, 1902.)

²⁴¹ After writing the above, I was gratified to find confirmation of my view by eminent authority in Benveniste's explicit and emphatic statement (in his review of *OP¹*, *BSL* 47.90): "aucun iraniste n'acceptera *casam* (au lieu de *casman-*)."

87. But whatever we think about the form *nāmă* used with masculine nouns and the form *nāmā* used with feminine nouns, when we come to the form *nāmă* used with neuter nouns we come to a grave difficulty. Even though I am not sure whether *nāmă* or *nāmā* was the inherited form, I am in general agreement with Debrunner's approach (as I have already indicated above, §§74 and 75) in thinking that only one form was inherited, and that it generated the other. But in explaining that *nāmă* was understood in the sense of 'nominatus', and that consequently *nāmā* was introduced in the sense of 'nominata', he certainly is guilty of a serious sin of omission in ignoring the need of a word for 'nominatum'! Original final *m*, unlike original final *n*, is written in Old Persian; and the neuter corresponding to masculine *kartă* and feminine *kartā* is *kartam*. Why, then, not *nāmam*?[242] It may be said that, though *nāma* and *nāmā* have come to be used respectively like the nominatives of corresponding adjectival stems in *ă* (from Indo-European *o*) and *ā*, still some connection with a neuter *n*-stem lingered on in the consciousness—or unconsciousness—of those using the forms; a case-form in -*m* would certainly seem abnormal (this is in line with Thumb's view, *KZ* 32.133, already quoted in fn. 235). Besides, these pseudo-adjectival forms may not have acquired complete adjectival force, and the tendency of masculine and neuter forms to resemble each other in opposition to the feminine may have carried over even into the nominative.[243] But above all—and here I think I may have found the real solution of the problem—the pronominal adjectives may have played a part,[244] for here the masculine (originally ending in -*aḥ*)

[242] The difficulty I think is inherent quite as much in Debrunner's explanation as in the reverse one (cf. above, fn. 233). It is true that if he is right in assuming that *nōmṇ* became not *nāmā* but *nāmă*, this *nāmă*, actually a neuter noun, could as an adjective serve as either masculine or neuter; but once he has posited a new feminine formation *nāmā* (like *kartā*) to serve as a feminine adjective, the corresponding adjective *nāmă* must be assumed to count as an *a*-stem (like *kartă*), and in that capacity it could be masculine only, and would demand a neuter **nāmam* (like *kartam*).

[243] Can there possibly be any connection with the fact noted by Wackernagel (*AiG* 3.32) that (presumably because of the identity of most of the cases of masculine and neuter adjectives) the neuter nominative-accusative singular adjective in Sanskrit sometimes borrows masculine forms? This is particularly true of adjectives in -*an*- (ib. 272); cf. e.g. *RV* 1.37.1 and 5.42.9.

[244] That Greek and Latin actually use pronominal forms (*tis* and *quidam* respectively) has already been noted in fn. 227. I protested there against the idea that the usage of one language can be adequately explained by a neat translation into another language; but I do not deny that it may be helpful to compare semantic developments in two different languages if they really present certain parallels.

and the neuter (originally ending in -*ad*) have come to be identical, since final -*d*, like final -*h* and unlike final -*m*, disappears.[245] Thus in *aniyă aniyā aniyă* 'other' we have an exact parallel for *nāmă nāmā nāmă*; cf. too such neuters as *avă* 'that', *aită* 'this', and *hamă* 'same', which probably have corresponding masculines in -*ă* and feminines in -*ā*, though these are not all attested.

88. But what I am really concerned with in viewing the variants *nāmă* and *nāmā* is not their phonological origin but their syntactical use. Most of the scholars who deal with their history,[246] apart from those (Bartholomae and Kent) who call them locatives, either specifically call them accusatives[247] or at least seem tacitly to infer and to imply that they are such. But I maintain that since they varied in gender along with the noun representing the bearer of the name, they must have been in agreement, either appositive or attributive, with this noun. And as the noun in question is nominative in every instance except one or possibly two,[248] so, too, must be *nāmă* and *nāmā*.

89. The fact that the noun with which *nāmă* or *nāmā* agrees is regularly nominative is tied up with a salient characteristic of Old Persian style. Normally when first we hear of a person or a place, he or it is introduced by a formula corresponding to the Latin *homo Iulius nomen*, usually followed by what Kent (97) calls a "resumptive". Thus the passage may run *homo Iulius nomen* (= *nominatus*), *is rex erat*, or *homo Iulius nomen* (= *nominatus*), *eum misi*, or *provincia Gallia nomen* (= *nominata*), *ibi pugnavi*. When *homo* and the "resumptive" are in different cases, as in the second passage just cited, such formulae are viewed by Kent as instances of anacoluthon, which he defines as "the use of a grammatical element in a form which does not find its justification in the remainder of the sentence" (99). Now it is true that the inscriptions were presumably composed by persons who could not read or write, and therefore must have been dictated to the scribes,[249]

---

[245] Once more I am assuming that if final consonants were not written, it was because they were not pronounced. Cf. above, §77.

[246] Of course Schmidt, with his bahuvrihi theory, and Gray, with his apposition theory, are exceptions.

[247] So e.g. Johnson (*GrAP* 202). Even Kent, though he believes *nāmā* to be a locative, does not completely rule out the possibility of its being an accusative (*OP* 80).

[248] See below, §§113 and 114.

[249] Darius the Great describes the process at the close of what must have been the original form of the Great Inscription at Bisitun (4.88–92): he made the inscription, and it was written and read to him. Cf. Sturtevant, *JAOS* 48.73.

and anything dictated may well abound in anacolutha; the verbatim reports that appear in newspapers of press conferences even with some of the highest officials can be punctuated only by dashes, and many a private secretary by quietly editing her stenographic notes saves her "boss" from the ignominy that would accrue if she typed what he really said. But none the less when a given tournure appears again and again in these royal inscriptions, I assume it must be true to the facts of the language;[250] and I believe such an introductory passage as *homo Iulius nomen* does not need to "find its justification in the remainder of the sentence", for I think it is itself a completely independent and self-sufficient element. Scholars argue as to whether we should regard such an expression as a nominative absolute[251] or as a nominal clause.[252] There is really not much difference between the two, since both involve predication;[253] but a nominative absolute cannot stand alone,

[250] After all, if that is the way Darius (for instance) dictated, that must be the way he talked; and what other guide have we to the "standard" language of his day? It is true his style seems to us wholly lacking in polish and grace. Is not that natural, however, in the member of a society neither literary nor even literate? Perhaps those who insist that the only true form of language is the spoken form forget the important influence that is exerted on the spoken form by contact, even in a limited way, with the written form. Even at a time when literature is beginning to be composed, the first works produced are likely to be choppy and almost childish in their structure; compare a Cato with a Cicero, an Ennius with a Vergil.

[251] On supposed examples of nominative absolutes in Homer, see my paper on partitive apposition, *TAPA* 85.204–10.

[252] The problem has already been referred to in fn. 208. Proponents of the nominative absolute include Spiegel, *GrAS* 408; Gray, *IF* 11.311; Benveniste, *MSL* 23.179–80 and *GrVP*[2] 14; Schaeder, *Ariaramnes* 638 fn. 2; Kent, *OP* 79 and 97. Proponents of the nominal clause include Meillet, *GrVP* 202–3; Schwyzer, *Parenth.* 12–13; Wüst, *WS* 20.249–53; Thieme, *KZ* 68.216; Hoffmann, *MSS* 9.79–80. Blümel, *IF* 33.16, also considers it conceivable to see a clause in the construction, but he apparently deals with it differently, for to him the clause is simply *Iulius nomen*; *homo* he ignores. With this clause he compares the Greek *Kydnos onoma* which with Brugmann he is willing to see as a clause; but Brugmann's interpretation (*IF* 27.144) 'Kydnos (ist) der (sein) Name' (on which see above, §6 and fn. 15) is not applied by Blümel to the Old Persian, for he expressly states that the meaning of the latter is not 'Gaumata ist der Name' but 'Gaumata ist er mit Namen'. In other words, he is not taking the Old Persian word for 'name' as a nominative.

[253] The element of predication is what distinguishes a Greek genitive absolute, or a Latin ablative absolute, from other genitives or ablatives. That is why we need two words to make an absolute construction—a substantive with another substantive or an adjective (to correspond to a nominal clause) or with a participle (to correspond to a verbal clause)—except in the case of the participle of an impersonal verb, which no more can agree with a substantive than a finite form of such a verb can agree with a subject. *Consule Planco* is as complete a predication as *deo volente*; the teachers who tell their students (as mine did me) that in an ablative absolute of the former type 'being'

and a nominal clause can; hence I think the second explanation is the better.[254] Then in the following clause the "resumptive" plays its syntactic part, but it is not needed to "resume" or complete the preceding clause.

90. An even more cogent reason for calling the nominative expression a clause is that in some instances the verb 'be' actually appears, and there is no distinction between these verbal clauses and the usual nominal clauses. I shall begin with examples of those which are just like the Sanskrit *āsīd rājā Nalo nāma* (*MBh.* 3.50.1).[255] It should be noted at the outset that in all these passages it is, as usual, possible to explain the construction by Brugmann's method of viewing the part equivalent to *Iulius nomen* as a second nominal clause, and in that case, when the verb 'be' appears, we may say that it is in this clause and not the other; but that is surely less simple than my usual method of viewing *nomen* as in apposition with *homo*. Examples follow[256] (in my translations I am keeping the Persian word order as far as possible[257]).

is "understood", only unfortunately (!) Latin has no word for 'being', are also those who explain that in a nominal clause 'is' is "understood".

[254] Hence I shall refer to these syntactic units as "naming clauses", though Kent (*OP* 97–98) calls them "naming phrases".

[255] Cf. above, fnn. 10 and 12, and §44.

[256] On the form of Old Persian citations, see fnn. 198 and 209.

[257] This varies (as has been noted by Bartholomae, *AiW* col. 1063, and Johnson, *GrAP* 234) between *homo Iulius nomen* and *Iulius nomen homo.* The position of *nomen* after *Iulius* seems to have become fixed in Old Persian, though I doubt that it represents the original state of affairs; cf. fn. 20. The Old Persian order is not surprising if *nomen* has really, as I believe with Debrunner (see §74), become an adjective meaning 'nominatus', for in that case it is almost like a participle and *Iulius* is almost like a predicate noun (cf. fn. 233), and the order just indicated as typical is in accordance with what Kent (*OP* 95) states is normal when a predicate noun is used, namely, *either* subject predicate verb *or* predicate verb subject. If the owner of the name is designated by *martiya* 'man', *martiya* always precedes the name, which in its turn, as just indicated, directly precedes the word 'name'. I suggest that this position for 'man' (already noted by Johnson 234) may have grown up as the result of the frequent placing after *nāma* of a word or words in apposition with *martiya*, giving the man's genealogy ('son' of so-and-so) or his nationality ('a Persian', 'a Babylonian', etc.); on this cf. fn. 28. There is only one instance of *martiya* alone, *homo Iulius nomen* and nothing else, 3.22 martiya Vahyazdāta nāma. But there are two examples of *homo Iulius nomen, Gaii filius,* 1.74 and 2.8–9; and there are five examples of *homo Iulius nomen, Romanus,* 2.14, 79, 3.12, 5.5–6, and (with an additional appositive, 'my subject', following *Romanus*) 7–8 (in the last two examples *martiya* is only a suppletion, but a very probable one). The two types are combined in 3.78–79 martiya Arxa nāma Arminiya Halditahya puça 'a man, Arkha by name, an Armenian, Haldita's son', in other words *homo Iulius nomen, Romanus, Gaii filius*; and in

91. 1.29–30 avahyā Kabūjiyahyā brātā Bardiya nāma āha 'of that
Cambyses a brother, Smerdis (his) name, there was'. This passage is
not typical, for it is not followed by a pronominal resumptive; instead,
the noun is repeated, appearing in the accusative, 31 avam Bardiyam
'that Smerdis'.

92. 1.35–36 pasāva[258] martiya magus āha Gaumāta nāma hauv

the well-known passage listing the men who helped Darius in the affair of the pseudo-
Smerdis (4.80–86), we have first (80) *imaiy martiyā tyaiy* 'these (are) the men who', and
then (83–86) there follow the six names, each in the form *Iulius nomen, Gaii filius,
Romanus*. A more unusual order, *homo Romanus, Iulius nomen, Gaii filius*, appears in
1.77–78 martiya Bābiruviya Naditabaira nāma Ainairahyā puça 'a man, a Babylonian,
Nidintu-Bel by name, Ainaira's son'; and *Romanus* also follows *homo* (perhaps because
of the interpolation of the verb *āha*) in 1.36 martiya Magus āha Gaumāta nāma 'a man,
a Magian, there was, Gaumata by name'. Oftener, *martiya* is not present, and then either
Gaii filius or *Romanus*, though it still stands after *nomen*, must serve in place of *homo*.
There is only one example with *Gaii filius*, 1.28 Kabūjiya nāma Kūraus puça 'Cambyses
by name, Cyrus' son'; we may compare with *Gaii frater*, which, however, precedes
Iulius nomen, probably because there has just been a reference to "Gaius", namely,
Cambyses, 1.29–30 avahyā Kabūjiyahyā brātā Bardiya nāma āha 'of that Cambyses a
brother, Smerdis by name, there was' (where again the presence of the verb *āha* may
make a difference). We may also note the genealogies (though here the verb is copulative), *XPf* 17–18 and 18–19 *Gaii pater Iulius nomen erat*. (These expressions of kinship are
the only instances of the use of any noun other than *martiya* preceding *Iulius nomen*,
unless we accept Kent's suppletion in 5.27 [math]ista [sām] S[ku]xa nāma 'their chief
Skunkha by name'; but this conjecture is so far out of line with regular Old Persian
usage as to seem to me distinctly dubious; note that Cameron, *JCS* 5.54, does not
attempt to complete a restoration.) Of the type *Iulius nomen Romanus*, there are numerous
instances, as 2.19 Vidarna nāma Pārsa 'Hydarnes by name, a Persian', and the famous
catalog of the nine liar-kings, 4.7–8, 10, 12–13, 15–16, 18, 20–21, 23–24, 26, 28–29.
Often, as in 5.7–8, noted above, *Romanus* is followed by an appositive, 'my subject'; we
meet this eight times, 2.19–20, 29–30, 49–50, 82, 3.13, 30–31, 55–56, 84–85. Corresponding to the order *Iulius nomen Gaii filius* or *Iulius nomen Romanus*, when a geographical
entity is involved the order *Roma nomen urbs* is invariable. The entity may be masculine,
used with *nāmă*, as *kaufa* 'mountain' (1.37, 3.44, *DSf* 31); feminine, used with *nāmā*, as
dahyaus 'district' (1.58–59, 2.27–28, 53, 58–59, 71–72, 3.11, 23, 66, 79–80, 5.4) and *didā*
'fortress' (1.58, 2.39, 44, 3.60–61, 72); or neuter, used with *nāmă*, as *āvahanam* 'village'
(2.33, *DSf* 46), *vardanam* 'town' (1.92, 2.9 probably, 22, 65–66, 95–96, 3.4–5, 22, 34,
51–52), and *rauta* 'river' (*DZc* 9). It is examples of this last category, in the form *Ostia
nomen oppidum* (he cites specifically 3.4–5 Patigrabanā nāma vardanam), that led Humbach to his explanation (dubious on other grounds) of the use of *nāmă* instead of *nāmā*
(see §75). But he errs in thinking that the invariability of this order is a peculiarity
involving the use of neuter nouns specifically; as we have just seen, it applies to all
nouns involving geographical entities, no matter what their gender, and if Humbach
were right in his view that *nāmă* instead of *nāmā* is used because of the close phonetic
connection with the following word *vardanam* or *āvahanam*, we ought likewise to find
nāmă instead of *nāmā* before *dahyaus* or *didā*.

[258] Note *pasāva* here. This involves a point to be taken up later; see fn. 266.

udapatatā 'then a man, a Magian, there was, Gaumata (his) name; he rebelled'. Here we have the usual resumptive, *hauv* 'he'.

93. Particularly interesting is the passage 4.7–31, in which Darius lists nine kings who rose against him, all of whom he ultimately conquered. Each king's crime was the same: he (resumptive *hauv* 'is' or 'ille') lied (his lying statement, claiming a name, or a kingdom, or both, to which he—at least according to Darius—had no right, is quoted), and he stirred up rebellion. The first of the nine is introduced in these words: 4.7–8 Gaumāta nāma magus āha hauv adurujiya 'Gaumata (his) name, a Magian, there was; he lied'. The second of the nine is introduced by these words: 10–11 Āçina nāma Ūvjiya hauv adurujiya 'Açina (his) name, an Elamite (there was); he lied'. These two passages differ from each other in that the first contains a verb *āha* 'erat' 'there was', and the second does not; but otherwise they are identical in form and in force—proving my earlier statement as to the complete equivalence of the nominal and verbal clauses, and disproving, I think, both Kent's anacoluthon theory, and the widely held nominative absolute theory.[259] The other seven kings are then enumerated (12–31), in each instance in a form exactly parallel to that of the passage about Açina, the second king—in other words without a verb.

94. Two other passages which involve the use of āha 'erat' are quite different, for in them the verb is purely copulative, not predicative;[260] the author, Xerxes, is giving his genealogy, not narrating as is Darius.[261] In neither instance does a statement relative to the owner of the name follow, so of course there is no resumptive. The two follow another which is like them except that it does not include either the word *nāma* or the verb *āha*[262] (again note the equivalence of the nominal and the verbal clause). I give all three: *XPf* 16–19 manā pitā Dārayavaus Dārayavahaus pitā Vistāspa nāma āha Vistāspahyā pitā

259 On the former, see §89; on the latter, fn. 252.

260 Cf. above, §7.

261 On the authorship of the examples, see fn. 209.

262 Since, as already noted in fn. 16 (with which, for Old Persian specifically, cf. Benveniste, Gr*VP*² 236), it is normal to use the nominal clause for present time (i.e. where the copula if employed would have been in the present) and the verbal clause for past time, it is perhaps natural for Xerxes to use the nominal form in speaking of his own generation, even though by the time of this inscription (which marks his ascent to the throne) Darius was already dead.

Arsāma nāma āha 'my father (was)[263] Darius, Darius's father was Hystaspes (his) name, Hystaspes's father was Arsames (his) name'.

95. I now turn to the far commoner type, with no verb.

96. The following have the resumptive *hauv* or its by-form *hauvam*. 1.28–29 Kabūjiya nāma Kūraus puça amāxam taumāyā hauvam idā xsāyathiya āha '(there was) Cambyses (his) name, Cyrus's son, (a member) of our family; he was king there'. 3.78–79 martiya Arxa nāma Arminiya hauv udapatatā '(there was) a man, Arkha (his) name, an Armenian; he rebelled'. Exactly parallel to this are the following: 1.74, 77–78, 2.79–80; also probably 2.14–15, where, however, *nāma* is restored.

97. Of course where the sense requires it, the "resumptive" is in the accusative instead of in the nominative, in which case the form *avam* 'illum' is regularly used.[264] I cite two examples. 2.19–20 Vidarna nāma Pārsa manā badaka avamsām mathistam akunavam '(there was) Hydarnes (his) name, a Persian, my subject; him I made chief of them'. 2.29–30 Dādarsis nāma Arminiya manā badaka avam adam frāisayam '(there was) Dadarshis (his) name, an Armenian, my subject; him I sent forth'. Very like the first are 2.82–83, 3.12, 30–32, 84–85, 5.5–6, 7–9. Very like the second is 2.49–50. One passage, which refers back to a group (the Scythians) just mentioned, is a little different from the norm. This is 5.27–28 mathistasām Skuxa nāma avam agarbāya. Here I think the meaning is 'the chief of these (was) Skunkha (his) name; him they seized' rather than the usual '(there was) the chief of these' etc.[265] Thus if we compare this nominal clause to a verbal clause, we shall liken it to the two examples in *XPf*, 17–18 and 18–19 (quoted in §94), rather than to 1.29–30 (quoted in §91) etc.

98. It should be noted that in a number of instances the "naming clause" is preceded by an expression of time, *pasāva* 'then, afterward' (this is particularly frequent),[266] or a temporal clause, introduced by

---

[263] Or, perhaps better, '(is)'? Cf. fn. 262. (We would hardly say of a dead father "my father *is* Darius", but we would say "I *am* the son of Darius".) However, in practically all the Old Persian nominal clauses, 'there *was*' is the only natural English translation.

[264] Kent evidently thinks that in such an instance the nouns denoting the person and his name should also be in the accusative, since he says of them (*OP* 97), "These phrases are always in the nominative case, whether or not that is their function in the sentence." But since I am of the opinion (as already indicated in §89 and fn. 254ˋ that they are clauses, not phrases, I believe their function *is* the nominative.

[265] Again (as in fn. 260) cf. §7.

[266] See fn. 258.

yathā 'when, after'.[267] A good example, in which both are present, is 1.73–74 yathā adam Gaumātam tyam magum avājanam pasāva martiya Āçina nāma Upadarmahyā puça hauv udapatatā 'after (*yathā*) I slew Gaumata the Magian, afterward (*pasāva*) (there was) a man, Āçina (his) name, Upadarma's son; he rebelled'. Since both the *yathā* clause and the adverb *pasāva* apply not so much to anything in the naming clause as to the verb (*udapatatā* 'rebelled') in the following clause, this might be taken as evidence that the naming clause might better be viewed as a nominative absolute.[268] But the same state of affairs prevails even when there is a verb in the naming clause, as in 1.35–36 (already quoted above, §92);[269] hence though we may say that the naming clause is interpolated parenthetically in a crude and clumsy way, still we cannot deny that a clause it is.

99. Even more awkward—at least so it seems to us—is a passage in which the naming clause is inserted in the heart of the sentence. The passage is 3.54–57 hauv Vahyazdāta hya Bardiya agaubatā hauv kāram frāisaya Harauvatim Vivāna nāma Pārsa manā badaka Harauvatiyā xsaçapāvā abiy avam 'this Vahyazdata who called himself Smerdis, he sent an army to Arachosia—(there was) Vivana (his) name, a Persian, my subject, in Arachosia, a satrap—against him'. We would have expected '(there was) Vivana (his) name, a Persian, my subject; against him this Vahyazdata who called himself Smerdis sent an army to Arachosia'. But the fact that Vahyazdata's exploits and, indeed, his death (by impalement)[270] have been the theme of the five preceding paragraphs, naturally leads to the present paragraph's beginning with a reference to him, and that is what results in the ensuing awkwardness of construction. The effect of awkwardness is enhanced by the circumstance that the "resumptive" is not in the nominative like the nouns in

[267] Less striking, but also not quite logical, is the use of *utā* 'and', as in 1.77.

[268] See fn. 252.

[269] Commented on in a different context in fn. 257.

[270] It is undoubtedly the fact that Vahyazdata's death has already been narrated (in 3.49–52) which leads to Kent's translation (*OP* 128) of *Vahyazdāta frāisaya* as 'Vahyazdata *had* sent' (italics mine). But this is to introduce into Old Persian a nuance that it apparently does not possess; the language seemingly has no variations for aspect, but uses the imperfect and aorist interchangeably, and has no pluperfect at all (perfective action in the passive may be conveyed, as in Hittite, by a combination of the participle and the copula, but this is not employed to show the priority in time of one action as compared with another).

the naming clause, but in the accusative; actually, however, the use here of the accusative is no more peculiar than it was in examples of the type of 2.19–20 (cited just above, in §97).

100. Still more peculiar and irrational in structure is a sentence in which there is no resumptive at all. That is what we have in 3.12–14 pasāva adam frāisayam Dādarsis nāma Pārsa manā badaka Bāxtriyā xsaçapāvā abiy avam 'after that I sent—(there was) Dadarshis (his) name, a Persian, my subject, in Bactria, a satrap—against him'; but apparently here again putting the verb before the naming clause upsets the structure of the sentence, so that the naming clause[271] is to be combined with it in lieu of an accusative.[272]

101. I believe this is the place to cite another puzzling (and much discussed) passage which involves a river not a man. This is DZc 8–10 adam niyastāyam imām yauviyām katanaiy hacā Pirava nāma rauta tya Mudrāyaiy danuvatiy abiy draya tya hacā Pārsā aitiy 'I ordered this canal to be dug from—(there is) the Nile (its) name, a river, which flows in Egypt—to the sea which goes from Persia'. Here it seems as if the preposition hacā 'from' needs an ablative[273] just as in the preceding

[271] Kent (OP 98) actually declares that "the nominative nāma-phrase ... functions as direct object". I think a clause can more easily be explained in this way than a phrase (cf. fn. 254).

[272] However, is it absolutely necessary that frāisayam have an object? It has none in 1.82 adam frāisayam Ūvjam 'I sent to Elam', i.e. 'I sent (a message) to Elam'. Ūvjam 'to Elam' in 1.82 and abiy avam 'to him' in 3.14 would correspond to each other; the absence of the preposition with the name of a place, and its presence with the name of a person, is of course regular (cf. Kent, OP 80). The preposition abiy can mean 'to' as well as 'against'; cf. 3.1–2 pasāva adam kāram Pārsam frāisayam abiy Vistāspam 'then I sent a Persian army to (abiy) Hystaspes'. Then the sentence would mean 'after that I sent (word)—(there was) Dadarshis (his) name, a Persian, my subject, in Bactria, a satrap'; the next clause, beginning abiy avam avāthasaiy athaham 'thus I spoke to him' and giving Darius' order, 'Go forth, smite that army' etc., would follow very logically. The interpolated naming clause still comes in awkwardly, but at least it does not have to serve as an object, and it is followed by the customary "resumptive".

[273] In 1887 and 1889 (in WZKM 1.224 and 3.148) respectively) Müller tried in two different ways to prove that Pirava actually is an ablative, postulating first a stem Piru- (with ablative Pirava standing for Piravat), and then a stem Pirāu- (inflected like dahyāu-). In 1901 Foy (IF 12.176–77) revived the second idea, assuming a nominative Piraus (cf. above, fn. 228). Bartholomae expressed disagreement with Müller in 1889 (BB 14.249), and with Foy in 1904 (AiW col. 1064 fn. 9), declaring in both places that Pirava is a nominative. The case of Pirava he discusses in detail in BB 14.249–50. He evidently views Pirava nāma rauta as a nominative absolute (cf. above, §89), and explains that the nomina- tive with nāmǎ and nāmā is used without reference "auf den syntaktischen zusammen- hang", as it is in 3.13 frāisayam Dādarsis nāma Pārsa (which I dealt with in the preceding

example the verb *frāisayam* needs an accusative.[274] There is no difficulty
with the preposition *abiy*; it needs an accusative, and seemingly *draya*
'sea' is right at hand to serve this purpose. But I think there is a simpler
way to handle this passage. We have *relative* clauses[275] in combination
with both prepositions; and in the old Indo–European pattern, the
antecedent of the relative is a part of the relative clause.[276] Thus *rauta*

---

paragraph). He also compares 1.37, where he seems to take the naming expression
Arakadris nāma kaufa with the preceding *udapatatā*, in 36, instead of with the following
one, in 38 (as I do; see below, §103). Actually the two passages are quite different, for
in 1.37 *Arakadris nāma kaufa* is *followed* by the "resumptive" *hacā avadasa* in the normal
way, whereas in *DZc* 9 *Pirāva nāma rauta* is *preceded* by *hacā*, and this I think needs a
complement (as a matter of fact I think it has one, the entire clause). So I agree with
Bartholomae as to the *form* of *Pirāva* and *rauta*, but not as to their syntax. On the other
hand Bang in 1889 (*ZDMG* 43.534), after declaring that *rauta* here can be nothing but
an accusative, tried to prove that *Pirāva* is an accusative too, like *dahyāva* (I do not understand this, because *dahyāva* is plural; see Kent, *OP* 63 and 190). He justifies the use of the
accusative with *hacā* here by its use in *DB* 1.50–51 kārasim hacā darsam atarsa 'the people
were much afraid of him'. It is true that *-sim* here is clearly an accusative (Kent begs the
question, giving two mutually contradictory explanations: in one place—*OP* 87—he
calls *-sim* "invariable", but elsewhere it is inflected; and in another place—*OP* 67—he
says it "functions as ablative", but in my opinion a case-form simply *is*, and does not
"*function as*" something else). It is also true that elsewhere (four passages in all) the verb
tars- is preceded by *hacā* and an ablative: *hacāma* 'de me' in *DPe* 9, *hacā avanā* 'de eo' in
DSe 38, *hacā aniyanā* 'de alio' in *DPd* 11 and *DPe* 20–21. Thus the one seemingly
anomalous use of the accusative in this particular idiom in *DB* 1.50 may justify what would
be a single seemingly anomalous use of the accusative in *DZc* 9, despite the overwhelm-
ing evidence against it; 47 instances (apart from the four with *tars-*) of *hacā* followed by
the ablative, locative, or instrumental, as against this one alleged instance of *hacā* accompanied by the accusative (for the list, see Kent, *OP* 212). But we need not go to such
lengths, for in my opinion *rauta* and *Pirāva* in our passage can be nothing but nominatives.

[274] Kent (*OP* 98) explains the second passage much as he did the first by saying that
"the nominative phrase functions as an ablative depending on *hacā*". For my objection
to this sort of explanation, see fn. 273; a prepositional phrase can indeed "function" as
any case (as the Latin *a. d. V Kal. Apr.* is used as an ablative or an accusative, respectively,
with the preposition *ex* or *ad*), but not in my opinion a *nominative* phrase. (Actually,
what "functions" here as an ablative depending on *hacā* is the entire clause, as we shall
see.) In his Lexicon (*OP* 197, 205, and 212), Kent pronounces the use of the nominatives
Pirāva and *rauta* "anacoluthic"; but I shall show directly that it is quite justified.

[275] Cf. 1.21–22 martiya hya agriya āha avam ubartam abaram 'homo qui egregius
erat, eum excelsum sustuli' 'whatever man was excellent, him I lifted on high'. Kent in
terming this an anacoluthon (*OP* 99) is unquestionably wrong (cf. just above, fn. 274;
also below, fn. 291).

[276] This is still the regular pattern in Hittite; cf. Sturtevant, *Curme Vol.* 142–46, and
Hahn, *Lg.* 22.70–71, especially 71 fn. 10. We also meet many instances of the same thing
in early Latin, and sporadic vestiges linger on in later literature, as in Vergil's well-
known passage (*Aen.* 1.573) urbem quam statuo vestra est. (I discuss this matter at
length in *TAPA* 95.111–41.)

'river', modified by the relative *tya*, is a nominative functioning properly as subject of *danuvatiy* 'flows'; and in that case the supposed accusative *draya* is not an accusative at all but likewise a nominative, functioning similarly with *tya* as subject of *aitiy* 'goes'. The meaning then is: 'I ordered this canal to be dug from which river, Nile (its) name, flows in Egypt, to which sea goes from Persia'—of course in English idiom 'from the river, Nile (its) name, which flows in Egypt to the sea which goes from Persia'.

102. This last example has taken us to instances involving geographical terms. They follow precisely the same pattern as those involving personal names, except that when the subject of the naming clause refers to a topographical or geographical entity instead of to a person, the pronominal resumptive is less likely to be the nominative or accusative. We meet the ablative of the demonstrative pronoun *ava-* 'ille' with the preposition *hacā* 'ab' in the phrase *hacā avanā* 'ab illo' 'from it'; but commoner with *hacā* is the ablatival adverb *avadasa* 'inde', in a seemingly tautological phrase like Latin *exinde* or English *from thence*. From the nature of the case, by far the most frequently used resumptive is the adverb *avadā* 'ibi'.

103. A masculine noun *kaufa* 'mountain' is met three times, as it happens with a different resumptive each time. The passage with *avadā* 'there' is perfectly simple and straightforward—3.44 Parga nāma kaufa avadā hamaranam akunava '(there was[277]) Parga (its) name, a mountain; there they joined battle'. The passage with *hacā avadasa* involves a rather clumsy clause: 1.37–38 Arakadris nāma kaufa hacā avadasa Viyaxnahya māhyā 14 raucabis thakatā āha yadiy udapatatā '(there was) Arakadri (its) name, a mountain; from thence of the month Viyakhna 14 by days [i.e. 14 days] were past when[278] he rebelled', i.e. 'from there he rebelled when 14 days of Viyakhna were past'. The passage with *hacā avanā* 'from it' contains a parenthetical clause which interrupts the main clause: DSf 30–32[279] tharmis hya naucaina hauv

---

[277] With the geographical entities, which are of course still there at the time of the composition of the inscription, it might be more natural to render '(there is) a mountain, a village', etc. But since these passages are absolutely parallel in construction with those that I have rendered '(there was) a man, a Persian', etc., I keep the same version here. The point is not important, even though a possible distinction has been noted in fn. 262.

[278] The conjunction *yadiy* 'when' is used like "*cum* inversum".

[279] On the building of Darius' palace. Cf. fn. 209, also fn. 281.

Labanāna nāma kaufa hacā avanā abariya 'which[280] timber (is) cedar, this—(there was) Lebanon (its) name, a mountain—from it it was brought', i.e. 'there is a mountain called Lebanon; from it the cedar timber was brought'.

104. We have two examples with the neuter noun *āvahanam* 'village' of which the first, with *avadā*, is just like the first example in the preceding paragraph, 3.44, and the second, except that it has *hacā avadasa* instead of *hacā avanā*, is just like the last example in the preceding paragraph, *DSf* 30–32.[281] These are 2.33–34 Zūzahya nāma āvahanam Arminiyaiy avadā hamaranam akunava '(there was) Zuzahya (its) name, a village, in Armenia; there they joined battle'; and *DSf* 45–46 stūnā athagainiya tyā idā kartā Abirādus nāma āvahanam Ūjaiy hacā avadasa abariya 'the stone columns which (were) made here—(there was) Abiradu (its) name, a village, in Elam—from there were brought'.

105. Far commoner than *āvahanam* 'village' is another neuter noun *vardanam* 'town'. The resumptive with this is always *avadā*. A typical example is 2.95–96 Vispauzātis nāma vardanam Parthavaiy avadā hamaranam akunaus '(there was) Vishpauzati (its) name, a town, in Parthia; there he joined battle'. Just like this is 3.4–5. There are also three more examples that follow *yathā* 'when' clauses, 1.91–94, 2.65–67, and 3.34–36. Here again we have an instance of a parenthetically interpolated naming clause, 3.50–52 pasāva adam avam Vahyazdātam utā martiyā tyaisaiy fratamā anusiyā āhata Uvādaicaya nāma vardanam Pārsaiy avadasis uzmayāpatiy akunavam 'after that I that Vahyazdata and the men who were his foremost allies—(there was) Uvadaicaya (its) name, a town, in Persia—there them I put on a stake [i.e. I impaled]'. Note that in such an instance *pasāva* 'then, afterward'[282] at the opening of the sentence is more in place, though the naming clause is perhaps less in place, than in the usual order.

106. In two instances we have a combination of the masculine noun *martiya* 'man' and the neuter *vardanam* 'village'; here we have two successive verbs, the first with the resumptive *avadā* referring

---

[280] The following pronoun *hauv* leads me to interpret *hya* in 30 as a relative, not—with Kent (*OP* 144 and 215)—as the definite article.

[281] Note that it is from the same inscription. See fn. 279.

[282] Cf. fn. 258 and §98.

to 'village', and the second with the resumptive *hauv* referring to 'man'.[283] The first is 2.8–10 martiya Martiya nāma Cicixrāis puça Kuganakā nāma vardanam Pārsaiy avadā adāraya hauv udapatatā '(there was) a man Martiya (his) name, the son of Cincikhri—(there was) Kuganaka (its) name, a village, in Persia; there he dwelled—he (*hauv*) rebelled'. (Here *vardanam* is a suppletion, but seems practically certain.) Exactly like this is 3.22–24, but there is still another element present here, a feminine noun with *nāmā*. The passage runs: martiya Vahyazdāta nāma Tāravā nāma vardanam Yautiyā nāmā dahyāus Pārsaiy avadā adāraya hauv duvitīyam udapatatā '(there was) a man Vahyazdata (his) name—(there was) Tarava (its) name, a town, (and) (there was) Yautiya (its) name, a district, in Persia; there he dwelled— he (*hauv*) rebelled for the second time' (i.e. 'he made the second rebellion').

107. This brings us to the feminine nouns employed with naming clauses. There are two of them: *dahyāus* 'province, district', as in the last example; and *didā* 'fortress'. Since both are geographical terms, we usually find them combined with adverbs, most often *avadā*, as in the last example; but there is one example with the personal pronoun *hauv*, 3.11 Margus nāmā dahyāus hauvmaiy hamiçiyā abava '(there was) Margiana (its) name, a province; it became hostile to me'. We find *avadā* after *dahyāus* in 2.53–54 Izalā nāmā dahyāus Athurāyā avadā hamaranam akunava '(there was) Izala (its) name, a province, in Assyria; there they joined battle'; so too 2.58–59 and 3.66. We find it after *didā* in 2.39 Tigra nāmā didā Arminiyaiy avadā hamaranam akunava '(there was) Tigra (its) name, a fortress, in Armenia; there they joined battle'; so too 2.44–45 and 3.60–61. And we find it with *didā* and *dahyāus* combined in 1.58–59 Sikayauvatis nāmā didā Nisāya nāmā dahyāus Mādaiy avadasim avājanam '(there was) Sikayauvati (its) name, a fortress, (there was) Nisaya (its) name, a district, in Media; there I slew him'.

[283] Kent (*OP* 123) punctuates as follows: "One man, by name Martiya, son of Cincikhri—a town by name Kuganaka, in Persia—there he abode. He rose up" etc. This puts the second verb in a separate sentence. I do not think this is right; in my opinion the *avadā* clause 'there he abode' balances the naming clause about the village, but we have to wait for the *hauv* clause 'he rebelled or rose up' to get the balance for the naming clause about the man. In English idiom, the sentence might run: 'a man named Martiya, who dwelt in a town named Kuganika, rebelled'.

108. An example like 3.50–52, cited in §105, with *pasāva* opening the sentence, an interrupting naming clause, and the resumptive *avadā*, is 2.27–28 pasāva hauv kāra hya manā Kapada nāmā dahyāus Mādaiy avadā mām amānaiya 'after that this army which (was) mine—(there was) Kampanda (its) name, a district, in Media—there awaited me'.

109. We also find, as with *kaufa* 'mountain' and *āvahanam* 'village', the phrase *hacā avadasa* with *dahyāus*, in 3.79–80 Dubāla nāmā dahyāus hacā avadasa hauv kārahyā avathā adurujiya '(there was) Dubala (its) name, a district; from there to the people thus he lied'. We also meet another adverb, *avaparā* 'along there', with both *dahyāus* and *didā*: 2.71–72 Ragā nāmā dahyāus Mādaiy avaparā asiyava '(there was) Raga (its) name, a district, in Media; along there he set forth'; and 3.72–73 Arsādā nāmā didā Harauvatiyā avaparā atiyāis '(there was) Arshada (its) name, a fortress, in Arachosia; along there he went'.

110. The foregoing examples surely make it clear that, gender apart, there is not the slightest difference syntactically between *nāmă* and *nāmā*, and certainly they cannot represent different cases.

111. Naturally, this use of 'name' is not necessarily confined to the naming clauses. There is one passage in which Darius lists the men who 'were there' when he killed Gaumata, the false Smerdia:[284] 4.82–86 imaiy martiyā hamataxsatā anusiyā manā Vidafarnā nāma Vāyaspārahyā puça Pārsa Utāna nāma Thuxrahyā puça Pārsa etc. 'these men cooperated as my allies: Intaphernes (his) name, Vayaspara's son, a Persian; Otanes (his) name, Thukhra's son, a Persian', etc. Darius lists six men in all, each in accordance with precisely the same formula. Here the succession of nominatives is to be analyzed as follows: *homo* is in this instance replaced by the plural *hi homines* (*imaiy martiyā* 'these men'), with which *socii mei* (*anusiyā manā*) is in predicative relation; *Iulius* is replaced by six successive proper names (Vidafarnā 'Intaphernes' etc.) in distributive apposition[285] with *homines*; *nomen* (*nāma*) appears with each proper name,[286] (*Vidafarnā* etc.), and so do the patronymic (*Vāyaspārahyā puça* 'Vayaspara's son' etc.) and the ethnicon (*Pārsa* 'a Persian' etc.). The relationship of *nāma* and *Pārsa* to *Vidafarnā*

---

[284] Herodotus lists them too (3.70) with agreement as to five out of the six.
[285] On this type of apposition see *TAPA* 84.101 fn. 41, and 102 fn. 52; 85.199 fn. 6, and 202–9.
[286] See fn. 257.

merits special attention; *puça* and *Pārsa* are clearly appositives of *Vida-farnā* (considered as representing a *homo* and not a *nomen*), and *nāma* is as clearly not,[287] despite its similar position after *Vidafarnā*,[288] for it adds no new detail, but must go back as a partitive appositive to *martiyā* 'men', the six partitive appositives constituting, so to speak, a distributive group of partitives.

112. All the examples considered so far have been from inscriptions of Darius the Great,[289] with the exception of a somewhat different type from Xerxes, which were part of a genealogy. We also have instances of *nāma* in genealogies of a later period, those of Xerxes' grandson and great-grandson, Artaxerxes II and III.[290] Whereas the inscriptions from Darius and Xerxes are on the whole clear and precise,[291] these later ones are loosely and vaguely constructed, and contain peculiarities that can hardly be accounted for except as downright errors,[292] though whether of form or of syntax it is sometimes hard to say.

[287] Any other example—and there are plenty in Old Persian—of the construction *homo Iulius nomen, Romanus*, or the more elaborate *homo Iulius nomen, Gaii filius, Romanus*, would likewise illustrate this distinction, but I choose the present passage because it seems to do so particularly well. This seems to me a conclusive argument against Gray's view (see above, fn. 19) that *nomen* is in apposition with *Iulius*.

[288] Again (as in fn. 286) cf. fn. 257.

[289] Cf. fn. 209.

[290] Again cf. fn. 209.

[291] Despite Kent's charges of anacoluthon on their part; cf. above, §89 and fn. 275. Kent (*OP* 97–98 and 99) finds anacolutha not only in the use of "naming phrases", which I have treated above, but also in the use of relative clauses, which I treat in *JAOS* 85.48–58. One passage, *DZc* 8–10, which involves both the relative construction and the naming construction, I treat there (§19, pp. 57–58) as well as here (§101). On the relative pattern in general, cf. above, fn. 276.

[292] Ware and Kent, *TAPA* 55.57, account for such "irregularities" as "either normal linguistic development or dialectal differences or misspellings due to carelessness"; Ware specifically declares (ib. 52) that "one may still identify the reasons for most of the errors, finding them akin to the reasons for the errors" in *DB*, but to me the style of these inscriptions is completely lacking in the neatness which I find in those of Darius (and so, I note with satisfaction, do Meillet, who speaks of them, *GrVP* 19, as "redigées dans une langue cohérente et manifestement correct", and Schaeder, who refers to the inscriptions of Darius and also of Xerxes, *Ariaramnes* 640, as exhibiting "einen grammatisch durchweg korrekten Sprachgebrauch"). Kent subsequently (*OP* 99) suggests a real difference in the later inscriptions, in that "apparently OP had by this time become virtually a dead language employed only in writing ceremonial official records". Others though they recognize a change in the language—called by Johnson (*GrAP* 196) "decline" and by Meillet (*GrVP* 19) and Benveniste (*GrVP*² 24) "évolution naturelle"—do not think this in itself an adequate explanation for what they regard as downright

113. Artaxerxes II in tracing his lineage to Darius the Great, begins with his personal name, Artaxerxes, in the nominative, and ends with his dynastic name, 'an Achaemenian', also in the nominative. Between the two he has a number of parallel phrases enumerating his ancestors in turn, generation by generation, the last three of which run as follows: 'son of Xerxes the king, of Xerxes the son of Darius the king, of Darius the son of Hystaspes'. Each proper name, it will be noted, is repeated, presumably for the sake of clearness; and each, as we would expect, is in the genitive. But the word *puça* 'son' is *not*, as we would also expect, in the genitive; it is in the nominative. Are we to explain it as a predicate nominative, translating 'son of Xerxes the king, of Xerxes—(he was) the son of Darius the king' etc.? Kent (*OP* 98) says no, because the final 'Achaemenian' refers back to the name with which we started. This would not trouble me, since I would be quite ready to view these clauses, as I do some of the naming clauses, as parenthetic interruptions. But I *am* troubled by the lack of predication: we need either a pronoun such as *hauv*, or a form of the verb 'be'. Whatever their explanation, these formulaic series occur, with very slight variations, in *A²Sa*, *A²Ha*, and *A²Hc*; but in *A²Hc* is inserted the word *nāma*, which does not appear in any other of this king's inscriptions. It is in 14–15 Dārayavausahyā Vistāspahyā nāma puça 'Darei Hystaspis nomen filius' 'of Darius the son of Hystaspes in name'. Since *Vistāspahyā* is a genitive, the nominative-accusative form *nāma* could not in the normal course of things be viewed as in apposition with it, and therefore we may feel compelled to say, as Blümel did (*IF* 33.16) of *Yt.* 13.120 (on which see above, §57), that here the word for 'name' is truly an accusative of specification. But since in *puça* 'filius' we certainly have a nominative used in quasi-apposition with the genitive *Dārayavausahyā* 'Darei', perhaps similarly we may say that in *nāma* we have a nominative used in quasi-apposition with the genitive *Vistāspahyā* 'Hystaspis'.[293]

corruption or barbarism; they (Johnson 195–96, Meillet 19–20), likewise Sturtevant (*JAOS* 48.71–73) and Schaeder (*Ariaramnes* 640), attribute these errors to a lack of knowledge of Persian on the part of foreign scribes, or possibly (see Benveniste 24) ignorant native ones. Foreign scribes must have written the earlier inscriptions too; so perhaps the suggestion that the later scribes were ignorant natives is preferable. Or possibly Darius and Xerxes were abler composers or more efficient supervisors than their descendants.
[293] We shall meet a similar piece of looseness in Old Irish. See below, §237.

114. Artaxerxes III in tracing *his* lineage (in *A³Pa*) behaves even more peculiarly than his father. He follows the same general formula, but *he* puts all the proper nouns into the nominative!—except the name of Hystaspes, which he puts whenever it occurs into the genitive![294] His phrases with *nāma* are as follows: A³Pa 18–20 Dārayavaus Vistāspahyā nāma puça Vistāspahyā Arsāma nāma puça 'Dareus Hystaspis nomen filius, Hystaspis Arsames nomen filius' '(of) Darius the son of Hystaspes in name, of Hystaspes the son (of) Arsames in name'. Here *nāma* appears first with *Vistāspahyā*, which is a genitive in form, and then with *Arsāma*, which is a nominative in form; but since the seeming genitive Vistāspahyā and the seeming nominative Arsāma have exactly the same function, there is no use in speculating at all on the construction of *nāma*, and we had probably better follow Bartholomae (*AiW* col. 1064) and dismiss the passage as 'worthless' ("ohne Wert") syntactically.[295]

115. There is also a seal, *Sa*: Arsaka nāma Āthiyābausnahyā [puça] 'Arsaces the name, son of Athiyabaushna'—or perhaps 'Arsaces (my) name', since some of the seals read 'I (am) Darius' etc. I do not think, however, that we need assume predication here, '(I) (am) Arsaces'; still less 'Arsaces (is) (my) name'. And an accusative of specification would be most unlikely. But of course in an abbreviated formula of this sort, we cannot really make a syntactic analysis. It is worth noting, however, that the names on the seals regularly appear in the full inflected nominative, not in the stem-form.

[294] Sturtevant (*JAOS* 48.68) thinks all these forms, the numerous nominatives and the one genitive, function sometimes as nominatives and sometimes as genitives, for he interprets the phrases in this final inscription as clauses, "Darius (was) of Hystaspes by name the son" etc. But I think it is better to assume as Kent does (*OP* 99) that we have now just one general case for each proper noun, which may resemble either the earlier nominative or the earlier genitive. Kent suggests that the name of Hystaspes took the form of the genitive rather than of the nominative because it occurred oftener in the genitive in the earlier inscriptions; this is very plausible, because Hystaspes never reigned, and so in the inscriptions we often hear of Darius the son of Hystaspes, but rarely of Hystaspes as himself performing any action. I certainly do not approve of Foy's explanation (*KZ* 35.55 and *IF* 12.174) that *Arsama* is in the nominative because it forms a compound with *nāma*; even if that could be true (which I doubt), it is vitiated by the fact that it fails to take cognizance of the genitive *Vistāspahyā* directly preceding it and absolutely parallel to it. Cf. above, §67.

[295] However, Foy (*IF* 12.173) uses it as proof that Gray is wrong in taking *nāma* as an appositive (cf. above, §67); and Blümel (*IF* 33.16), though he quotes Bartholomae, apparently does so only to express disagreement.

III. GREEK

116. Greek[296] is the language which developed the most clearly, and used the most frequently, the accusative of specification, in the case of 'name'[297] as in many other respects. Yet though Homer abounds in instances of the "accusativus graecus",[298] he has not so far as I know a single indubitable instance of 'name' so used.[299]

117. He has several examples of the construction *Iulius nomen est*. Each of these clauses follows an earlier clause in which there is a common noun—'man', 'mistress', etc.—designating the person to whom the name belongs. This type of expression occurs the first time we hear about the person in question, and gives the effect of the Hittite '(there was) a man Appu his name',[300] or of the Sanskrit 'there was a king Nala (his) name',[301] though Homer's narrative style is not so simple and bare as that of the anonymous authors of the Appus tale and of the *Mahabharata*. All the examples are from the *Odyssey*.[302] They

[296] In citing Greek, I write connected passages as Greek, for I fancy my fellow-classicists find it as difficult and disagreeable as I do to try to read transliterated Greek with understanding; but, in the interest of economy, I transliterate individual words (even in quotations from writers who employ Greek characters) using *h* for the rough breathing and (in conformity with the *TAPA* style-sheet) *ê* and *ô* for eta and omega, and regularly omitting accents—as well as smooth breathings—in authentic pre-Hellenistic fashion.

[297] For 'call by name' in the sense not of 'entitle' but of 'address', where for 'name' Hittite uses the dative (cf. §20 and fn. 61) and Latin the ablative (cf. fn. 391), we might expect the dative in Greek, but we do not find it in Homer (indeed, he cannot use the dative of *onoma* in any connection, since it is metrically impossible). We do find an adverb, *(ex)onomaklêdên*, with *onomazô* in *Il.* 22.415 and *Od.* 4.278, and with *kaleô* in *Od.* 12.249–50.

[298] Once more I refer to my study of the Homeric usage, *TAPA* 85.254–79.

[299] Blümel (*IF* 33.27) gives reasons for thinking that *onoma* had very little to do with the development of the accusative of specification in Greek. I have come to the same conclusion (see *TAPA* 85.242 fn. 159, and 288), though not for precisely the same reasons.

[300] Cf. above, fn. 12 and §23.

[301] Cf. above, §44.

[302] This is not surprising. As was noted in fn. 12, the tournure belongs fundamentally to the language of the folk-tale—'once upon a time there was a man, and his name was John'—and the *Odyssey* is closer to this than the *Iliad*.

follow. *Od.* 20.287–88 ἦν δέ τις ἐν μνηστῆρσιν ἀνὴρ ἀθεμίστια εἰδώς, Κτήσιππος δ᾽ ὄνομ᾽ ἔσκε 'there was among the suitors a man versed in lawlessness, and he was Ktesippus (his) name' (i.e. 'he was named K.'). *Od.* 7.53–54[303] δέσποιναν μὲν πρῶτα κιχήσεαι ἐν μεγάροισιν· Ἀρήτη δ᾽ ὄνομ᾽ ἐστὶν ἐπώνυμον 'first of all you will find the lady of the house in the hall, and she is Arete (her) name'. *Od.* 15.256 τοῦ μὲν ἄρ᾽ υἱὸς ἐπῆλθε, Θεοκλύμενος δ᾽ ὄνομ᾽ ἦεν 'his son came up, and he was Theoclymenus (his) name'. *Od.* 18.1–5 ἦλθε δ᾽ ἐπὶ πτωχὸς πανδήμιος, Ἀρναῖος δ᾽ ὄνομ᾽ ἔσκε 'then there came up a common beggar [a description of him follows], and he was Arnaius (his) name'. *Od.* 19.244–47 καὶ μέν οἱ κῆρυξ εἵπετο· Εὐρυβάτης δ᾽ ὄνομ᾽ ἔσκε 'and him an attendant followed [description of him], and he was Eurybates (his) name'. All of these are of the ambiguous type,[304] and scholars debate whether 'name' is (a) a nominative, subject of the verb 'be', or (b) an accusative of specification, the subject of the verb 'be' being contained within the verb, 'he' or 'she'.[305] I believe that it is perfectly

[303] The combination of *onoma* and *epônymon* here gives an effect of redundancy which may remind us of the Sanskrit *nāma nāmnā* and *nāma nāmatas* discussed above (§52); but actually it is quite different, for *epônymon* is an adjective modifying, and reinforcing, *onoma*. Blümel (*IF* 33.25) views *epônymon* both here and in *Il.* 9.562 (which, however, is quite different, for there is no *onoma* there) as superfluous, and *onoma epônymon* may be merely a matter of epic fullness; yet it should be noted that wherever *epônymon* is used, whether alone as in *Il.* 9.562 (on which see §118 and fn. 312), or in combination with *onoma* as in *Od.* 7.54 (the present example) and 19.409 (quoted below, in §123), it always applies to a name which is justified by etymology (or at least folk-etymology), Alcyone, Odysseus, Arete—so too the Cyclopes in Hesiod, *Theog.* 144 (quoted in §133; see also fnn. 366 and 369).

[304] Cf. fn. 17.

[305] Delbrück, *Grund.* 3.388, declares he cannot come to a decision in the matter (and for that reason he renounces all attempts to find the beginning in Greek of the use of *onoma* in the sense of 'mit Namen'). Other scholars have been less timorous. Merry (on *Od.* 7.54) favors the interpretation 'Arete is her name' because "the only passages which are decisive point this way". The passages that he lists (they will be discussed below, in §123) are those in which the person is designated by a dative, as *Od.* 9.366. But these are "decisive" precisely because the dative is present! Kieckers (*IF* 30.364–65) follows— with much more justice—an exactly opposite line of reasoning: he interprets *Od.* 7.54 as "Arete ist sie dem Namen nach", with 'name' as an accusative of specification, precisely because no dative is present; for 'name' to be subject and therefore nominative, we must in his opinion have a dative personal pronoun. Blümel (*IF* 33.24) is not convinced by Kieckers; he says the latter's examples with a dative prove only that this construction exists, and he believes *Od.* 9.366 has to have a dative because it has no copula. Actually, we could argue, and I would argue, just the other way, that 9.366 does not need a copula precisely because it has a dative, which serves, as does any "dative of possession", as a predicate, 'the name Noman (is) to me', i.e. 'belongs to me', or, *anglice*, 'I have the name Noman', i.e. 'I am called Noman'.

possible to interpret as I have done with 'he' or 'she' as subject as in (b), and 'name' in partitive apposition with it and therefore a nominative as in (a).

118. I would deal in the same way with Homer's examples of the construction *hominem Iulium nomen nominant*,[306] all of which[307] as it happens have a demonstrative or a relative pronoun to represent *hominem*.[308] All of these are in the *Iliad* except for one (*Od.* 5.273)

[306] Cf. above, §13 and fn. 35. As pointed out in fn. 35, the construction outside Greek is common only in Avestan. Oddly enough, Avestan and Greek resemble each other in the tendency to use the relative pronoun *quem* rather than the noun *puerum*; see fn. 203 for Avestan, and fn. 308 for Greek.

[307] Unless we are to see an instance of the construction in *Od.* 8.550 εἴπ᾽ ὄνομ᾽ ὅττι σε κεῖθι κάλεον μήτηρ τε πατήρ τε. There are three ways of analyzing the passage. (1) Possibly we may interpret it as meaning 'say what your father and mother yonder called you, (your) name', with pronouns representing the nouns of our formula, *se* standing for *hominem* and *hotti* for *Iulium*. The *hotti* clause would then be an indirect question parallel to those in 573 and 577 just below (both also after *eipe*). (2) A different interpretation of the indirect question would combine *hotti* and *onoma* (as we combine *hon tina* and *potmon* in *Od.* 3.16), and the meaning would then be 'say what name your father and mother yonder called you'. (3) The *hotti* clause may be a relative clause and not an indirect question at all. In that case *onoma* is the object of *eipe*, like the accusatives in 8.555, just below; we may compare *teon ounoma eipe* in *Od.* 9.355, and, for the following indefinitive relative, a parallel example with *genos*, *Od.* 19.162 εἰπὲ τεὸν γένος ὁππόθεν ἐσσί. Of course if this is the right interpretation, the relative *hotti* represents *onoma*, and its relation to the verb is the same as that of *onoma* in interpretation 2.

[308] It may be worth noting, though what its significance is I do not know, that Homer says *Iulius nomen est* but not *homo Iulius nomen est*, and, correspondingly, *eum* (or *quem*) *Iulium nomen nominant* but not *puerum Iulium nomen nominant*. I have also noted, though I realize it may be purely a matter of chance, that similarly Aristophanes, in a passage (*Av.* 809–17) containing a number of different naming constructions concerning the new city, uses (a) the triple accusative *urbem Romam nomen nominant* only where the word corresponding to *urbem* is a pronoun, but where it is a noun chooses (b) the construction *urbi Romam nomen dant* or (c) its variant *urbi Roma nomen est*. Thus we have (a) in 814 Σπάρτην ὄνομα καλῶμεν αὐτήν; 'Shall we call it, (its) name, Sparta?', i.e. 'Shall we call it Sparta by name?' But when in the echo of this (though with the word 'name' omitted) in the very next line, 815, the noun 'city' is employed, we find (b): Σπάρτην γὰρ ἂν θείμην ἐγὼ τῆμῇ πόλει; 'Should I give (the name) Sparta to my city?' When the name of the city is represented by a pronoun, either indefinite or interrogative, we have (b) in 809–10 ἄγε δὴ τί χρὴ δρᾶν; πρῶτον ὄνομα τῇ πόλει θέσθαι τι μέγα καὶ κλεινόν 'Come, what ought we do?—First give a name to the city, something great and distinguished'; and in 817 τί δῆτ᾽ ὄνομ᾽ αὐτῇ θησόμεσθ᾽; 'What shall we give as a name to it?' And we have (c) in 812 τί δ᾽ ἡμῖν τοὔνομ᾽ ἔσται τῇ πόλει; 'What will be the name to the city (to be chosen) by us?' (It might be suggested that *ti* and *tí* in 810 and 817 are simply adjectives modifying *onoma*, but this is hardly possible in 812.) It will be noted that in 817 *urbi* is represented by a pronoun, as *urbem* is in 815. I am not suggesting that the triple accusative construction is *preferred* when the word for *hominem* or *urbem* is a pronoun, merely that it is apparently avoided when this word is a noun. To these examples from

which is identical with one of those in the older epic (*Il.* 18.487). And
in all of them we have not *onoma* but *epônymon* or *epiklêsin*.[309] The latter

Aristophanes I can add a few miscellaneous ones from various other classical Greek
authors, although I do not claim to have made an exhaustive or even a systematic search.
Instances in which, as in Homer, *hominem* is represented by a relative pronoun, are
Aristotle, *Cael.* 293A ἐναντίαν ἄλλην ταύτῃ γῆν ἦν ἀντίχθονα ὄνομα καλοῦσιν 'another
earth opposite this one, which (its) name, they call counter-earth'; and Ps.-Plato, *Epin.*
990D ἐφεξῆς ἐστιν ὃ καλοῦσι μὲν σφόδρα γελοῖον ὄνομα γεωμετρίαν 'next is what
they call, (its) very absurd name, geometry'. A corresponding example in the passive,
with the relative pronouns the subject instead of the object, is Thucydides 1.122.4
καταφρόνησιν ἣ τὸ ἐναντίον ὄνομα ἀφροσύνη μετωνόμασται 'disdain which has been
renamed, (its) opposite name, folly'. (In these last two instances, where *onoma* has its
own adjective with it, my feeble attempts at what I think may be a literal translation are
particularly unhappy; the English equivalent is of course rather 'which they call by the
very absurd name of geometry' and 'which has been renamed by the contrasting name
of folly'.) In some other instances *hominem* is represented by a pronominal form in agreement with *onoma*. This is interrogative, as in *Av.* 812 and 817, in Euripides, *Ion* 259
ὄνομα τί σε καλεῖν ἡμᾶς χρεών; 'what shall we call you, (your) name?' and *Ion* 800
ὄνομα δὲ ποῖον αὐτὸν ὀνομάζει πατήρ; 'of what sort does your father call you, (your)
name?, i.e. 'by what sort of name does your father call you?' The pronoun is relative in
Plato, *Crat.* 383B ὅπερ καλοῦμεν ὄνομα ἕκαστον, τοῦτό ἐστιν ἑκάστῳ ὄνομα; 'whatever
we name each one, (his) name, is this the name for each one?'; and 402D τόν τε Ποσειδῶ
καὶ τὸν Πλούτωνα καὶ τὸ ἕτερον ὄνομα ὃ ὀνομάζουσιν αὐτόν 'both Poseidon and Pluto
and the other name which they name him'. The last instance is different from all the
others in that *nomen* (*onoma*) is in the main clause along with *hominem* (*Ploutôna*), the
latter repeated in the relative clause in the form of *eum* (*auton*). This is particularly
interesting because *Ploutôna* as parallel to *Poseidô* refers to the god, but as parallel to
onoma refers to the name, being used in a double sense as are the proper nouns in the
passages from Vergil quoted below in §§151–53; and the fact that *nomen* here is coordinated with *homo* seems to me good evidence that elsewhere it is in apposition with it.
When an active example with a personal or demonstrative pronoun as object is shifted
to the passive, no subject for the verb is needed at all. An instance is Sophocles, *Phil.*
604–6 μάντις ἦν τις εὐγενής, Πριάμου μὲν υἱός, ὄνομα δ' ὠνομάζετο Ἕλενος 'there
was a certain high-born seer, Priam's son, and he, (his) name, was called Helenus'. This
is a paratactic counterpart to the hypotactic example from Thucydides cited above, and
reminds us of the Homeric examples quoted in §117, except that the verb is 'was
named' instead of 'was'; perhaps such simple and choppy style is suitable for the suffering
Philoctetes.

309 These words are not completely synonymous with *onoma*; probably the prefix *epi*
gives an added force in both cases. We have already noted (fn. 303) that *epônymon* (on
which see further below, fn. 312) is used of a name that is bestowed because of its
etymological fitness, real or fancied; *epiklêsis* on the other hand is a sort of nickname
bestowed because of its suitability to the character of the bearer ('clubber') or to its
shape in the case of a star or constellation ('wain', 'dog'). Also, *epônymon* in the case of
Cleopatra (called Alcyone), and *epiklêsin* in the case of Areithous (called 'Clubber') and
the Bear (called the 'Wain'), designate an additional name, a surname. But this slight
difference in meaning, which could not affect the syntax, certainly does not justify
Blümel in his insistence that *epiklêsin* is not like *onoma* (*IF* 33.24), and that it and *epôny*-

is of course unquestionably an accusative, and so may be used as an argument by those who believe that the ambiguous *onoma*, though not an accusative in origin, had come to be interpreted as one in Homer, and consequently had induced the use of the accusative *epiklêsin*. But it is surely significant that in Homer, though the ambiguous nominative-accusative *epônymon* may accompany a nominative,[310] the indubitable accusative *epiklêsin* always accompanies an accusative substantive, and so may be viewed in accordance with my theory as being in partitive apposition with it.[311] We find the following examples of the two words: *Il.* 9.561–62 τὴν δὲ τότ᾽ ἐν μεγάροισι πατὴρ καὶ πότνια μήτηρ Ἀλκυόνην καλέεσκον ἐπώνυμον[312] 'whom, (her) name, her father and lady-mother called Alcyone'; *Il.* 7.138–39 τὸν ἐπίκλησιν Κορυνήτην ἄνδρες κίκλησκον 'whom, (his) name, men were wont to call Korynetes'; *Il.* 18.487 = *Od.* 5.273 ἄρκτον θ᾽, ἣν καὶ ἄμαξαν ἐπίκλησιν καλέουσιν 'and the bear, which, (its) name, they also call the Wain'; *Il.* 22.26–29 ἀστέρ᾽ ὅν τε κύν᾽ Ὠρίωνος ἐπίκλησιν καλέουσιν 'the star which, (its) name, they call the dog of Orion'.

---

miên (which does not occur in Homer) must be separated from *onoma* (ib. 14 and 21). He holds (ib. 21) that, unlike *onoma*, *epiklêsin* and (probably) *epônomiên* "schon in sehr alter Zeit" were adverbs, which seems to me pointless, for they must have been accusatives in the beginning. After all, what is the difference between an adverbial accusative (which is what Merry calls *epiklêsin* in *Od.* 5.273) and an accusative that is used as an adverb? So to term a case-form that clearly retains its original meaning an adverb seems a mere begging of the question; if it has lost all substantival force, like Sanskrit *nāma* in the sense of 'really, truly' (cf. above, §43 and fn. 156), that is different. But I agree with Blümel that they *are* unlike *onoma* in that they demonstrably became accusatives of specification (in the Homeric Hymns; see §134) much sooner than it did (in Plutarch; see §139).

310 It modifies *onoma*, which may be a nominative in *Od.* 7.54 (cf. fn. 303) and must be in *Od.* 19.409 (cf. §123).

311 Delbrück (*Grund.* 3.388), though he takes Avestan *nama* in the parallel construction as an appositive, cannot decide whether to view *epiklêsin* as an appositive or as an inner accusative with *kaleô*. Kieckers rejects the first explanation and approves the second (*IF* 30.361). Blümel approves of Kieckers' rejection (*IF* 33.21 fn. 1) but is skeptical about his approval (ib. 21 fn. 2); he himself has different views about *epiklêsin* and *epônymiên* (see above, fn. 309).

312 I view *epônymon* as a neuter noun here, equivalent in meaning to the phrase *onoma epônymon* in *Od.* 7.54 and 19.409, and in syntax to *epiklêsin* in the other examples here cited. In Herodotus its function is taken over by *epônymiên* (cf. fn. 372), which does not occur in Homer (cf. fn. 309). Most authorities cite for Homer only an adjective *epônymos* (on which cf. fn. 366); so LSJM, also Gehring, who in his *Index Homericus* classes *epônymon* here in *Il.* 9.562 as feminine, i.e. an adjective in agreement with *Alkyonên*—which may remind us of the use of *nāmā* with feminine nouns in Old Persian.

119. Naturally, the partitive appositive *nomen* is not absolutely necessary.[313] Examples of its omission of course abound.[314] We find one passage without it that is otherwise precisely similar to those just listed above, namely, *Il.* 6.401-3 [315] Ἑκτορίδην ἀγαπητόν, τόν ῥ᾽ Ἕκτωρ καλέεσκε Σκαμάνδριον, αὐτὰρ οἱ ἄλλοι Ἀστυάνακτ᾽, 'the beloved child of Hector, whom Hector called Scamandrius, but the others Astyanax'. Perhaps the omission of the word for 'name' is particularly natural here, since both the *onoma* (Scamander) and the *epônymon*[316] (Astyanax) are given.

120. But much harder to understand is the omission of the word for *Iulium*. That is what we seem to have in *Il.* 22.506[317] Ἀστυάναξ, ὃν Τρῶες ἐπίκλησιν καλέουσιν 'Astyanax, whom (his) name, the Trojans (so)[318] call'. Myers in the LLM translation (449) renders the line "Astyanax—that name the Trojans gave him",[319] but would not that demand *hên* rather than *hon*?

121. Finally we must note one other rather peculiar passage, *Il.* 16.173-77 Μενέσθιος, ὃν τέκε Πολυδώρη Σπερχειῷ, αὐτὰρ ἐπίκλησιν Βώρῳ 'the son Menesthius, whom Polydore bore to Spercheius, but (whom), (his) name, she bore to Borus', in other words she bore the

---

However, there can be no doubt that *epônymon* is a neuter noun meaning 'name' in *Theogony* 282 τῷ μὲν ἐπώνυμον ἦν.

[313] I think it is more easily to be dispensed with if it is an appositive than if it is an inner object.

[314] I note here just three: *Il.* 1.403 ὃν Βριάρεων καλέουσι θεοί, 4.477 τοὔνεκά μιν κάλεον Σιμοείσιον, and *Od.* 9.366-67 (referred to again in fn. 325) Οὖτιν δέ με κικλήσκουσιν μήτηρ ἠδὲ πατὴρ ἠδ᾽ ἄλλοι πάντες ἑταῖροι. (I am assuming that in *Il.* 1.403, *Briareôn* is an accusative, for *Briareôi* with transfer of quantity, as Seymour says ad loc. Schwyzer, *Gr. Gr.* 2.66, calls it a nominative, which would make it a close parallel for the Avestan *kahrkatās* in *Vd.* 18.15, quoted in §55, and a fair one for the Latin *aurea* in Ovid, *Met.* 15.96, quoted in §162, both presumably examples of the "nominativus tituli"; see fn. 205. But anything of the sort is quite unparalleled in Homer.)

[315] Paley thinks these lines "read very like an interpolation", but Bolling accepts them.

[316] Cf. fn. 309.

[317] It would be much simpler if we might read *Astyanakt'* at the beginning of the line, as in 6.403. Then the antecedent of the relative *hon* would be the subject of the verb *pathêisi* in the preceding line (22.505). The reading *Astyanax* before *hon*, at the beginning of line 506, if wrong, might have got into the text through the copyist's eye being caught by *Astyanax* before the relative *hos* at the beginning of line 500 just a little above.

[318] In English we need some such word as *so*; cf. the use of *sic* in two Vergil passages, *Aen.* 6.441 and 7.607 (discussed below in §146).

[319] Similarly Blümel (*IF* 33.21 fn. 2) declares that *hon* is "sicherlich Prädikatsakkusativ" and translates "wie ihn die Troer mit dem Beinamen nennen", explaining that 'wie' represents *hon* and 'ihn' is to be supplied; he also offers the alternative explanation, which is even less satisfactory, that *hon* "vertritt beide Akkusative".

child himself to his real father Spercheius, but that part of him constituted by his name was attributed to his putative father Borus.[320] Here *epiklêsin* comes particularly close to an accusative of specification, 'whom she bore to Borus so far as his name went', 'in name only'.

122. But nevertheless in not a single one of the Homeric examples cited above is it *necessary* to call *onoma*, *epônymon*, or *epiklêsin* an accusative of specification, However, there may be one reason for so viewing them, which will be presented later.[321]

123. There are also examples in which the representatives of *homo* and *nomen* are in different cases. The type is not *homo nomen Iulium habet*,[322] but its equivalent *homini nomen Iulius (est)*.[323] I cite the following, all from the *Odyssey*: 9.366[324] Οὖτις ἐμοί γ' ὄνομα 'the name Noman is to me', i.e. 'my name is Noman', 'I am called Noman';[325] 19.409 τῷ δ' Ὀδυσεὺς ὄνομ' ἔστω ἐπώνυμον 'and the name Odysseus shall be to him',[326] i.e. 'Odysseus shall be his name', 'he shall be called Odysseus'; and 24.306 αὐτὰρ ἐμοί γ' ὄνομ' ἐστὶν Ἐπήριτος 'but the name Eperitus is to me', i.e. 'but my name is Eperitus'. These are all straightforward, with no irregularities or peculiarities. I do not find instances of attraction of the type *homini nomen Iulio (est)*, with the

---

[320] For a possible parallel in Latin, see below, §159.

[321] I.e., the use of *geneên* as an accusative of specification. See below, §130.

[322] Cf. the anomalous Sanskrit *homo nomen Iulius habet* (§§17 and 48, and fn. 49).

[323] In these instances, I assume that *nomen* is the subject, with *Iulius* in apposition with it. Were one of these nouns the subject and the other the predicate nominative, a genitive (as *hominis* or *eius*) or a possessive adjective agreeing with *nomen* (as *meum*) would be in order to indicate the bearer of the name rather than the dative (*homini*). On the difference between the construction with the genitive and that with the dative, see fn. 25.

[324] Blümel (*IF* 44.260) compares this with the Sanskrit *āsīd rājā nalo nāma* (*MBh* 3.50.1), in which, as I have already said (see fn. 162), he, like Brugmann, takes *nāma* as a predicate nominative; but the presence of a dative in *Od.* 9.366 certainly constitutes an important difference between the two passages (cf. above, fn. 305).

[325] This is followed by a parallel of the type *hominem Iulium nominant* (without *nomen*), namely 9.366–67, already quoted above in fn. 314.

[326] This clause, with the imperative *esto*, reminds us of the Hittite clauses with the cognate imperative *esdu* in *KUB* 24.8.3.10 (see above, §24); in both instances the pronouncing of the name follows a ritual ceremony in which the child is placed on the knees of the person who is to name him (cf. Laroche, *Onom.* 7 and fn. 10). In both instances too there is perhaps a comparable touch of tenderness in the use of certain adjectives as stock epithets—'sweet' name in Hittite (cf. fn. 94), 'dear' child in Greek. In *KUB* 24.8.3.16, also with *esdu* (again see §24), the general sense is again 'he shall be called Julius', but the formula is not the same, for in Hittite there is no dative and the literal meaning must be, as I have already shown, 'he, his name, shall be Julius', not 'the name Julius shall be to him'.

name in agreement with *homini* instead of with *nomen*,[327] to correspond
with the Sanskrit *homo nomen Iulius habet*;[328] but I have noted one
instance of a sort of reverse attraction, with an adjective in agreement
with the name instead of with *homini*, i.e., *homini nomen (est) Iulius,
minor natu* (for *minori natu*). This is *Od.* 19.183–84 ἐμοὶ δ' ὄνομα κλυτὸν
Αἴθων, ὁπλότερος γενεῇ 'to me is the famous name Aethon, (being)
the younger in birth'. Doubtless the shift of the adjective to the nominative from the dative demanded by logic, like the shift in Sanskrit of
the name to the nominative from the accusative demanded by logic,
was induced by the fact that the expression 'to me the name is X', like
the Sanskrit 'I have the name X', is equivalent in sense to 'I am called
X'.

124. We also have the type *homini nomen Iulium indunt*,[329] as *Od.*
19.403–4 [330] ὄνομ' εὕρεο, ὅττι κε θῆαι παιδὸς παιδὶ φίλῳ 'find a name
which you will give to your child's dear[331] child'.[332]

125. The close parallelism between *nomen* and *genus* has already been

---

[327] Cf. above, §17. We do find this in Latin; cf. below, §142.

[328] Cf. above, §17 and fnn. 49 and 322. I know of two possible examples from the
classical period (already referred to in fn. 186): Euripides, *Tro.* 1233 τλήμων ἰατρὸς ὄνομ'
ἔχουσα 'having the name (of) physician'; and Plato, *Leg.* 956B–C αἱρετοὶ δικασταὶ
γίγνοιντ' ἄν, διαιτηταὶ δικαστῶν τοὔνομα μᾶλλον πρέπον ἔχοντες 'there would be
selected judges, having the name arbitrators, (a name) much more suitable than judges'.
In both passages, as regularly in instances of the kind, we cannot be sure whether we
have a nominative by attraction or an indeclinable name-form ("nominativus tituli", as
some call it; see fn. 205). But only the second explanation is possible in Xenophon, *Oec.*
6.14 (cited again below in fn. 519) τοὺς ἔχοντας τὸ σεμνὸν ὄνομα τοῦτο τὸ καλός τε
κἀγαθός 'those having the stately name of gentleman', where the presence of *to* proves
that *kalos te kagathos* is used as an indeclinable locution, and where, furthermore, the case
of this phrase could under no circumstances be due to attraction into the nominative,
since there is no nominative to attract it!

[329] Cf. above, §14 and fn. 39.

[330] In reading *thêai*, I am accepting the lectio difficilior, a rare subjunctive form, since
I think the context demands the subjunctive (note both the sequence, and the parallelism
with the subjunctive in 406). See in defense of the subjunctive Monro ad loc. and
Goodwin, *GMT* 217; in defense of the common reading, the optative *theio*, Ameis
ad loc.

[331] See fn. 326.

[332] Cf. for an example without *homini* the parallel passage *Od.* 19.406 τίθεσθ' ὄνομ'
ὅττι κεν εἴπω, also 18.5 Ἀρναῖος δ' ὄνομ' ἔσκε· τὸ γὰρ θέτο πότνια μήτηρ, and for one
without *Iulium*, and with *nomen* also absent but implied by the context, *Od.* 8.552–54
οὐ μὲν γάρ τις πάμπαν ἀνώνυμός ἐστ' ἀνθρώπων, ἀλλ' ἐπὶ πᾶσι τίθενται ἐπεί κε
τέκωσι τοκῆες. We may note too that 18.5 is followed by an example of *Iulium nominant*
without either *hominem* or *nomen*, namely 18.6 Ἶρον δὲ νέοι κίκλησκον ἅπαντες.

indicated.[333] When one meets a stranger, the first things to ask him are his name and his ancestry, and these are the first things he may be expected to tell;[334] the two ideas often stand side-by-side, as in *Od.* 19.183–84,[335] and may even get somewhat confused, as in *Il.* 10.68 πατρόθεν ἐκ γενεῆς ὀνομάζων ἄνδρα ἕκαστον 'naming each man from his *ancestry*'; and in the noble hero both his *onoma* and his *genos* live on and are not lost or disgraced.[336] It is not strange, then, to find *genos*,[337] and its synonym *geneê*, used in much the same way as *onoma*.[338]

126. Parallel to *homo nomen Iulius* (*est*) is *homo genus malus* (*est*), as in *Il.* 14.126 με γένος γε κακὸν καὶ ἀνάλκιδα φάντες 'declaring me (my) race base and cowardly'. But as a rule we find corresponding to *Iulius* a genitive, usually though not always accompanied by *ek*; one's name is *Iulius* but one's race or descent is *e Iulio*.[339] A typical example is

[333] See fn. 28.

[334] Cf. as objects with a verb of asking *onoma* in *Od.* 9.364, *genos* in *Od.* 19.116, *geneên* in *Il.* 6.145, 7.128, and 21.153; with a verb of telling, *onoma* or *ounoma* in *Il.* 3.235, *Od.* 8.550 (on which see fn. 307), 9.16, 9.355, *genos* in *Od.* 19.162.

[335] Quoted in §123.

[336] See on preserving the *onoma Od.* 4.710 and 24.93; on preserving the *genos* and the *geneê*, *Il.* 15.141 and *Od.* 4.62; and on not disgracing the *genos*, *Il.* 6.209, and *Od.* 24.508 and 512.

[337] When *genos* is used in different constructions, we are likely to give it different translations, as 'race', 'ancestry', 'breed', 'blood', 'birth', 'offspring', 'son', etc., but these are doubtless misleading, for they are chosen more with an eye to English idiom than to Greek sense. I do not deny that there are passages where nothing but a word for an individual—e.g. 'offspring'—will do: e.g., *Od.* 16.401–2 δεινὸν δὲ γένος βασιλήϊόν ἐστιν κτείνειν. Here, incidentally, the BL translation does try to keep the notion of 'race'; but its rendering (272), "it is a fearful thing to slay *one of the stock of kings*" (italics mine), is just a makeshift. So too the LLM rendering (by Myers, 389–90) of *Il.* 19.122–24, "To-day is born a man ... of thy lineage" (see fn. 360). My guess is that the use of the word in the sense of 'offspring, son' developed from a misunderstanding of its use as a partitive appositive; thus this type of expression generated a new meaning as well as a new construction. But just to make sure that I am not loading the dice, I shall try regularly to render *genos* by 'race', regardless of idiom.

[338] Just as *onoma* can be omitted (cf. §119), so too can *genos*. Cf. *Od.* 1.406–7 ποίης δ' ἐξ εὔχεται εἶναι γαίης; 'from what country does he claim to be?' and 20.192–93 τέων δ' ἐξ εὔχεται εἶναι ἀνδρῶν; 'from what men does he claim to be?'.

[339] The parallelism with the use of *onoma* also includes a construction to correspond with *homini nomen est Iulius*. This may appear, like *homo genus malus est*, in the form *homini genus malum est*, as in *Il.* 13.354 ἦ μὰν ἀμφοτέροισιν ὁμὸν γένος, and also, like *homo genus e Iulio est*, in the form *homini genus e Iulio est*, as in *Il.* 21.157 αὐτὰρ ἐμοὶ γενεὴ ἐξ Ἀξιοῦ. But *e Iulio* is generally replaced by an adverb (like *pothen* 'whence' in *Od.* 17.373); adverbs so used include *hothi* 'where' (*Od.* 6.35, 15.175), *pou* 'where' (*Od.* 1.407 = 20.193), or *enthen* 'thence' and *hothen* 'whence' *Il.* 4.58). We also find one instance of a phrase showing place, *epi limnêi* (*Il.* 20.390).

Il. 5.544–45 γένος δ’ ἦν ἐκ ποταμοῖο ’Αλφειοῦ, which is exactly like *Od.* 7.54 and raises exactly the same questions.[340] I think the meaning here was originally ‘he (his) race was from the River Alpheus’ (*genos* nominative, in partitive apposition), even if it ultimately became ‘he was from the River Alpheus in race’ (*genos* accusative of specification). I believe the meaning was certainly not (as is clearly the idea of Leaf, *LLM* 99) ‘(his) race was from the River Alpheus’; a change of subject from *patér* with the preceding verb *enaien* to *genos* with *én* is most unlikely, and besides there are a number of other examples where *genos* cannot possibly be the subject of ‘be’ because the latter has an expressed subject, as in *Il.* 23.347 ὃς ἐκ θεόφιν γένος ἦεν ‘who, (his) race, was from the gods’, or because the verb is first or second person,[341] as in *Od.* 15.267 ἐξ ’Ιθάκης γένος εἰμί ‘I, (my) race, am from Ithaca’, *Il.* 5.896 ἐκ γὰρ ἐμεῦ γένος ἐσσί ‘you, (your) race, are from me’, *Od.* 4.63 ἀνδρῶν γένος ἐστὲ διοτρεφέων βασιλήων ‘you, (your) race, are from men (who were) Zeus-nourished kings’.[342] I have once more made translations in keeping with what I believe to have been the original force of the construction; I do not deny that it is possible also to render ‘who was from the gods in race’, ‘I am from Ithaca in race’, ‘you are in race from men’ etc.[343]

127. This type of expression is particularly likely to occur in connection with the stereotyped locution ‘I claim to be’, as in *Il.* 14.113–14 πατρὸς δ’ ἐξ ἀγαθοῦ καὶ ἐγὼ γένος εὔχομαι εἶναι, Τυδέος. In such a construction, *genos* cannot be viewed as in partitive apposition with the subject. Can we call it a predicate? We can do it if we use the somewhat

---

There is a parallel not only for *homini nomen est* but also for *homini nomen indunt*, the same verb, *tithémi*, being used with *genos* as with *onoma*; this is *Od.* 1.222–23 οὐ μέν τοι γενεήν γε θεοὶ νώνυμνον ὀπίσσω θῆκαν ‘assuredly the gods did not set upon you a race henceforth nameless’.

[340] See §12 and fnn. 17 and 305.

[341] Cf. the Sanskrit and Avestan examples quoted in §§45, 52, and 54; and see §15. An additional example is *Od.* 6.35 if we read Φαιήκων, ὅτι τοι γένος ἐσσὶ καὶ αὐτή, but the usual lection Φαιήκων, ὅτι τοι γένος ἐστὶ καὶ αὐτῇ seems to me preferable, and on that assumption I am classing the passage elsewhere (fn. 339).

[342] Here we have the simple genitive without *ek*; cf. below, fn. 456. (However, the genuineness of this line is questioned, in part because of the syntactic peculiarities; it is in a passage rejected by Aristarchus.)

[343] Cf. above, fn. 337. But arguments against this are provided in the case of the first passage by *Il.* 6.180, and in the case of the second by *Il.* 19.122–24 (on both see §131).

tricky translation 'son, scion, offspring'.[344] But that is hardly what *genos* is—as is made clear by *Od.* 21.335 πατρὸς δ' ἐξ ἀγαθοῦ γένος εὔχεται ἔμμεναι υἱός, where 'son' is actually present.[345] And yet it might be argued that if *Od.* 15.267[346] means 'I—(my) race—am from Ithaca', *Od.* 24.269 εὔχετο δ' ἐξ Ἰθάκης γένος ἔμμεναι must have the general meaning 'he claims that he—(his) race—is from Ithaca'; but the trouble is that there is no 'he' present in the Greek for 'race' to be in apposition with, and I do not believe we can substitute partitive predication for partitive apposition! Hence perhaps we must conclude that in these passages we have a fully developed accusative of specification: *Il.* 14.113 πατρὸς δ' ἐξ ἀγαθοῦ καὶ ἐγὼ γένος εὔχομαι εἶναι 'I claim to be from [i.e. sprung from] a noble father in race', *Od.* 21.335 πατρὸς δ' ἐξ ἀγαθοῦ γένος εὔχεται ἔμμεναι υἱός 'he claims to be the son (sprung) from a noble father in race', *Od.* 24.269 εὔχετο δ' ἐξ Ἰθάκης γένος ἔμμεναι 'he claimed to be from Ithaca in race'. Yet where we have a simple genitive instead of an *ek* phrase, its use alone in the predicate seems very bald, as in *Od.* 14.204 Κάστωρ Ὑλακίδης, τοῦ ἐγὼ γένος εὔχομαι εἶναι 'Castor, son of Hylax, of whom I claim to be in race', and *Od.* 17.373 αὐτὸν δ' οὐ σάφα οἶδα, πόθεν γένος εὔχεται εἶναι 'I do not clearly know him, whence he claims to be in race' ('offspring of whom I claim to be, he claims to be', the type of rendering that I am religiously eschewing, would certainly be more satisfactory[347]).

128. Rather odd too is one example without any infinitive, *Od.* 14.199 ἐκ μὲν Κρητάων γένος εὔχομαι εὐρειάων (repeated almost verbatim, 16.62). Here the omission of 'be' is doubtless to be compared with that which occurs in a nominal clause.

129. If in any of the foregoing examples instead of *genos* its synonym *geneê* had been used, that would have settled the problem: we would know whether we had a nominative or an accusative. But with *geneê* Homer uses a different construction: *Il.* 6.211 = 20.241 ταύτης τοι γενεῆς τε καὶ αἵματος εὔχομαι εἶναι 'I claim to be of this race and blood', 19.103-5 ἄνδρα τῶν ἀνδρῶν γενεῆς, οἵ θ' αἵματος ἐξ ἐμεῦ

---

[344] See fn. 337.
[345] To be sure, it fits in rather clumsily. Cf. Monro ad loc.
[346] Quoted in the preceding paragraph.
[347] Cf. fn. 337.

εἰσίν 'a man of the race of those men who are of blood from me',³⁴⁸
5.265–66 τῆς γάρ τοι γενεῆς, ἧς Τρωί περ εὐρύοπα Ζεὺς δῶχ' 'they
are of that breed which Zeus gave to Tros'. Just once he does employ
genos and *geneê* in exactly parallel ways in two successive verses, but,
alas, the reading is not certain.³⁴⁹ The verses are *Il.* 21.186–87 φῆσθα σὺ
μὲν ποταμοῦ γένος ἔμμεναι εὐρὺ ῥέοντος, αὐτὰρ ἐγὼ γενεὴ μεγάλου
Διὸς εὔχομαι εἶναι. I think the reading *geneê* is favored by 191 just
below, κρείσσων αὖτε Διὸς γενεὴ ποταμοῖο τέτυκται. Here *Dios*
must modify *geneê*, which suggests that the same thing should be true
of 187; but that can *not* be true if we have *geneên*, an accusative of
specification.

130. We do, however, find three instances of *geneên* so used: *Od.*
15.225 ἀτὰρ γενεήν γε Μελάμποδος ἔκγονος ἦεν 'but he was a descendant of Melampus in descent'; *Il.* 14.474 αὐτῷ γὰρ γενεὴν ἄγχιστα
ἐῴκειν 'he resembles him most closely in race'; 23.470–71 δοκέει δέ
μοι ἔμμεναι ἀνὴρ Αἰτωλὸς γενεήν 'he seems to me to be a man Aetolian
in race'. But it must be noted that there is reason to read *phyên* not
geneên in the second passage,³⁵⁰ and to reject line 471 altogether in the
third.³⁵¹ At all events, we obviously have at least one sure example³⁵²
to prove that *geneê* had produced an accusative of specification by

³⁴⁸ See further on this passage below, fn. 363.
³⁴⁹ The mss. favor *geneên*. The reading *geneê* is Bekker's emendation, accepted by
Christ and Paley. A copyist of a later date would certainly find *geneên* more natural than
geneê, and so a change from an original nominative to an accusative might have been
more likely than the reverse.
³⁵⁰ So Aristarchus, followed by Bolling. On *phyên*, cf. fn. 352.
³⁵¹ The line is athetized by Aristarchus, as attested by Scholiasts A and T. See Bolling,
Athetized Lines 181.
³⁵² However, *geneên* as an accusative of specification was not so well-established as
e.g. *phyên* was (with seven instances). As a case-form of *geneê* expressing specification,
Homer definitely prefers the dative. We have a number of examples with adjectives:
one with *hyperteros* 'superior' (*Il.* 11.786), and ten with adjectives meaning 'older' or
'oldest', 'younger' or 'youngest' (cf. the Latin use of *natu* with *maior* and *maximus*,
minor and *minimus*). A particularly interesting instance is in an expression of claiming,
Il. 9.161 γενεῇ προγενέστερος εὔχομαι εἶναι 'I claim to be the older in race [i.e. in birth,
in age]'. The form *geneêi* occurs seven times (*Il.* 2.707, 6.24, 7.153, 9.161, 15.166 = 182,
Od. 19.184), and *geneêphi(n)* three times (*Il.* 9.58 14.112, 21.439). There is one similar
expression with *genos*, *genei hysteros* (*Il.* 3.215). We also find the dative *geneêi* expressing
specification in *Od.* 1.387 ὅ τοι γενεῇ πατρώιόν ἐστιν, and, probably with an admixture
of a causal notion, in *Il.* 4.60–61 = 18.365–66 ἀμφότερον, γενεῇ τε καὶ οὕνεκα σὴ
παράκοιτις κέκλημαι.

Homer's time, though we cannot be certain that this applied to the commoner[353] *genos* or to any word for 'name'.[354]

131. On the other hand, there are three examples which prove absolutely that in them at least *genos* is *not* an accusative of specification, but is in apposition with the subject of the sentence—in partitive apposition if we keep to the interpretation 'race', which is, however, next to impossible to employ in these instances.[355] The first of these is *Il.* 6.180 ἡ δ' ἄρ' ἔην θεῖον γένος οὐδ' ἀνθρώπων 'she, (her) race, was divine, not of men'. Had we had the genitive *theôn* to balance *anthrôpôn* we might well have translated 'she was of the gods, not men, in respect to race', treating it as many would treat *ek theophin* in *Il.* 23.347;[356] but the use of the adjective *theion*,[357] which modifies *genos* and not the subject *hê*, precludes any such interpretation.[358] Neither can we hedge here as is sometimes done by translating *genos* as 'offspring'; this would have little point in connection with the subject, the Chimaera. I believe that an exact parallel to *theion genos* here is provided by *dion genos* in *Il.* 9.538–39 ἡ δὲ χολωσαμένη δῖον γένος ἰοχέαιρα ὦρσεν ἔπι, χλούνην σῦν ἄγριον ἀργιόδοντα, though here some translation such as 'offspring' does make for smoothness: 'and she in wrath, (her) divine race, the arrow-shooting one, stirred up a grass-tenanting (?), white-tusked wild boar'. Stressing Artemis' divine ancestry here enhances the awfulness of her wrath, and the magical means which she took to satisfy it. It might also be possible, though the word order is

[353] There are 32 instances of the nominative-accusative form *genos*, vs. 26 of nominative *geneê* plus accusative *geneên*. I am not taking cognizance of cases other than the nominative and accusative singular.

[354] Therefore to assume as do Delbrück (*Grund.* 3.390) and, following him, Kieckers (*IF* 30.363) that *onoma* provided the model for *genos* and *geneê* seems to me extremely doubtful. So far as chronology goes, one might rather pronounce *geneê*, and therefore presumably *genos*, the model for *onoma* (and *epiklêsis*); but this too seems questionable to me (as to Blümel, *IF* 33.27). I would rather think that both 'name' and 'race' began as appositives, and developed naturally and independently into accusatives of specification.

[355] Once more, cf. fn. 337.

[356] Quoted in §126. Cf. fn. 343.

[357] This use of the adjective with 'race' reminds us of the use of an adjective with 'name' already noted in Hittite (§§32 and 35) and perhaps in Sanskrit (§51). So too in *Od.* 16.401 (quoted in fn. 337), where the adjective *basilêis* is equivalent to the genitive *basileôn*.

[358] To be sure, Seymour ad loc. compares *Il.* 5.544 and 896, in which he classes *genos* as an accusative of specification; but I simply cannot find any justification for this.

against it, to take *dion genos* with the object rather than with the subject, and in that case *dion* might agree with *syn* and *genos* be an accusative of specification; but I think the parallelism with *theion genos* in *Il.* 6.180 points in the opposite direction, what is said of the Chimaera there applying to the Calydonian Boar here, so that we would still have *genos* in apposition, in this case with *syn*,[359] and the apposition would still be partitive. The third example is *Il.* 19.122–24 ἤδη ἀνὴρ γέγον᾽ ἐσθλός, σὸν γένος 'already has been born a noble man, (his) race yours' ('his race springing from you', i.e. 'your descendant').[360] Here again *genos* must be in apposition with the subject, though had *son* 'your' been replaced by *ek seu* 'of you, from you', we would have had a passage that would have to be called ambiguous, exactly like 5.896[361] ἐκ γὰρ ἐμεῦ γένος ἐσσί.

132. Thus we have indubitable evidence from Homer that, though one word for 'race' (*geneê*) had already (at least in the *Odyssey*) generated an accusative of specification,[362] the other (*genos*) continued (at least in the *Iliad*) to be used as an appositive;[363] in other words, Homer

[359] So Leaf in his translation (LLM 177) "sent against him a creature of heaven, a fierce wild boar".
[360] Myers (in LLM 389–90) dodges the issue by his free rendering "To-day is born a man of valour ... *of thy lineage*" (italics mine). Cf. fn. 337.
[361] Cf. above, fn. 343.
[362] See the three examples—of which only one is certain—quoted in §130.
[363] And that *geneê* too might perhaps be used as an appositive is indicated by at least one passage, already cited above (§129). This is a remarkable instance, because the form of *geneê* in question is a genitive. The passage (uttered by Zeus of Heracles) is *Il.* 19.103–5

σήμερον ἄνδρα φόωσδε μογοστόκος Εἰλείθυια
ἐκφανεῖ ὃς πάντεσσι περικτιόνεσσιν ἀνάξει
τῶν ἀνδρῶν γενεῆς οἵ θ᾽ αἵματος ἐξ ἐμεῦ εἰσίν.

The apposite part of this I translated in §129 'a man of the race of those men who are of blood for me', but the literal meaning may be 'of the men (their) race, who are from me (my) blood'—i.e. 'a member of the race of men who are (descended) from my blood'. I believe that in this line we may have not one but two instances of partitive apposition, though the second pair exhibits unusual order, with the whole following the part, and though it involves in one of its members a prepositional phrase instead of the simple genitive. I admit that when we meet a combination of two substantives in the genitive, it is particularly hard to demonstrate that we have an instance of partitive apposition and not the construction that superseded it, with the 'whole' substantive a genitive modifying the 'part' substantive (cf. *TAPA* 84.101–2, 85.211–12); but it may well be that this passage is to be added to those which I listed in *TAPA* 85.212–14 as illustrating the use of the genitive in partitive apposition. These genitives have troubled the commentators. In the first pair *geneês* is taken by Paley and Clapp with *andra* two lines back; by Doederlein with *periktionessin* one line back (he regards it as a sort of quasi-appositive with a dative that is equivalent to a genitive, *not* as a "genitive of quality or apposition" as Paley says he does); and by Heyne, 7.628, as equivalent to *kata geneês* (presumably 'according to race, in race') with *haimatos ex emeu* (though elsewhere, 2.380, he admits the alternative possibility that it belongs with *andra*). Of these three possibilities I would choose the first; but I am here offering a fourth, that *andrôn* belongs with *andra* (as genitive of the whole), and *geneês* with *andrôn* (as a partitive appositive). Doederlein's explanation seems to me very dubious syntactically (the parallel that he offers, 20.180–81, where an abstract genitive and a concrete dative are combined, is hardly cogent, even if the passage is genuine), and quite out of the question on the basis of content, for the point is surely that the hero to be born will be descended from Zeus, not that the men whom he is to rule will be. Heyne's explanation involves a rather odd use of the genitive *geneês* to express specification (I would have expected rather a dative or an accusative) and a very awkward piling up of genitives; Heyne himself says (2.380) that it is the harsher (*durior*) of the two alternative explanations. As for the second pair of genitives, Doederlein, Paley, and Clapp all believe *haimatos ex emeu* may involve a confusion of two constructions, but the two as offered on the one hand by Doederlein and (supposedly but not exactly follow-ing him) Paley, and on the other hand by Clapp, do not agree. Heyne translates *haimatos* by 'sanguine', and Paley and Clapp by 'in blood'; this seems to me open to the same objection as Heyne's 'progenie' for *geneês*.

Hera responds to Zeus as follows, 109–11

ἦ μὲν τὸν πάντεσσι περικτιόνεσσιν ἀνάξειν
ὅς κεν ἐπ' ἤματι τῷδε πέσῃ μετὰ ποσσὶ γυναικὸς
τῶν ἀνδρῶν οἳ σῆς ἐξ αἵματός εἰσι γενέθλης.

The order here seems to me to confirm the view that the ruler, not the subjects, will be descended from Zeus; but otherwise Hera's words do not help very much with the construction of Zeus's, for she alters the form of expression. This in part I am sure she does deliberately, since her point is quite different from her husband's. Zeus is interested in saying, 'a man will be born today who will rule over his neighbors'; Hera shifts the emphasis to suit *her* interest by saying, 'that man who is born today will rule over his neighbors'. There seems less point in the variations that she introduces into 111 as compared with 105 (though this does not seem to me to justify Heyne's extensive emendation of 111 to make it conform to 105). She keeps *tôn andrôn* and *hoi*, but re-places *geneês* by *genethlês*, *haimatos* by *ex haimatos*, *ex emeu* by *sês*. Though Clapp takes *haimatos* here as a "gen. of reference" like *haimatos* in 105, the presence of *ex* with it seems to me to indicate that *haimatos* in both places, and also presumably *geneês* and *genethlês*, indicate source and not specification. Since her possessive *sês* does away with one of Zeus's genitives (*ex emeu*), she can fit the genitive with which she combines it, *genethlês*, into the relative clause with *hoi* instead of placing it with *tôn andrôn* outside the relative clause as Zeus places *geneês*, and thus provide a new set of genitives in partitive apposition, once more, like his second set, with the whole following the part, 'of those men who are of your race from (your) blood'. But it cannot be denied that there is a sort of tautology here in the use together of *haimatos* and *genethlês* which did not exist in Zeus's speech, where *geneês* particularized *andrôn* and *haimatos* particularized *ex emeu*. Perhaps Hera is too much concerned with her hidden meaning, which she has safely covered in her earlier lines, to bother about voicing the outer meaning at the end as clearly and logically as Zeus does.

represents a transitional period so far as 'race' goes. So far as 'name' goes, we must leave the problem unsettled; there is in Homer no such clinching proof either way.[364] However, I believe the original appositional use of 'race' must have been modeled on that of 'name'; see above, §12 and fn. 28.

133. But that 'name' later became an accusative of specification in Greek cannot be doubted. Delbrück (*Grund.* 3.388) cites as a decisive example of the accusative use of *onoma*, provided the reading is correct,[365] Hesiod, *Theog.* 144 Κύκλωπες δ' ὄνομ' ἦσαν ἐπώνυμον, but it is still possible according to my manner of analysis to interpret *onoma epônymon* as a nominative here—'they, (their) name, were Cyclopes'.[366] If the subject consists of two entities in apposition with each other, as whole and part, the verb naturally agrees with the one denoting the whole, which may be in the first or second person,[367] or, as here, in the plural number.[368] However, the seeming clumsiness of combining such a form with the singular noun denoting the part (*onoma*)[369] may have been a powerful factor in the transfer of this noun from nominative to accusative.

[364] This is true also of Homer's imitator Vergil; see §160. Could this possibly indicate an awareness on Vergil's part that a Greek construction that became common later did not exist in Homer?

[365] The genuineness of this line has been questioned (see e.g. Wolf ad loc.; and cf. fn. 369). To be sure, as Blümel says (*IF* 33.24), even if it is not "echthesiodisch", still it is "echtgriechisch". However, one would like to be able to date it.

[366] The line is thus a perfect parallel for *Od.* 7.54 Ἀρήτη δ' ὄνομ' ἐστὶν ἐπώνυμον, which I similarly explain as meaning 'she (her) name is Arete' (cf. §117). On *onoma epônymon* in the latter passage, see fn. 303. However, some would emend the Hesiod passage by changing *epônymon* to *epônymoi*, a reading thought to be supported by *EtymMag.* on *Kyklôpes*, which has ἔσαν οὔνομ' ἐπώνυμοι. This is the only reading listed in LSJM; and Paley, though he does not adopt it in his text, refers to it with some favor in his notes, and even goes so far as to suggest that in *Od.* 7.54 the original reading might have been *epônymos*. If Paley is right, his view provides an argument in favor of Gehring's interpretation of *epônymon* in *Il.* 9.562; see fn. 312. But *EtymMag.* in any case fails to represent *Theogony* 144 accurately; and I would rather assume that *Od.* 7.54 as it stands offers good support for *Theogony* 144 as it stands than change them both on the basis of *EtymMag.*

[367] Cf. fn. 341.

[368] Cf. e.g. *Il.* 2.775–77 (the singular is possible too, as in 16.264–65, but this is less common). See my discussion of this type of apposition in *TAPA* 85.201–2 for Greek, 84.100–1 for Latin.

[369] It is the supposed awkwardness of *onom' epônymon* "after the plural" *Kyklôpes êsan* that leads Paley in his edition of Hesiod to favor *epônymoi* (see fn. 366). Just how or why Paley believes this emendation would alleviate awkwardness I cannot tell, for he

134. As for *epiklêsin*, there is a certain example of its use as an accusative of specification, since it accompanies a dative, in the Homeric Hymn to the Pythian Apollo, 3.385–86[370] ἔνθα δ᾿ ἄνακτι πάντες ἐπίκλησιν Τελφουσίῳ εὐχετόωνται 'there all men pray to the lord (as) Telphusius by name [i.e. under the name of Telphusius]'. Accordingly we are probably to view *epônymon* also as an accusative of specification just above, in 372–73 οἱ δὲ ἄνακτα Πύθιον καλέουσιν ἐπώνυμον 'and they call the lord Pythius by name'.[371]

135. By the time of Herodotus, the accusative of specification, as exemplified by *epiklêsin* and the non-Homeric *epônymiên*,[372] was

---

does not inform us how he analyzes either the Hesiod passage or its parallel from the *Odyssey*. The latter, as I have already said (§117), has been viewed as ambiguous by some scholars, who debate as to the relative values of two alternative intepretations (neither of them right in my judgment): 'she is Arete by given name' and 'Arete is (her) given name'. But no such problem should arise in regard to the Hesiod passage: here only the first type of interpretation would be possible, 'they were Cyclopes by given name'. However, perhaps Paley's difficulty is that he is trying to force upon this line too the alternative explanation, 'Cyclopes was their given name'; and then of course a line which from this point of view could mean only 'Cyclopes *were* their given name' would naturally cause him difficulty. But with the shift proposed by him from *epônymon* with *onoma* to a form in agreement with *Arêtê* or *Kyklôpes*, he would certainly seem to be shifting the two proper names from subjects to predicate nominatives, 'she was named Arete in name' and 'they were named Cyclopes in name'; and I do not see why he could not have accepted this version even if he kept *epônymon* with *onoma*. Whether one agrees with me in taking *onoma* in the two passages as a nominative in partitive apposition with the proper noun (*Arêtê* and *Kyklôpes* respectively) or whether one prefers to view it as already an accusative of specification, in either case I think there can be no doubt that both *Arêtê* and *Kyklôpes* are predicate nouns; the subject of *êsan* in *Theog.* 144 is the same (*hoi*) as that of *êsan* in 143: they were like the gods in other respects, but they had just one eye in the middle of the forehead; and they were Cyclopes in name given (because of this), that they had a cyclical (circular, round) eye in their forehead. (That Hesiod's etymology may be incorrect is of course irrelevant.) I admit that the couplet 144–45 *is* awkward and perhaps suspicious because of the cacophonous echo of 142–43, and because of the tautology in *spheôn* and *heeis*; but the use of *onoma* does not trouble me.

370 Cited by Blümel, *IF* 33.22.

371 Here, however, it would have been possible to consider *epônymon* an appositive to the object (or if one insists, an adjective modifying the object) precisely as in *Il.* 9.562 (on which see fn. 312).

372 In Herodotus these two words are somewhat different in connotation from *ounoma*, their use reminding us of that of *epiklêsin* and *epônymon* in Homer (on which see fn. 309), though not precisely identical with it. Herodotus uses *epiklêsin* in 4.181.4 in explaining why the Spring of the Sun is so called; but when etymology is involved— in 1.14.3, 1.173.3, and 5.92e.1—he uses *epônymiên*, just as Homer uses *epônymon* (see fnn. 303, 309, and 312). His use of *epiklêsin* in 1.114.1 to denote an erroneously given name

completely established as a part of the Greek speech pattern. In his
work we find *epiklêsin* not only with an accusative, as in 1.114.1 οἱ
παῖδες εἵλοντο βασιλέα εἶναι τοῦτον δὴ τὸν τοῦ βουκόλου ἐπίκλησιν
παῖδα 'the children chose this (boy), the cowherd's son in name [i.e.
the so-called son of the cowherd], to be king', but also, as in the
Homeric Hymn, with a different case, namely, the genitive, in 1.19.1
ἅψατο νηοῦ ᾿Αθηναίης ἐπίκλησιν ᾿Ασσησίης 'it set on fire the temple
of Athena, (Athena) Assesia in name'. Similarly we find *epônymiên* with
a dative in 2.44.5 τῷ μὲν ὡς ἀθανάτῳ ᾿Ολυμπίῳ δὲ ἐπωνυμίην θύουσι
'they sacrifice to the one [Heracles] as to an immortal, Olympius in
name'. Both accusatives are also met with the passive of *kaleô*, the first
in 4.181.4 ἐπίκλησιν δὲ αὕτη ἡ κρήνη καλέεται ἡλίου 'in name this
spring is called (the Spring) of the Sun', and the second in 1.173.3 κατὰ
τοῦ Λύκου τὴν ἐπωνυμίην Λύκιοι ἐκλήθησαν 'after Lycus they were
called Lycians in name', and 1.14.3 ὁ δὲ χρυσὸς οὗτος καὶ ὁ ἄργυρος
τὸν ὁ Γύγης ἀνέθηκε καλέεται Γυγάδας ἐπωνυμίην 'this gold and
the silver which Gyges dedicated is called *Gygadas* [(gift) of Gyges] in
name'. Distinctly odd is 5.92e.1 οἱ ἀπὸ τῆς κυψέλης ἐπωνυμίην
Κύψελος οὔνομα ἐτέθη 'to him was given the name Cypselus in name
after the chest (*kypselê*)'. In this passage *epônymiên* is used in combination not with *homini Iulio* or with *homo Iulius nominatur* but with
homini Iulius nomen inditum est.[373]

136. In the light of this use of other nouns in the accusative, it is
probable, though of course not certain, that we should interpret
ounoma too as an accusative of specification and not as a nominative

('the so-called or supposed son of the cowherd') reminds us of Homer's use in *Il.* 16.177
(on which see §121). Either noun can be used to denote an additional epithet of a deity,
just as either *epiklêsin* or *epônymon* can in the Hymn to Apollo (see §134); Herodotus
thus employs *epiklêsin* in 1.19.1 and *epônymiên* in 2.44.5, with which we may compare
epônymôi in 5.45.1. (5.45.1 is quoted in fn. 373; all the other passages from Herodotus
here cited are quoted in §135.)

[373] Here the seemingly redundant *epônymiên ounoma* reminds us of Homer's *onoma*
epônymon in *Od.* 7.54 and 19.409 (on which see fn. 303), and perhaps suggests that
epônymon there is a noun, as I think it may be in *Il.* 9.562 (see fn. 312). On the other hand,
the interpretation of *epônymon* as an adjective in the passage from the *Iliad* (no matter
what we think about the two from the *Odyssey*) is favored by Herodotus 5.45.1 ᾿Αθηναίῃ
ἐπωνύμῳ Κραθίῃ, where *epônymôi* is probably an adjective in agreement with *Athênaiêi*
in the sense 'for Athena called Crathia' rather than 'for Athena in name Crathia'.
Incidentally, for the seeming redundancy, we may perhaps, despite syntactic difference,
compare the Sanskrit *nāma nāmnā* and *nāma nāmatas*, noted in §52.

appositive in its comparable occurrences in Herodotus. There are three of these:[374] 4.12.1[375] ἔστι δὲ καὶ χώρη οὔνομα Κιμμερίη 'there is also a country in name Cimmeria'; 7.176.5[376] κώμη δέ ἐστι ἀγχοτάτω τῆς ὁδοῦ, 'Αλπηνοὶ οὔνομα 'very near the road is a village, Alpeni in name'; and 8.138.3 ὑπὲρ δὲ τῶν κήπων ὄρος κέεται, Βέρμιον οὔνομα 'above the gardens a mountain is situated, Bermion in name'.

137. When we come to Xenophon, who in the *Anabasis* uses this tournure frequently, there is again probability but not certainty that *onoma* is an accusative of specification. We find passages parallel to those of Herodotus, e.g. 1.4.11 πόλις αὐτόθι ᾠκεῖτο Θάψακος ὄνομα 'there was an inhabited city there, Thapsacus in name', and 2.4.28 πόλις ᾠκεῖτο ὄνομα Καιναί 'there was an inhabited city, in name Caenae'.[377] In the case of rivers, Xenophon, who generally had the job of crossing them, is apt to inform us as to their breadth as well as their name, and *euros* behaves just like *onoma*.[378] Thus we find two

[374] Blümel (*IF* 33.16) attaches importance to the word order in these three examples from Herodotus, which he says are the earliest instances of the sort known to him "und können hinsichtlich der Wortstellungsform noch als Sätze gelten". This he evidently thinks may be used in support of Brugmann's view of *Iulius* and *nomen* as originally constituting subject and predicate of a subordinate clause; cf. above, fn. 15. (I myself doubt whether it matters much which comes first, subject or predicate, or even whether it matters much which we consider the subject and which the predicate; on the latter point cf. §6 and fn. 17.) Blümel's own comment on the comparative lateness of the earliest instances of the usage in question would seem to militate against his conclusion. But at all events any argument based on the word order seen in these three passages loses all point, for it actually varies (cf. fn. 20); Blümel quotes 4.12.1 as parallel to the others, with *Kimmeriê ounoma*, but I find no support for this lection.

[375] The use here of a variant construction in the following member (despite its close parallelism in thought), ἔστι δὲ Βόσπορος Κιμμέριος καλεόμενος 'and there is a Bosporus [an "ox-ford", a strait] called Cimmerian', is interesting, but does not give us a clue to the syntax of the first member.

[376] This passage reminds one particularly of the Old Persian naming clauses, except that the Greek employs the copula, which does occur in such clauses in Old Persian (see §§90–93) but not with a geographical expression (see §§101–9). Note the presence in the following clause ἐκ ταύτης δὲ ἐπισιτιεῖσθαι ἐλογίζοντο οἱ Ἕλληνες 'and from this the Greeks expected to obtain food', of the "resumptive" *ek tautês*, parallel to Old Persian *hacā avana* (see §§102–3). Of course this parallelism is simply the result of the common heritage from Indo–European; I am not suggesting that Herodotus could have been linguistically familiar with, or stylistically influenced by, the inscriptions of Darius!

[377] Here again, as in fn. 374, note the free variation in word order. Cf. fn. 20.

[378] Cf. *mêkos* in Herodotus 6.36.2 ἡ Χερσόνησος ἔσω πᾶσά ἐστι σταδίων εἴκοσι καὶ τετρακοσίων τὸ μῆκος 'the Chersonese within [i.e. on this side (of the isthmus)] is in its entirety of four hundred and twenty stadia in length'. On these neuter dimension nouns, cf. above, §§12 and 13. Since their use seemingly as an accusative of specification is met in Avestan also, it looks as if the usage might be inherited from Indo–European; but

almost identical passages, 1.2.23 διὰ μέσου δὲ τῆς πόλεως ῥεῖ ποταμὸς Κύδνος ὄνομα, εὖρος δύο πλέθρων 'through the middle of the city flows a river, Cydnus in name, of two plethra in breadth', and 1.4.4 διὰ μέσου δὲ ῥεῖ τούτων ποταμὸς Κάρσος ὄνομα, εὖρος πλέθρου 'through the middle of these [i.e. between these (gates)] flows a river, Carsus in name, in breadth of a plethrum'. Brugmann (*IF* 27.144; cf. 147) cites the first of these passages (along with 2.4.28) as exemplifying what he thinks constituted "die altertümlichsten Wendungen", that is, the occurrence of an interpolated "Satz".[379] But, simple though Xenophon's style is, I do not think it would permit such choppiness as these supposed paratactic parentheses.[380] Note Brugmann's translation (*IF* 27.148): "durch die Stadt fliesst ein Fluss, Kydnos (ist) der (sein) Name, die (seine) Breite (beträgt) zwei Plethren". If *onoma* and *euros* really mean respectively not just '*der* Name' and '*die* Breite' but '*sein* Name' and '*seine* Breite', I think we would need some word to denote such possession.[381] This word might be a demonstrative (parataxis) as in

---

whether it did actually develop in Indo–European or evolved independently in Avestan and Greek, I believe that in either case it originally stemmed from partitive apposition. Presumably whatever conclusion we reach about o(u)noma in Herodotus and Xenophon must also apply to dimension words such as *mêkos* and *euros*: if it still stands in partitive apposition with a nominative or an accusative, so do they; if it has already developed into an accusative of specification, so have they. Thus it can be said that in the Herodotus passage quoted just above, *to mêkos* represents an original partitive apposition with the nominative *Chersonêsos*, and in the *Anabasis*, *euros* represents an original partitive apposition with the accusative *potamon* in 1.4.9 ἐξελαύνει ἐπὶ τὸν Χάλον ποταμόν, ὄντα τὸ εὖρος πλέθρου 'he marches to the Chalus River, being [*anglice* which is] (its) breadth of a plethrum', but the paratactic partitive apposition construction has been replaced by the hypotactic genitive construction just below in 1.4.10 and also in 1.2.5 (both quoted at the end of §137). It is perhaps significant that with the genitive construction we find the measure in the nominative in 1.2.5 instead of in the genitive as it usually is: this may be because, though the *breadth* (of the river) can be equated with two plethra, the *river* cannot be. But Xenophon is willing to call the river as well as the breadth *plethriaion* 'a plethrum long, extending a plethrum', as in 1.5.4 ἀφικνοῦνται ἐπὶ τὸν Μάσκαν ποταμόν, τὸ εὖρος πλεθριαῖον 'they come to the Mascas River, extending a plethrum in breadth', and the almost identical 4.6.4.

[379] Yet this type appears comparatively late in Greek (cf. above, fn. 15). As a matter of fact, I do not suppose that Brugmann would actually analyze this particular passage in this particular way, but I think he chose badly in citing it as an illustration of what he believes the original construction to have been. (On his view concerning this original construction, see above, §6 and fn. 15.)

[380] Cf. above, fn. 15. Even Hittite and Old Persian, artless though they are, especially in comparison with Greek, knit their sentences together in the semblance of a period.

[381] It is true that there is no such word in 1.5.10 ἦν πόλις εὐδαίμων, ὄνομα δὲ Χαρμάνδη, but this can be explained like the examples quoted from Homer in §117, as

1.5.4 ἐνταῦθα ἦν πόλις ἐρήμη, ὄνομα δ᾽ αὐτῇ Κορσωτή 'there there was an uninhabited city, and the name *to it* [i.e. its name] (was) Corsote', and 1.2.5 ἐξελαύνει ἐπὶ τὸν Μαίανδρον ποταμόν· τούτου τὸ εὖρος δύο πλέθρα 'he marches to the Maeander River, *of it* the breadth [i.e. its breadth] (was) two plethra'; or a relative (hypotaxis) as in 2.4.13 πόλις ἦν μεγάλη ᾗ ὄνομα Σιττάκη 'there was a large city, *to which* the name [i.e. the name of which] (was) Sittace', and 1.4.10 ἐξελαύνει ἐπὶ τὰς πηγὰς τοῦ Δάρδατος ποταμοῦ, οὗ τὸ εὖρος πλέθρου 'he marches to the source of the Dardas River, *of which* the breadth (was) of a plethrum'.[382]

138. I think my system of analyzing the original construction would account more satisfactorily than Brugmann's for the Xenophon passage, which could be explained as meaning 'through the middle of the city there flows a river, (its) name Cydnus, (its) breadth of two plethra', with *Kydnos* in apposition with *potamos* and *duo plethrôn* modifying *potamos*, and with *onoma* and *euros* inserted as partitive appositives to *potamos*. However, since *epiklêsin* had certainly become an accusative of specification by Herodotus's time, I think we may assume that *onoma* has probably become an accusative of specification by Xenophon's— and so then has *euros*.

139. Of course, just as the one thing that proved *epiklêsin* to be an accusative of specification was its use in combination with a noun not in the accusative (dative in the Homeric Hymn, nominative and genitive in Herodotus), the one thing that could prove *onoma* to be an accusative of specification would be its use in combination with a noun not in the nominative or the accusative. I know of just one example: Plutarch, *Solon* 12.4 παῖδα νύμφης ὄνομα Βάλτης 'child of the nymph Balte in name'.[383] Whether the apparent dearth of examples before this late date is purely an accident of course cannot be known.

---

having meant originally 'there was a prosperous city, and it (its) name (was) Char-mande', which later may have come to mean 'there was a prosperous city, and it was Charmande in name' (not 'there was a prosperous city, and the name was Charmande').

[382] Xenophon uses the dative with *onoma* and the genitive with *euros*. In the NT too, the tendency is to combine with *onoma* the dative rather than the genitive, whether of the demonstrative or of the relative; see §185.

[383] Cited by Blümel, *IF* 44.260. Cf. above, fn. 15.

IV. LATIN

140. Latin,[384] just as it lacks the accusative of specification in general,[385] lacks the special variety of it exemplified by 'name' in particular;[386] exceptional instances are assuredly borrowings from Greek. But none the less there are certain features of Latin usage with respect to *nomen* that are not irrelevant.

141. Latin to express the idea 'in name' uses not the accusative but the ablative.[387] My artificial formulae *homo nomen Iulius est* and *hominem nomen Iulium nominant* appear in genuine Latin not with *nomen* but with *nomine*. Both are rare in Plautus.[388] I can cite for the first only *Capt.* 288 nam ille[389] quidem Theodoromedes fuit germano nomine, and for the second only its version in the passive, *Stich.* 242 nunc Miccotrogus nomine e vero[390] vocor. There are a number of other

[384] For the purpose of sampling Latin usage, I have made an exhaustive study of Plautus and Vergil, though naturally I have not confined myself to these writers. Plautus, as the earliest author of whom we possess a body of works and not mere fragments, is of course the logical starting-point for any syntactic investigation. Vergil I selected for examination in order to check on the influence of Greek, especially Homer, upon Latin.

[385] See *TAPA* 84.104–5, 85.198 fn. 2.

[386] As was stated at the outset of this study, §2.

[387] This of course represents the instrumental, which I believe was the case originally used in this construction. Cf. §12 and fn. 26.

[388] So too in Vergil. Cf. below, especially §146.

[389] The codices have an adverb here, either *illi* or *illic*, which a number of editions retain; but Camerarius' correction *ille*, adopted by Goetz and Schoell, seems to me to make better sense (cf. *Capt.* 573). However, see Lindsay ad loc. I certainly agree with Lindsay's argument against deleting the line, as was done by Bothe and Leo.

[390] I think the substantive depending on *e* here is *vero*, the meaning being 'I am now called Miccotrogus (and not Gelasimus) in accordance with the true state of affairs'. Lodge (2.851) takes *vero* as an adjective and (2.180) joins the preposition with *nomine*— or *nomen* as he prints it in 2.180, but that is obviously a slip (elsewhere—1.555, 2.852, and 2.899—he has *nomine* correctly). But Miccotrogus is *not* the bearer's *real* name as Theodoromedes in *Capt.* 288 is. He was named Gelasimus as a child by his father (174), and his profession as a parasitic buffoon rendered this name appropriate (176–77). It is only when, in a moment of hunger and misery, he is hailed by Crocotium as Gelasimus that he denies this is his name; he admits it used to be, but now he is (more appropriately)

examples of *nomine* with *sum, appello*, or *voco*,[391] but not with a proper noun corresponding to our formulaic *Iulius* or *Iulium*.

142. What is of special interest in Latin is the fact that the formula *homini nomen Iulius est* usually, though not always, appears in the form *homini nomen Iulio est*,[392] precisely as in Sanskrit the equivalent formula *homo nomen Iulium habet* appears in the form *homo nomen Iulius habet*;[393] in other words, with the noun denoting the name attracted into the case of the noun or pronoun denoting the possessor of the name.[394] The "logical" type *homini nomen Iulius est*, as in *Rud.* 32–33 huic esse nomen urbi Diphilus Cyrenas voluit, is rare in Plautus; I know of only three other instances (all to be quoted below), *Trin.* 889 (which, as we shall see, is a special type), *Truc.* 12, and *Mil.* 86. But the type *homini nomen Iulio est*, as in *Men.* 1096 huic Menaechmo nomen est, is very common; other examples (in addition to those to be quoted below) are *Amph.* 19, 332, *Men.* 297, 1068, 1107, 1122–23 (with *hoc* standing for *hoc nomen*), *Rud.* 5. Probably in *Trin.* 889 Pax, id est nomen mihi, the presence of *id*[395] accounts for the use of the nominative, as opposed to the dative in

called Miccotrogus (239–42). Of course he does not expect to be taken seriously; he refers to himself as Gelasimus in 398, 498, and 631 (though in an unhappy frame of mind in all these passages), and he answers to this name when so addressed by Pamphilippus (585). Also, the use of the preposition *e* seems more natural with the noun denoting the source of the *nomen* than with *nomine* itself; cf. e.g., though it is not an exact parallel, *Merc.* 517 ex forma nomen inditumst, and—a closer parallel, though to be sure much later—Ovid, *Fasti* 2.859 ex vero positum permansit Equiria nomen.

[391] Respectively *Capt.* 590, *Men.* 1122; *Amph.* 813, *Men.* 298 and 383, *Mil.* 435, *Pseud.* 185, *Trin.* 927; *As.* 652, *Men.* 44 and 1135, *Rud.* 236. However, in none of these is *nomine* an ablative of specification. It is rather an ablative of quality in the first two, with *sum*, and an ablative of means in the others, with *appello* and *voco*. Further, in all the examples with *appello* and *voco* except *Men.* 44, the verb is used in the sense of 'address' rather than of 'name' (cf. above, fn. 297). For the comparable construction in Vergil, see §146 and fn. 404; and on the usage in general, fn. 61.

[392] Cf. above, §17 and fn. 50. For the "logical" construction, cf. fn. 17.

[393] Cf. above, fn. 49.

[394] I find very strange the alternative explanation proposed by Gildersleeve-Lodge (224) that the usage is "on the analogy of the Double Dative". Surely that would demand not nomen mihi est Iulio but Iulius mihi est nomini.

[395] The pattern id est nomen mihi is not uncommon; cf. *Cist.* 465 (where, however, the reading is doubtful), *Stich.* 239, and, with slight variation, *Pseud.* 655 and *Most.* 70. The nominative case is of course obligatory for the demonstrative, and practically so for the proper noun used in conjunction with the demonstrative. In any event Pax rather than Paci is absolutely required in *Trin.* 889, because of the pun on the interjection pax just below, in 891. An interesting variety of the use of the formula id est nomen mihi is found in *Pseud.* 637, discussed below, §144.

e.g. *Cist.* 154 mihi Auxilio est nomen; but in general there seems to be absolutely no difference between the passages with the nominative and those with the dative.[396] Cf.: *Truc.* 12 mulier nomen quoi est Phronesium, vs. *Poen.* 92 hominis quoi Lyco nomen siet; *Mil.* 86 Alazon Graece huic nomen est comoediae, vs. *As.* 10 huic nomen Graece Onagost fabulae (also *Trin.* 18, quoted in the next paragraph). After the question *quid est tibi* (or *ei*) *nomen?*, or some variation of it, the answer may be in the nominative, as in *Capt.* 285, *Cist.* 773, *Pers.* 700–5, *Pseud.* 653 and 977, *Trin.* 889 (already quoted in part), or in the dative, as in *Men.* 1131, *Merc.* 516, *Pseud.* 744. The attraction must have become firmly established, for we find *Iulius* appearing in the dative even in some sentences in which *homini* does not appear at all (though it may be implied in a preceding clause): namely, *Curc.* 76–77 anus hic solet cubare custos ianitrix, nomen Leaenaest (i.e. Leaenae est); *Trin.* 390–91 haec sunt aedes, hic habet; Lesbonico est nomen; and *Pers.* 624 (in answer to the question in 623 quid nomen tibist?) Lucridi nomen in patria fuit. So too *Mil.* 436 Diceae nomen est, in answer to a question which means *quid nomen tibist?* but has the quite different form *quis igitur vocare?*[397] In *Bacch.* 704 quid mi refert Chrysalo esse nomen, *mi* with *esse nomen* is implied by the preceding *mi* with *refert*; but in *Pseud.* 989–90 (if the reading is correct) Polymachaeroplagidi nomen est, there is no preceding dative at all, only a nominative (in 988–89 Polymachaeroplagides purus putus est ipsus).

143. Precisely the same attraction takes place in the formula *homini nomen Iulium indunt* (or, in the passive, *homini nomen Iulius inditur*), which usually appears as *homini nomen Iulio indunt* (or *homini nomen Iulio inditur*).[398] For this I can cite no active example in which Plautus uses the accusative, and only one passive example in which he uses the nominative, namely *Aul.* 164 sit paratum nomen puero Postumus. For examples with the dative I quote the following: *Men.* 77 iuventus

---

[396] Cf. Gellius' comment, 15.29 duae istae in loquendo figurae notae satis usitataeque sunt: 'mihi nomen est Iulius' et 'mihi nomen est Iulio'. (The remainder of Gellius' discussion of this point will be taken up below, §163.)

[397] On the form of this question, cf. above, fn. 45, and below, fn. 402. We may note the reverse situation in *Amph.* 364–65, where, in answer to the question, *quid nomen tibi est?*, Sosia answers, *Sosiam vocant Thebani*, with *me* to be supplied as if the question had been *quid te vocant?* Cf. too *Capt.* 983–84 (discussed below, §143). Still more anomalous is *Pseud.* 636–37 (discussed below, §144).

[398] Cf. above, §17 and fn. 51. For the "logical" construction, cf. §14 and fn. 39.

nomen fecit Peniculo mihi, *Capt.* 69 iuventus nomen indidit Scorto mihi, *Stich.* 174 Gelasimo nomen mi indidit parvo pater, and, in the passive, *Men.* 1126 Menaechmo nomen est factum tibi, and *Men.* 263 huic urbei nomen Epidamno inditumst.[399] Here again,[400] we find *Iulio* without *homini* (to be sure shortly after the full formula, *homini nomen Iulio est*, discussed in the preceding paragraph), in *Trin.* 18–20 huic Graece nomen est Thensauro fabulae, Philemo scripsit, Plautus vortit barbare, nomen Trinummo fecit. We may compare a passage which lacks *nomen* as well as *homini*: *Capt.* 984 (in answer to the question in 983 *quid erat ei nomen?*) Paegnium vocitatust, post vos indidistis Tyndaro.

144. Still more remarkable is the attraction of an implied *nomen* to *homo* in gender[401] in *Mil.* 436 quis igitur vocare?[402] 'who are you called?' for 'what are you called?'. More or less the reverse confusion is seen in a passage in which the question 'what is your name?' is answered as if it had been 'who are you?' In this passage the following dialogue takes place, *Pseud.* 636–37: quid est tibi nomen?—Surus sum. —Surus?—id est nomen mihi. Here to the question *quid est tibi nomen?*, which would be properly answered by *Surus est*, Pseudolus instead responds *Surus sum*, as if he had been asked, *quis es?* Yet when his interlocutor echoes, *Surus?*, Pseudolus replies, *id est nomen mihi*, as if he had actually said *Surus est* in the first place. In other words, *Surus* in his first response stands for the *homo*, but in his second for the *nomen*.

145. When we come down to Vergil,[403] we find many of Plautus' usages still current.

146. Specification is still regularly expressed by the ablative, *nomine*[404] (or *cognomine*[405]), the construction being *hominem Iulium*

---

[399] Other examples are: with *nomen facio*, *Bacch.* 945, *Trin.* 843, and, in the passive, *Men.* 1126; with *nomen indo*, *Capt.* 820, *Men.* 42–43, *Rud.* 934, *Trin.* 8, and, in the passive, *Capt.* 726.

[400] As in the examples in the form *Iulio est nomen*, quoted at the end of the preceding paragraph.

[401] As happens to *nomen* in Old Persian. Cf. above, §17 and fn. 54.

[402] This question, as already noted (§142), is answered as if it ran *quid nomen tibi est?* We may compare in the Vulgate translation of *Luke* 1.62–63 the inquiry directed to Zacharias, *quem* vellet vocari eum, and his answer, Ioannes est nomen eius; on this see further below, fnn. 500 and 596.

[403] Cf. fn. 384. In quoting Vergil, I designate passages from the *Eclogues* by *Ecl.* and those from the *Georgics* by *Georg.*; all not specially marked are from the *Aeneid*.

[404] We also, just as in Plautus (see fn. 391), meet *nomine* with *voco* in the sense of

'rufen', as in 4.383–84 nomine Dido saepe vocaturum, 11.731 = 12.759 nomine quemque vocans. So too with *clamo* (4.674) and with *imploro* (12.652). Cf. above, fn. 61.

405 Plautus does not use *cognomine* as an ablative of specification; indeed, there is only one occurrence of this noun in any use in his extant works (*Capt.* 878). In Vergil, the fundamental difference between *nomine* and cognomine as ablatives of specification, and indeed, in a broader sense between any of the case-forms of *nomen* and *cognomen*, is somewhat like that between *onoma* and *epônymon* in Greek (cf. fn. 309). Where only a single name and nothing else is involved, we find *nomen*; where two names are involved, one of which serves as a basis for the other, or where a single name is involved but is thought of as clearly a derivative from an earlier name or from some ordinary word, the earlier name (if included) is regularly designated as *nomen*, and the derived name as *cognomen*. A good example is 8.330–32 Thybris, a quo post Itali fluvium cognomine Thybrim diximus; amisit verum vetus Albula nomen; the river is named after Thybris and is therefore so called *cognomine*, having lost its original *nomen* of Albula (on the construction of *Albula*, see fnn. 417 and 460). Another good example is the very similar passage (discussed along with 8.330–32 in fn. 407) 3.334–35 Chaonios cognomine campos Chaoniamque omnem Troiano a Chaone dixit; here there can be no question of an earlier *nomen* replaced by the *cognomen*, since Chaonia, named after Chaon, is a new settlement never known by any other name. The same is true of Pergamea, mentioned in 3.132–34 muros molior urbis Pergameamque voco, et laetam cognomine gentem hortor amare focos; it is clearly implied here, though not expressly stated, that Pergamea gets its name from Pergamum (hence Knapp's comment ad loc. that *cognomine* here = *nomine* is certainly wrong). There are, to be sure, a few instances where *cognomen* as an ablative of source (not specification) is used not of the later name as we would expect, but of the earlier one. We have two examples of this in combination with the passive participle of *dico*: 3.702 Gela fluvii cognomine dicta, and 7.671 fratris Tiburti dictam cognomine gentem. 3.702 has been thought to be spurious, for various reasons summed up conveniently by Page ad loc.; the use of *cognomine* instead of *nomine* might seem to be a more cogent reason than any of those listed by Page were it not for the parallel provided by 7.671 (the five passages compared by Forbiger, including one, 12.845, which is also compared by Conington, are definitely not parallels; all are discussed elsewhere in the present note). The two passages seem to involve contamination of (a) *Gela fluvii nomine dicta* and *fratris Tiburti nomine dictam gentem*, and (b) *Gela a fluvio cognomine dicta* and *a fratre Tiburto dictam cognomine gentem*; for the first construction cf. 11.542–43 matris vocavit nomine Casmillae Camillam, and for the second 8.330–32 Thybris a quo fluvium cognomine Thybrim diximus (cited just above). Perhaps the confusion in our examples was furthered by the close proximity in each case to *dico* (in the forms *dicta, dictam*) of the ablative of source *cognomine* (on which see again fn. 408), suggesting the common use and position of this word as an ablative of specification, e.g. in 8.331, just cited. The same use of *cognomine* but without *dico* is met in 11.246 and possibly in 3.350; on these see fn. 411. I know of no other exception in Vergil to the distinction that I have just indicated. It holds good in 6.383 gaudet cognomine terra (or terrae) whether we think of *cognomine* here as a noun or as an adjective (cf. fn. 422). 1.530 =.3.163 Hesperiam Grai cognomine dicunt, and 12.845 dicuntur geminae pestes cognomine Dirae, are not exceptions; in the first, the derivation of *Hesperia* from a stem meaning 'west' is surely implicit (cf. Hahn, *CW* 13.209–12), and in the second, that of *Dirae* from an adjective meaning 'dreadful'. So, too, in the one occurrence of the genitive *cognominis*, in 8.48 Ascanius clari condet cognominis Albam, *Albam* is clearly thought of as echoing *alba* in 8.45 alba, solo recubans, albi circum ubera nati (just as *ter denis* in 47 echoes *triginta* in 44); the position of *alba* at the beginning of its line, and of

nomine dicunt[406] or *homo Iulius nomine dicitur*, as in *Georg.* 3.280–81 hippomanes vero quod nomine dicunt pastores, and 6.242 unde locum Grai dixerunt nomine Aornon (a line, however, of doubtful authen-

Albam at the end of its, intensifies the effect. In the two instances of *cognomen* as a nominative (both quoted in §150), the reference is to an additional second name, a *cognomen* in the later, Roman use: in 1.267–68 Ascanius gets the *cognomen Iulus*, and Numanus in 9.592–93 has the *cognomen Remulus*. In the case of Ascanius, the derivation of *Iulus*— from *Ilus*, allied to *Ilium* (*res Ilia* = *Ilium*)—is distinctly stressed. In the case of Numanus, there is no indication that his *cognomen* has any particular significance, etymological or otherwise; there are two other men named Remulus in the *Aeneid* (9.360 and 11.636). Yet I cannot but wonder whether the Numanus surnamed Remulus who from outside the walls so boastfully and scornfully taunted Ascanius until the latter was provoked into killing him, may not be meant to suggest that Remus who was later to have a similar encounter with Ascanius' descendant Romulus (for their relationship, cf. the reference to Ascanius in 1.267–71, followed closely by that to Romulus, 275–76 inde Romulus excipiet gentem; also the introduction of Romulus in 6.777–79 as the culmination of the line of Alban kings). To be sure, Romulus is ultimately to be reconciled with Remus (1.292; cf. *Georg.* 2.533); but the final peace, even for Aeneas, is still far off at the moment when Ascanius sturdily kills Remulus.

When we turn to Vergil's use of *nomen*, we find it is not quite so consistent as that of *cognomen*, since of the 106 occurrences of *nomen* in the major works of Vergil, there are eleven in which *cognomen* might have been used, 1.288, 3.18, 5.121, 6.242 (perhaps a spurious line), 7.63, 8.329, 338, 358, 422, 10.145, 12.194, plus five others which are less certain, since in them *nomen* seems to do duty at once for the name of the original bearer of the name and for that of the namesake, 5.564, 6.235, 381, 768, 10.200 (but that might be said also of 3.350, where *cognomine* is used: cf. fn. 411). At all events it is more natural to use the word of less narrow denotation (*nomen*) for that of more narrow (*cognomen*), than would be the reverse. Of course in a number of these instances the choice may be a mere matter of metrical convenience: *Chaonios cognomine campos* (3.334) vs. *Volcania nomine tellus* (8.422), *Grai cognomine dicunt* (1.530) vs. *Romani nomine portam* (8.338).

[406] Vergil uses *memoro* in 8.338–39, and *voco* in 11.542–43 (where, however, the accompanying *nomine* is an ablative of source rather than specification, as already noted in fn. 405); but his usual verb for 'call' in this sense is *dico*. This verb also figures in a rather odd passage, *Georg.* 4.356 te crudelem nomine dicit. Conington translates ad loc. "He is crying on thee by name for thy cruelty"; but, although a Greek adjective with *onta* might easily have this meaning, one may well hesitate to read such a meaning into the Latin. It would be more natural to interpret the passage, in the light of those here cited, as 'he is calling you cruel'; but *nomine* makes this a little difficult, since such an epithet as *crudelem* is by no means a name, and especially since Aristaeus did not specifically address his mother as *crudelis*. I am led to wonder whether there may not be a confusion of *te crudelem dicit* 'he calls you cruel' (*crudelem* quoting Aristaeus), and *te crudelis, nomine dicit* (*crudelis* quoting the speaker Arethusa, whose viewpoint is fused with that of Aristaeus). Other passages, to be sure of a somewhat different nature, in which a word that would logically be vocative gets incorporated into the sentence as an accusative are *Ecl.* 1.5 formosam resonare doces Amaryllida silvas and *Georg.* 4.525–27 Eurydicen vox et lingua a miseram Eurydicen! anima fugiente vocabat; Eurydicen referebant ripae; see my discussion of both of these, *CW* 22.132, and cf. further below, fn. 461.

ticity); and, in the passive, 12.845 dicuntur geminae pestes cognomine
Dirae, and—probably—3.210–11 Strophades Graio stant nomine
dictae insulae Ionio in magno. In the last example, I think *Strophades* is
the predicate nominative (*Iulius*), with *insulae* the subject (*homo*); but
it is just possible that *Strophades* is the subject, with *insulae* in apposition
with it. In that case, the member *Iulius* is lacking, as often happens in
Vergil: this may also be true of 3.334–35 Chaonios cognomine campos
Chaoniamque omnem Troiano a Chaone dixit, and 8.330–32 Thybris,
a quo post Itali fluvium cognomine Thybrim diximus;[407] and it is

[407] The ambiguity in these two passages has already been referred to in §13. The question is whether 3.334–35 means (a) 'he called the Chaonian Fields in name after Chaon'
or (b) 'he called the fields "Chaonian" in name after Chaon'; and whether 8.331–32
means (a) 'we name the River Tiber (or the Tiber River) after him' or (b) 'we name the
river "Tiber" after him'. (It is easier to make the distinction in speech than in writing.)
The (a) versions may involve a slight touch of prolepsis, since it might be argued (as
noted in fn. 13) that the Chaonian Fields as such and the Tiber River as such do not
exist until after they have received their names; but this is carrying logical analysis too
far, and after all the (nameless) fields and river (before naming) and the Chaonian Fields
and Tiber River (after naming) respectively represent exactly the same thing. In the (a)
versions *Chaonios* is an attributive adjective and *Thybrim* is an appositive; in the (b)
versions they are predicate accusatives. Or, to put it differently, in (a) we have "accusatives of affect", and in (b) we have "accusatives of effect". In the case of 3.334 I am
inclined to favor interpretation (a), since that appears to me the only natural one for the
following line 335 (Knapp's explanation that this is "briefly put for *called the whole
region Chaonia*" seems very dubious to me); but in the case of 8.331–32, it seems impossible to choose between the two interpretations. If 3.335 points toward (a), 1.530 and
1.532–33 point toward (b). In the passive too, we have both varieties: (a) the two
passages to be cited directly as certain examples of the omission of the name, 3.702 and
7.671; (b) 12.845 dicuntur geminae pestes cognomine Dirae, in which the predicate
nominative *Dirae* corresponds to the predicate accusative with the active voice.
    This is a rather difficult passage, because the *geminae pestes* have not been mentioned
before; I assume it is a shortened form standing for *sunt geminae pestes quae dicuntur
cognomine Dirae*, just as Conington explains 6.106–7 hic inferni ianua regis dicitur by
equating *hic dicitur* with *hic est quae dicitur*. I suppose this would be in full *hic est (ianua)
quae inferni ianua regis dicitur* ('here is the gate which is called the nether king's'), with the
predicate genitive *inferni regis* corresponding to the predicate nominative *Dirae* in 12.845.
The school editions, Fairclough and Brown on 6.106–7, and Knapp on both passages,
give a different explanation, in accordance with which *dicitur* must be viewed as a vivid
substitute for *est* adding an idea of fame: in Knapp's rendering, "here is the far-famed
gateway", "two plagues there are, widely heralded". But if we accept this, we must,
with Knapp, put a comma after *pestes* and separate *cognomine Dirae*, 'Furies in name',
from *dicuntur*, which seems most unnatural, and, as will be pointed out in the following
paragraph (§147), quite contrary to Vergil's practice. Conington in his translation of the
Aeneid gives a similar interpretation (despite the paraphrase quoted just above from the
note ad loc. in his edition): "since here it is that Fame tells of the gate of the infernal
monarch" (241). However, he deals differently with 12.845, which he renders about as

certainly true of 3.702 Gela fluvii cognomine dicta, and 7.671 fratris
Tiburti dictam cognomine gentem.[408] On the other hand, the member
hominem is lacking, though it is readily supplied in thought from the
preceding clause, in 1.530 = 3.163 est locus, Hesperiam Grai cognomine
dicunt,[409] where we have a quaint paratactic construction suggesting
a folk-tale.[410] Cf. too the interpolated clause in which *sic* replaces
Iulium, 6.440–41 monstrantur lugentes campi, sic illos nomine dicunt,
and (without a word for *hominem*) 7.607 sunt geminae Belli portae, sic
nomine dicunt. Rather odd is 3.350 Xanthi cognomine rivum, where
the school-texts, Fairclough-Brown and Knapp, which have to account
precisely for the syntax of every word, explain that we have an
ablative of characteristic in *cognomine* accompanied by the genitive
Xanthi (instead of by an adjective in the ablative).[411]

I would, "There are two fiends known as the Furies" (421). Both passages are handled
in the same way by Mackail in his translation: "since here is the gate named of the
infernal king" (122) and "twin monsters there are called the Awful Ones by name"
(296).

[408] These two passages differ from the others here cited (as already pointed out in
fn. 405) in that *cognomine* is an ablative of source, not specification. In other words,
cognomine here is not used as is *cognomine* in e.g. 1.530 Hesperiam Grai cognomine dicunt,
but is equivalent to *de nomine* in 1.532–33 nunc fama minores Italiam dixisse ducis de
nomine gentem and 3.18 Aeneadasque meo nomen de nomine fingo (cf. too *a quo
nomine* in 5.117, discussed below in fn. 422). On the substitution of *cognomine* for the
normal *nomine*, again see fn. 405.

[409] Is this an argument in favor of Brugmann's view (cf. above, §6) that we have a
clause in *Nalo nāma* and *potamos Kydnos onoma*? I think not, because there is a real point
in adding a statement here: it is the *Greeks* who call the country Hesperia (this helps to
localize Italy, as I tried to prove long ago, in 1920, *CW* 13.210–11).

[410] Cf. above, fn. 12.

[411] Fairclough and Brown specifically state that the genitive *Xanthi* is equivalent to an
adjective (the reverse of the substitution of an adjective for a genitive which we have
already noted, fn. 357). As for *Xanthi* itself, it may be an appositional genitive, 'a stream
with the name of Xanthus' (cf. below, fn. 467); but I would rather suggest that it is a
true possessive (like the genitive in 11.246, quoted just below) referring not to this
pitiful dry little stream, a mock-Xanthus, but to the whirling Xanthus back home in
Troy whose proud name it humbly bears. Support for this interpretation is lent by
11.246 urbem Argyripam patriae cognomine gentis, where *patriae gentis*, denoting the
source of the name (cf. fnn. 405 and 414), provides an excellent parallel for *Xanthi* if this
refers to the great Trojan river, not its little namesake stream in Epirus. There is nothing
in 3.350 to correspond to *Argyripam*, but nothing is needed, since presumably the western
river is called Xanthus exactly as the eastern one is, and to say *Xanthi cognomine rivum
Xanthum* instead of just *Xanthi cognomine rivum* would involve intolerably banal tautology. But in 11.246 *Argyripam* of course is needed, since only part of the region's name
could be traced back to Diomedes' ancestral home in Argos (already suggested by

147. But what Vergil hardly ever, if ever, says (and again in this he resembles Plautus)[412] is *homo Iulius nomine* without a verb of calling for *nomine* to relate to.[413] It is worth noting that in the example just cited, he did *not* write *Xanthum cognomine rivum*.[414] We do perhaps have this construction in 8.422 Volcani domus, et Volcania nomine tellus, where *domus* and *tellus* may be taken as in apposition with *insula* in 416 or, as Conington suggests, loosely with the whole sentence. But this is not a bare statement 'an island the home of Vulcan, and a land Vulcania by name'; the emphasis is on the relation with Vulcan, who appears in the next line; the genitive *Volcani* and the adjective *Volcania* are emphatic, and almost suggest predication: 'Vulcan's is (this) abode, and Volcanian is the land by name'.

148. Still, two other possible examples are 3.613–14 sum patria ex Ithaca, comes infelicis Ulixi, nomine Achaemenides, and 12.514–15 maestum mittit Oniten, nomine Echionium. But the reading *nomen* is also found in both these passages; and, as Conington says in regard to both (though he himself adopts *nomen* only in the second), *nomen* would be more likely to get altered in the manuscripts than *nomine*. Since the construction *homo Iulius nomine* is also rare in Vergil, as I have just pointed out, I would be quite ready in these two instances to accept the likewise rare construction *homo Iulius nomen*, with *nomen* as an accusative of specification.[415] In the first of these, Vergil may well have had in mind a specific passage from the *Odyssey*, or possibly two specific passages, in which Homer used what the Latin poet would probably have taken as an accusative of specification, whether it actually is or is not to be so explained. The earlier one is particularly apposite, for here too an unhappy individual far from home claims

---

Argiva in 243, and therefore not requiring specific reference in 246). The substitution of *gentis* with its overtone of sentiment for the logically demanded but perhaps less affecting toponym is of course readily comprehensible.

[412] The Plautine *Theodoromedes fuit germano nomine* (*Capt.* 288), quoted above in §141, is hardly a parallel, for the presence of the adjective *germano* makes a difference.

[413] The corresponding Greek construction *homo Iulius nomen* does not occur in Homer at all. Blümel seems to be quite right in his statement (*IF* 33.27) that its first appearance is after Hesiod, perhaps not till Herodotus.

[414] In 11.246 he does write *urbem Argyripam patriae cognomine gentis*, but here *cognomine* is an ablative of source, not of specification. See fn. 411.

[415] Conington, who, as I have said, adopts *nomen* in 12.515, explains it as in apposition with *Oniten*, but this I consider out of the question. See below, §153.

origin in Ithaca and close relationship with its chief, namely, *Od.* 15.267
ἐξ Ἰθάκης γένος εἰμί, πατὴρ δέ μοί ἐστιν Ὀδυσσεύς. The second
passage applies to Odysseus himself, namely, *Od.* 24.269 εὔχετο δ᾽ ἐξ
Ἰθάκης γένος ἔμμεναι. In each of these, the putative accusative of
specification, which, however, can be given a quite different interpretation (see §§126 and 127), is not the word for 'name', which, as already
indicated (§122), Homer probably did not so use, but the word for
'race', which he probably did so use, at least in the case of *geneē* if not
in that of *genos* (see §130). On the close connection between 'name'
and 'race', cf. §§12 and 125 (on Greek) and §§157–60 (on Latin).
In the second Vergilian passage, the reading *nomen* seems to me far
preferable to *nomine* on the basis of internal evidence, for reasons which
I shall give later (§159). If we adopt *nomen* rather than *nomine* in either
one of these two passages, that furnishes an additional argument for
adopting it in the other too. Hence in these two passages Vergil in
my opinion is departing from the earlier Latin usage, and copying
Greek.[416]

149. In his use of the constructions *homini nomen est Iulius* (or *Iulio*)
and *homini nomen indunt Iulium* (or *Iulio*),[417] Vergil again agrees with
Plautus.[418] He sometimes uses the "logical" nominative or accusative,
as in 8.358 Ianiculum huic, illi fuerat Saturnia nomen, and in 7.63
Laurentisque ab ea nomen posuisse colonis (in the latter passage, however, absolute logic is violated by *ab ea*, on which see below, fn. 420).
In this connection we may note also *Georg.* 1.137–38 navita tum stellis
numeros et nomina fecit Pleiadas, Hyadas, claramque Lycaonis Arcton.
This follows the general pattern of 7.63, but *nomina* here, coordinated

---

[416] For another possible example (though of a quite different type) of *nomen* as an
accusative of specification in Vergil, see §156.

[417] In 10.200 matrisque dedit tibi, Mantua, nomen, there is neither dative nor accusative, the place of one of these cases being taken by the vocative *Mantua*. The form
Mantua could also be explained as a *nominativus tituli*, the name cited as a name (cf. fn.
205), here used in apposition with the accusative *nomen*; but that is most unlikely, in
view of the indubitable vocative in the following line, *Mantua dives avis*. Another
possible example of a *nominativus tituli* in apposition with *nomen* is 8.332 amisit verum
vetus Albula nomen, where the word order seems to favor this explanation; but more
probably *Albula* is the subject of *amisit*, since to supply a subject *fluvius* from the preceding clause (331–32 fluvium cognomine Thybrim diximus) would be rather clumsy.
More likely instances of the *nominativus tituli* in apposition with nomen are Ovid's
lactea, probably, and his *aurea*, positively, in *Met.* 1.169 and 15.96 respectively (on both
of which see below, §162).

[418] Cf. above, §§142 and 143.

with *numeros*, is more forceful and impressive than *nomen* there; in 7.63 the emphasis is on *Laurentis*, the point being that *Laurentes* was the particular name given the colonists, whereas in *Georg.* 1.137 the emphasis is on *nomina*, the point being that names were now assigned to the hitherto nameless stars in general, a few of the specific names being added rather casually in partitive apposition as examples. There is an added complication here too, occasioned by the presence of *claram*, which will be dealt with below (§154).

150. But Vergil, like Plautus, uses *Iulio* oftener than *Iulius* or *Iulium*, thus joining it with *homini* instead of with *nomen*; note two parallel passages in the *Georgics*, in the first of which the dative replaces a nominative, and in the second of which it replaces an accusative, namely, *Georg.* 3.146–48 est lucos Silari circa volitans, cui nomen asilo Romanum est, and *Georg.* 4.271–72 est etiam flos in pratis, cui nomen amello fecere agricolae; also two more examples from the *Aeneid*, 9.592–93 Numanum, cui Remulo cognomen erat, and 1.267–68 puer Ascanius, cui nunc cognomen Iulo additur.[419]

151. A quite different type of confusion of *homo* and *nomen*—stylistic rather than syntactic—is also met in Vergil. Doubtless because *Iulius* in one sense may represent the *homo* and in another sense the *nomen*, the poet often uses *Iulius* in a sort of *apo koinou* way to refer first to the man and then to the name. Thus we may find the word corresponding to *Iulius* in apposition with the word corresponding to *homo*, and thereafter *nomen* in apposition with the word corresponding to *Iulius*. A good example—in which, as it happens, the word corresponding to *Iulius* actually *is Iulius*—is 1.286–88 nascetur Caesar, Iulius, a magno demissum nomen Iulo.[420] Precisely like this is 6.760–63 iuvenis proxima tenet loca, Silvius, Albanum nomen, tua postuma proles.[421] Very

---

[419] It is rather interesting, though I suppose not significant, that all these examples occur in relative clauses, like the Homeric passages exemplifying *epiklêsin* (cf. above, §118 and fn. 308).

[420] There is a second confusion here, since rigorous precision would demand *a magno* (or *magni*) *nomine demissum nomen Iuli*. Cf. 5.121 Sergestusque, domus tenet a quo Sergia nomen, where *a quo* represents *a cuius nomine*; and 7.63 Laurentisque ab ea nomen posuisse colonis (already cited above, §149), where *ab ea* (i.e. *a lauro*) represents *ab eius* (i.e. *lauri*) *nomine*. The more cumbersome logical form is met in 3.18 Aeneadasque meo nomen de nomine fingo.

[421] Here another complication is provided by the additional appositive *proles*, which relates back to *iuvenis Silvius* as a man and not to *Silvius* as a name. Cf. the English examples cited above in fn. 56.

similar is 5.116–17 Mnestheus agit Pristim, mox Italus Mnestheus, genus a quo nomine Memmi.[422]

152. In all these instances, there is a departure from strict logic;[423] but of course strict logic should not be expected of poetry. On the contrary, the passages gain by the overtones implicit in a manner of expression that consists of the blending of two others, suggesting both. Thus the first passage may be called a fusion[424] of (*homo*) *Iulius, a magno Iulo ortus*, and (*nomen*) *Iulius, a magni Iuli nomine* (or *a magno Iuli nomine*) *demissum*;[425] but obviously it is infinitely superior to either.[426] The effect is furthered by the fact that *nomen* can mean 'fame' as well as 'name' (e.g. in 2.89 and 12.226, on which see below, §§159 and 157 respectively). This artificial and artistic type of apposition, in whch *Iulius* used in two senses forms a connecting link between *homo* and *nomen*, is altogether different from the choppy paratactic type, with

[422] Here again there is a second confusion which is precisely the reverse of that in 1.286–88 and the other examples cited in fn. 420. There the name was said to be descended from the man: here the men, the race, are said to be descended from the name. It is possible, to be sure, to view the substantive introduced by *a* as *quo*, not *nomine*, and to take *nomine* as an ablative of specification as I advocate doing in Plautus, *Stich.* 242 nomine e vero vocor (see above, fn. 390); but the word order in Vergil is certainly against separating *quo* and *nomine*. The same possible ambiguity arises in connection with 8.330–32 Thybris, a quo post Itali fluvium cognomine Thybrim diximus; but in this passage the word order would rather lead us to separate *quo* and *cognomine*, and to interpret *cognomine* as an ablative of specification (as has already been done above, §146). Conington ad loc. suggests still another possibility, namely, that *cognomine* is an adjective here (modifying *quo*), as he believes it to be (following Servius) in 6.383 gaudet cognomine terra. Others—e.g. Henry—call *terra* in 6.383 a nominative, which (despite the possible parallelism of 3.133 laetam cognomine gentem) seems to me very unsatisfactory, as we are interested in Palinurus' feelings, not in the region's; still others—e.g. Ribbeck —adopt the variant reading *terrae*, which seems the most satisfactory, despite the testimony of Servius. But whatever we may decide about *cognomine* in 6.383, I think the evidence of the numerous parallel passages is completely against taking it as an adjective in 8.331, and the word order favors its separation from *quo* just as much if *cognomine* is an adjective modifying *quo* as if *quo* is an adjective modifying *cognomine*.

[423] As has been seen in fnn. 420, 421, and 422.

[424] The usual term is confusion or contamination, but I avoid these because both have themselves an overtone of disparagement.

[425] The other passages here cited may be dealt with in the same way.

[426] Vergil has numerous other blendings of the sort which it would take us too far afield to catalogue here; I hope to treat them elsewhere. Such fusions are particularly characteristic of this poet; but the interchange of the *homo* and his *nomen* are common enough in many authors and many languages. One comes across them repeatedly in modern English newspapers, especially in reference to the titles of books. Several examples have been given above (fn. 56).

nomen in partitive apposition with *homo*, and *Iulius* in apposition with either or both, which I have posited as the starting-point from which developed the accusative of specification

153. Additional examples are 7.717 quosque secans infaustum interluit Alia nomen, and 7.412 et nunc magnum manet Ardea nomen if *nomen* is in apposition with *Ardea*; it might, however, be a predicate nominative, 'Ardea remains a great name', indicating that the city has lost not merely its prosperity (cf. the following statement, 413 sed fortuna fuit) but even its very existence—a more poignant interpretation, and therefore probably the right one, especially as it may also suggest the poetic justice of the subsequent fate of Turnus's capital.[427] To these Conington, as I have already said (fn. 415), would add 12.514–515 maestum mittit Oniten, nomen Echionium, with which he specifically compares 1.288 and 6.763; but they are not alike at all. *Oniten* does not effect a transition from man to name, for surely *it* is not an 'Echionian name'; the man Onites is 'Echionian in name', and the point of this I shall discuss later (§159; cf. fn. 448).

154. In general in the preceding passages, the irregularity, if such it can be called, lay in the placing of *nomen*, usually with an accompanying adjectival modifier (*demissum, Albanum, infaustum, magnum*), in apposition with *Iulius* or its equivalent referring to the *homo* or *res* (a man, a river, a town) and not to the *nomen*. A different variety occurs in *Georg.* 1.137–38 navita tum stellis numeros et nomina fecit, Pleiadas, Hyadas, claramque Lycaonis Arcton (already treated above, §149), Here we have several nouns corresponding to *Iulius* as a name, precisely used in apposition with *nomina*; but one of them (*Arcton*) is accompanied by an adjective (*claram*) which applies to the noun considered not as a name but as the object which bears the name (a star).

155. Another indication of the interchangeability or equivalence of *homo* and *nomen* is provided by their correlation in 6.776 haec tum nomina erunt, nunc sunt sine nomine terrae,[428] and by their coordina-

---

[427] Both possibilities are of course ruled out if we accept the reading *tenet*, which also has good MS authority, but which I think is less effective than a reading which places the two contrasting nouns, *nomen* and *fortuna*, in the same case. 6.235 aeternumque tenet per saecula nomen is hardly a satisfactory parallel, since the promontory named for Misenus not only retains the name but is still of course in full existence itself.

[428] The four towns here listed, to be founded by Aeneas's descendants, have a very different fate from Turnus's capital, the luckless Ardea referred to just above (§153). In

tion in 12.529–30 atavos et avorum sonantem nomina. These are instances of typical Vergilian blending:[429] the former representing a fusion of *haec tum nomina habebunt, nunc sunt sine nomine terrae*, and *haec tum nomina erunt, nunc non sunt*; the latter representing a fusion of *atavos et avos sonantem*, and *atavorum et avorum sonantem nomina*. But how commonplace and colorless these prosaic substitutes are as compared with Vergil's poetic and picturesque expressions! On the other hand, *nomina* in the phrase *gentis nomina*, used as a periphrastic equivalent for *gens* and as an inexact parallel for the practically synonymous *proles*, is almost otiose in *Georg*. 3.34–36 stabunt et Parii lapides, spirantia signa, Assaraci proles demissaeque ab Iove gentis nomina, Trosque parens et Troiae Cynthius auctor. This is a loosely constructed (as well as a singularly frigid) passage; but apparently *proles* and *nomina* are in apposition with *Parii lapides* (subject of *stabunt*) or with its appositive, *spirantia signa*. Since in no case could *stabunt nomina* be logical, the use of *demissae ab Iove gentis nomina* as a substitute for *demissa ab Iove gens* cannot be logically accounted for; and there is no proper noun here to soften the inconcinnity by serving as a connecting link between *homo* and *nomen* (here *lapides* or *signa*, and *nomina*) as in the slightly reminiscent but vastly superior passage 1.286–88 nascetur pulchra Troianus origine Caesar, Iulius, a magno demissum nomen Iulo (already treated above, §151). There and elsewhere, the employment of the abstract *nomen* provides overtones suggesting fame, as I have already pointed out (§152); but I do not think that justifies the use of *nomina* in so

---

Aeneas's own day, these colonies of the *Prisci Latini* are of course nonexistent *as of now* (*nunc* in 776); their sites are mere empty and homeless expanses of land (*sine nomine terrae*); but some day (*tum*) Nomentum and the rest will have names—more poetically, will *be* names—which implies flourishing existence. Ardea, on the other hand, was founded and named long before Aeneas's time, by the legendary Danae; in Aeneas's day it is the capital of Turnus's Rutulian kingdom, and has both *nomen* and *fortuna*; but now in Vergil's day (*nunc* in 7.412, used quite differently from *nunc* in 6.776) it has ceased to be, and exists as a name only. In both passages the use of the word for 'name' is extremely effective, though in the one case it implies prosperity and in the other desuetude.

[429] Cf. above, fnn. 424 and 426. That such blendings are in Vergil's case the result of deliberate preference, and not due to the exigencies of the meter, is evidenced by the fact that in the second of the two passages quoted here, a perfectly parallel form of expression, with *atavorum* substituted for *atavos*, though possibly the additional elision might have seemed objectionable, none the less would have been metrically possible. For other instances of such collocations, see my *Coordination* passim, especially 191, 194, and 195–99; this particular example is there treated on 196–97.

concrete a context as the one under discussion. If this passage is really, as it assuredly seems to be, a hint of the epic that is to come, Vergil certainly improved immeasurably between the promise and the fulfilment!

156. There remains to consider one passage involving a use of *nomen* which is quite without a parallel in Vergil:[430] 3.692–94 Sicanio praetenta sinu iacet insula, nomen dixere priores Ortygiam. This, including the necessity of turning back to the preceding clause to find the definition of the place that receives the name, may remind us of 1.530 = 3.163 est locus, Hesperiam Grai cognomine dicunt;[431] but there is the great difference that in the one instance we have the usual ablative (*cognomine*) and in the other we have the accusative (*nomen*). Have we here once more an example of *nomen* used as an accusative of specification[432]—'the men of old called (it) Ortygia by name'? Or is *nomen* the object of *dixere*?[433] In that case Vergil is probably imitating Homer's use of *onoma* with *kaleo*,[434] but the idiom is quite alien to Latin,[435] which, as we have seen, uses *nomen facio* or *indo*[436] (with the dative of the person)[437] or *nomine dico* (with the accusative of the person).[438] As for the full Greek construction with *three* accusatives,

---

[430] Conington compares 3.18 Aeneadasque meo nomen de nomine fingo (cited above, fn. 420), but *nomen fingo* seems more in keeping with the usual Latin idiom than *nomen dico*.

[431] Cf. above, fn. 12 and §146.

[432] Cf. fn. 416.

[433] This is evidently Conington's view; cf. fn. 430. It is also supported by Livy 1.1.11 stirpis virilis, cui Ascanium parentes dixere nomen.

[434] This is the type of accusative that according to Delbrück (*Grund.* 3.388) may be, and according to Kieckers (*IF* 30.361) must be, an inner object; cf. above, fnn. 13 and 37. I view it as an appositive with the direct object *hominem* when the latter is present; when, as here, *hominem* is not present, being provided by the preceding clause (see fn. 431), then *nomen* of course takes its place as direct object, but it does not differ fundamentally from *hominem*, of which it represents a part, and I therefore would not differentiate the two by calling *hominem* an outer, and *nomen* an inner, object.

[435] Plautus, *As.* 780 nomen nominet, and Terence, *Phorm.* 739 meum nomen nominat, are quite different, not only for the reason pointed out by Delbrück (*Grund.* 3.382) with reference to the Terence passage, namely, that there is no second accusative present, but also because *nomino* here means 'rufen', not 'nennen' (cf. above, fn. 61, and, specifically in regard to Early Latin, fn. 391).

[436] This corresponds closely to the Greek *onoma tithêmi*: the verbs even come from the same root (cf. fn. 39).

[437] See §149 for Vergil, and §143 for Plautus.

[438] See §146 for Vergil, and §141 for Plautus.

hominem nomen Iulium nominant (on which see §§13 and 118 and fn. 35),
I know of nothing like it in Latin[439] until Marcus Aurelius, who wrote
in a letter to his tutor (Fronto 2.11): *arborem multorum ramorum,
quam ille suum nomen catachannam nominabat.* (Delbrück, *Grund.*
3.381–82, wrongly ascribes this to Fronto.) Of course Marcus Aurelius,
like Vergil, was steeped in Greek literature; but whether his employment of the locution is also a Grecism one can hardly say.

157. In Vergil as in Homer, the use of *genus* is so close to that of
nomen[440] that it too must be studied. Vergil employs the two as
parallels in 5.621 *cui genus et quondam nomen natique fuissent*, 10.149
et regi memorat nomenque genusque,[441] and 12.515 *nomen Echionium
matrisque genus Peridiae*;[442] cf. too 12.529–30 *avorum antiqua
sonantem nomina per regesque actum genus omne Latinos*,[443] and
12.225–26 *cui genus a proavis ingens clarumque paternae nomen erat
virtutis*, where, however, as already noted (§152), *nomen* is used in the
sense of 'fame' rather than of 'name'. Note also their juxtaposition in
Georg. 2.240 *nec Baccho genus aut pomis sua nomina servat* and 5.621
cui genus et nomen natique fuissent; the reference to a *nomen* as descended from a *genus* in 5.117 *Mnestheus, genus a quo nomine
Memmi*;[444] and the use of *nomen* in 10.618 *ille tamen nostra deducit
origine nomen*, where, as Conington says ad loc., it seems to have the

[439] Is Delbrück's view that 'name' as an accusative of specification developed from its
use as an inner object favored by the fact that Greek possessed both and Latin neither?
However, in refutation of this suggestion it may be pointed out that partitive apposition
is also much commoner in early Greek than in early Latin; contrast my findings for
Greek (*TAPA* 85.200–239; on the accusative alone, 219–39) with those for Latin (*TAPA*
84.99–103, 105–7; on the accusative specifically, 101–3), and see also my discussion of the
origin of the "Greek accusative" in Latin (*TAPA* 91.221–38, especially 227).

[440] Cf. above, §§125–28; also fn. 28. Note too Horace's use of *genus* in the mock-epic
passage *Serm.* 2.5.62–63 *iuvenis ab alto demissum genus Aenea*, corresponding to
Vergil's use of *nomen* in *Aen.* 1.288 *Iulius, a magno demissum nomen Iulo.* The former
sounds like a parody of the latter, but the publication of the second book of *Satires*
antedates by a year the beginning of composition of the *Aeneid*, so we must simply
conclude that the two poets are following the same formula, one in jest and one in
earnest.

[441] Cf. for a similar combination of ideas 11.249 *nomen patriamque docemus.*

[442] Discussed in detail below, §159.

[443] Here the use of the plural *nomina* (for which cf. *Georg.* 1.137, discussed in §149)
changes the pattern somewhat, since it involves a reference not to the individual's own
name but to the names of his ancestors. The coordination of *avorum nomina* with the
preceding *atavos* has already been treated (§155).

[444] I am assuming that *quo* and *nomine* belong together. Cf. above, fn. 422.

sense of *genus*. We also find, at the outset of an impressive passage that naturally stresses the two ideas of name and race, *nomen* balancing *gens*, which is used as a synonym of *genus* (just as in Homer *geneê* is used as a synonym for *genos*, as noted in §129), and likewise *proles*, in 6.756–58 Dardaniam prolem quae deinde sequatur gloria, qui maneant Itala de gente nepotes, inlustris animas nostrumque in nomen ituras. Here Anchises seems to be emphasizing the two-fold origin of the Romans by his use on the one hand of *Dardaniam prolem*, echoed by *nostrumque in nomen*, and on the other hand of *Itala de gente*; and Servius may well be right in his statement that *nomen* here is used in the sense of *gens* (he compares its use in 12.515, but here I think he is wrong; see §159). The same collocation of ideas recurs directly afterward, referring to a specific individual instead of to the whole group, in 762–63 Italo commixtus sanguine surget, Silvius, Albanum nomen, tua postuma proles; and we may also note 766 genus, 768 nomine, 784 felix prole virum (balanced by 786 laeta deum partu), 788 gentem, 789–90 Iuli progenies, and, as the grand climax, 792 Augustus Caesar, divi genus, where the syntactic construction employed in the reference to the last of the line of Aeneas' descendants echoes that employed in the reference to the first, 763 Silvius, Albanum genus. (On this appositional use, see §151 for *nomen*, and §158 for *genus*.)

158. Probably to an even greater extent than Homer, [445] Vergil uses *genus* to refer to individuals: a group, as in 5.45 Dardanidae magni genus alto a sanguine divom; and, oftener, an individual, as in the similar verse, 6.500 Deiphobe armipotens, genus alto a sanguine Teucri. [446] In both of these passages, *genus* might be thought to be an accusative of specification; [447] but it cannot be anything but a nominative or vocative appositive in 8.51 Arcades his oris, genus a Pallante profectum (of a group) and 7.213 rex, genus egregium Fauni (of an individual, Latinus); and even more clearly *genus* stands for *filius* in 7.556 egregium Veneris genus et rex ipse Latinus, where *egregium Veneris genus* (of Aeneas) is not even an appositive, but is subject of the verb (*celebrent*, in 555) and coordinate with *rex ipse Latinus*. Other

[445] See fn. 337.
[446] But in 4.230–31 genus alto a sanguine Teucri proderet, *genus* stands for the race, as indeed seems more natural with the prepositional *a* phrase.
[447] Cf. Conington on 6.500; also see above, §148.

examples are: of a group, 6.580 genus antiquum Terrae, Titania pubes, and 9.603 durum a stirpe genus natos; of two persons (twins), 12.198 Latonaeque genus duplex; of an individual, 4.12 credo equidem genus esse deorum (of Aeneas), 6.25-26 mixtumque genus prolesque biformis Minotaurus, 6.792 Augustus Caesar, divi genus, 6.839 ipsumque Aeaciden, genus armipotentis Achilli, and 12.127 genus Assaraci Mnestheus. (We may also note the similar use of *gens* in 10.228-29 deum gens, Aenea.)

159. Conington classes with these examples of *genus* (of which he singles out 7.213 as a specimen) 12.515, a line which it is now time to take up in its entirety.[448] The whole passage runs thus: 12.513-15 neci maestum mittit Oniten, nomen Echionium matrisque genus Peridiae. Servius offers two explanations for *nomen Echionium*. The first interprets *nomen* in the sense of *gloria* (as Servius also takes it, doubtless rightly, in 2.89, already referred to in §152), and *nomen Echionium* as equivalent to *Thebana gloria*, on the ground that Onites' ancestry may be traced back to Echion, king of Thebes (reputed to be one of the heroes who sprang from the dragon's teeth sowed by Cadmus); this is to attribute to our poet an Alexandrian obscurity worthy of Propertius but unworthy of Vergil.[449] The second explanation (which, however, according to Thilo does not belong to the genuine Servius) suggests that Vergil uses *nomen* in the sense of *genus*, "ut ostendatur eum Echionis esse et Peridiae filium vel ab Echione genus ducentem"; but that is precisely what I think he does not do. Conington's explanation is banal in the extreme: if *nomen* is used as in 6.763 Silvius, Albanum nomen, and *genus* as in 7.213 rex, genus egregium Fauni,[450] the passage means 'Onites, an Echionian name[451] and son of his mother Peridia', and seems possessed of neither point nor poetry. On the contrary, I

[448] For an earlier reference, see §148.

[449] Since Echion was the father of Pentheus, the man of sorrow (cf. Euripides, *Bacch.* 367), it might be suggested as the crowning bit of Alexandrianism that this accounts for the epithet *maestus* of Onites!

[450] On these respectively, see §151 and §158.

[451] If this really is the meaning, we have an example of the shift of the substantive *Iulius* (here a third declension form *Echion*) to an adjective in agreement with *nomen*, like that seen in *Tarquinio nomine* as interpreted by Gellius in 15.29 (see §163). But the parallelism is not complete, for the man to whom Gellius refers was really named Tarquinius (Lucius Tarquinius), whereas Onites presumably had only one name, Onites, and so was not named Onites Echion or Onites Echionius.

would take both *nomen* and *genus* as accusatives of specification;[452] they must, I think, be strictly parallel,[453] but not, as Servius makes them, synonymous. My suggestion is that *nomen* here is used like *epiklêsin* in Homer, *Il.* 16.177 (quoted and discussed above in §121). Echion (presumably another Echion, not Agave's husband) was merely Onites' putative father, as Borus in the Greek passage was Menestheus'; hence Onites' *genus* can be traced only to his mother.[454] Conington says, "we have no clue to the reason why Onites is called 'maestus'"; if being 'sent to death' by Aeneas is not reason enough (and probably it is not, since three other warriors are recorded in the preceding line as meeting the same fate, and there is no indication of sadness on *their* part), perhaps the reason may be sought in his illegitimacy. The

[452] Like the corresponding accusatives in the Greek parallel cited by Conington, Apollonius Rhodius 1.202–3

σὺν δὲ Πυλαιμόνιος Λέρνου πάις Ὠλενίοιο,
Λέρνου ἐπίκλησιν, γενεήν γε μὲν Ἡφαίστοιο.

But the parallelism lies only in general form; there is no likeness between descent from Hephaestus and from Peridia!

[453] Cf. above, §157.

[454] Otherwise there seems no point in mentioning the name of the warrior's mother—a detail hardly ever given by Vergil, as Conington notes. Conington suggests that there might be a reason for referring to her if (with Ribbeck) we accept Peerlkamp's transposition of lines 515 and 516, for this would make Peridia the mother of the 'brothers from Lycia', and Lycians (according to Herodotus 1.173) are named after their mothers, not their fathers. But line 515 does not assign Peridia's *name* to the Lycian brothers; the name is Echionian. Peerlkamp evidently thinks this name fits the Lycian brothers, who are fighting on Aeneas' side (cf. 516), better than it does Onites, who is fighting against Aeneas (cf. 513–14), for he says, "sic *Echionium* et *Peridia* fiunt Graeca, seu Asiatica". But Greek and Asiatic are by no means synonymous! If *Echionium* is to be interpreted as Theban, it does not fit the Lycian brothers any better than it does Onites; the Lycians were allies of the Trojans (*Il.* 2.876–77) but the men from Hyperthebe (a name variously explained, but doubtless in some way connected with Thebes) were of course their enemies (*Il.* 2.505), and would hardly have become Aeneas' allies (the Arcadians' friendliness was surely exceptional). Furthermore, if Forbiger is right in identifying these brothers with Clarus and Thaemon of 10.126, then, since these are termed *germani Sarpedonis ambo* 'both (full) brothers of Sarpedon' (10.125), they must be the children of Zeus and Laodamia (cf. *Il.* 6.198–99), unless Vergil is nodding; but of course Forbiger's identification is not certain. The main argument against the transposition is that, in my opinion, it results in impossible syntax. I cannot follow Peerlkamp in his comment, "*Nomen* et *genus* melius dantur *fratribus* quam uni." In combination with *Oniten, nomen* might be an appositive, and *Echionium* an adjective modifying it, or (as I believe) *Echionium* might be an appositive, and *nomen* an accusative of specification; but in combination with *fratres*, neither is possible (*nomen* can be *only* an accusative of specification, but would we not need *Echionios* instead of *Echionium?*).

passage would then mean 'sad Onites, an Echionian in name (only), and of his mother Peridia[455] [i.e. son of his mother Peridia, sprung from his mother Peridia] in descent'. The meaning would be equally well conveyed if we read *nomine*, but *nomen* seems to me far preferable as a parallel for *genus*. I have already admitted that the only other Vergilian examples of *nomen* as an accusative of specification are also doubtful,[456] but for *genus* as an accusative of specification there are three practically positive instances: 5.285 Cressa genus, 8.114 qui genus?, 12.25 nec genus indecores.[457]

160. It is rather interesting to note that in Vergil as in Homer,[458] 'name' as an accusative of specification is not certain but 'race' probably is. However, all this is significant merely in revealing to us how Vergil understood Homer's constructions, but not perhaps in revealing what Homer's constructions really were, and still less in revealing what the originals of Homer's constructions really were.

161. There remain to be noted three Latin passages, two from Ovid and one from Gellius, which perhaps have a bearing—extremely slight, to be sure—on the question whether Sanskrit *dhenu* and Hittite HUL-*lu*, *Ullakummi*, etc., are stem-forms or adjectives in agreement with 'name'.[459] The passages from Ovid perhaps favor the first theory, and the one from Gellius the second.

162. The first passage, Ovid, *Met.* 1.168–69, runs as follows: est via sublimis, caelo manifesta sereno; lactea nomen habet, candore notabilis ipso. It is possible that the nominative *lactea* is here used as an indeclinable form designating a word as a word;[460] a modern writer might mark it off as such by the use of quotes or italics.[461] However, it cer-

---

[455] This use of the genitive may seem rather awkward, but we have Greek parallels, *Od.* 4.63 (see §126 and fn. 342) and *Argonautica* 1.203 (see fn. 452).

[456] See above, §§148 and 156.

[457] To be sure, even these instances of *genus might* conceivably be classed as nominatives in partitive apposition. If they really are such, we may compare with the second and third respectively the combination in Sanskrit of *nāma* with an interrogative in *Br.* 11.5.4.1 (see §45), and the combination in Greek of *onoma* with a plural in *Theogony* 144 (see §133). However, by Vergil's time such a usage seems extremely unlikely.

[458] Cf. fn. 364.

[459] Cf. above, §17 and fn. 53.

[460] There is a possibility, but a very remote one, that *Albula* and *Mantua* are similarly used by Vergil in *Aen.* 8.332 amisit vetus Albula nomen and 10.200 matris dedit tibi Mantua nomen; see fn. 417, and, on the construction in general, the so-called *nominativus tituli*, fn. 205.

[461] We may perhaps compare Propertius 1.18.31 resonant mihi Cynthia silvae (in contrast to Vergil, *Ecl.* 1.5 resonare doces Amaryllida silvas, already referred to in fn.

tainly remains a case-form rather than a stem-form; it is questionable whether the latter can have an independent existence.⁴⁶² Besides, there is a quite different way, and possibly a better one, of accounting for the nominative here; it may be the result of attraction, like the dative in the type *homini Iulio nomen est*.⁴⁶³ In that case Latin (at least Ovidian Latin) possesses also the type *homo nomen Iulius habet*, just as Sanskrit does.⁴⁶⁴ But I admit that this explanation is rendered less·likely by the second example from Ovid, *Met.* 15.96 aetas cui fecimus aurea no-men.⁴⁶⁵ Here the only explanation is that *aurea* is used as an inde-clinable; for were attraction at work, we would have had not *aurea* but *aureae*.

163. The remaining passage⁴⁶⁶ is Gellius 15.29, and runs as follows: duae istae in loquendo figurae notae satis usitataeque sunt: *mihi nomen est Iulius* et *mihi nomen est Iulio*; tertiam figuram novam hercle repperi apud Pisonem in secundo annalium. verba Pisonis haec sunt: L. Tarquinium, collegam suum, quia Tarquinio nomine esset, metuere; eumque orat, uti sua voluntate Roma concedat. Gellius then concludes (with reference to the words *Tarquinio nomine esset*): hoc proinde est, tamquam si ego dicam: *mihi nomen est Iulium*. If Gellius is right, Piso's *Tarquinio nomine* forms a close parallel, and his own *nomen Iulium* a closer one, for the Hittite *Sintalimeni* as an adjective in *KUB* 33.121.1.5 SAL-*as* SUM-*se-it Si-in-ta-li-me-ni* etc. (cited above in §23; see also

---

406), and Horace, *Epis.* 1.7.37–38 rexque paterque audisti. In both these passages the nouns may be nominatives, though they may also be vocatives, like those in Horace, *Serm.* 2.6.20 Matutine pater seu Iane libentius audis (I have discussed this problem elsewhere, *CW* 22.132). With the use of *pater* in the two Horace passages just quoted, we may contrast that of *patre* in Ovid, *Met.* 10.402 Myrrha, patre audito, suspiria duxit, where the word, though used as a word, is declined (like *Amaryllida* in *Ecl.* 1.5). The point is not that Myrrha has heard her father; it is her old nurse that was just speaking to her. But she has heard the word *pater*, in the nurse's final sentence (10.401 vivunt genetrixque paterque). Cf. Schulze, *Kl. Schr.* 91 fn. 1.
⁴⁶² This seems even less likely in Latin than in Hittite (see §§31–32) or in Sanskrit (see §51). Latin compounds of the type of *calefacio* and *videlicet* have been thought to exhibit the verb stem as a separate entity, but this seems to me extremely doubtful, and I have tried to find a different explanation for them (see *TAPA* 78.301–35 and 79.308–37, respectively).
⁴⁶³ Cf. above, §17.
⁴⁶⁴ Cf. above, §17 and fnn. 49 and 186. Two possible examples from classical Greek, subject to the same reservations as the one from Ovid, are quoted in fn. 328. The usage also occurs in the *New Testament*, both Greek and Latin; examples are quoted in fn. 519.
⁴⁶⁵ Already cited, along with the previous example, in fn. 417.
⁴⁶⁶ Already referred to above, fnn. 52, 129, and 451.

§§30 and 35). But the difficulty is that any Latin *nomen* (I am using *nomen* here in the technical sense, as contrasted with the *praenomen* and the *cognomen*) is adjectival in form; and *Tarquinio* therefore may be a noun in apposition with *nomine* rather than an adjective modifying it. Gellius probably thought of *Tarquinio nomine* as an adjective and noun jointly constituting an ablative of quality; but it is possible to say that the usual ablative adjective is replaced by an ablative appositive here, just as it is by an appositional (or possibly possessive) genitive in Vergil, *Aen.* 3.350 Xanthi cognomine rivum.[467]

164. Finally, we must take cognizance of the fact that in addition to the common type *homini nomen est Iulio*, one passage has been cited as an instance of the supposed type *hominis nomen est Iulii*.[468] Thus in Harper's *Latin Dictionary*, s.v. *nomen*, we find listed a group of examples characterized as used "with *dat.*",[469] which include a number of instances already noted above as illustrative of the type *homini nomen est Iulio*;[470] and then as a parallel to them one example characterized as used "with *gen.*", and thus evidently viewed as illustrating the supposed type *hominis nomen est Iulii*. This example, which is from the

---

[467] Cf. above, fn. 411. The appositional genitive is probably commoner with *nomen* than with any other word, and in combination with *nomen* it may often be equatable, as in this passage, with a possessive genitive. Thus in 6.381 aeternumque locus Palinuri nomen habebit, the proper noun *Palinuri* is doubtless a possessive genitive just as is the common noun *avi* in 5.564 nomen avi referens Priamus; similarly in Livy 40.54.9, *sub nomine Flaminini* may mean 'under the name (actually) belonging to Flamininus'. (The true appositional genitive with *nomen* occurs for the first time, according to Krebs-Schmalz, *Antibarbarus* 2.154, in Velleius Paterculus 1.11.2 cui ex virtute Macedonici nomen inditum.) Other instances of the appositional genitive, such as *Aen.* 1.247 urbem Patavi and 7.714 flumen Himellae, cannot so readily be explained as possessives (despite Wunsch, *RhM* 69.130–33), and probably have a quite different origin. I have tried to trace them too to partitive apposition, but of a different sort (*TAPA* 84.97–98). At all events the use of this genitive with *nomen* has no bearing on constructions with *nomen* in general, though Gray does include it in his discussion thereof (*IF* 11.313).

[468] Or *Iuli* if one prefers to cite the genitive in this form.

[469] These follow some examples characterized as used "with *nom.*" in connection with the locutions *est mihi nomen*, *inditur mihi nomen*. But the use of *mihi* is inaccurate, since a dative is lacking in *Trin.* 391 (already discussed above in §142), and is replaced by a genitive in *Gen.* 24.62 (the passage from the Vulgate with which the present paragraph is primarily concerned).

[470] Namely, *Rud.* 5, *Cist.* 154, and *Trin.* 391 (on which see fn. 469), all cited in §142; *Men.* 77, cited in §143; and *Trin.* 843, cited in fn. 399. However, *Men.* 263, which belongs with *Men.* 77 and is cited with it above, §143, is listed elsewhere by the dictionary.

Vulgate, is given as *Gen.* 25.11 cuius nomen est Viventis, but 25.11[471] is an error for 24.62. Nor is the citation apposite at all. *Viventis* does not bear the same relation to the relative *cuius* as does e.g. *Lyco* to the relative *quoi* in *Poen.* 92 quoi Lyco nomen siet.[472] The entire passage runs as follows: deambulabat Isaac per viam quae ducit ad puteum cuius nomen est Viventis-et-Videntis. The name of the man mentioned in *Poen.* 92 was *Lycus*, but the name of the well was not *Vivens-et-Videns*, which after all would not make much sense, but *Viventis-et-Videntis*— in complete form *Puteum Viventis-et-Videntis*,[473] as is made perfectly clear by *Gen.* 16.14 appellavit puteum illum Puteum Viventis-et-Videntis-Me. The genitive recurs in *Gen.* 25.11 habitabat iuxta puteum nomine Viventis-et-Videntis, where it is clearly *not* to be considered, as some might suggest, appositional. The *me* which is present only in 16.14 really is needed in all three passages, both to make complete sense and to do justice to the original Hebrew.[474]

[471] 25.11, which is quoted just below, is quite different.

[472] Likewise listed above in §142, and cited here rather than one of the similar examples in the dictionary because of the close parallelism in construction with the passage from *Gen.*

[473] We have a similar ellipsis elsewhere in the Vulgate, in *Lk.* 19.29 ad montem qui vocatur Oliveti (discussed below in fn. 498), and much the same in *Lk.* 21.37 and *Acts* 1.12 (all discussed below in fn. 498).

[474] The Hebrew reading of these three passages offers no certain clue as to the constructions of the Latin versions. We have in all three Be'er La-hai-roi, literally 'the well to the living one who sees me', the name of the well consisting not of a genitive as in the Latin, but of a prepositional phrase, la 'to the' plus a dative. The words *cuius nomen est* in 24.62 and *nomine* in 25.11 correspond to nothing in the Hebrew. (I owe this information to the courtesy of Dr. Harry Blumberg, Professor of Hebrew at Hunter College; I myself unfortunately have no knowledge of Hebrew.) The King James Version is much closer than the Vulgate to the construction of the original Hebrew, and it actually retains the Hebrew name of the well, rendering 16.14 "the well was called Be'er-la-hai-roi", glossed by note *f* "i.e. *the well of him that liveth and seeth me*"; 24.62 "the way of the well La-hai-roi"; 25.11 "by the well La-hai-roi". (In citing the Hebrew, I omit diacritics.) The Septuagint rendering is freest of all, and seems to me to involve an actual error (inasmuch as it in part makes Hagar do the seeing instead of the Lord). 16.13–14 runs as follows: καὶ ἐκάλεσεν Ἁγὰρ τὸ ὄνομα Κυρίου τοῦ λαλοῦντος πρὸς αὐτήν Σύ ὁ θεὸς ὁ ἐπιδών με· ὅτι εἶπεν Καὶ γὰρ ἐνώπιον ἴδον ὀφθέντα μοι. ἕνεκεν τούτου ἐκάλεσεν τὸ φρέαρ φρέαρ οὗ ἐνώπιον ἴδον. This seems to mean: 'And Hagar called the name of the Lord who spoke to her, "Thou the God who seest me"; because she said, "For I saw face to face him who appeared to me". Therefore she called the well "the well of him whom I saw face to face".' In the other two passages the well is simply, and ambiguously, called *to phrear tês horaseôs* 'the well of vision'.

V. GERMANIC

165. In Germanic[475] there seems to be hardly any evidence for the accusative of specification in general, and none at all for our special 'in name' construction in particular. The various works on Germanic syntax that I have examined,[476] with two exceptions,[477] make no

[475] It is customary, probably for historical and/or geographical reasons, to list Germanic after Celtic, but I am departing from the usual order because on the whole the Germanic documents that I am dealing with are older than the Celtic: that is, the earliest Germanic material is doubtless earlier than the earliest Celtic, and the latest Celtic material is doubtless later than the latest Germanic. Incidentally, since considerable attention is paid in this chapter to the Greek and Latin versions of the Bible, it is perhaps convenient to have it directly follow the chapters on Greek and Latin.

[476] However, there seems a woeful paucity of publications on syntax in Germanic, amazing to the classicist accustomed to working with such *magna opera* on Greek and Latin syntax as those of Schwyzer and of Hofmann and Szantyr, not to speak of all the special studies in the field. To mention but one example, the stimulating *Comp. Germanic Gram.* of Prokosch ignores syntax completely.

[477] The exceptions are the Gothic grammars of Bernhardt and Wright (strangely, Streitberg in his admirable *Gotisches Elementarbuch*, which by its thoroughness belies its name, ignores the construction altogether). Bernhardt (*Got. Gr.* 78) says, "Der accusativ der näheren bestimmung findet sich im Gotischen äusserst selten"; and Wright (*Gr. Goth.* 182) translates him word for word, though without giving him credit, "An accusative of closer definition occurs very rarely in Gothic". Both cite two instances, *Jn.* 11.44 gabundans handuns jah fotuns faskjam, and *Eph.* 6.14 ufgaurdanai hupins izwarans sunjai, which Wright translates respectively, "bound as to hands and feet with bandages" and "girt as to your loins with truth". These are close renderings of the Greek, *Jn.* 11.44 δεδεμένος τοὺς πόδας καὶ τὰς χεῖρας κειρίαις and *Eph.* 6.14 περιζω-σάμενοι τὴν ὀσφὺν ὑμῶν ἐν ἀληθείᾳ. Bernhardt suggests that possibly it was the presence of a dative in each instance, *faskjam* (representing *keiriais*) and *sunjai* (representing *en aletheiai*), that led Wulfila to employ the accusative instead of a second dative for the body-part involved. In this connection it is worth comparing with the second example (*Eph.* 6.14) the following passage (6.15), which is parallel to it, jah gaskohai fotum in manwithai aiwaggeljons gawairthjis, literally 'and shod as to feet in the preparation of the gospel of peace'. This represents the Greek ὑποδησάμενοι τοὺς πόδας ἐν ἑτοιμασίᾳ τοῦ εὐαγγελίου τῆς εἰρήνης. In this case Wulfila does not use a simple dative like *sunjai*, but a dative introduced by a preposition, *in manwithai*, to render the Greek prepositional phrase *en hetoimasiai*; and perhaps it is because of this that he employs the more natural Gothic dative, *fotum*, as a substitute for the Greek accusative *tous podas*. It is interesting to note that in all three passages the Vulgate follows the Greek exactly and employs the

accusative, though this is certainly not a natural construction for Jerome (cf. below, §182): *Jn.* 11.44 ligatus pedes et manus institis, *Eph.* 6.14 succincti lumbos vestros in veritate, 6.15 et calceati pedes in praeparatione Evangelii pacis. It is also interesting to note that on the other hand none of the OE translations of the Vulgate that I have examined (cf. below, §192) preserves the accusative. The Northumbrian version uses the dative singular: the Lindisfarne MS has gebundeno foet & hond, and the later Rushworth MS, which in its rendering of *Jn.* is modeled on the Lindisfarne, has gibundenne foet & honda (*honda* rather than *hond* is the form one would expect; but see Sievers, *OEGr.* 153, Wright, *OEGr.* 187). The West Saxon version uses the dative plural, gebunden handan & fotan (on -*an* for -*um* in the West Saxon dative plural, see Sievers 130). This substitution of the dative of specification for the accusative of specification would seem to indicate that the latter construction was entirely lacking in OE; perhaps it was lacking in natural Gothic too, and Wulfila's employment of it may be a bit of what may be called "translation Gothic" after the "translation English" all too familiar to the teacher of Latin.

In *Eph.* 6.14 there is a third phrase coordinated with the two just discussed, ἐνδυσάμενοι τὸν θώρακα τῆς δικαιοσύνης. Jerome and Wulfila deal with *thôraka* just as they do with *osphyn*; the former uses an accusative, induti loricam iustitiae; and the latter uses a dative, gapaidodai brunjon garaihteins. But *thôraka* and *loricam* are not accusatives of specification, they are direct objects. In Greek, verbs of clothing, like those of asking, teaching, etc., take two accusatives in the active, one of the person and the other of the thing, as in Homer, *Od.* 21.339 ἔσσω μιν χλαῖνάν τε χιτῶνά τε, εἵματα καλά (see Schwyzer, *Gr. Gr.* 2.83); in the middle, which is equivalent to an active verb plus a reflexive object, they naturally take the accusative of the thing. In Latin, which uses the double accusative much more sparingly than does Greek (as already noted in §47), they can in the active take the accusative of the person and the ablative (means) of the thing (regularly an article of raiment or armament), as in Livy 44.41.9 induissent se hastis 'they would have equipped themselves with spears', or, once more with the middle substituted for the active plus the reflexive, Vergil, *Aen.* 12.947 spoliis indute. But, by a sort of hypallage, these verbs can also take the accusative of the thing, as Plautus, *Cas.* 695 loricam induam 'that I don a breastplate'. Since donning is an act performed for one's own benefit, it is not surprising that the middle may be used instead of the active: Vergil has both galeam induit (9.365–66) and galeam induitur (2.392–93). The construction seen in the variant galeam induitur is surely a native Italic one; we meet it in Umbrian also (Buck, *OU* 199). It is especially common with the past passive participle, with which it occurs at all periods: e.g., Plautus, *Men.* 511–12 te indutum pallam, Vergil, *Aen.* 11.487 thoraca indutus, Jerome, *Eph.* 6.14 induti loricam. The locution *vestem induor* or *indutus* is in my opinion completely different from the Grecism *corpus induor* or *indutus*, with which a number of scholars have sought to equate it; I discuss this question in detail in *TAPA* 91.224–32.

Elsewhere, in the comparatively few instances in which Wulfila found an accusative of specification in the Greek, he substituted a dative for it, just as he did for *tous podas* in *Eph.* 6.15. This happens in *Mk.* 8.36 ἐὰν ζημιωθῇ τὴν ψυχὴν αὐτοῦ (another reading exists, with a passive infinitive instead of a conditional clause; but that does not affect the point under discussion here), *Lk.* 4.18 τοὺς συντετριμμένους τὴν καρδίαν (a phrase missing in some versions), 1 *Tim.* 6.5 διεφθαρμένων ἀνθρώπων τὸν νοῦν, and the very similar 2 *Tim.* 3.8 ἄνθρωποι κατεφθαρμένοι τὸν νοῦν (all cited by Bernhardt, *Got. Gr.* 78). Wulfila's renderings of these are as follows: *Mk.* 8.36 gasleitheith sik saiwalai seinai (with the Greek passive rendered by the active plus the accusative of the reflexive), *Lk.* 4.18 thans gamalwidans hairtin, 1 *Tim.* 6.5 frawardidaize manne ahin, 2 *Tim.* 3.8

mention of such a construction, and the Germanic scholars whom I have consulted personally deny its existence. There would be little reason for devoting a chapter to this language group were it not for the fact that a supposed example (not of the accusative of specification but) of the type *homo nomen Iulius* has been cited for Old English by one scholar[478] and quoted from him by others.[479] This is *Beowulf* 1457 waes thaem haeft-mece Hrunting nama, translated by Gray "war ihm ein Heftschwert, 'Hrunting' sein Name".[480] If West Germanic actually exhibited either an appositional nominative (or accusative) of the sort,[481] or a fully developed accusative of specification, the evidence would be of infinite value, since in this language group our word for 'name' has shifted from the neuter to the masculine, hence we can unfailingly distinguish a nominative from an accusative.[482] In view of Gray's testimony, it may be worth while to test out first some branches of Germanic in general, and then the specific Old English work, *Beowulf*, from which Gray's example is taken.

166. I have decided to make my test of Germanic by examining (1)

---

mannans frawaurthanai ahin—his datives being *sailwalai, hairtin, ahin, ahin*. The Vulgate uses a quite different tournure in *Mk.* 8.36 (si detrimentum animae suae faciat), and an ablative in each of the others (sanare contritos corde, hominum mente corruptorum, homines corrupti mente); but in one passage not extant in Wulfila, it does keep the accusative: this is *Hebr.* 10.22 ἐρραντισμένοι τὰς καρδίας καὶ λελουμένοι τὸ σῶμα, rendered in Latin aspersi corda et abluti corpus. The Old English translations of the Gospels afford us no help: in *Mk.* 8.36 they of course adhere to the aberrant rendering of the Vulgate, and in *Lk.* 4.18 they omit altogether the relevant Latin phrase *sanare contritos corde*. (Does this omission, which may reflect the similar omission, already noted, of the corresponding Greek phrase in some versions of the original, suggest that a version of the Vulgate slightly variant from ours may have been used by *both* N and *W*? Cf. fn. 589.)

[478] Gray, *IF* 11.309 (1900). Cf. above, fn. 7, and below, §§207-21.

[479] Foy, *IF* 12.178 (1901); Brugmann, *IF* 27.144 (1910). Cf. further, Humbach, *MSS* 5.91 (1954), who writes as if he were dealing with a commonplace, and Schmidt, *ZCP* 28.230 (1961). See below, §222, and fnn. 698-702.

[480] *IF* 11.309 fn. 478.

[481] Whether one interprets it as I do, with *nomen* viewed as an appositive (partitive) of *homo*, or, as Gray does, with *nomen* viewed as an appositive of *Iulius* (see fn. 19), does not affect the case.

[482] For this very reason, however, we would not expect to find an accusative of specification 'in name' in these languages, if I am right in my explanation of such an accusative as not inherited from Indo-European but derived independently, from a misunderstood nominative-accusative appositive, in such groups as used it.

all extant remains of Gothic, which consists almost exclusively of remnants of Wulfila's translation of the *New Testament*; (2) three translations, into different dialects of Old English, of the Gospels in the Vulgate edition. Since the *NT* abounds in instances of the locution 'in name', it seems as if we might expect this to appear as an accusative of specification somewhere in the course of these renderings into Germanic languages if the construction existed in any of them. It may be argued that the value or validity of this test is lessened by the extreme rarity of the accusative of specification meaning 'in name' in the Greek original, and its complete absence in the Latin version. Yet it is probably significant that in the one possible instance of the construction whch Wulfila met, he perhaps did not recognize it as an accusative, and he certainly did not render it as one,[483] though usually[484] he seems to have followed the Greek syntax with a slavish literalness reminiscent of a college freshman. As for the Old English translators, they show a fair amount of variation in their idiom both from their original and from one another, so we may conclude that had an accusative of specification been natural to one or the other of them, he might well have used it. Quite apart from the question of the accusative of specification, a study of naming constructions in the *NT*, and of the manner in which Jerome and Wulfila dealt with them, and in which three Old English writers dealt in turn with Jerome, may be not without interest for its own sake.

167. As a preliminary to treatment of the Gothic and Old English translations, it may be desirable rapidly to consider the constructions

---

[483] See below, §§183 and 191. Cf. Streitberg, *Got. El.* 161–62: "Es muss in jedem Falle untersucht werden, was als *unmittelbare Nachahmung* des griech. Textes zu gelten habe und was beanspruchen könne, als *echt germanisch* betrachtet zu werden. Von besonderer Bedeutung für die Entscheidung dieser Grundfrage sind jene Fälle, *wo die gotische Konstruktion in irgendeinem Punkte von der griechischen abweicht. Denn allein diese Abweichungen* geben uns den Schlüssel zum Vertständnis der wahren gotischen Syntax."

[484] To be sure, not invariably. We shall see below some passages in which Wulfila definitely departs from the construction of the Greek. Real changes in sentence structure are noted in the following passages: *Mt.* 27.57 probably (§§183 and 189); *Mk.* 5.9 (§188), 8.36 (fn. 477); *Lk.* 1.5 (§189), 1.26 (§187), 1.62 (§172), 4.18 (fn. 477), 8.30 (§188), 16.20 (§181), 19.29 (§172); *Jn.* 18.10 (§188); *Eph.* 6.14 (fn. 477) 6.15 (fn. 477); 1 *Tim.* 6.5 (fn. 477), 2 *Tim.* 3.8 (fn. 477). There are also slight changes in the following passages: *Mt.* 9.9 (§172); *Mk.* 3.16 (§175), 11.1 (fn. 498); *Lk.* 1.5 (§181), 1.27 (§187), 2.25 (§187), 6.15 (§172), 8.41 (§187), 19.29 (fn. 498); *Eph.* 1.21 (§ 174).

employed by the Greek and Latin originals[485] which they were
reproducing.[486]

[485] Obviously, the only reason for citing the language of the Greek *NT* and of the
Latin translation is their bearing on subsequent Germanic versions. It goes without
saying that *koine* Greek and the Latin of the Vulgate can have practically no value as
revealing either inheritance from Indo-European or natural native development within
Greek and Latin.

[486] For the convenience of the printer, here as in Chapter III (cf. fn. 296), I am translit-
erating isolated Greek words, except in fn. 498, where the APA method of transliter-
ating cannot make the necessary distinction between ἐλαιῶν and ἐλαιών.

A. GOTHIC

168. The Greek accusative of specification, which always "com-peted" with the dative,[487] had been practically ousted by the latter in Hellenistic times.[488] As for the particular type of accusative of specifi-cation 'in name', we shall look in vain for either of the two main types to which I believe it owes its origin, (est) *homo nomen Iulius*[489] and *puerum nomen Iulium*[490] *nominant.*[491] The former perhaps appears in the variation *homo in Italia incolit nomen Iulius,*[492] the latter not at all.

169. In relation to this latter construction, we may note that with a verb meaning *nomino,*[493] Biblical Greek uses two accusatives but never

---

[487] The two may serve as equivalents as early as Homer (cf. *Il.* 3.194 and 3.227); but the very strong tendency there to use the dative in combination with a dative of refer-ence, and the accusative in combination with a direct object, indicates that they are rather employed in partitive apposition than as independent expressions of specification. I have pointed out and illustrated the phenomenon in *TAPA* 85.219 and 226, also fnn. 67, 105, 111, 210, 231.

[488] Cf. Schwyzer, *Gr. Gr.* 2.86 and 168. We do find adverbial accusatives in the *NT*, such as *tên archên* or *ton arithmon*; see on these Buttmann 153. And even the general type is not wholly lacking: cf. the nine examples cited in fn. 477. Those who distinguish between the accusative of specification and the direct object of the middle voice (which I do not; cf. *TAPA* 85.198 and fn. 4) may class as examples of the latter the two parallel instances in *Eph.* 6 (14 and 15) and the two almost identical ones in 1 and 2 *Tim.* (6.5 and 3.8), as well as the two coordinate instances in *Hebr.* 10.22 and perhaps even the one in *Lk.* 4.18 (if the reading is accepted); but certainly the infinitive in *Mk.* 8.36 and the participle in *Jn.* 11.44 must be passive, and therefore the accusatives cannot be objects.

[489] In dealing with the nouns corresponding to *Iulius* and *Iulium*, I am somewhat hampered by the fact that the Semitic names are usually indeclinables in Greek, Latin, and Germanic; but I am assuming that their case is what the context manifestly demands. Cf. below, fnn. 494, 519, 620. The case of the indeclinable form may sometimes be pointed up by the use of the definite article (cf. fn. 551). On the other hand some occur-rences of the nominative where we would expect another case may be explained as the use not of an undeclined form but of a so-called "nominativus tituli" (see fnn. 497 and 519).

[490] Cf. fn. 489.

[491] Cf. above, §§4 and 13; also, for Greek specifically, §§117–18.

[492] Cf. above, §8, and below, §182.

[493] The verb is in the Greek version of the Bible almost always *kaleô*, in the Vulgate almost always *voco*, in Wulfila almost always *haitan*. We may note some exceptions: with *legô* and *dico* in *Rev.* 8.11 (on this see fn. 514); with *onomazô, nomino* or *cognomino*, and *namnjan, Lk.* 6.13 and 14, in both of which the sense is 'bestow a name', and in *Eph.* 1.21 in combination with the cognate noun (on this see fn. 516). The participle 'called' may be either (a) *kaloumenos* (as in *Lk.* 6.15, 19.2, *Acts* 9.11, 10.1) or (b) *legomenos* (as in

three; it can say either (a) *puerum Iulium nominaverunt* or (b) *nomen Iulium nominaverunt*, but in (a) it occasionally replaces the accusative *nomen* by a dative of specification, or, far more commonly, omits anything of the sort altogether, and in (b) it replaces the accusative *puerum* by a genitive of possession.

170. As for (a) in the active, I can cite *Mt.* 10.25 τὸν οἰκοδεσπότην Βεελζεβούβ[494] ἐπεκάλεσαν,[495] *Lk.* 1.59 ἐκάλουν αὐτὸ [= τὸ παιδίον] ἐπὶ τῷ ὀνόματι[496] τοῦ πατρὸς αὐτοῦ Ζαχαρίαν, 6.13 ἀπ᾽ αὐτῶν δώδεκα, οὓς καὶ ἀποστόλους ὠνόμασε, 6.14 Σίμωνα, ὃν καὶ ὠνόμασε Πέτρον.[497] There are numerous examples in the corresponding passive: with finite verbs, *Mt.* 2.23 Ναζαραῖος κληθήσεται, 27.8 ἐκλήθη ὁ ἀγρὸς ἐκεῖνος Ἀγρὸς αἵματος, *Lk.* 1.32 υἱὸς ὑψίστου κληθήσεται, 1.60 κληθήσεται Ἰωάννης, 2.4 εἰς πόλιν Δαβίδ, ἥτις καλεῖται Βηθλεέμ, *Jn.* 1.42 σύ κληθήσῃ Κηφᾶς; with the infinitive, *Lk.* 1.62 ἐνένευον δὲ τῷ πατρὶ αὐτοῦ, τὸ τί ἂν θέλοι καλεῖσθαι αὐτόν. Instances with participles abound, and I cite just a few:[498] *Mt.* 2.23

Mt. 2.23, 9.9, 10.2, 27.33, *Jn.* 20.24); Latin, which cannot render the participle literally (see below, §171), uses a finite passive form of *voco* twice for *kaloumenos* (*Lk.* 6.15, *Acts* 9.11) and once for *legomenos* (*Mt.* 2.23), and of *dico* once for *kaloumenos* (*Acts* 10.1) and three times for *legomenos* (*Mt.* 10.2, 27.33, *Jn.* 20.24), but no verb at all in *Lk.* 19.2 and *Mt.* 9.9 (on these see §171). In the three passages extant in Wulfila (*Mt.* 9.9, *Lk.* 6.15, 19.2) he as usual employs *haitan* (participle *haitans*).

494 Also read *Beelzeboul.* (Jerome has *-b*, Wulfila *-l*; see §§171 and 172 respectively.) As frequently happens (cf. fn. 489), the Hebrew (or Aramaic) noun is treated as an indeclinable, but I assume it is to be regarded as accusative, like *Zacharian* in the next example. It might also be a nominative—a *nominativus tituli* (cf. fn. 205); but this seems less likely, in view of the parallels with accusatives.

495 *Cod. Vat.* reads with the dative *tôi oikodespotêi* in place of the accusative (and similarly in the following clause, which is parallel). This if right must represent a contamination of the normal construction with the accusative *kaleô tina ti*, and *epitithêmi tini ti*, but it seems to me unlikely that it can be right, and I believe Buttmann (151) is justified in categorically rejecting it.

496 On the prepositional phrase, cf. below, fn. 499.

497 A striking variant is *hominem Iulius nominant*, seen in the *Septuagint* 1 *Sam.* 9.9 and in *Jn.* 13.13, quoted and discussed in fn. 519. Both passages exemplify the so-called "nominativus tituli", on which see fn. 205.

498 A particular problem is presented by *Lk.* 19.29 and 21.37. 19.29 is usually printed πρὸς τὸ ὄρος τὸ καλούμενον Ἐλαιῶν, and 21.37 is identical with it except that it has *eis* instead of *pros*. Those who would read *Ἐλαιῶν* as representing (τὸ ὄρος) Ἐλαιῶν. The only difficulty about this lies in the similar passages *Mk.* 11.1, *Lk.* 22.39, and *Jn.* 8.1 πρὸς [or εἰς] τὸ ὄρος τῶν Ἐλαιῶν, and *Lk.* 19.37 πρὸς τῇ καταβάσει τοῦ ὄρους τῶν Ἐλαιῶν, which suggest that we need the article *tôn* in *Lk.* 19.29 and 21.37 also. To be sure, the NT is not wholly consistent in its use of the definite article (as we shall note

again in §190); why, for instance, do we find πρὸς (εἰς) τὸ ὄρος τὸ καλούμενον in our two Lk. passages, but ἀπὸ ὄρους τοῦ καλουμένου (not apo tou orous) in Acts 1.12, a passage to be discussed just below? The alternative is to read not 'Ελαιῶν ('Olivarum') but 'Ελαιών ('Olivetum'), as, e.g., Streitberg does in Lk. 19.29 in his admirable bilingual edition of Wulfila (Got B 156). That this nominative exists is proved by the passage that has just been partially quoted in another connection, namely Acts 1.12, which runs completely ἀπὸ ὄρους τοῦ καλουμένου 'Ελαιῶνος. Here the original nominative represented by the genitive expression obviously cannot be ὄρος τὸ καλούμενον (τὸ ὄρος) 'Ελαιῶν ('Mons Olivarum, the Mount of Olives'); but the question is whether it is (a) ὄρος τὸ καλούμενον (τὸ ὄρος) 'Ελαιών ('Mons Olivetum, Mount Olivet'), 'Ελαιών being in predicate agreement with oros, or (b) ὄρος τὸ καλούμενον (τὸ ὄρος) 'Ελαιῶνος ('Mons Oliveti'), 'Ελαιῶνος being an appositional (or possessive?) genitive used predicatively. The second on the whole seems more likely. I question whether a predicate noun in the genitive of the type that would be posited by (a) is possible; and for (b) we have a perfect parallel in classical Greek, Herodotus 4.181 ἡ κρήνη καλέεται ἡλίου (already quoted in §135). Yet ὄρος 'Ελαιῶνος 'Mons Oliveti' does not correspond to either ὄρος 'Ελαιών 'Mons Olivetum, Mt. Olivet' as posited by Streitberg for Lk. 19.29 (Got B 156) and therefore presumably for 21.37, or ὄρος (τῶν) 'Ελαιῶν 'Mons Olivarum, the Mount of Olives' as perhaps met in these two passages, and certainly in Mk. 11.1, Lk. 22.39, and Jn. 8.1. Is it perhaps a contamination of the two? Furthermore, since the proper noun is presumably masculine, and therefore nominative, its use in the two Lk. passages may be deemed peculiar; here the nominative designating a name must be viewed as either coming from an indeclinable noun (which is not likely, since elsewhere this noun varies for case) or as a nominativus tituli. The same problem arises in connection with Mt. 10.25 (on which see §170 and fn. 494), Mk. 3.17 (§175 and fn. 519), and Rev. 9.11 (fn. 519), for which last, however, still a third explanation is possible and perhaps preferable (fn. 205). The NT grammarians are divided about the Lk. passages. They recognize the occasional anomalous use of the nominative in naming constructions, Winer (210) citing Jn. 13.13, and Buttmann (151) and Blass (84) adding to this Rev. 9.11 (the two, however, are not necessarily identical; see below, fn. 519). Winer (210) thinks Lk. 19.29 probably illustrates the same usage (that of nominativus tituli) as Jn. 13.13, and therefore reads 'Ελαιών, and his translators Moulton (Winer-Moulton 226 fn. 4) and Lünemann (Winer-Lünemann 182 fn. 1) seem to prefer this, though they deem 'Ελαιῶν not positively wrong; however, his later reviser Schmiedel (Winer-Schmiedel 256) considers 'Ελαιῶν equally possible. Buttmann (22) is willing to accept 'Ελαιών in the Luke passage as an indeclinable (this is not the same as a nominativus tituli; again see fn. 519), but he notes that "recent editors" have rejected this form and written 'Ελαιῶν. Blass (84), on the basis of 'Ελαιῶν in Lk. 19.37, pronounces an indeclinable 'Ελαιών "unglaublich" in Lk. 19.29 and 21.37, and not only would read 'Ελαιῶν there, but would also substitute it for 'Ελαιῶνος in Acts 1.12, which seems to me much too arbitrary. Debrunner in his revision of Blass (Blass-Debrunner 95) modifies the latter's extreme views: he too prefers 'Ελαιῶν in Lk. 19.29 and 21.37 on the basis of 19.37, but he considers 'Ελαιών possible, and he accepts 'Ελαιῶνος in Acts 1.12. Funk in his English revision of Blass-Debrunner (Blass-Funk 79) follows Debrunner absolutely. (Incidentally, Debrunner's reference, retained by Funk, to 'Ελαιῶνα in Lk. 19.29 would seem to be an error.)

The translators appear to have had their difficulties with the passages in question. Jerome is quite inconsistent. For τὸ ὄρος τῶν 'Ελαιῶν in the three similar passages Mk. 11.1, Lk. 22.39, and Jn. 8.1, he has the literal montem Olivarum in the first two, but montem Oliveti in the third, and likewise in Lk. 19.37 he has montis Oliveti; and he has montem (or monte) qui vocatur Oliveti not only in Acts 1.12, where Oliveti corresponds to

εἰς πόλιν λεγομένην Ναζαρέτ, 9.9 εἶδεν ἄνθρωπον καθήμενον ἐπὶ
τὸ τελώνιον, Ματθαῖον λεγόμενον, 10.2 Σίμων ὁ λεγόμενος Πέτρος,
27.33 εἰς τόπον λεγόμενον Γολγοθᾶ, Lk 6.15 Σίμωνα τὸν καλούμενον
Ζηλωτήν, 10.39 τῇδε ἦν ἀδελφὴ καλουμένη Μαρία, Jn. 20.24 Θωμᾶς
δέ, εἷς ἐκ τῶν δώδεκα, ὁ λεγόμενος Δίδυμος, Acts 10.1 ἐκ σπείρης
τῆς καλουμένης ᾽Ιταλικῆς. As was noted in the preceding paragraph,
the dative *onomati* may appear. I know of only one instance, Lk. 19.2
ἰδού, ἀνὴρ ὀνόματι καλούμενος Ζακχαῖος. A variant construction
employs this dative but omits the name itself; again I know of a
single instance, Lk. 1.61 οὐδείς ἐστιν ὃς καλεῖται τῷ ὀνόματι τούτῳ.
(Of course here *toutôi*, referring to the preceding *Iôannês*, replaces
the name.)

171. The Vulgate rendition follows most of these very closely:
Mt. 10.25 patrem familias Beelzebub vocaverunt, Lk. 1.59 vocabant
eum nomine [499] patris sui Zachariam, 6.13 duodecim ex ipsis, quos et
Apostolos nominavit, 6.14 Simonem, quem cognominavit Petrum;
Mt. 2.23 Nazaraeus vocabitur, 27.8 vocatus est ager ille Haceldama,
hoc est ager sanguinis, Lk. 1.32 Filius Altissimi vocabitur, 1.60 vocabitur
Ioannes, 1.62 innuebant patri eius quem [500] vellet vocari eum, 2.4 in
civitatem David, quae vocatur Bethlehem, Jn. 1.42 tu vocaberis
Cephas, and (using the ablative *nomine* to correspond to the dative
onomati) Lk. 1.61 nemo est qui vocetur hoc nomine. But where the
Greek uses the present passive participle, naturally the Latin, which

---

the Greek, but also in the two disputed Lk. passages, 19.29 and 21.37, where it does not.
(With the genitive here, we may compare his use of the genitive in Gen. 24.62 puteum
cuius nomen est Viventis et Videntis, already discussed in §164 and fn. 474). Wulfila too
probably reads ᾽Ελαιῶν in Lk. 19.29 (despite Streitberg), for in his version he renders
Lk. 19.29 and Mk. 11.1 in the same way, in both alike employing an adjective: for the
former he has *at fairgunja thatei haitada alewjo* 'ad montem qui vocatur Olivarius', and
for the latter *at fairgunja alewjin* 'ad montem Olivarium'. However, in Lk. 19.37 he
translates ᾽Ελαιῶν by *alewabagme*, the genitive plural of a compound noun meaning
'olive-tree'. (These three passages are the only ones of the group here discussed that are
extant in Wulfila.) The King James Version is closer to the Greek than is either the Latin
or the Gothic: it has *the mount of Olives* in all six Gospel passages, with the words *the
mount* italicized in Lk. 19.29 and 21.37, showing that they are to be supplied, while in
Acts 12.1 it has *the mount called Olivet.*

[499] Of course *nomine* here (corresponding to *epi tôi onomati* of the Greek, on which
cf. fn. 496) is an ablative of source, not specification. Cf. below, §193 and fn. 598.

[500] The use of the masculine *quem*, while not affecting the general structure, is still an
interesting departure from the Greek neuter *ti*. Cf. Plautus, Mil. 436 quis igitur vocare,
discussed above in §144 and fn. 402. See further on this below, fn. 596.

lacks such a form, departs from its original, usually substituting a relative clause, as in *Mt.* 2.23 in civitate quae vocatur Nazareth, 10.2 Simon, qui dicitur Petrus, 27.33 in locum qui dicitur Golgotha, *Lk.* 6.15 Simonem, qui vocatur Zelotes, *Jn.* 20.24 Thomas, unus ex duodecim, qui dicitur Didymus, *Acts* 10.1 centurio cohortis quae dicitur Italica.[501] In the one place where *onomati* accompanies the participle, the Latin reproduces only this and omits any rendering of the participle, *Lk.* 19.2 ecce vir nomine Zachaeus; and it substitutes *nomine* for the participle[502] in *Mt.* 9.9 vidit hominem sedentem in telonio, Matthaeum nomine, and in *Lk.* 10.39 huic erat soror nomine Maria, which is thus made parallel to the preceding 10.38 mulier quaedam Martha nomine (cited below in §180).

172. Wulfila's translation into Gothic,[503] wherever we have it,[504] is almost always thoroughly literal. Thus he preserves the active with two accusatives, *Mt.* 10.25 gardawaldand Baiailzaibul haihaitun, *Lk.* 1.59 haihaitun ina afar namin[505] attins is Zakarian, 6.13 us im twalib, thanzei jah Apaustuluns namnida, 6.14 Seimon thanei jah namnida Paitru; and the passive with predicate nominative, *Mt.* 27.8 duththe haitans warth akrs jains akrs blothis und hina dag, *Lk.* 1.32 sah wairthith mikils jah sunus hauhistins haitada, 1.60 haitaidau Iohannes. In two passages in which he found a present participle, he replaced it by a past participle,[506] otherwise reproducing the Greek exactly: these are *Mt.* 9.9 gasahv mannan sitandan at motai, Maththaiu haitanana, and *Lk.* 6.15 Seimon thana haitanan Zeloten. However, in a third passage he replaces the participle by a relative clause, just as Jerome does: this is *Lk.* 19.29 at fairgunja thatei haitada alewjo.[507] In the two passages, one

[501] So too in *Lk.* 19.29 and 21.37, and *Acts* 1.12, all discussed above, fn. 498.

[502] Hence here the Latin uses the same construction as it does in rendering the type *homo nomine Iulius* (for examples see §180). This construction, incidentally, is rare in Plautus and Vergil; see §§141 and 147.

[503] In the transliteration of Gothic, I use *hv* and *th* to replace the corresponding Gothic characters.

[504] When I cite no passage from Wulfila corresponding to a given Greek original, this is because it is not preserved.

[505] Here the Gothic is closer to the Greek than the Latin is (cf. fn. 499), since it represents the original prepositional phrase *epi tôi onomati* by a prepositional phrase *afar namin attins*.

[506] It is rather odd that Latin did not do the same thing instead of substituting a relative clause. Cf. above, §171.

[507] Already quoted and discussed in fn. 498.

with a predicate nominative and the other without one, in which the Greek uses the dative *onomati*, the Gothic uses the dative *namin*: *Lk.* 19.2 guma namin haitans Zakkaius, and 1.61 ni ainshun ist saei haitaidau thamma namin. Only in the passage in which the verb of naming appears in the infinitive does Wulfila introduce a notable variation: he employs an adverb *hwaiwa* 'how' (*quomodo*) instead of the predicate adjective *ti*, and the so-called active infinitive *haitan*[508] instead of the passive infinitive *kaleisthai*. The passage runs: *Lk.* 1.62 gabandwidedun than attin is thata[509] hvaiwa wildedi haitan ina. A Latinist may wonder whether the meaning is 'quo modo vellet *vocare* eum' or 'quo modo vellet *vocari* eum', but probably it must be the latter, in the first place because Wulfila regularly keeps as close to the Greek as he can,[510] and in the second place because there are parallels elsewhere in Gothic of the infinitive with subject-accusative after verbs of wishing.[511]

173. Type (b) *nomen Iulium nominant*,[512] accompanied by the genitive, is common. We meet it twice in the *Septuagint*,[513] and eight times in the *NT*. As an example we may cite *Mt.* 1.21 = *Lk.* 1.31 καλέσεις τὸ ὄνομα αὐτοῦ Ἰησοῦν. Exactly like this except for occasional changes in the person or tense of the verb and, of course, variations in the proper

---

[508] Gothic has no true passive infinitive (see Streitberg, *Got. El.* 208-9, Wright, *Gr. Goth.* 194); to render this Greek form, it sometimes has recourse to periphrases, but sometimes uses the form called the active infinitive. Is not the true explanation that actually the Gothic infinitive is voiceless, as it is in Hittite, in Sanskrit, and sometimes even in English? (For English, cf. *the boys are ready to eat* and *the apples are ready to eat*.) Wulfila was struggling to adapt his translation from a language whose infinitives possessed distinctions of voice to one of which this was not true. The same observation applies to the Gothic use of participles; Gothic grammarians (e.g. Streitberg 215, Wright 194) tell us, as do Hittite grammarians (e.g. Friedrich, *El.* 1.81), that the participle of intransitive verbs is active and (at least by implication) that that of transitive verbs is passive, but surely the true explanation is that they are alike voiceless, and it is only our native types of expression that force us to inject the category of voice into our interpretation and translation. (See my discussion of the voice of nonfinite verb forms in *TAPA* 74.269-306.)

[509] This corresponds to the Greek *to*. Both seem superfluous here.

[510] However, he sometimes does shift voice, either from active to passive or vice versa. See Streitberg, *Got. El.* 190.

[511] E.g. *Mk.* 7.24 ni wilda witan mannan, corresponding to οὐδένα ἤθελε γνῶναι.

[512] Buttmann (151) holds that the construction must be borrowed from Hebrew or from the *Septuagint*, "for the classic use of *kalein onoma* is manifestly of a different nature". But the usage, at least with the dative, is not unexampled in classical Greek: cf. Plato, *Pol.* 279E τουτοισὶ τὸ μὲν ὄνομα ἱμάτια ἐκαλέσαμεν and, in the passive, Euripides, *Hec.* 1271-73 τύμβῳ δ᾽ ὄνομα σῷ κεκλήσεται κυνὸς ταλαίνης σῆμα.

[513] On the *Septuagint* cf. fn. 512.

names, are, from the *OT*, *Gen.* 17.19 and 1 *Sam.* 1.20, and, from the *NT*, *Mt.* 1.23, 1.25, *Lk.* 1.13. The corresponding passive is met in *Lk.* 2.21 ἐκλήθη τὸ ὄνομα αὐτοῦ ᾽Ιησοῦς, so, too, *Rev.* 8.11 τὸ ὄνομα τοῦ ἀστέρος λέγεται[514] ὁ ῎Αψινθος and 19.13. The Vulgate translates all these passages literally: *Mt.* 1.21 = *Lk.* 1.31 vocabis nomen eius Iesum, *Lk.* 2.21 vocatum est nomen eius Iesus, etc. So too does Wulfila, so far as the remains go:[515] *Lk.* 1.31 haitais namo is Iesu, 2.21 haitan was namo is Iesus.

174. The same construction underlies *Eph.* 1.21, although it follows a different pattern: ὑπεράνω παντὸς ὀνόματος ὀνομαζομένου.[516] Here again Latin substitutes a relative clause for the impossible Greek present passive participle:[517] supra omne nomen quod nominatur. Wulfila follows the Greek word for word, except that he substitutes plural genitives for the singular of the Greek: ufaro allaize namne namnidaize.

175. In just one passage we find neither *hominem Iulium nominant* nor *nomen hominis Iulium nominant*, but *nomen homini Iulium indunt*[518] (or perhaps rather, as we shall see, *nomen homini Iulius indunt*), followed by the even stranger *nomina hominibus Iulii nominant*. This is *Mk.* 3.16 ἐπέθηκε τῷ Σίμωνι ὄνομα Πέτρον, followed almost directly by 3.17 ἐπέθηκεν αὐτοῖς ὀνόματα Βοανεργές. Remarkable here is the use of the apparent nominative *Boanerges*;[519] and I venture the conjecture that

---

[514] Note the use of *legó* here instead of the usual *kaleô*, and of *dico* in the corresponding Latin, nomen stellae dicitur Absinthium. Cf. fn. 493.

[515] The only passages extant in Wulfila are *Lk.* 1.13, 1.31, 2.21.

[516] Here, and so far as I know only here, *onoma* is accompanied by a verb of kindred etymology, *onomazô*, instead of the usual *kaleô*. Similarly Latin uses *nomino* instead of *voco*, and Gothic uses *namnjan* instead of *haitan*. Cf. fn. 493.

[517] Cf. above, §171.

[518] Cf. above, §14 and fn. 39.

[519] It is not certain that *Boanerges* is a nominative, for it presents the problem already noted in fnn. 494 and 498. It may be an indeclinable noun here serving as an accusative, like *Beelzeboub* in *Mt.* 10.25 (see §170 and fn. 494); the Greek form is an approximation of the original Aramaic, and was in its turn simply transliterated by Jerome (perhaps) and Wulfila (certainly). But *Boanerges* differs from *Beelzeboub* in that it *looks* like a Greek nominative, and that may be the case that Jerome intended to use when he too wrote *Boanerges* (though of course in the Latin version this form may even be the accusative demanded by logic). If *Boanerges* is the nominative, then it must be an example of the *nominativus tituli* (on which see fn. 205). This is what we must have in the case of common nouns, as in *Jn.* 13.13 (already referred to in fn. 497) ὑμεῖς φωνεῖτέ με, ῾Ο διδάσκαλος, καὶ ῾Ο κύριος. Wulfila renders this literally, jus woreid mik, laisereis jah frauja; but the Vulgate substitutes vocatives for the nominatives, perhaps using them in direct quotation, vos vocatis me magister et domine (so too Horace, *Serm.* 2.6.20, Matutine pater,

Petron must have originally been a nominative too, *Petros*, for both the Vulgate and Wulfila render it by the nominative: imposuit Simoni nomen Petrus, and imposuit eis nomina Boanerges; gasatida Seimona namo Paitrus, and gasatida im namna Bauanairgais. Also noteworthy is the use of the plural *nomina*; since the two men have the same name, the singular *nomen* would have been in order,[520] and the use of the plural is a sort of attraction pointing once more to the identification of the *homo*—or, in this instance, the *homines*—and the *nomen*.

176. We may now turn to the construction *homo Iulius nomen*. This is almost wholly lacking in the Scriptures[521]—almost but possibly not quite, as we shall see later (§191). The word meaning 'in name'

seu Iane libentius audis, cited also above, fn. 461; on the confusion of direct and indirect discourse, see Sturtevant, *CW* 20.24, and Hahn, *CW* 22.131–32, where this particular example is dealt with 132 and fn. 2). Buttmann (151) compares with *Jn.* 13.13 a passage from the *OT*, 1 *Sam.* 9.9 (already referred to in fn. 497) τὸν προφήτην ἐκάλει ὁ λαὸς ἔμπροσθεν ὁ βλέπων. Here it occurs to me that the employment of the nominative instead of a second accusative may be useful as a means of avoiding ambiguity (the Vulgate avoids it by recasting the entire sentence, qui enim Propheta dicitur hodie vocabatur olim Videns; so too the King James Version, he that is now called a Prophet was beforetime called a Seer).

Another passage in which the nominative is anomalously used is *Rev.* 9.11 ἐν τῇ Ἑλληνικῇ ὄνομα ἔχει Ἀπολλύων. This follows an example of the much more common construction, ὄνομα αὐτῷ Ἑβραϊστὶ Ἀβαδδών (to be referred to again in §185 and fn. 558), and the two clauses are rendered alike in the Latin, angelum abyssi cui nomen Hebraice Abaddon, Graece autem Apollyon (partially quoted again below in §186); but there is an anacoluthic Latin interpolation which echoes the Greek construction with *Apollyon*, Latine habens nomen Exterminans. Possibly Jerome felt that in departing from the letter of the Greek, he was being truer to its spirit; the reference to the usage in a foreign language (Hebrew for the writer of *Rev.*, both Hebrew and Greek for the writer of the Vulgate) is worded in a perfectly normal way, but the reference to the writer's own language (Greek for the writer of the original *Rev.*, Latin for the writer of the Vulgate) is worded in an unusual and striking way. However, these passages with *echei* and *habens* seem less strange syntactically than the others cited before them in this footnote, since we may recognize in them the familiar type *homo nomen Iulius habet* (see §17 and fn. 49). Blass evidently believes that *Rev.* 9.11 as well as *Jn.* 13.13 involves the *nominativus tituli*, since he compares with both (84) Xenophon, *Oec.* 6.14 (already cited above in fn. 328) τοὺς ἔχοντας τὸ σεμνὸν ὄνομα τοῦτο τὸ καλός τε κἀγαθὸς ἐπισκεψαίμην (here again the departure from grammar may mean an advance in sense; possibly *kalon te kagathon* if used might at first glance appear to modify *onoma* instead of being in apposition with it). Blass may be right; but Thayer's comparison (447) with the two Biblical passages of Xenophon, *An.* 1.4.11 (quoted above, §137) seems utterly pointless.

520 Of course the plural in *Mt.* 10.2 (quoted in fn. 574) is quite in order, since there a number of different names are enumerated. For the plural in *Mk.* 3.17, we can cite a similar use in Hittite (fn. 151) and an identical one in Middle Irish (fn. 720).

521 Here the Aramaic influence seems.absent. Cf. above, fn. 208.

regularly appears not in the accusative but in the dative (*onomati*), rendered by the ablative (*nomine*) in Latin and by the dative (*namin*) in Gothic.[522] Since there can be no question of apposition here, there is no essential significance for our purpose in examining the case of the word corresponding to *homo*; none the less, it is of interest to note that we find it in every case, nominative, accusative, genitive, and dative.

177. The nominative is the commonest case. It is used several times as the subject of the verb 'to be' in our familiar formula 'there was a man Julius in name'.[523] Thus the third Gospel, after a prefatory dedicatory paragraph, begins its narrative proper[524] as follows: *Lk.* 1.5[525] ἐγένετο ἐν ταῖς ἡμέραις Ἡρώδου ἱερεύς τις ὀνόματι Ζαχαρίας. Cf. too *Acts* 9.10 ἦ δέ τις μαθητὴς ἐν Δαμασκῷ ὀνόματι Ἀνανίας; also, with a departure from the initial position of 'be' usual in such expressions, *Lk.* 16.20 πτωχὸς δέ τις ἦν ὀνόματι Λάζαρος, ὃς ἐβέβλητο[526] and *Acts* 9.36 ἐν Ἰόππῃ δέ τις ἦν μαθήτρια ὀνόματι Ταβιθά, and, with a nominal clause replacing the verbal clause with 'be', *Lk.* 23.50–52 καὶ ἰδού, ἀνὴρ ὀνόματι Ἰωσήφ, ἀνὴρ ἀγαθὸς καὶ δίκαιος, οὗτος ᾐτήσατο τὸ σῶμα τοῦ Ἰησοῦ.[527] But verbs other than 'be' are much

---

[522] Schirlitz in his *Wört. NT* (243) deals with this construction in the most amazing way. He obviously believes that the name (*Iulius*) logically modifies the word for 'name' (whether the Greek form is *onomati* or the very rare *onoma*, to be dealt with below, §§182–91), and he therefore expects it to be "nach dem Gesetze der Abhängigkeit im Genitiv" (this would be with 'name' the rare "appositional genitive", not really a natural dependent; on this see above, fn. 467, and, for a similar mistake made by Gaedicke in regard to Sanskrit, cf. fn. 184). Since the word for *homo*, with which the name *Iulius* really does agree, is frequently in the nominative, and therefore *Iulius* is frequently in the nominative too, he calls it "Nominativus Tituli", and cites as examples *Mt.* 27.57, *Mk.* 14.32, *Lk.* 1.5, 1.26, 1.27, 1.63, *Rev.* 9.11. These actually present a variety of constructions, and are accordingly dealt with here in a number of different places: *Mt.* 27.57, §182; *Mk.* 14.32, §185; *Lk.* 1.5, §177; 1.26 and 1.27, §185; 1.63, fn. 562; *Rev.* 9.11, fn. 519. The last one cited is the only one of the group that might be viewed as actually containing a "Nominativus Tituli", and even this can be disputed (cf. fnn. 48, 205, and 519).

[523] Cf. above, §6.

[524] Note the omission of a connective particle.

[525] The construction shifts directly, however, the sentence continuing rather unskillfully: καὶ γυνὴ αὐτῷ ἐκ τῶν θυγατέρων Ἀαρών, καὶ τὸ ὄνομα αὐτῆς Ἐλισάβετ. For the latter locution, see below, §185.

[526] There is also a reading πτωχὸς δέ τις ὀνόματι Λάζαρος ἐβέβλητο (referred to again in fn. 530); but the Latin and Gothic translations certainly support the form with *erat* and the relative. (For these see below, §§180 and 181.)

[527] Because of the loose and naïve style, it is also possible to assume that *anêr* here is the subject of the subsequent verb (in 52) *êitêsato*; this verb has as its subject *houtos*,

commoner in this use: *Lk.* 10.38 γυνὴ δέ τις ὀνόματι Μάρθα ὑπεδέξατο αὐτὸν εἰς τὸν οἶκον αὐτῆς, *Acts* 10.1 ἀνὴρ δέ τις ἐν Καισαρείᾳ ὀνόματι Κορνήλιος εἶδεν ἄγγελον,[528] 12.13 προσῆλθε παιδίσκη, ὀνόματι ʽΡόδη, 18.24 Ἰουδαῖος δέ τις Ἀπολλὼς ὀνόματι, Ἀλεξανδρεὺς τῷ γένει,[529] ἀνὴρ λόγιος, κατήντησεν εἰς ˮΕφεσον. Other examples are *Mk.* 5.22, *Lk.* 24.18, *Acts* 5.1, 5.34, 8.9, 11.28, 16.14, 20.9, 21.10.[530] A passage departing from the usual pattern is *Acts* 19.24 Δημήτριος[531] γάρ τις ὀνόματι, ἀργυροκόπος, παρείχετο ἐργασίαν, where we would have expected ἀνήρ τις, Δημήτριος ὀνόματι, or possibly ἀργυροκόπος τις, ὀνόματι Δημήτριος. The order is unusual in *Acts* 17.34, where the main verb precedes, τινὲς δὲ ἄνδρες ἐπίστευσαν, ἐν οἷς καὶ Διονύσιος ὁ Ἀρεοπαγίτης, καὶ γυνὴ ὀνόματι Δάμαρις.

178. As examples with the accusative, we may cite *Mt.* 27.32 εὗρον ἄνθρωπον Κυρηναῖον, ὀνόματι Σίμωνα, *Lk.* 5.27 ἐθεάσατο τελώνην, ὀνόματι Λευίν, καθήμενον ἐπὶ τὸ τελώνιον, *Acts* 9.11 ζήτησον ἐν οἰκίᾳ Ἰούδα Σαῦλον[532] ὀνόματι, Ταρσέα, 9.12 εἶδεν ἄνδρα Ἀνανίαν ὀνόματι, 9.33 εὗρε ἄνθρωπόν τινα Αἰνέαν ὀνόματι, 18.2 εὑρών τινα

---

which in that case must be viewed as a tautological resumptive introduced after the long interpolation. However, in the passage *Mt.* 27.57-58 ἦλθεν ἄνθρωπος πλούσιος ἀπὸ Ἀριμαθαίας, τοὔνομα Ἰωσήφ· οὗτος ᾐτήσατο τὸ σῶμα τοῦ Ἰησοῦ, *êlthen anthrôpos* is perhaps in thought even though not in form a parallel for *idou*, *anêr*; and *houtos êitêsato* unquestionably is in a wholly separate clause. Cf. too *Mk.* 15.43 ἐλθὼν Ἰωσὴφ ὁ ἀπὸ Ἀριμαθαίας ᾐτήσατο τὸ σῶμα τοῦ Ἰησοῦ, and *Jn.* 19.38 ἠρώτησε ὁ Ἰωσὴφ ὁ ἀπὸ Ἀριμαθαίας ἵνα ἄρη τὸ σῶμα τοῦ Ἰησοῦ.

[528] This has been taken as resembling *Lk.* 23.50 (cf. fn. 527). Thus Souter evidently viewed *anêr* as subject of a nominal clause, for in his edition of the NT he placed a period before *eiden*; and Jerome actually inserted the verb 'be', translating *vir autem quidam erat in Caesarea, nomine Cornelius: is vidit.* But the absence of a sentence connective with *eiden* seems to me to militate against such an interpretation.

[529] This is an interesting passage because of the coordination of 'in name' and 'in race', recalling similar combinations in Homer (see §125) and in Vergil (see §157). So too, in the same chapter, *Acts* 18.2, quoted just below in §178. For the Vulgate renderings, with *nomine* and *genere*, see §180. On the collocation in general, see fn. 28.

[530] Also *Lk.* 16.20 if we accept the variant reading πτωχὸς δέ τις ὀνόματι Λάζαρος ἐβέβλητο, but on this see above, fn. 526.

[531] Like this nominative is the accusative in *Acts* 9.11 and the genitive in *Acts* 18.7, both quoted in the following paragraph. In 19.24 and in 18.7 we may say that *tis* and *tinos* replace the usual substantives, i.e. that 19.24 means not 'a certain Demetrius by name' but 'a certain (man), Demetrius by name'; but nothing of the sort is present in 9.11, where no indefinite occurs.

[532] See fn. 531.

'Ιουδαῖον ὀνόματι 'Ακύλαν, Ποντικὸν τῷ γένει.[533] I have found one example with the genitive, Acts 18.7 ἦλθεν εἰς οἰκίαν τινὸς ὀνόματι Τίτου 'Ιούστου,[534] and two with the dative, Acts 27.1 παρεδίδουν τὸν Παῦλον ἑκατοντάρχῃ, ὀνόματι 'Ιουλίῳ, and 28.7 ὑπῆρχε χωρία τῷ πρώτῳ τῆς νήσου, ὀνόματι Ποπλίῳ.

179. The examples quoted above reveal the tendency to use an indefinite pronominal form in combination with the 'in name' construction—not simply homo nomine Iulius but homo quidam nomine Iulius.[535] The indefinite usually employed is tis. We have just seen it in Lk. 1.5, 10.38, 16.20, Acts 9.10, 9.33, 9.36, 10.1, 16.1, 18.2, 18.7, 18.24, and 19.24; and it is also met in Acts 5.1, 5.34, 8.9, 16.14, 20.9, 21.10. It is regularly used as an adjective (practically an indefinite article) modifying anêr, mathêtês, etc.; but in two passages, Acts 18.7 and possibly 19.24,[536] it perhaps serves itself as the substantive to which onomati refers. We also find heis similarly used (but always as a substantive): it possibly keeps its force as a numeral when combined with a partitive genitive, as in Mk. 5.22 ἔρχεται εἷς τῶν ἀρχισυναγώγων, ὀνόματι 'Ιάειρος, or with an equivalent prepositional phrase, as in Jn. 20.24 (quoted in §170) and Acts 11.28 ἀναστὰς δὲ εἷς ἐξ αὐτῶν, ὀνόματι "Αγαβος, but it is an indefinite pure and simple in Lk. 24.18 (where it replaces a noun) ἀποκριθεὶς δὲ εἷς, ὀνόματι Κλεόπας.

180. The Vulgate for the most part keeps very close to the Greek original. Its translations of the passages quoted above follow: with the nominative, subject of the verb 'to be', Lk. 1.5 fuit in diebus Herodis sacerdos quidam nomine Zacharias, Acts 9.10 erat quidam discipulus Damasci, nomine Ananias, Lk. 16.20 erat quidam mendicus, nomine Lazarus, Acts 9.36 in Ioppe fuit quaedam discipula, nomine Tabitha, 16.1 ecce discipulus quidam erat ibi, nomine Timotheus; with the nominative, subject in a nominal clause, Lk. 23.50 ecce vir nomine Joseph, vir bonus et iustus; hic accessit ad Pilatum, Acts 17.34 quidam viri crediderunt, in quibus et Dionysius Areopagita et mulier nomine

[533] See fn. 529.

[534] See fn. 531.

[535] This shows how inaccurate it is to equate the use of nomen itself with that of quidam, as has been done by certain scholars. Cf. above, fn. 227.

[536] On this see fn. 531. But Acts 9.11, classed with them in that fn., differs from them in this respect, for in it there is no substantive to correspond with homo at all, unless we so regard the following Tarsea (which seems less likely).

Damaris; with the nominative, subject of verbs other than 'be',537
Lk. 10.38 mulier quaedam, Martha nomine, excepit illum, Acts 12.13
processit puella, nomine Rhode, 18.24 Iudaeus quidam, Apollo
nomine, Alexandrinus genere, devenit Ephesum, 19.24 Demetrius
quidam nomine, argentarius, praestabat quaestum;538 with the accusative, Mt. 27.32 invenerunt hominem Cyrenaeum, nomine Simonem,
Lk. 5.27, vidit publicanum, nomine Levi, sedentem ad telonium, Acts
9.11 quaere Saulum nomine Tarsensem,539 9.33 invenit hominem
quendam, nomine Aeneam, 18.2 inveniens quendam Iudaeum nomine
Aquilam, Ponticum genere; with the genitive, 18.7 intravit in domum
cuiusdam nomine Titi Iusti;540 with the dative,541 Acts 27.1 iudicatum
est tradi Paulum centurioni nomine Iulio. In all these passages (as in
Lk. 1.61 and 19.2, commented on in §171), onomati is regularly represented by nomine;542 tis is always translated quidam, while heis is translated quidam once (Mk. 5.22 venit quidam de archisynagogis nomine
Iairus) and unus twice (Lk. 24.18 unus cui nomen Cleophas543 dixit,
Acts 11.28 unus ex eis nomine Agabus significabat; so too in Jn. 20.24,
quoted in §171).

181. As for the Gothic, we unfortunately have only four passages
preserved to correspond to the many cited above for Greek and
Latin544 as illustrations of onomati and nomine. These four545 all have
the dative namin.546 Mk. 5.22 qimith ains thize swnagogafade namin
Jaeirus, Lk. 1.5 was in dagam Herodes gudja namin Zakarias, and 5.27
gasahv motari, namin Laiwwi, sitandan ana motastada are word-for-
word translations of the Greek, except that in the second tis is not

---

537 On the change in Acts 10.1 see fn. 528.
538 Cf. fn. 531.
539 Cf. fnn. 531 and 536.
540 Cf. fn. 531.
541 In my second example of this usage (§178), Acts 28.7, the Greek datives are replaced in the Latin by genitives: erant praedia principis insulae, nomine Publii.
542 There is only a single exception: in Lk. 24.18 unus cui nomen Cleophas dixit, the
clause cui nomen Cleophas is used instead of the normal nomine Cleophas to translate
onomati Kleopas. This cannot be due to an unwillingness to use nomine with unus, for we
do have it in Acts 11.28 (quoted in §180).
543 See fn. 542.
544 This is not surprising, for 21 of these 29 are from Acts, which is wholly wanting
in our remains of Wulfila.
545 Cited above in §§177, 177, 178, and 177 respectively.
546 Cf. Winkler, Germ. Casussyntax 111.

reproduced. *Lk.* 16.20 ith unleds sums was namin haitans Lazarus; sah atwaurpans was is somewhat freer; this time *tis* is represented (by *sums*), but the past participle *haitans*, 'called' or 'named', is inserted, so that we have 'there was a certain poor man *called* Lazarus in name' [547] instead of simply 'there was a certain poor man Lazarus in name'.[548]

182. So far, we have had no sign of *nomen* in the accusative. But there is just one possible example, *Mt.* 27.57 ἦλθεν ἄνθρωπος πλούσιος ἀπὸ Ἀριμαθαίας, τοὔνομα Ἰωσήφ.[549] Despite the presence of the article,[550] I venture to think that *onoma* here may be an accusative of specification[551] equivalent to the very common *onomati* elsewhere, e.g.

[547] Thus the construction is precisely the same as that in *Lk.* 19.2 guma namin haitans Zakkaius, which translates literally ἀνὴρ ὀνόματι καλούμενος Ζακχαῖος (on which see above, §170).

[548] Also, sah, properly a compound demonstrative, corresponds to the relative *hos*, but that is common. See Streitberg, *Got. El.* 226; Wright, *Gr. Goth.* 127. (Old English too can use a compound demonstrative much like a relative; on this see fnn. 601 and 622.)

[549] This was referred to above, §166. In the corresponding passages *Mk.* 15.43 and *Jn.* 19.38 he is simply called Ἰωσήφ ὁ ἀπὸ Ἀριμαθίας, without the word meaning 'in name'. (*Jn.* prefixes the article *ho*; cf. fn. 582.)

[550] On this cf. below, §190.

[551] So most of the *NT* lexica, Cremer (473), Berry (154), Bauer (col. 905), and the English adaptation of Bauer, Arndt and Gingrich (574); also the *NT* grammar of Blass (92), and its revisers Debrunner (105) and Funk (87). Buttmann (139 and 153) calls it an adverbial adjunct like *tên archên* or *ton arithmon* (cf. above, fn. 488), and Robertson (487) calls it an adverbial accusative, both of which amount to much the same thing as an accusative of specification. Thayer (447) calls it an accusative absolute, which, if I understand his use of the term, would force us to regard *Iôsêph* as an accusative also; this may seem possible, since (as noted above in fn. 489) a foreign proper noun of the sort is indeclinable, but in its case, when other than nominative, is likely to be indicated by a definite article in the interest of clarity (cf. Winer-Lünemann 113), and so I would expect *ton Iôsêph* here, as in *Lk.* 2.16 (cf. too the dative *tôi Iôsêph* in *Mt.* 1.18, etc.). Or does he simply mean by accusative absolute, strange though this would seem, what others mean by accusative of specification or adverbial accusative? Robinson (508) would supply *kaloumenos*, which seems to me merely to increase our difficulties; not only do I consider it methodologically unsound to explain syntactical problems by "supplying" something that manifestly is not there, but *anthrôpos kaloumenos tounoma Iôsêph* would imply an active *anthrôpon kaleô tounoma Iôsêph*, a construction non-existent in the *NT* (cf. §169).

It is of interest to note that Blass-Funk cites as an example of an accusative of respect not only *tounoma* in *Mt.* 27.57 (87) but also *genos* in *Acts* 17.28, which he reads ἐκ σοῦ γὰρ γένος ἐσμέν (Souter has τοῦ γὰρ γένος ἐσμέν, where I find the first word rather puzzling.) Parallelism in use of *onoma* and *genos* is not surprising (cf. above, fn. 529), but in this particular passage I believe *genos* is more probably a predicate nominative, as in the following sentence also, 17.29 γένος οὖν ὑπάρχοντες τοῦ Θεοῦ. It is certainly so interpreted both in the *Vulgate*, 17.28 ipsius enim et genus sumus, and 17.29 genus ergo cum simus Dei (in both of which Jerome would probably have used the ablative *genere* had he

in the parallel passage *Lk.* 23.50–51 ἰδού, ἀνὴρ ὀνόματι 'Ιωσήφ, ἀπὸ 'Αριμαθαίας. Certainly they are dealt with as equivalents in the Vulgate, which uses the ablative *nomine* in both instances: *Lk.* 23.50–51 ecce vir nomine Ioseph, ab Arimathaea civitate Iudaeae; *Mt.* 27.57 venit quidam homo dives ab Arimathaea, nomine Ioseph.

183. But Wulfila apparently interprets *onoma* in *Mt.* 27.57 quite differently, as a nominative not an accusative;[552] in other words he handles it as the subject of an interpolated clause.[553] His translation runs qam manna gabigs af Areimathaias, thizuh namo Iosef, literally 'venit homo dives ab Arithmathaea, illius[554] nomen Ioseph'.

184. Has Wulfila any justification for this interpretation?

185. Common variants in the *NT* for *homo nomen Iulius* are (1) the paratactic form *homo, nomen ei Iulius* and (2) the hypotactic form *homo nomen cui Iulius*.[555] For the former we may cite[556] *Jn.* 1.6 ἐγένετο ἄνθρωπος ἀπεσταλμένος παρὰ Θεοῦ, ὄνομα αὐτῷ 'Ιωάννης, 3.1 ἦν δὲ ἄνθρωπος ἐκ τῶν Φαρισαίων, Νικόδημος ὄνομα αὐτῷ, perhaps *Rev.* 6.8 ὁ καθήμενος ἐπάνω αὐτοῦ, ὄνομα αὐτῷ ὁ Θάνατος,[557] 9.11

---

thought that *genos* expressed *specification*); also in the King James Version, 17.28 for we are also his offspring, and 17.29 forasmuch then as we are the offspring of God.

[552] This view places the proper noun in a predicative relationship to the word meaning 'name'—which is not very different from, though it seems preferable to, Thayer's view (referred to in fn. 551) that *tounoma Iôséph* is an accusative absolute.

[553] This is in line with Brugmann's view of the origin of the accusative of specification. But of course *koine* Greek, especially as employed by foreigners, has no bearing on questions of origins of ancient constructions.

[554] Or *cuius*; *thizuh* is the genitive of *sah*, on which see fn. 548. Of course *thizuh*, whether used as a demonstrative or as a relative, corresponds to nothing in the Greek On this see below, §189.

[555] We meet both in classical Greek also, but I think more rarely. For the demonstrative we may cite Xenophon, *An.* 1.5.4 ἐνταῦθα ἦν πόλις ἐρήμη, μεγάλη, ὄνομα δ' αὐτῇ Κορσώτη. For the relative we may cite Herodotus 3.85 Δαρείῳ δὲ ἦν ἱπποκόμος ἀνὴρ σοφός, τῷ οὔνομα ἦν Οἰβάρης.

[556] A variant is *Jn.* 18.10 ἔπαισε τὸν δοῦλον, καὶ ἀπέκοψεν αὐτοῦ τὸ ὠτάριον. ἦν δὲ ὄνομα τῷ δούλῳ Μάλχος. If this clause had followed *doulon* directly, we would doubtless have had the usual form, ὄνομα αὐτῷ Μάλχος, but, because of the intervention of the second clause, this is set off as an independent one, with a conjunction and a copula, and with the noun *tôi doulôi* replacing the usual *autôi*. Of course we must separate wholly from this paratactic use of a logically subordinate clause the use of a genuine principal clause, as in the examples with the dative of a first or second person pronoun, in *Mk.* 5.9 and *Lk.* 8.30, cited below, §188.

[557] I frequently find the form of *Revelations* as confused and confusing as I do its content, and I am not certain whether *onoma autôi ho thanatos* is a parenthetical paratactic clause or a principal clause. The trouble lies in the looseness and lack of parallelism

τὸν ἄγγελον τῆς ἀβύσσου, ὄνομα αὐτῷ Ἀβαδδών,[558] for the latter,
Lk. 1.26 εἰς πόλιν τῆς Γαλιλαίας, ᾗ ὄνομα Ναζαρέτ, 1.27 ἀνδρὶ ᾧ
ὄνομα Ἰωσήφ,[559] 2.25 ἰδού, ἦν ἄνθρωπος ἐν Ἰερουσαλὴμ ᾧ ὄνομα
Συμεών, 8.41 ἰδού, ἦλθεν ἀνὴρ ᾧ ὄνομα Ἰάειρος, 24.13 εἰς κώμην
ἀπέχουσαν σταδίους ἑξήκοντα, ᾗ ὄνομα Ἐμμαούς, Acts 13.6 εὗρον

---

characterizing the famous "Four Horsemen" passage (6.1–8). Each horse with his rider is
heralded by a different beast, and each of the four beasts says 'come and see' (erchou kai
ide); then three times follows 'behold' (ἰδού, to be distinguished from the true imperative ἴδου), which in the NT has lost all trace of its verbal origin, and (less logical than
French voici and voilà) is followed just like Latin ecce by a nominative not an accusative.
The apposite portions run as follows: (a) 6.2 ἰδού, ἵππος λευκός· καὶ ὁ καθήμενος
ἐπ᾽ αὐτὸν ἔχων τόξον· καὶ ἐδόθη αὐτῷ στέφανος, (b) 6.4 ἐξῆλθεν ἄλλος ἵππος
πυρρός· καὶ τῷ καθημένῳ ἐπ᾽ αὐτὸν ἐδόθη αὐτῷ λαβεῖν τὴν εἰρήνην· καὶ ἐδόθη
αὐτῷ μάχαιρα, (c) 6.5–6 ἰδού, ἵππος μέλας· καὶ ὁ καθήμενος ἐπ᾽ αὐτὸν ἔχων
ζυγὸν ἐν τῇ χειρὶ αὐτοῦ· καὶ ἤκουσα φωνήν, (d) 6.8 ἰδού, ἵππος χλωρός· καὶ ὁ
καθήμενος ἐπάνω αὐτοῦ, ὄνομα αὐτῷ ὁ Θάνατος, καὶ ὁ Ἅδης ἠκολούθει μετ᾽
αὐτοῦ· καὶ ἐδόθη αὐτοῖς ἐξουσία. The fourth horse, hippos chlôros, is parallel to
hippos leukos and hippos melas, being used with idou, but not to (allos) hippos pyrros, which
is subject of the verb exêlthen. The riders, too, are designated in different ways.
The first and third riders are made syntactically parallel to their mounts: ho kathêmenos,
accompanied by a subordinate participle echôn, is a nominative with idou just like
hippos. This I think is true of the fourth rider too, only here there is no subordinate
participle; there is introduced what I believe is a paratactic parenthesis, 'his name
is Death'. Then in each of these three instances there follows an independent clause
introduced by kai and containing a finite verb. The second rider, like the second horse,
is differently treated from the others. Here we have no nominative but a dative, tôi
kathêmenôi, and the kai preceding it of course does not join it to the preceding hippos but
introduces the verb edothê, on which tôi kathêmenôi depends, though there is a second,
redundant dative autôi after edothê; but later on there is another kai edothê clause like the
one in the first passage. On the basis of this second passage, it might be argued that in
ours similarly we have a principal clause onoma autôi ho Thanatos, corresponding to
edothê autôi labein tên eirênên of the second rider; and this seems to be the view of both the
Vulgate and the King James Version (both of which struggle manfully to introduce some
balance and logic into the passage). But this interpretation would involve a still graver
inconcinnity than any other in the passage, for the use of the nominative in ho kathêmenos would involve a serious anacoluthon; we would need the dative as in the red
horse passage. So I believe I am right in viewing 'his name (was) Death' as paratactic and
parenthetical.
[558] This is followed by a second clause, involving more inconcinnity (cf. fn. 557).
See above, fn. 519.
[559] After this the construction shifts, the sentence reading καὶ τὸ ὄνομα τῆς παρθένου
Μαριάμ. Possibly a relative clause (hêi onoma Mariam) might have fitted in rather awkwardly with parthenou in view of its rather long modifier memnêsteumenên andri etc.; yet
plenty of parallels exist. We may compare the shift earlier in the same chapter, 1.5,
already commented on in fn. 525; also the clumsier one in Rev. 9.11, commented on in
fn. 558.

ἄνδρα τινὰ[560] μάγον ᾧ ὄνομα Βαριησοῦς.[561] The use of the genitive instead of the dative in such expressions seems to be much rarer. I have found no instances of the asyndetic paratactic form[562] *homo, nomen eius Iulius*,[563] but perhaps we may note an example in which the coordinate clause is introduced by *kai*: *Lk.* 1.5 ἐγένετο ἱερεύς τις· καὶ γυνὴ αὐτῷ ἐκ τῶν θυγατέρων Ἀαρών, καὶ τὸ ὄνομα αὐτῆς Ἐλισάβετ.[564] An instance of the hypotactic variety, *homo nomen cuius Iulius*, is *Mk.* 14.32 εἰς χωρίον οὗ τὸ ὄνομα Γεθσημανῆ.

186. The Vulgate keeps the paratactic form in the example with the genitive, *Lk.* 1.5 fuit uxor illius de filiabus Aaron, et nomen eius Elisabeth, but it changes it in the examples with the dative: it substitutes the hypotactic form in *Jn.* 1.6 fuit homo missus a Deo, cui nomen erat[565] Ioannes and *Rev.* 9.11 angelum abyssi, cui nomen Hebraice Abaddon,[566] while in *Jn.* 3.1 erat homo ex Pharisaeis, Nicodemus

[560] On *tina* cf. above, §179.

[561] With this particular passage Thayer (447) compares Xenophon, *Mem.* 3.11.1 γυναικὸς δέ ποτε οὔσης ἐν τῇ πόλει καλῆς, ᾗ ὄνομα ἦν Θεοδότῃ.

[562] Again as in fn. 556 on *Mk.* 5.9 and *Lk.* 8.30, we must differentiate from this type a true principal clause, as *Lk.* 1.63 ἔγραψε λέγων, Ἰωάννης ἐστὶ τὸ ὄνομα αὐτοῦ. An example with a noun instead of a pronoun, like *Jn.* 18.10 (quoted in fn. 556), is *Mt.* 10.2 (quoted in fn. 574).

[563] We have already noted (§§22–23) the occurrence in Hittite of this construction, or at least of its variant *homo nomen suum Iulius* (as I write even at the expense of Latin idiom, in order to represent the possessive adjective used in Hittite; cf. fn. 63). It is of course possible that in the *NT* the rare form *homo nomen eius Iulius*, and the common form *homo nomen ei Iulius*, really go back to the same sort of partitive apposition as the Hittite does, and that the hypotactic forms, in which the demonstrative is replaced by a relative, developed from a misunderstanding of what was originally an instance of partitive apposition. But the use of the genitive or the dative in expressions of the sort seems peculiar to *koine* Greek as opposed to Homeric Greek (see fn. 305), and so had better not be explained as an inheritance from Indo–European (cf. fn. 485). The seeming parallelism is doubtless pure coincidence, as is surely that of an English passage that I have noted, in *This Is Goggle* by Bentz Plagemann (New York, 1955) 170: "His name, this teacher of mathematics, was Andrew Sadowsky", where *teacher* probably is loosely used in apposition with *his*, not with *name*.

[564] Already quoted in fn. 525. Cf. too the use of *kai* in *Jn.* 18.10, quoted in fn. 556.

[565] The Greek nowhere uses the verb 'be', but the Latin employs it here and in *Lk.* 1.27 and *Acts* 13.6.

[566] The clause in *Rev.* 6.8 is rendered word for word, *nomen illi Mors*, but the interpretation of the general structure of the sentence is (as already noted, fn. 557) entirely different from the one I favor. It may be remarked incidentally that once more (cf. above, §171) a relative clause is substituted for each of the four participles; this is practically obligatory here, for Latin has no other satisfactory way of dealing with the Greek combination of article and participle.

nomine, it introduces a different construction, *homo Iulius nomine*, as also in one hypotactic passage, *Lk.* 24.13 in castellum quod erat in spatio stadiorum sexaginta, nomine Emmaus. The other hypotactic passages with the dative are rendered literally: *Lk.* 1.26 in civitatem Galilaeae cui nomen Nazareth, 1.27 viro cui nomen erat[567] Ioseph, 2.25 ecce homo erat in Ierusalem cui nomen Simeon, 8.41 ecce venit vir cui nomen Iairus, *Acts* 13.6 invenerunt quendam virum magum, cui nomen erat[568] Bariesu. The hypotactic example with the genitive it treats like those with the dative, thus departing from the Greek: *Mk.* 14.32 in praedium cui nomen Gethsemani.

187. It happens that all the paratactic examples with the dative are missing in Wulfila; the one with the genitive, *Lk.* 1.5, he renders literally, qeins is us dauhtrum Aharons, jah namo izos Aileisabaith. In dealing with the hypotactic examples with the dative, he once substitutes a relative clause of quite different structure: *Lk.* 1.26 in baurg Galeilaias sei haitada Nazaraith.[569] All the other instances (so far as we have them in his translation) he handles alike, invariably where he finds the Greek saying *cui nomen Iulius* substituting the genitive *cuius nomen Iulius.*[570] This occurs in *Lk.* 1.27 abin, thizei namo Iosef, 2.25 tharuh was manna in Iairusalem thizei namo Swmaion, 8.41 sai qam wair thizei namo Iaiirus. Unfortunately, our single hypotactic example with the genitive, *Mk.* 14.32, is wanting in Wulfila;[571] it seems likely that he kept the genitive, since the fact that he used it even where he found a dative in the Greek original would appear to suggest that the genitive was his natural idiom.

188. Elsewhere too there is evidence that the locution *homini est nomen Iulius*[572] is alien to Wulfila.[573] Thus in *Jn.* 18.10 ἦν δὲ ὄνομα τῷ

---

[567] Cf. fn. 565.

[568] Cf. fn. 565.

[569] Yet in *Lk.* 1.27, which follows directly, he keeps more closely to the Greek, as we shall see. Is there a difference between personal names and place names? Unfortunately, *Lk.* 24.13 and *Mk.* 14.32, which also involve place names, are not preserved in Wulfila; there are a few fragments of the former, which some scholars have tried to restore (cf. Wrede 115), but of course their suppletions are of no use for our purpose.

[570] It is odd that the Latin does exactly the reverse, in a hypotactic passage substituting a dative where it found a genitive, as we have just seen (in the preceding paragraph).

[571] Cf. fn. 569.

[572] Cf. fn. 25.

[573] This is not for lack of the dative of possession in his idiom as a whole. Note for

δούλῳ Μάλχος, rendered literally in the Vulgate, erat nomen servo Malchus,[574] Wulfila once again changes the construction, saying sah than haitans was namin Malkus 'this man however was called in name Malchus', just as if he had found in the Greek ὁ δοῦλος ὀνόματι ἐκαλεῖτο Μάλχος;[575] and where the Greek has the dative of a personal pronoun, Wulfila substitutes the possessive adjective. Thus we find the question τί σοι ἐστὶν ὄνομα; in Lk. 8.30, and the question and its answer τί σοι ὄνομα; Λεγεὼν ὄνομά μοι in Mk. 5.9. The Vulgate follows the Greek closely, rendering both questions (Mk. 5.9 and Lk. 8.30) quod tibi nomen est?, and the answer (Mk. 5.9) Legio mihi nomen est. But Wulfila[576] has for the questions hva ist namo thein? (Lk. 8.30) and hva namo thein? (Mk. 5.9), and for the answer namo mein Laigaion (Mk. 5.9). Of course the possessive adjectives mein 'meum' and thein 'tuum' correspond to the genitive of a substantive, e.g. the genitive of the relative pronoun thizei 'cuius', which we find in the passages quoted in §187.

189. As we have seen (§183), the construction with the genitive that Wulfila uses in rendering homo nomen eius Iulius and homo nomen cui Iulius he also uses in rendering homo nomen Iulius. Note once more Lk. 1.5 καὶ τὸ ὄνομα αὐτῆς Ἐλισάβετ, rendered jah namo izos Aileisabaith; 2.25 ἄνθρωπος ᾧ ὄνομα Συμεών, rendered manna thizei namo Swmaion; Mt. 27.57 ἄνθρωπος τοὔνομα Ἰωσήφ, rendered manna thizuh namo Iosef. (The genitives are, in succession: izos, personal pronoun; thizei, relative pronoun; thizuh, emphatic demonstrative, often equivalent to a relative.[577]) Does this mean that in the light of the

---

instance Lk. 1.7 οὐκ ἦν αὐτοῖς τέκνον, which he translates ni was im barne. Not infrequently, Wulfila even uses the dative where the Greek has a genitive, as in 2 Thess. 3.2 οὐ γὰρ πάντων ἡ πίστις, which he translates ni auk ist allaim galaubeins; on this cf. Streitberg, Got. El. 168.

[574] In another passage both the Greek and, following it, the Latin versions use not homini nomen est Iulius but hominis nomen est Iulius. This is Mt. 10.2 τῶν δὲ δώδεκα ἀποστόλων τὰ ὀνόματά ἐστι ταῦτα, duodecim autem Apostolorum nomina sunt haec (already referred to in fn. 562). One wonders whether Wulfila would have rendered this literally; unfortunately the passage is not extant in Gothic. To be sure, here a dative would not really be in place, for the genitive is attributive, not predicative.

[575] Cf. Lk. 1.61 and 19.2 (both cited in §170) and Wulfila's rendering of them (cited in §172).

[576] In one respect he keeps closer to the Greek than the Vulgate does: he uses the verb 'be' only when he finds it in the original (contrast fn. 565).

[577] Cf. above, fnn. 548 and 554.

other passages Wulfila interpreted *Mt.* 27.57 as standing for ἄνθρωπος, τοὔνομα αὐτῷ 'Ιωσήφ[578] (or its less common variant with the genitive pronoun instead of the dative)?

190. I question whether such an interpretation is justified. If *autou* or *autôi* were implied, I think it would have been employed.[579] We have found 11 examples where a demonstrative or relative pronoun, either genitive or dative, was used, presumably because it was needed; I do not think that this one passage would or could do without it, were it parallel in construction to the others. I believe it is much easier to equate *tounoma* here with *onomati* elsewhere, as I have suggested doing (§182). We know that in classical Greek the two "specification" constructions were really equivalent to each other, and that even in Hellenistic Greek the accusative did not wholly disappear.[580] It is true that *tounoma* differs from *onomati* not only in case but also in the presence of the article; but in the examples of the type *nomen ei Iulius*, as in *Jn.* 1.6 ἄνθρωπος, ὄνομα αὐτῷ 'Ιωάννης etc., the article is also lacking. To be sure, it does occur in *Mk.* 14.32 εἰς χωρίον οὗ τὸ ὄνομα Γεθσημανῆ, as well as in the slightly different[581] type *Lk.* 1.5 καὶ τὸ ὄνομα αὐτῆς 'Ελισάβετ, but this merely goes to show that the NT use with respect to the article is not completely consistent, and may furnish support for equating *tounoma* in *Mt.* 27.57 with *onomati* elsewhere.[582]

191. I therefore hold that *onoma* in *Mt.* 27.57 really is an accusative of specification.[583] Presumably Wulfila did not recognize it as such; or,

---

[578] Cf. §§ 185 and 189, and fn. 553.

[579] It is precisely because in *Od.* 7.54 'Αρήτη δ' ὄνομ' ἐστὶν ἐπώνυμον there is nothing to correspond to *autês* in the otherwise similar passage *Lk.* 1.5 καὶ τὸ ὄνομα αὐτῆς 'Ελισάβετ that I have refused to accept the view held by some that *onoma* is the subject of *estin*. Cf. above, §117.

[580] Cf. above, fnn. 477 and 488.

[581] Because not asyndetic (see §185).

[582] Cf. further what has already been said on the subject in fn. 498. For other examples of inconsistency in the use or non-use of the article, see fnn. 549 and (on Old English) 607 (a perhaps possible but extremely dubious one is noted in fn. 551).

[583] Bauer (col. 905) and Arndt and Gingrich (574), who so take it (as already noted, fn. 551), cite as a parallel for it *onoma* in 2 *Macc.* 12.13 ἐπέβαλε δὲ καὶ ἐπί τινα πόλιν, ὄνομα δὲ Κασπιν. But, if this passage (which seems poorly written to me) is to be dealt with as normal *koine* Greek, I do not see how *onoma* here can be an accusative of specification. The *de* indicates that the three words constitute a separate clause, and a clause requires predication. On the other hand, if *onoma* and *Kaspin* are in the relation to each other (either way) of subject and predicate, then once more I feel the need of *autês* or *autêi* (cf. above, §190 and fn. 579). The dilemma seems insuperable, unless we emend by

if he did, he deliberately departed from it in his translation. Either reaction on his part would strongly suggest, though neither would indubitably prove, that his own idiom did not include the use of an accusative of specification in the sense of 'in name'.

---

inserting *autêi*. The Vulgate translation, aggressus est autem et civitatem quandam, cui nomen Casphin, reads as if Jerome had found a dative demonstrative *autêi* with *de*, for which he substituted a relative *cui* (cf. his treatment of *Jn*. 1.6, quoted above, §186). If this emendation is accepted, the text is enormously improved.

B. OLD ENGLISH

192. We have now observed and compared constructions involving the word 'name' in the *NT* and in its translations into Latin (Jerome) and Gothic (Wulfila), and have used the Gothic rendering specifically in a search for evidence in Gothic as to the possible existence of an accusative of specification 'in name'. Next we shall similarly observe and compare such constructions in the Vulgate and in several of its translations into various dialects of Old English,[584] all dating from the tenth century, and shall use the latter in a similar search in Old English. The documents to be employed are as follows:[585] (1) *N*, a translation of the four Gospels into Old Northumbrian made by Aldred, a priest, probably with three collaborators working under his supervision, about 950;[586] (2) *M*, a translation of the Gospel according to Matthew into Old Mercian, made by Farman, a priest, some time in the latter half of the tenth century;[587] (3) *W*, a translation of the four Gospels into West Saxon (miscalled "Anglo-Saxon"), made in great part by Aelfric, a monk, before 1000.[588] In studying these we shall of course deal only with the Latin version which they were representing,[589]

[584] In the transcription of Old English, I use *th* for "thorn", *dh* for "edh", and *ae* for the corresponding ligature.

[585] They are conveniently collected in parallel form in Skeat's *Gospels*; see especially the Preface to this work. In quoting them I follow the text as found in Skeat.

[586] This is known as the Lindisfarne MS or the Durham Book, and is now in the British Museum. See Skeat, *Gospels*, Pref. to *Mk.* xi–xii, and *Dialects* 22.

[587] This is known as the Rushworth MS, and is now in the Bodleian Library at Oxford. It includes also a translation of the other three Gospels, begun by Farman and continued and completed by Owun; but this portion is in Northumbrian and is based on the Durham Book, so, as Skeat says (*Dialects* 23), "it is best in this case to rely, for our knowledge of Old Northumbrian, on the Durham book *alone*" (see on the Rushworth MS Skeat, *Gospels*, Preface to *Mk.* xii–xiii, and *Dialects* 22–23 and 70). Where I have occasion to refer to this Northumbrian version, I shall call it *N²*.

[588] This is known as the Corpus MS, and is now in the Library of Corpus Christi College at Cambridge. Skeat in his *Gospels* adds to this a subsequent translation in West Saxon, known as the Hatton MS; but as this is later than 1150, nothing is gained by using it in addition to its much earlier predecessor. See Skeat, *Gospels*, Pref. to *Mk.* v–vi and x.

[589] In the case of *N* and *M*, this is unquestionably the Vulgate practically as we have it (but see the end of fn. 477). Since the two West Saxon versions (cf. fn. 588) show certain peculiarities of their own, Skeat in his *Gospels*, Preface to *Mt.* x, suggests that they may have been made "from a Latin text which is really distinct from that contained in the Lindisfarne and Rushworth MSS., though of course it much resembles them upon the

without any consideration of the Greek original.[590]

193. These Old English glosses, being interlinear translations,[591] generally correspond as closely as possible to the Latin, which they frequently reproduce word for word.[592] Where the Latin says *hominem Iulium vocant*, or *homo Iulius vocatur*, the Old English regularly keeps the same construction.[593] The former type occurs in *Mt.* 10.25, *Lk.* 6.13, 6.14; the latter in *Mt.* 2.23,[594] 10.2, 27.8, 27.33,[595] *Lk.* 1.32, 1.60, 1.62,[596]

---

whole". The hypothesis has even been advanced that this may have been the Vetus Italica on which Jerome based his Vulgate (see Corson 494–95); but Skeat simply assumes that there were variant versions of the Vulgate. At all events there are hardly any noticeable discrepancies, apart from variations in the spelling of proper names, between *N* and *M* on the one hand, and *W* on the other, either as compared with the Vulgate as we have it or as compared with each other, in the Latin text of the passages that I discuss here; the only ones of any significance whatsoever are the following, all, as it happens, in *Lk.*: the erroneous *virgo* instead of *viro* in the original version of *N* (corrected in *N*²) in 1.27 (see fn. 649); the omission of the phrase *sanare contritos corde* in both *N* and *W* in 4.18 (see fn. 477, close); and the insertion of *othrum naman* in *W* in 5.27 (see §197 and fn. 640). We may also note the change of the genitive *eius* to the dative *ei* in *N*² as compared with *N* in 1.5 (see §201): also, incidentally, the incorrect translation of both *eius* and *ei* by the masculine *his* and *him* in *N* and *N*² respectively, as compared with the correct feminine *hyre* for *eius* in *W* (again see §201).

[590] However, as a matter of interest we shall occasionally recall important departures from the Greek on the part of the Latin.

[591] When a proper name is included in the original Latin, this is not always reproduced in the interlinear translation; obviously in such instances its appearance in the Latin text is expected to carry over into the OE translation. In such cases I supply the Latin form of the name in my OE quotations.

[592] Cf. Skeat, *Dialects* 23–24.

[593] There is no consistency as to choice of the verb for 'call'. Latin (as already noted in fn. 493) almost always uses *voco*, the only exceptions being *nomino* (with its compound *cognomino*) and *dico*. We meet the former in two of the four active examples, both of which refer to the adoption of a new name, *Lk.* 6.13 *duodecim quos et Apostolos nominavit*, and, directly after it, 6.14 *Simonem, quem cognominavit Petrum*. We meet the latter in three of the ten passive examples, *Mt.* 10.2 *Simon, qui dicitur Petrus*, 27.33 *in locum qui dicitur Golgotha*, and *Jn.* 20.24 *Thomas, qui dicitur Didymus*. OE verbs for 'call' include *ciegan*, *clipian*, *hatan* (with compounds); also *cwethan*, really (like Greek *legô* and *dico*) 'say, speak'. *N* regularly has *ciegan*, but it adds a variant *nemnan* in *Mt.* 1.21 (on which see further below, fn. 602), and elsewhere uses *nemnan* three times (*Mt.* 2.23, *Lk.* 2.4 and 6.13), with a seemingly corrupt compound (*getor-nomade*) in *Lk.* 6.14; and, in the three places where Latin has *qui dicitur* (*Mt.* 10.2 and 27.33, and *Jn.* 20.24) it uses the OE word for 'say', *cwethan*. *M* regularly has *nemnan*, but it uses *hatan* twice (*Mt.* 2.23 and 27.33) in the unique medio-passive *hatte* 'is called, s'appelle, heisst'; also in *Mt.* 27.57 *waes haten* 'was called'. *W*, too, regularly has *nemnan*, but it uses *clipian* in *Mt.* 10.25, *hatan* in *Mt.* 27.8, and (like *N*) *cwethan* in *Jn.* 20.24.

[594] In this passage, and in *Mt.* 27.33 and *Jn.* 20.24, the Latin finite verb replaces a Greek participle. Cf. above, §171.

2.4, *Jn.* 20.24.[597] In two passages Latin adds the ablative *nomine*, which the OE replaces by a dative, Northumbrian *noma*, West Saxon *naman*. In *Lk.* 1.59 *nomine* is an ablative of source:[598] vocabant eum nomine patris sui Zachariam, *N* ge-ceigde[599] hine noma fadores his Zachariam, *W* nemdon hyne hys faeder naman Zachariam. In *Lk.* 1.61 (where it replaces a predicate nominative; cf. §170), *hoc nomine* is an ablative of means:[600] nemo est qui vocetur hoc nomine, *N* ne aenig is sedhe[601] ge-ceiged dhisum noma, *W* nis nan thyson naman genemned.

194. The type *vocant nomen eius Iulium* is also closely maintained:[602] e.g. *Mt.* 1.21 vocabis nomen eius Iesum, *N* ge-ceig dhu[603] noma is[604]

---

[595] See fn. 594.

[596] This is the passage in which Latin replaced the Greek neuter *ti* by the masculine *quem*, saying *quem vellet vocari eum* (cf. above, fn. 500). It is interesting to note that *N* keeps the masculine, saying *huoelcne [qualem] waelde ge-ceiga hine*; but *W* substitutes the neuter, saying *hwaet [quid] he wolde hine genemnedne beon*.

[597] See fn. 594.

[598] It represents a prepositional phrase of the Greek: cf. above, fn. 499. Therefore I think it implies a slightly different relationship from *nomine* in the next example, which represents a Greek dative.

[599] The use of the singular seems odd. It is replaced by the plural *cegdun* in *N²*.

[600] We may contrast with this passage the *W* rendering of *Lk.* 5.27 geseah publicanum he waes othrum naman Leui gehaten. Here the OE translation involves a syntactic departure from the Latin original, which runs vidit publicanum nomine Levi (i.e. not *homo Iulius vocatur* but *homo Iulius nomine*, the construction to be treated below, §§196–198; on this particular passage, see §198).

[601] *N* reproduces the relative construction of the original, as well as OE can; *W* omits it. Thus *ge-ceiged* in *N* must represent a finite verb, *ge-ceiged is*; but *genemned* in *W* is a true participle. (For this quasi-relative use of the compound demonstrative *sedhe* in OE, see fn. 622.)

[602] There are, to be sure, variations in the verb forms used. Thus *vocabis* (*Mt.* 1.21, *Lk.* 1.13, 1.31) and *vocabunt* (*Mt.* 1.23) present difficulties, since there is no future in the Germanic languages involved. Wulfila, quoted above (§173), uses for *vocabis* the present subjunctive *haitais* (*Lk.* 1.13 and 1.31). *M* (in *Mt.* 1.21) and *W* use the present indicative, *nemnest* or *nemst* or *genemnest*, for *vocabis*, and *nemnath* or *nemnadh* for *vocabunt* (*nemnath* may also mean *vocatis* or *vocate*, but the parallelism of the other forms, and in *W* the presence of the subject *hi* 'ei', make it practically certain that here it means *vocant*). *N* shows more variety: for *vocabis* it has two alternate forms, the imperative *geceig* and the present subjunctive *genemne*, in *Mt.* 1.21 (cf. fn. 593), and the present subjunctive *ge-ceige* in *Lk.* 1.13 and 1.31; while for *vocabunt* it has the present indicative *geceiges* in *Mt.* 1.23, a dialectal form (see Sievers, *OEGr.* 196). But this has no bearing on the point here under consideration.

[603] Also *genemne dhu*. On the variants see fn. 602.

[604] The form *is* is unusual; we regularly find *his* (or its variant *hys*), as in the other two versions of this passage, and in both versions of the next passage cited, *Lk.* 1.31. Cf. Sievers, *OEGr.* 117.

Haelend, *M* thu nemnest his noma Haelend, *W* thu nemst hys naman Haelend. That the OE translators are by no means consistent in their rendering of their original [605] is shown by the variations of their versions of the identical Latin passage in *Lk.* 1.31: *N* ge-ceige dhu noma his Haelend, *W* his naman Haelend genemnest. But there is never any departure from the syntactical pattern of the Latin except in the case of *Lk.* 2.21 vocatum est nomen eius Iesus: *N* is perfectly literal,[606] ge-ceigd waes noma his se Haelend, but *W* unaccountably changes to his nama waes Haelend 'eius nomen erat Iesus'.

195. OE also preserved, at least in part, the rare type *homini nomen Iulium indunt*,[607] met in *Mk.* 3.16–17 imposuit Simoni nomen Petrus, imposuit eis nomina Boanerges. This is rendered in *N* gesette to Symone noma Petre, ge-sette him [noma [608]] Boanerges; it will be noted that, while the dative pronoun *eis* in the second clause is represented by the corresponding dative *him*, the dative noun *Simoni* in the first clause is represented by the prepositional phrase *to Symone*.[609] The *W* version is he nemde Simon Petrum, him naman onsette Boaneries; here the Latin construction is preserved in the second clause, but in the first clause is replaced by the commoner variant *hominem Iulium nominant*.

196. OE is completely at odds with the Latin when we come to the construction *homo nomine Iulius*, which seems to have been as alien to OE as was *homo nomen Iulius* to Latin (and, presumably, to OE[610]). Wulfila in translating the corresponding Greek expressions replaced *onomati* by a dative (*namin*), but the OE glosses never deal thus with *nomine*. This is all the more striking because they do render *nomine* by

---

[605] Cf. fn. 603.

[606] Except for the interpolation of the definite article *se* before *Haelend* ('the Saviour'), which does not appear in any of the parallel passages. On similar inconsistency in the use of the article in Gothic, see fn. 582.

[607] Cf. above, §14 and fn. 39.

[608] While the Latin singular accusative *nomen* is glossed by *noma*, the Latin plural *nom[i]na* is not provided with a gloss, but I am venturing to supply the Northumbrian plural accusative *noma*, which does appear in *N*².

[609] But we find *to* with a pronoun in *Lk.* 1.26 (again in *N* only), quoted in §199. Cf. fn. 650.

[610] I find no sure trace of the accusative of specification in OE. As already noted above (fn. 477), in *Jn.* 11.44, in which Wulfila retained the accusative in translating δεδεμένος τοὺς πόδας καὶ τὰς χεῖρας κειρίαις, OE apparently did not retain it in translating *pedes et manus*. N has the dative singular *foet & hond*, and *W* has the dative plural *handan & fotan*.

a dative in two passages[611] in which it is combined with *voco, Lk.* 1.59 and 1.61 (both quoted above in §193), as does *W* (though not *N*) in a third passage, *Lk.* 5.27, where it adds the dative with *waes gehaten.*[612]

197. The Latin passages containing *nomine* as an ablative of specification are: *Mt.* 9.9, 27.32, 27.57,[613] *Mk.* 5.22, *Lk.* 1.5, 5.27, 10.38, 16.20, 19.2,[614] 23.50, 24.13,[615] *Jn.* 3.1.[616] In translating them, OE has three ways of dealing with *nomine*. (1) It occasionally uses a prepositional phrase.[617] *N* has *midh noma* (dative) in *Mt.* 9.9[618] and *Lk.* 1.5; and *W* has *on naman* (dative[619]) followed by the proper name[620] in *Lk.* 1.5, 10.38, 10.39, 16.20, 19.2, 23.50, 24.13.[621] (2) It often uses a paratactic or quasi-hypotactic[622] clause with a verb meaning 'vocatus erat'[623] or *vocatus* without a copula, or (once[624]) *vocabatur.*[625] Examples are: *N*,

---

[611] As we have just seen (§193).

[612] See above, fn. 600, and below, §197.

[613] This is the passage in which Greek has *tounoma* instead of *onomati*. See above, §182.

[614] This is the passage in which Greek has *onomati kaloumenos* instead of simply *onomati*. See above, §170.

[615] In this passage Greek has a relative clause. See above, §185.

[616] In this passage Greek has a paratactic clause with a demonstrative. See above, §185.

[617] Professor Elliott Van Kirk Dobbie of Columbia University tells me that Old Icelandic can also use a preposition and dative, *at nafni*, although it too more often employs a clause.

[618] However, with the variants *waes genemned* and *benemned*.

[619] *On* can govern the accusative as well as the dative, and *naman* can be an accusative as well as a dative, but I think we may safely assume it is a dative here. On the use of *on* in general, see Grein 2.322–39.

[620] These proper names are often treated as indeclinables. Cf. above, fn. 489.

[621] It is interesting to note that all instances of *on naman* are confined to the *W* version of *Lk.*, and that this version never renders the Latin *nomine* in any other way except in 5.27, which is a special case. See below, §198.

[622] True hypotaxis is impossible, as OE has no genuine relative; but the demonstrative, or the particle *dhe*, or the two combined, may seem to serve instead (see Sievers, *OEGr.* 188; Wright, *OEGr.* 231). For the former, cf. §197 and fn. 632; for both used in the same sentence, fn. 648; for the two in combination in a single compound, fn. 601 (and for the similar use of a compound demonstrative in Gothic, fnn. 548 and 554).

[623] Cf. from the *OT Gen.* 38.2 filiam hominis Chananaei, vocabulo [instead of the usual *nomine*] Sue, rendered an Chananeisc wif, seo waes genemned Sue; and *Gen.* 38.6 dedit autem Iudas uxorem primogenito suo Her, nomine Thamar, rendered Iudas sealde Here his suna wif, seo waes genemned Thamar. (These examples were given to me by Professor Dobbie.)

[624] In the *W* version of *Mk.* 5.22. The form used, *hatte* (on which see fn. 593) is here doubtless past in its force, though it may also serve as a present (see Sievers, *OEGr.* 200; Wright, *OEGr.* 236).

[625] Cf. from the *OT Gen.* 29.24 dans ancillam filiae, Zelpham nomine, rendered and scalde hyre ane dhinane, seo hatte Zepha; and *Gen.* 30.21 peperit filiam, nomine Dinam

Mt. 9.9 gesaeh monno sittende, Matthaeum (sic!)[626] waes genemned (benemned),[627] *Mk.* 5.22 cuom sum monn of hehsomnungum, genemned waes Iarus, *Lk.* 5.27 gesaeh dhone baersynnig genemned waes Leui, 10.38 wif sum odhero Mardha waes genemned, also, without the copula, *Jn.* 3.1 monn of Pharisaeis, Nicodemus genemned;[628] in *M*, without the copula, *Mt.* 9.9 gesaeh monnu sittende, Matheus haten; in *W*, *Jn.* 3.1 man, waes genemned Nichodemus, and, with a subject expressed (the personal pronoun *he*[629]), *Lk.* 5.27 geseah publicanum, he waes othrum naman[630] Leui gehaten, also, with the simple verb, *Mk.* 5.22 dha com sum Iairus hatte.[631] *M* has a similar clause with a subject expressed, the demonstrative *se*, which approaches a relative in use,[632] *Mt.* 27.57 cuom sum monn waelig se waes haten Ioseph 'ille (= qui) erat vocatus Ioseph'. (3) OE also often uses a pseudo-relative clause of the type just cited meaning 'illius (= cuius) nomen erat Iulius', or (once[633]) 'illi (= cui) nomen erat Iulius'. Examples in *N* are *Mt.* 27.32 gemoeton monno dhaes waes noma Symon, 27.57 cuom summ monn wlong dhaes waes noma Ioseph, and, with commoner order, *Lk.* 16.20 waes sum dhaerfe dhaes noma waes Lazarus, 19.2 wer dhaes noma waes Saccheus, 23.50 heono wer dhaes noma waes Ioseph, 24.13 in woerc dhaes [noma][634] waes Emmaus. Examples in *W* are *Mt.* 9.9 geseah aenne man sittende, thaes nama waes Matheus, 27.32 gemetton aenne mann thaes nama waes Symon, and 27.57 com sum weli mann thaes nama waes Iosep. The only example of a clause

rendered he gestrynde ane doktor, Dina hatte. (I owe these references too to Professor Dobbie; cf. fn. 623.)

[626] See fn. 627.

[627] Cf. fn. 618. In changing *midh noma* to *waes genemned*, the translator overlooked the fact that now the Latin accusative *Matthaeum*, which had no gloss (cf. fn. 591), needed to be replaced by the nominative *Matthaeus*.

[628] Here *genemned* might be viewed as simply the participle, in agreement with the preceding *monn*, but I think it is better to take it as equivalent to *waes genemned* in view of the fairly common occurrence of the finite form elsewhere (in this very passage in *W*, quoted just below, and in the other passages from *N*, quoted just above). Skeat has the 'or' sign after *genemned* in *N*, but I do not see why.

[629] Cf. fn. 632.

[630] On the phrase *othrum naman* see below, fn. 640.

[631] On *hatte* cf. fn. 624.

[632] It thus differs from the personal pronoun *he*, met in *W* in *Lk.* 5.27. See fn. 622; also, on Gothic, fnn. 548 and 554.

[633] In the *M* version of *Mt.* 27.32.

[634] The omission of *noma* here is evidently a piece of inadvertence on the part of the writer. It is supplied in *N²*.

of this sort in *M* is also the only example with a dative instead of a genitive,[635] *Mt.* 27.32 gemoettun monn thaem wes noma Symon.

198. Of all the examples cited in the previous paragraph, one, the *W* version of *Lk.* 5.27, geseah publicanum he waes othrum naman Leui gehaten, merits special comment, because of the occurrence in it of the dative *othrum naman*.[636] However, it must be stressed that the dative here belongs with the verb *waes gehaten*,[637] and thus does not correspond to the Latin *nomine*, which belongs with the nouns *publicanum Levi*. In none of the other OE versions of Latin passages illustrating the construction *homo Iulius nomine* does the dative appear, and presumably the translator inserted the dative phrase *othrum naman*[638] here because he wished to introduce[639] the notion that Levi was the publican's *other* or *second* name,[640] thus harmonizing the passage in *Lk.*[641] with the parallel passage *Mt.* 9.9,[642] where the publican similarly treated by Jesus is called Matthew.[643]

199. The same sort of translation as we have just noted (§197) for

[635] Cf. fn. 633.

[636] Already referred to, fnn. 600, 612, and 630.

[637] Just as in *Lk.* 1.61 the dative belongs with *ge-ceiged* or *genemned*; see above, §193 and fn. 600.

[638] Professor Dobbie, whom I consulted in regard to this rather unusual use of the dative, cited as a parallel the OE translation of Gregory's Pastoral Care (ed. by Sweet) 173.16 Gregorius, se waes odhrum noman genemned Nanzanzenus; also an example with the almost non-existent instrumental (merged with the dative in *naman*, but here preserved in the pronominal form *odhre*), the OE translation of Boethius (ed. by Sedgefield) 10.8 hatadh morgensteorra, thone ilcan we hatadh odhre naman aeiensteorra.

[639] Or to reproduce if he really found a corresponding word in the Latin original with which he was dealing. See fn. 640.

[640] There is no such word as 'other' or 'second' in the Vulgate, or in *N* (*N²* is lost). Its presence in *W* might suggest, though Skeat does not cite it, some support for his idea (on which see fn. 589) that the *W* version of the Gospels goes back to a different Latin original from the *N* version. The Hatton MS follows the earlier *W* version, reading ge-seah publicanum the waes odher name Leuj ge-haten. I am not sure of the form of *odher name*: *name* might be a rare form of the nominative (Sievers, *OEGr.* 154), but in late West Saxon it could also be a dative (ib. 153); *odher* certainly seems to be a nominative. Probably *odher name* is an instance of the break-down of the OE inflectional system, and thus cannot be cited (much though I wish it could!) as evidence for my theory that *nomen* was originally in partitive apposition with *homo*.

[641] However, he made no such attempt in the similar passage in *Mk.* 2.14, where the man whom Jesus saw "sedentem ad telonium" and bade follow him is called Levi as in *Lk.* 5.27. In *Mk. W* reads simply he ge-seah Leuin Alphei sittende aet his cep-setle.

[642] Quoted in Latin in §171 and in OE in §197.

[643] Matthew is also called the publican in the list of the twelve Apostles in *Mt.* 10.3 (though not in the similar lists in *Mk.* 3.18, *Lk.* 6.15, and *Acts* 1.13).

nomine frequently serves for *cui nomen* and the rarer *cui nomen erat*, met in *Mk.* 14.32,[644] *Lk.* 1.26, 1.27, 2.25, 8.41, 24.18,[645] *Jn.* 1.6, of course always with the proper noun following. This is at times rendered literally with the dative, 'illi [= cui] nomen est'; but at other times the translator shifts to the genitive (which we found so frequently in translations of *nomine*), 'illius (= cuius) nomen est'.[646] *W* has the genitive in every instance, *thaes nama waes*, or, in the one instance where the feminine is called for (*Lk.* 1.26), *thaere*[647] *nama waes*. *N* on the other hand regularly has the dative: *Mk.* 14.32[648] dhaem is noma is on Ebrisc Gesamini, *Lk.* 1.27 dhaere[649] noma waes Ioseph, 2.25 dhaem noma Simeon, 8.41 dhaem noma waes Iairus, 24.18 dhaem waes noma Cleophas, *Jn.* 1.6 dhaem noma uaes Iohannes; also in one instance, instead of the simple dative, a combination of the preposition *to* with the dative,[650] namely in *Lk.* 1.26[651] to dhaer noma Nazareth.[652]

---

[644] This had a genitive in the Greek. Cf. above, §185; also below, fn. 646.

[645] Here the Greek had *onomati*, not a relative clause. Cf. above, §177 and fn. 542.

[646] It is worth noting once more that, while the Latin always has the dative, the Greek fluctuated between the genitive and the dative. Cf. fn. 644.

[647] To be sure, *thaere* can also be dative; but I assume that here it is the genitive, in keeping with the practice of *W* everywhere else.

[648] This is a very complicated passage. The Latin is simple enough, in praedium cui nomen Gethsemani. But the translator into *N* apparently took *praedium* 'estate' (representing Greek *chórion*) as a proper noun corresponding to the Hebrew *Gethsemani*, for he rendered the passage on th lond dhe is genemned predium dhaem is noma th is on ebrisc Gesemani 'to the property which is called Predium, to which is the name which is in Hebrew Gethsemane'. (The first word that I am rendering 'which' is the particle *dhe*, the second the demonstrative *dhaem*; on both see fn. 622.) The translator of *N*² followed him closely. The *W* version is perfectly straightforward and exact: to anum tune thaes nama waes Gezemasi 'to an estate whose name was Gethsemane'.

[649] Just as I assumed, on the basis of parallel passages, that *thaere* was a genitive in *W* (cf. fn. 647), so I assume that its variant *dhaere* is a dative here. Of course we should not have a feminine at all, but the trouble came about through the faulty recording (already noted above in fn. 589) of the preceding *viro* (the antecedent of *cui* in the Latin) as *virgo*, a mistake perhaps contributed to by the presence of *ad virginem* before *desponsatam viro*. This was changed to *viro* by a later hand in *N*, and is correctly given in *N*², which also properly replaces the *dhaere* by *dhaes* in the translation.

[650] We meet the same variant in *Mk.* 3.16 (§195), where *N* has *to Symone* and *N*² has *to Simoni*. The *to* phrase here is of course quite different from the one in *Mk.* 5.9 (cited in the following paragraph), where the phrase is equivalent to a dative of purpose, not a dative of indirect object; see fn. 654. On the use of *to* plus dative instead of the simple dative, cf. fn. 609; also the not dissimilar use of *do* plus dative in Old Irish (§228 and fn. 732).

[651] Referred to above in fn. 609, and below in fn. 653. It is rather odd that this variant construction immediately precedes the normal one (i.e. the simple dative) in *Lk.* 1.27, cited just above.

However, in *Lk.* 24.18, *dhaem waes noma Cleophas* is followed by the variant *dhaes noma Cleophas*, i.e. the dative has been replaced by the genitive.[653]

200. This distinction between genitive and dative is carried out in other instances too where the Latin uses the dative of possession: *Jn.* 18.10 erat nomen servo Malchus, *Mk.* 5.9 quod tibi nomen est? Legio mihi nomen est, *Lk.* 8.30 quod tibi nomen est? N employs the dative uniformly: *Jn.* 18.10 uaes noma dhaem esne Malchus, *Mk.* 5.9 huaetd dhe to noma is? here to noma me is,[654] *Lk.* 8.30 huaed dhe noma is? But *W* replaces the dative noun by a genitive in *Jn.* 18.10 thaes theowan nama waes Malchus, and replaces the dative pronouns by possessive adjectives in *Mk.* 5.9 hwaet is thin nama? min nama is Legio and in *Lk.* 8.30 hwaet is thin nama?[655]

201. There is just one passage where, though N^2 clings to the dative, *N* agrees with *W* in using the genitive. This is a passage in which Latin, following the Greek original word for word,[656] employs a pronoun in the genitive: *Lk.* 1.5 fuit uxor illius de filiabus Aaron, et nomen eius Elisabeth. However, the text of the Vulgate used by the N^2 translator substitutes the dative *ei* for *eius*.[657] Very strangely,[658] both *N* and N^2 use a masculine pronoun for the ambiguous *eius* or *ei* of the Latin:[659] the former has *noma his* (genitive) Elizabet, the latter has *noma him* (dative) Elizabeth. The *W* version, *hyre nama waes Elizabeth*, correctly employs the feminine *hyre*; this may be either genitive

---

[652] On the treatment of this passage in N^2, see directly below, fn. 653.

[653] Similarly, N^2 has dhaes noma waes Cleopas. The writer of this elsewhere changed the dative of *N* to a genitive: in *Lk.* 1.27, where he replaced the ambiguous but presumably dative feminine *dhaere* (cf. fn. 649) by the masculine genitive *dhaes*, and perhaps in *Lk.* 1.26, where he replaced the prepositional phrase *to dhaer* (in which *dhaer* is an indubitable dative form) by the ambiguous *dhaere* (cf. fn. 647).

[654] In this passage the use of the preposition *to* (also referred to in fn. 650) shows us that *noma* must be a dative not a nominative. In other words we have the "double dative" construction (cf. Corson's glossary, 460, s.v. *to*), as if the Latin had been *quod tibi nomini est? Legio mihi nomini est*. However, I do not believe Latin ever uses the "double dative" with *nomen* (the second dative in *Iulio mihi nomen est*—on which see §142—is of course quite different).

[655] We shall find the same usage in *Beowulf*, 343 Beowulf is min name (see below, §220).

[656] See above, §185.

[657] Cf. above, fn. 589.

[658] Cf. similar examples of carelessness noted earlier (fnn. 634 and 649).

[659] This cannot be accounted for by an error in the Latin text, as may be the reverse use of a feminine pronoun to refer to a man in *Lk.* 1.27 (on which see fn. 649).

or dative, but, as usual in dealing with *W*, I assume[660] it is a dative on the basis of parallels elsewhere.

202. In the one place where Latin, following the Greek literally, has a genitive and not a dative, all three OE dialects, following the Latin literally, also have genitives. This is *Mt.* 10.2[661] duodecim Apostolorum nomina sunt haec, rendered into OE as follows: *N* tuelfe dhara Apostolorum noma sint dhas, *M* thara twelf Apostola noma thonne sindun thas, *W* dhis synt sodhlice thaera twelf Apostola naman. Here a dative would not really be in place, for the predicate is *haec*, not *Apostolorum*.

203. Having now completed my investigation of the Gothic and early OE translations of the *NT*, I wish to state most emphatically that I am not laboring under the delusion that it is in any way conclusive. Based on only two Germanic languages, and on an infinitesimal proportion of the remains of one of them, and at that depending on the *argumentum e silentio*, it could not possibly lay any claim to complete cogency.[662] Yet none the less so far as it goes it certainly seems to

---

[660] Cf. above, fn. 649.

[661] See above, fn. 574.

[662] However, it is perhaps significant that the evidence furnished by the West Saxon translation of the Gospels finds confirmation in the evidence furnished by the Alfredian translation of Bede's *Ecclesiastical History*. When Alfred found the ablative of specification *nomine*, and also when he found the clause *cui nomen*, *cui nomen est*, or *cui nomen erat*, he rendered the Latin by a clause of one of two types, (a) *thaes noma waes* 'cuius nomen erat', or (b) *(se) waes haten* '(ille or qui) erat vocatus', or *hatte* 'vocabatur'. Examples (all supplied by Professor Dobbie) follow (I cite the Latin passages by page and line in Plummer's edition of Bede, and the Old English passages by line as in Schipper's). (1) The Latin has *nomine*. Translations of type a. 1.25 (45.25–26) cum episcopo nomine Liudhardo; (1159–63) mid thy biscope, thaes nama waes Leodheard. 3.2 (130.10–12) quidam de fratribus nomine Bothelm; (147–49) waes sum of tham brothrum, thaes nama waes Bothelm. 3.7 (140.19–20) venit pontifex quidam, nomine Agilberctus; (587–90) tha com sum bisceop, thaes nama waes Aegelberht. Translations of type b. 2.9 (98.43–99.1) missus a rege Occidentalium Saxonum nomine Cuichelmo; (894–95) waes he sended fram Westseaxna cynincge, se waes haten Cwichelm. 3.1 (127.7–9) regnum suscepit filius Aedilfridi, nomine Aeanfled; (15–17) feng to rice Aethelfrithes sunu, Eanfridh waes haten. 2.15 (116.18) occisus est a viro gentili nomine Ricbercto; (1603–5) waes ofslegen fram sumum haethenum men, Ricbyrht hatte. (2) The Latin has *cui nomen* (*est* or *erat*). Translations of type a. 2.9 (99.19) pepererat regina filiam, cui nomen Aenfled; (928–30) cende sio cwen dohtor, thaere noma waes Eanflaed. 2.16 (117.6–7) praefectum Lindocolinae civitatis, cui nomen erat Blaecca; (1653–55) Lyndcylene ceastre gerefan, thaes nama waes Blecca. 3.19 (168.16–17) in villa sua, cui nomen est Perrona; (2177–78) on his tune, dhaes noma is Perrona. Translations of type b. 3.7 (140.13–14) secessit ad regem Orientalium Anglorum, cui nomen erat Anna; (575–76) da gewat he to Eastengla cyninge, se

confirm my informants who assured me that the Sanskrit and Greek construction of 'in name' does *not* appear in Germanic.[663]

204. Wulfila actually found one example (*Mt.* 27.57) in which the word for 'name' at least could be (and in my opinion should be[664]) interpreted as an accusative of specification. Either he did not interpret it as a potential accusative of specification,[665] or, if he did so recognize it, he still did not see fit to render it as such in Gothic. This is not the way he dealt with the accusatives of specification in *Jn.* 11.44 and *Eph.* 6.14 (both quoted above in fn. 477), which he translated literally *gabundans handuns jah fotuns* 'bound hands and feet' and *ufgaurdanai hupins izwarans* 'girt up as to your loins', thus suggesting that he could use the accusative of specification (whether or not it accorded with his native idiom) for parts of the body but not for 'name'. It is also not the way he dealt with the dative of specification *onomati*, which, as we have seen (§181), he regularly rendered literally as *namin*.

205. On the other hand the translators of the Gospels into OE, when they met the corresponding Latin construction, the ablative of specification *nomine*, did not use a dative of specification.[666] Neither did they find any consistent way of rendering this ablative, but employed a variety of devices. To paraphrase in Latin their renderings, *N* said *cum nomine Iulius, vocatus Iulius, vocatus erat Iulius*, and *illius (cuius) erat nomen Iulius*; *M* said *ille erat vocatus Iulius* and *illi erat nomen Iulius*; and *W* said *in nomine Iulius, Iulius vocabatur, erat vocatus Iulius, illius (cuius) nomen erat Iulius*. Obviously, their invariable failure, in translating the expression 'in name', to use for the Latin ablative of specification its closest parallel in Germanic, the dative, shows that this construction was wholly alien to OE. Had the accusative of specification not been equally alien, is it not highly probable that they would have employed

---

waes Anna haten. 4.1 (203.28–29) ad portum cui nomen est Quentauic; (173–74) to tham porte, the is nemned Cwentawic. A Latin passage similar to the *cui nomen* type, 5.12 (310.25) hoc erat viro nomen, is rendered by the (a) type of translation, (1897–98) waes thaes weres nama.

[663] Cf. above, §165.

[664] Cf. above, §191.

[665] Evidently Jerome *did*, for, as we have seen (§182), he treated it just as he did the dative of specification elsewhere, and not, like Wulfila, as a nominative.

[666] Cf. above, §197. *Lk.* 5.27 in the *W* version is only an apparent exception; on this see §198.

it at least occasionally? It would have been closer to the Latin than any of the forms they did use (with the possible exception of the prepositional phrases), and they did on the whole keep as close to the Latin as they could.[667] On the other hand, as we have just seen, they were not slavishly consistent in their methods; they could depart from their Latin model, or from one particular method of following that model, in a manner unpredictable and unaccountable. Which makes all the more striking the total absences from their renderings of anything suggesting an accusative of specification.

206. I conclude therefore that the probabilities are that Germanic, or at least Gothic and Old English, lacked the type of expression *homo Iulius nomen*,[668] whether in it we interpret *nomen* as a nominative in apposition with *homo*, or as an accusative of specification. If I am right in believing that the second construction was a development of the first (and a natural development, arrived at independently in at least one language group and possibly two[669]), then we would expect that under usual circumstances a language which had the one at an early stage would at a later stage have the other. These usual circumstances prevailed in Gothic. They did *not* prevail in the West Germanic languages, because in them there is lacking the necessary concomitant for such development—to wit, the neuter gender of the word for 'name'. So even if OE did possess the first locution *homo Iulius nomen*, with *nomen* a nominative (*nama*), it could not have produced the second, with *nomen* an accusative (*naman*).

207. But did it possess the first?[670] According to Gray,[671] it did. He, as we have seen (fnn. 19 and 40, and §165), interprets *nomen* as in apposition with *Iulius*, not with *homo* as I do; but no matter which way we analyze it, an expression of this type has the same appearance.

---

[667] Cf. Skeat, *Dialects* 23–24.

[668] The validity of this method of checking Germanic syntax by noting the consistent departures of the Gothic and Old English translations of the Bible from their respective Greek and Latin originals seems to be attested by the uniformity with which the Vulgate replaces the present passive participle of the Greek (such as *kaloumenos*) by a relative clause (such as *qui dicitur*); cf. §171. From this observation we might have safely inferred, even did we not already know it, that Latin lacks a present passive participle.

[669] Indo–Iranian (possibly) and Greek.

[670] I have already (in fn. 640) expressed the conviction that *odher name* as recorded in *Lk.* 5.27 in the Hatton MS cannot be an instance.

[671] The material here presented in detail I have summarized in the course of an article which I published in *Lg.* 37.476–83; see especially 479–83.

208. As examples illustrating his thesis that the word for 'name' was "ursprünglich bloss ein Wort in Apposition mit dem Nomen proprium" (*IF* 11.307), Gray quotes two passages from *Beowulf* (ib. 309): 78 scop him Heort naman, which he translates "gab ihm den Namen 'Heort'", and 1457 waes thaem haeft-mece Hrunting nama, which he translates "war ihm ein Heftschwert, 'Hrunting' sein Name".

209. The first of these passages presents no problem at all. It is of the type *homini nomen Iulium indunt*, which we have already met in the renderings of *Mk.* 3.16–17.[672] Gray's translation is perfectly acceptable, although the fundamental meaning of the verb *scyppan* is 'make, create'[673] rather than 'give'. But how he could think that the passage which he correctly rendered as he did illustrates the view that 'name' is in apposition with the proper name, I do not see.[674] Surely in this passage, as in all others of the sort, the word denoting the proper name (*Iulium*, here *Heort*) is in apposition with the word for 'name' (*nomen*, here *naman*), and not the other way around.[675] It is not *Heort* that we give him, or make for him; it is a name.

210. In the second passage, Gray clearly takes *haeft-mece* as a nominative, used as subject of the verb *waes*, and *thaem* as a dative demonstrative pronoun referring to Beowulf, used as a dative of possession: 'erat illi gladius Hrunting nomen'. But it is equally possible (and, as we shall see infinitely more probable) that *haeft-mece* is a dative of possession, and *thaem* a demonstrative adjective (or article), used as a modifier of *haeft-mece*: 'erat illi gladio Hrunting nomen'.[676] And this is obviously the view of all the OE scholars whose works I have consulted in

[672] In *N* in both 3.16 and 3.17 (the simple dative in the latter, the dative with *to* in the former); in *W* in 3.17 only. See above, §195; and, on the construction in general, §14 and fn. 39.

[673] 'Make' is also the fundamental meaning of Latin *facio* and Breton *ober*, commonly used in the same construction. See fn. 39.

[674] He similarly attributes (ib.) to the original interpretation of *nomen* "in appositioneller Bedeutung" the variant constructions in Latin seen in *Aul.* 164 sit paratum nomen puero Postumus vs. *Capt.* 69 iuventus nomen indidit Scorto mihi. Again I fail to follow him. Clear proof (should any be needed) that the proper noun and not *nomen* is the appositive is furnished in *Aul.* 164 by the gender of *paratum*, and in *Capt.* 69 by the shift of *Scorto* away from the case of *nomen* to that of *mihi*. My own view on the implications of the double construction has been given above, §17; see also §143.

[675] So too I believe in opposition to Delbrück that *Iulium* is in apposition with *nomen* in the construction *puerum nomen Iulium nominant*; see fnn. 37 and 40.

[676] Cf. above, §200, and below, §220.

this matter, so far as they commit themselves, the editors in their glossaries,[677] and the translators in their versions.[678] The editors apparently do not consider that any problem is involved,[679] since they do not discuss it in their commentaries.[680]

211. The question therefore arises as to whether Gray has any justification for offering an opinion counter to the obviously unanimous one of OE specialists—or indeed whether he has any realization that he is so doing!

212. There are a few points in his favor; but none is cogent, and all can be counterbalanced or even refuted.

213. (1) The initial position of the verb 'to be' (*waes*) perhaps suggests that it is used predicatively, not copulatively:[681] literally, 'there was a sword to him, named Hrunting' (rather than 'the name to the sword was Hrunting'). Cf. 2493 naes [= *ne* 'not' + *waes*] him aenig thearf 'there was not to him any lack'. On the other hand, this order is by no means proof that *waes* means 'there was', since usage varies. Indeed, the verb can have this meaning even when not initial; in particular contrast 2493 with 201 him waes manna thearf 'to him there was lack of men'.

214. (2) *Haeft-mece* can of course be a nominative. Cf. the nominative *mece* in 1937-38 waes mece gethinged 'the sword was appointed'. On the other hand, it can equally well be a dative.

215. (3) *Thaem* can be a substantive; the demonstrative is frequently so used in *Beowulf*. I cite a few other instances in the dative: 12 dhaem

---

[677] A number of the glossaries that I have seen classify their entries by form, and all those that do so call *haeft-mece* in line 1457 a dative. These glossaries are in editions prepared by the following scholars: Harrison and Sharp, Heyne-Schücking, Holder, Klaeber, Sedgefield. The same classification is given in Grein's thesaurus (2.20).

[678] The following translators show clearly that such is their interpretation of the line: Botkine, Child, Crawford, Ettmüller, Garnett, Genzmer, Gering, Gummere, Hall, Hall-Wrenn, Huyshe, Kirtlan, Morgan, Morris and Wyatt, Pierquin, Steineck, Strong, Thorpe, Tinker. The translation by Ayres is too free to help, and that by Leonard ("a good sword hafted, and Hrunting its name") is too vague.

[679] Just one edition (that of Harrison and Sharp) has a note to the effect that the line contains a dative of possession; this is not identified in the note, but the glossary, as we have seen (fn. 677), classes *haeftmece* as a dative.

[680] This applies to all the editors cited in fn. 677, and also to the following, who either do not classify words as to form in their glossaries, or lack glossaries altogether: Dobbie, Holthausen, Hoopes, Wrenn, Wyatt-Chambers.

[681] Cf. above, §6.

aefera waes cenned 'to him a son was born', 59–60 dhaem feower bearn wocun 'for him (or from him) four children sprang', 374–75 dhaem forgeaf Hrethel dohtor 'to him Hrethel gave (his) daughter'. On the other hand, *thaem* can equally well be an adjective with *haeft-mece*; this use of the demonstrative is common in *Beowulf*. Cf. e.g. 197 = 790 = 806 on thaem daege thysses lifes 'on this day of this life'.

216. (4) *Thaem* is normally used with a noun—i.e. as an adjective meaning 'this' or 'the'—only when the noun designates an entity that has already, and fairly recently, been mentioned (possibly under a different name); but the *haeft-mece* of 1457 has not previously received any explicit reference. Examples of this usage are innumerable; here are a few samples, all in the dative: 143 thaem feonde 'from the fiend' (cf. 101 feond 'a fiend' [682] and subsequent references to Grendel) and 425 widh tham [683] aglaecan 'against the monster' (cf. 424 Grendel); 270 to thaem maeran 'to the famous one' (cf. 268 sunu Healfdenes 'Haelfdene's son'); 824 aefter tham wael-raese 'in consequence of the bloody conflict' (just narrated at length) and 1073 aet tham lind-plegan 'in the battle' (implied in 1068–70); 1421 on tham holm-clife 'on the sea-cliff' (implied by the preceding description); above all the numerous references to Hrothgar's famous hall, whose construction is told of at the outset of the poem (we first hear of his intention of building his palace in 68, where it is called *heal-reced* 'a hall-house'), e.g. 695 in thaem win-sele 'in the wine-hall', 713 and 1016 in (or on) sele tham hean 'in the high hall'; similarly of Hygelac's palace, 1984 in sele tham hean (cf. 1976 flet innan-weard 'the inner hall' *without* a demonstrative, and thereafter 1981 geond thaet heal-reced 'through the hall-house' *with* a demonstrative). On the other hand, the demonstrative adjective with *haeft-mece* is not out of order, even though we have not heard of the hilted sword before; we *have* just heard in the two preceding lines of a useful loan made to Beowulf by Unferth, and this loan, as we shall

---

[682] This is the second reference to Grendel in the poem. At the first reference in 86, he is called *se ellengaest* 'the bold spirit'; but that is in keeping with a feature of the narrative style (somewhat like the classical epic plunging *in medias res*) in accordance with which the poet first refers to an important figure as familiar to the hearers or readers, and then formally introduces him (cf. Klaeber lxvi); informal story-tellers today sometimes start with "now there was *this* man" or the like. Such a usage, however, would hardly apply to a sword.

[683] A variant form of *thaem*.

see later (§221), was unquestionably Hrunting. Furthermore, the loan is thus characterized, 1455–56 naes thaet thonne maetost maegen-fultuma thaet him on dhearfe lad dhyle Hrodhgares 'nor was that then the least of mighty aids that to him in need lent Hrothgar's *dhyle*'. The demonstrative *thaet* in 1455 refers to Hrunting; and consequently it seems to me practically out of the question that the demonstrative *thaem* in 1457 could refer to Beowulf rather than to Hrunting.

217. (5) *Thaem* can be a dative of possession. Cf. 2137 thaer unc waes hand-gemaene 'there to us was a common-hand' (i.e. a hand-to-hand fight); also the two examples quoted under point 1 (§213), 201 and 2493. On the other hand, the alternative explanation also involves a dative of possession (*haeft-mece*).[684]

218. (6) The use of the dative of possession in the construction *est ei gladio Hrunting nomen* is quite unexampled in *Beowulf*. On the other hand, so is the construction *est ei gladius Hrunting nomen*, and the latter is assuredly the more unlikely of the two.[685]

219. The last point brings us back to our main subject, constructions with 'name'. As has been said (§208), Gray groups 78 scop him Heort naman and 1457 waes thaem haeft-mece Hrunting nama. As has also been said (§§209 and 210), the first belongs to the type *indunt homini Iulium nomen*,[686] the second according to Gray's interpretation to the type *est homo Iulius nomen*. But the first construction, in which *homini* is in a different case from *Iulium nomen*, in no way parallels or justifies the second, in which all three nouns are in the same case;[687] only *hominem nomen Iulium nominant*[688] would do that. Much closer to *homini Iulium nomen indunt* is *homini Iulius nomen est*.

220. Now *Beowulf* has no example of the latter construction either.

---

[684] Cf. above, fn. 679.

[685] This will be further discussed below, §220.

[686] We have met this construction in Wulfila (§175) and in the OE versions of the Gospels (§195).

[687] Latin, for instance, has the first construction and not the second.

[688] In our examination of Wulfila and of the OE Gospels (as well as their Greek and Latin originals) we found no passage with three accusatives, only passages with two, either *hominem* and *Iulium* or *nomen* and *Iulium* (§§169–73, 193–94). The former construction is met in *Beowulf* also: 363–64 thone yldestan oret-mecgas Beowulf nemnadh 'the warriors call the chief Beowulf', 1354–55 thone Grendel nemdon fold-buende 'the earth-dwellers called him Grendel', 2806–7 thaet hit sae-lidhend hatan Biowulfes biorh 'that the seafarers may call it Beowulf's mound'.

It usually employs a quite different tournure, *homo Iulius vocatur*:[689]
102 waes se grimma gaest Grendel haten 'this savage spirit was named
Grendel'; 262-63 waes min faeder Ecgtheow haten 'my father was
named Ecgtheow', echoed in 373 waes his eald faeder Ecgtheo haten
'his old [or late?] father was named Ecgtheow'; 2602 Wiglaf waes
haten Weoxstanes sunu 'Weohstan's son was named Wiglaf'. It also
says (as already remarked in fn. 655) 343 Beowulf is min name 'Beowulf
is my name'. *Iulius est nomen meum* would of course correspond to
Iulius est nomen hominis, not to *Iulius est nomen homini*. We have already
noted (§200) that the West Saxon version of the Gospels invariably
uses a genitive or a possessive adjective where the Anglian versions
(Northumbrian and Mercian) almost invariably use a dative.[690] Hence
Beowulf 343 corresponds to *Mk.* 5.9 in the West Saxon version, *min*
['meum'] *nama is Legio*, not in the Northumbrian version, *Here to
noma me* ['mihi'] *is*; but Beowulf 1457 waes thaem haeft-mece Hrunting
nama corresponds to *Jn.* 18.10 in the Northumbrian version, *uaes
noma dhaem esne* ['illi servo'] *Malchus*, not in the West Saxon version,
thaes theowan ['illius servi'] *nama waes Malchus*. However, this does not
need to arouse our suspicions. There is plenty of dialect mixture in
Beowulf; the consensus of opinion seems to be that the poem as we have
it is primarily in West Saxon (the dialect of the greater part of OE
literature), but that in origin it was Anglian (the probability inclining
slightly to Northumbrian rather than to Mercian).[691] It may be worth
noting that the form *mece* (instead of *maece*) in this very same line is
Anglian, not West Saxon.[692] Furthermore, even though the West
Saxon version of the Gospels, in contrast with the Northumbrian,

[689] The OE Gospels too show this construction frequently (§§193 and 197), and
Wulfila also has it (§172). It of course corresponds in the passive to the examples cited
in fn. 688.

[690] This occurs (1) in clauses serving as paraphrases for *nomine*, where *W* has three
examples of *thaes nama waes*, and *N*, contrary to its usual custom, has six, but *M* has one
example of *thaem wes noma* (see §197); (2) in clauses rendering *cui nomen (erat)* where
invariably (seven times) *W* has the genitive *thaes* or *thaere naman waes*, and *N* the dative
(once with a preposition) *thaem* or *thaer* or *thaere* (see §199); (3) in other clauses involving
a dative of possession, where invariably (four times) W has a genitive or a possessive, and
N has a dative (see §200).

[691] See e.g. Klaeber lxxii, xc, xci, cxxi; Dobbie lvii.

[692] See Klaeber on *mece*, lxxix fn. 2: "This, the invariable form in OE., has become
stereotyped through its use in English poetry." Cf. also Sweet, *Dict.* 115 s.v.; Wright,
OEGr. 59.

lacks the construction with the dative,[693] we do find it elsewhere in West Saxon, both in prose[694] and in poetry.[695]

221. Hence on linguistic grounds we may conclude that our line means 'this sword was called Hrunting'. But there are other grounds as well for adopting this interpretation. We have only to examine the situation, the context, and we perforce must come to the same con-

[693] As does also Alfred's translation of Bede's *Ecclesiastical Hist.* On this see fn. 662.

[694] We find examples of the construction in both of Plummer's versions of the *Chronicles* (the so-called *Anglo-Saxon Chronicle*), A (the Parker MS) and E (the Laud MS). The older of the two, A, is definitely West Saxon; but E is more complicated. Though begun, according to Plummer (2.l and liv), at Canterbury, E is associated with Peterborough; and in this form, though it has West Saxon features, it is thought to have been originally Anglian. Skeat (*Dialects* 73) pronounces it Mercian; and Clark in the course of her very thoughtful and thorough discussion (xxx–lxvi) of the language of the *Peterborough Chronicle* (= E from 1070 on) agrees (xxx) that its writers were probably natives of the East Midland, though she points out parallels (xxxi–xxxii) with the Northumbrian Lindisfarne Gloss of the Gospels as well as with the Mercian Rushworth Gloss of the first Gospel (already noted above in fnn. 586 and 587 respectively), and she concludes that "the language of this text appears to be basically Anglian, although certainly influenced by the [West Saxon] Schriftsprache" (xlix). At all events not only in E but in A as well we find agreement with the Northumbrian as opposed to the West Saxon version of the Gospels (cf. §§199 and 200) and to the thoroughly West Saxon Alfred (cf. fn. 662) in the employment of the construction *ei erat nomen* rather than *eius nomen erat*. As examples may be cited the following: 465A tham waes noma Wipped, E tham waes nama Wipped; 508A tham was nama Natanleod, E tham waes nama Nazaleod; 975A tham waes Eadweard nama (a line of verse incorporated in the Chronicle); 1118E tham waes odher nama Gelasius; 1119E tham weardh nama Calixtus. However, E seems definitely to prefer the locution 'he was named', met also in all three versions of the Gospels (see point 2 in §197) and in Alfred (see fn. 662): note e.g. *het* 'vocatur', 777, 963, 1086 (twice), 1124; *hatte* 'vocabatur', 656, 1070, 1106; *is gehaten* 'est vocatus', 495 (A here has *is gecueden*), 1086; *waes* (or *was*) *gehaten* 'erat vocatus', 656 (four times), 777 (twice), 963 (three times), 1070 (three times), 1085, 1086, 1124. A rather odd variation, in the form *ei nomen erat vocatum*, seems almost like a contamination of the two constructions: this is 794A tham was other noma nemned Praem, E tham waes odher nama nemned Praem. (This seems to me less natural than the construction *eius nomen erat vocatum*, as in the Northumbrian version of *Lk.* 2.21, quoted in §194). The fact that the West Saxon A as well as the Anglian E at times agrees with Northumbrian as opposed to West Saxon serves definitely to illustrate dialect mixture; the existence of this is of course not surprising, in view of the Chronicles' lack of homogeneity in both time and place.

[695] As examples may be cited: *Genesis* 1106 tham waes Seth noma; *Andreas* 1322 tham waes Crist nama; *Elene* 418 dham waes Iudas nama, 437 tham waes Sachius nama. (All these examples I owe to Professor Dobbie.) All the passages cited here are from works of literature regularly regarded as West Saxon in their existing form; if the attributions of *Genesis* to Caedmon, and of *Elene* (as seems certain) and *Andreas* to Cynewulf, are correct, these works, like Beowulf (cf. just above, in this paragraph), have an Anglian origin and may exhibit dialect mixture.

clusion. Beowulf is getting ready for his fight with Grendel's mother. He puts on his armor (1441–42); there is a special description of the corselet or coat-of-mail which is to protect his body (1443–47) and of the helmet which is to protect his head (1448–54). Then we read (1455–57) 'nor was that then the smallest of powerful helps that to him in need Hrothgar's *dhyle* lent; this hilted sword's name was Hrunting.' Hrothgar's *dhyle* (apparently some sort of spokesman or major domo [696]) was a man named Unferth (cf. 1165 Unferth thyle). What he lent Beowulf was certainly the sword Hrunting; cf. 1467–68 he thaes waepnes onlah selran sweord-frecan 'he made a loan of this weapon to a superior swordsman'.[697] It would therefore be absurd to think that after the lines telling about the valuable aid, namely, the sword, lent Beowulf by Hrothgar's *dhyle*, the poet would have added a line meaning 'he had a sword named Hrunting', as if he was telling us something new. Nor do I see how anyone who actually read the scene *could* think such a thing.

222. I fear that Gray (in 1900) copied the line out of some sort of lexicon or concordance, that Foy the following year copied the line out of Gray's article,[698] that Brugmann nine years later copied it out of

---

[696] The meaning is not certain; it has even been suggested that he is a kind of court jester, which to me seems not impossible. See Klaeber's interesting discussion (145–46) of this very interesting figure.

[697] This loan is generally viewed as an act of courtesy and magnanimity on Unferth's part, which is surprising after his earlier malicious attack on Beowulf (506–28). Beowulf is grateful, and in directing what shall be done with his treasures in case of his death, says that his own sword is to be given to Unferth; meanwhile he will fight with Hrunting (1488–91). But when he is actually engaged in battle with the horrible she-monster, the sword fails him (1522–28), and only a miracle (the finding with God's help of another and better weapon) saves his life (1553–62), as he afterwards reports (1655–64). He expressly says that Hrunting is good (1660), and in returning it to Unferth thanks him and praises him, and does not blame the sword (1807–12); yet I cannot help wondering whether there may not be an implication of some sort of trick on Unferth's part, which Beowulf is too chivalrous to recognize.

[698] Foy, *IF* 12.178, cites as a possible source for the use of Sanskrit *nāma* "im Sinne von 'mit Namen'" "solche Sätze wie *Beow.* 1457" (as if there were other instances of the sort as reported by Gray and Foy!). He then, after quoting the line, offers as a translation "es war ihm ein Heftschwert, Hrunting (war) der Name". It will be seen that this reproduces (with the insignificant addition of a preliminary expletive *es*) Gray's impossible version of the first part of the line, but substitutes for Gray's also impossible version of the second part, "Hrunting sein Name", an equally impossible but quite different rendering, "Hrunting (war) der Name", which presupposes a wholly dissimilar analysis of the structure.

Foy's,[699] and that none of them examined the text! Error dies hard: the error perpetrated by Gray and perpetuated by Foy and Brugmann is still alive, more than half a century later, as witness Humbach, *MSS* 5.91 (1954),[700] and Schmidt, *ZCP* 28.230 (1961).[701] Furthermore, it is evident that Foy alone had actually read Gray's article; the others manifestly had not, Brugmann depending on Foy, and Humbach (presumably) and Schmidt depending on Brugmann,[702] without checking.

223. If this chapter, futile though I fear it may be in other respects, serves to register a resounding protest against such methods in the field of linguistics or of philology, it will not have been written in vain.

[699] Brugmann, *IF* 27.144, seizes upon the line from *Beowulf* and Foy's translation of it (which he copies exactly) as an illustration, parallel to Xenophon, *An.* 1.2.23 ῥεῖ ποταμὸς Κύδνος ὄνομα (cited above, §137), in favor of his thesis (on which cf. above, §6) that originally the proper noun and the word for 'name' were in the relationship to each other of subject and predicate. "Passend verweist Gray auf Beowulf 1457," says he (ib.), without knowing either how Gray actually explained the passage, or how the passage really ought to be explained.

[700] Humbach, *MSS* 5.91, offers as examples of "Namenparenthese" *MBh.* 3.50 āsīd rājā Nalo nāma (on which see above, §44), which he translates "es war ein König, Nala der Name", and Beowulf 1459 (sic!), which he translates "es war ihm ein Heftschwert, Hrunting der Name". His translation of the first part of the line is identical with Foy's and Brugmann's; his translation of the second part is identical with Gray's (except for the use of "der" instead of "sein" before "Name") and is obviously based on Gray or on some copyist of Gray, but none the less he clearly agrees with Brugmann's interpretation. He does not mention Gray, Foy, or Brugmann by name, simply saying that the line is "gut bekannt und oft zitiert". "Oft zitiert" is, alas, true, frighteningly true; and "gut bekannt" is true so far as the words of the line go, but not so far as its meaning goes or the context in which it occurs.

[701] Schmidt, *ZCP* 28.230, cites the line with Brugmann's translation and apparently knows only Brugmann's discussion, not Gray's, for he says the line, cited "*seit Gray* [emphasis mine] und Brugmann", is taken by Brugmann and others as evidence for the development of the accusative of specification from a nominal parenthesis.

[702] That they without checking misinterpreted Gray, who had himself without checking misinterpreted *Beowulf*, is perhaps poetic justice!

VI. CELTIC

A. GAELIC

224. Gaelic[703] provides a fertile field for the investigation of naming constructions, since the Old and Middle Irish sagas, like the Old Persian royal annals,[704] have the habit whenever a person or a place is mentioned for the first time of using a fixed formula which may be translated 'a man named So-and-So', 'a city named So-and-So'. Before we proceed to a study of these conventional expressions, some preliminary remarks should be made in regard to the manner of denoting the owner of the name.[705]

225. When the owner of the name is indicated by a pronoun, the possessive[706] is regularly employed, as in the following.[707] *First*

[703] In Celtic as in Indic, my competence is unfortunately too limited to permit me to undertake systematic independent research on an exhaustive scale. I have perforce confined myself in the main to Old and Middle Irish, the only branches of this language of which I have any knowledge at all. Professor Robert T. Meyer of the Catholic University of America has graciously placed at my disposal a group of examples which served as a starter, and these I have augmented by a number of others which I have personally collected. These passages I believe I am qualified to interpret. I have in every instance made an independent translation, which, however, has often coincided in whole or in part with the one kindly provided by Professor Meyer for the passages which he sent me. He has also been most helpful in answering my queries.

On my still scantier treatment of Welsh, Cornish, and Breton, see fn. 796.

[704] See above, §89. We have met the same phenomenon in Hittite, Indic, and Greek (for references see fn. 12); but its regular and repeated usage is most striking in Old Persian and in Old and Middle Irish.

[705] Some of the examples here noted will be returned to later when the entire passages in which they occur are under discussion. Cf. fnn. 710, 715–17, 721, 722, 724, 726–30, 733, 735.

[706] Irish possessives are substantives rather than adjectives, being old genitives of the personal pronouns and therefore indeclinables. See Thurneysen 276–79, especially 276.

[707] In quoting Old and Middle Irish, I omit accents, which in any case are not employed consistently (Thurneysen 20). I use our own sign for *and* (&) to represent the Irish sign for *ocus* 'and'. Citations of texts are made from the following publications. *Alex.* = *Lebar Brecc*, ed. by Kuno Meyer (*IT* 2.2.1–93). *BBal.* = *Book of Ballymote*, ed. by Kuno Meyer (*IT* 2.2.94–108). *BDD* = *Togail Bruidne Da Derga*, ed. by Eleanor Knott

183

singular. Tain (St. 10.7–8) maith lem cid ed mo ainm '(it's) all right with me what it[708] (is) my name', i.e. 'what my name is'. *Second singular. Tain (St.* 3.12) cia th'ainm-siu? 'what (is) thy name?' *Tain (St.* 10.6–7) bid Cu Chulainn t'ainm-siu 'Cu Chulainn will be thy name'. In these last two examples, the possessive is reinforced by the emphasizing particle[709] (Thurneysen 252–53). *Third singular. Usn.* 5 (69.24) = *Uisl.* (44.52) bid Derdriu a hainm[710] 'Deirdre will be her name'. *Tain (St.* 12.12–13) for-biad a ainm Herinn co brath 'his name would be upon Ireland forever'. *Second plural. Wb.* 5a.17 is hed for n-ainm in sin 'it[711] is your name that' *(latine* 'est id vestrum nomen illud'), i.e. 'that is your name'.

226. All the passages listed in §225 employ the type of verbal or nominal clause *(est) nomen suum*[712] *(meum, tuum, vestrum) Iulius* 'his (my, thy, your) name (is) Julius'. Quite different is the formulaic use[713] *homo Iulius suum nomen* 'a man Julius his name', in which many scholars see a nominal clause,[714] but which I think as a rule does not

---

(*IS* 8). *Em. = Tochmarc Emire,* ed. by A. G. Van Hamel (*IS* 3.16–68). *Et. =* Tochmarc *Etaine,* ed. by Ernst Windisch (*IT* 1.113–33). *LL = Book of Leinster,* excerpt "The Power of Women", ed. by Julius Pokorny (*Historical Reader* 12–15). *Mer. Uil. = Merugud Uilix Maic Leirtis,* ed. by Robert T. Meyer (*IS* 17). *Patrick = The Tripartite Life of Patrick,* ed. by Whitley Stokes. *ScM = Scel mucci Mic Datho,* ed. by Ernst Windisch (*IT* 1.93–112); also = *Scela Mucce Maic Datho,* ed. by Rudolf Thurneysen (*IS* 6). *Tain* (St.) = *Stories from the Tain,* ed. by John Strachan, 3rd edition, rev. by Osborn Bergin. *Tain* (*YBL*) = *The Tain Bo Cuailnge from the Yellow Book of Lecan,* ed. by John Strachan and J. C. O'Keeffe. *Thes. = Thesaurus Palaeohibernicus,* ed. by Whitley Stokes and John Strachan. *Troi = Togail Troi,* ed. by Wh. Stokes (*IT* 2.1.1–142). *Uisl. = Longes Mac n-Uislenn,* ed. by Vernam Hull. *Uisn. = Oided mac nUisnig,* ed. by Whitley Stokes (*IT* 2.2.109–84). *Usn. = Longes mac n-Usnig,* ed. by Ernst Windisch (*IT* 1.59–92). *Wb. = Würzburg Glosses,* ed. by Whitley Stokes. I may add that *IS = Mediaeval and Modern Irish Series,* and *IT = Irische Texte.* The figures directly following the name of the work refer to the paragraph or section number of the text when there is one; the figures in parentheses refer to the pages and lines, or lines alone where these are numbered continuously (as in *YBL*), of the volume in which the text is published. For additional details see the Bibliography.

[708] The unidiomatic 'it' is my not very successful attempt to render *ed,* Latin 'id'. Is the French *c'* (before *est*) in *ce que c'est que ça* and *qu'est-ce que c'est que ça?* a faint echo of the Celtic construction?

[709] Referred to further below in fnn. 719 and 774.

[710] For the entire passage, see below, §239.

[711] Again I have had a struggle in rendering *(h)ed*; see fn. 708. Cf. Thurneysen 302.

[712] On my (frequently non-Latin) use of Latin *suum* to represent the Old Irish possessive, cf. below, fn. 746.

[713] Referred to in §224, and illustrated in §233.

[714] Schmidt (*ZCP* 28.231) gives as an argument for this view the fact that *ainm* is nominative. I suppose he has in mind the shift of neuter *ainm* to masculine in Middle

involve a clause at all. For the third singular we may cite, in addition
to the repeated examples of the typical formula quoted in §233, the
following passages: *Tain* (*YBL* 811) Ferteidhil a ainm;[715] the three
parallel locutions,[716] *Tain* (*St.* 17.6, 23, 15) Foill a ainm, Tuachell a
ainm, Fannall a ainm-side; *Tain* (*St.* 12.22) Ibor a ainm-side.[717] In the
last two examples the possessive *a* is reinforced by the genitive demonstrative *side*;[718] this may seem tautological to us, but *side* cannot stand
without the possessive[719] (Thurneysen 304). We also find occasional
instances of the third plural of the type *homines Iulius et Claudius
nomina sua*[720] 'men Julius and Claudius their names', as *Tain* (*St.*
15.11) Foill & Fannall & Tuachell a n-amman,[721] and *Alex.* 4 (19.45–
46) Parmenion & Amintai & Atalir a n-anmunda-side.[722] Here again
we find the reinforcing genitive *side*, this time a plural.[723]

227. When the owner of the name is indicated by a noun, we would
expect to find the genitive case of this noun to correspond to the
possessive pronoun just exemplified. We do indeed sometimes meet
such a genitive, as in *Tain* (*St.* 15.6–7) ad-fet do dano ainm cech
phrimdune 'he then tells him the name of every chief fort'; *Alex.* 26
(39.343–44) Protolomeus ainmm cech fir[724] 'Ptolemy (was)[725] the

Irish (see Pedersen, *KG* 2.66, and cf. Thurneysen 154), but I find no citation of any
accusative singular except *ainm* (on the gender of 'name' in general in the Indo–European languages, see above, fn. 14). At all events the fact that *ainm* is nominative suits my
thesis quite as well as his.
[715] For the entire passage, see below, §236.
[716] On these too see below, §236.
[717] For the entire passage, see below, §235.
[718] The form *side* is certainly used here in the masculine, though according to Thurneysen (304) the regular genitive form is *sidi* in the masculine and neuter, *side* in the feminine.
[719] We may compare the use with the possessive of the emphasizing particle *siu*
noted in §225.
[720] Of course when several persons share the same name, we expect the singular *ainm*
'nomen', as in *Wb.* 5a.17 (§225) and *Alex.* 26 (§249); but I have noted one illogical use
of the plural *anmunda* 'nomina', in *BBal.* following 272b (101.19–20) Itcifai a n-ammunda
'Ichthyophagi their *names*', as if we had *Romani nomina sua*. This shift of *nomen* to
nomina by attraction into the number of *homines* or *Iulii* (in this instance rather *Romani*
than *Iulii*) has already been noted in Hittite (fn. 151) and in *koine* Greek (§175 and fn.
520); the Hittite parallel is not so close to the Irish passage as is the Greek one.
[721] For the entire passage, see below, §236.
[722] See below, §241.
[723] For this Thurneysen (304) gives the regular form as *ade*. Cf. fn. 718.
[724] Listed below (fn. 780) in another connection.
[725] Irish apparently does not adhere to the rule (noted above in fn. 16 as a general
norm, and in fn. 262 as applied specifically to Old Persian) that nominal clauses are

name of each man'; *ScM* 1 (1.2) Aelbe ainm in chon[726] 'Aelbe (was) the dog's name'; *Alex.* 60 (69.798) Buicefalis ainmm in eich[727] 'Bucephalus (was) the horse's name'; *Uisn.* 8 (122.8) is iadso aṅimanna na bfiled[728] 'these are the names of the poets'; *Alex.* 80 (21.87–88) batar he anmandai na ceithre litre sin[729] 'these were the names of those four letters'; *Troi* 4 (9.209–10) it he anso a n-anmand na ndorus[730] 'these are the names of the gates'. The last passage shows us that the genitive[731] of a noun can be combined with the possessive *a* just as can be the genitive of a pronoun, again (as remarked in §226) in a way that seems tautological to us. The last three examples show the same use of the plural 'names' as was noted in §226.

228. But instead of the genitive we also meet a phrase consisting of the preposition *do* 'to'[732] and the dative, as in *Alex.* 33 (45.432) don choin sin is ainmm Bemoth[733] 'the name to that dog is Bemoth', i.e. 'that dog's name is Bemoth'. Or should we say rather 'the name Bemoth is to that dog', i.e. 'that dog has the name Bemoth'?[734] We also find *do* in one instance very similarly used in conjunction with a personal pronoun, namely in *Alex.* 38 (50.511) ainmm ele di ï Minotha[735] 'another name (was) to her, namely Minothaea', i.e. 'she had another name, namely Minothaea'; here the presence of *ele* 'other' would seem to have ruled out the use of the possessive *a*.

229. The situation is complicated by the fact that there is a second preposition, *di* 'of', also governing the dative, which sometimes cannot be distinguished from *do* "to'. Semantically though not syn-

---

regularly used only to refer to the present. Note that no mention of tense or time is included in Thurneysen's statement (494): "The copula is often omitted, especially when it would have been a form of the 3rd person indicative."

[726] For the entire passage, see below, §238.

[727] For the entire passage, see below, §244.

[728] For the entire passage, see below, fn. 780.

[729] For the entire passage, see below, fn. 780.

[730] For the entire passage, see below, fn. 780.

[731] The form *dorus* must be a genitive plural here, though Thurneysen (194) lists it in the plural only as nominative and accusative.

[732] On the occasional similar use of the preposition *to* 'to' in Old English, see above, §195 with fn. 609, §199 with fn. 650, also fn. 653.

[733] For the entire passage, see below, §245.

[734] In that case the phrase *don choin* is used in the predicate, somewhat like the Latin dative of possession.

[735] On this see further below, §241.

tactically, a phrase with *di* corresponds to the genitive, and a phrase with *do* to the dative. But we cannot tell which we have in certain compounds with the article, with a suffixed personal pronoun,[736] or with the relative particle -*a* (on these, respectively, see Thurneysen 505 and 506, 274, and 312). Thus in the two preceding examples we might say that the meaning is rather 'the name of that dog' and 'another name (was) hers'. I think this is less likely, however. The regular compound of *di* plus the article is apparently *din* rather than *don*;[737] and though *di* may certainly stand for either *di* or *do* plus the feminine dative pronoun of the third person singular, a dative relation seems called for there rather than a genitive.[738]

230. However, when we come to the relative formula involving the use of *dia*, with or without a suffixed (conjunctive) copulative verb, which became so common in Middle Irish,[739] it is really impossible to say whether the meaning is 'cuius nomen (est) Iulius' or 'cui nomen (est) Iulius'.[740]

231. Now it is time to return to the formulaic usage referred to above (§224). This formula runs: *erat rex Iulius suum nomen*, and is frequently cited as a parallel for the familiar Sanskrit *āsīd rājā Nalo nāma* (quoted above in §44).[741] However, *nāma* in Sanskrit, like *onoma* in Greek,[742] is regularly viewed as an accusative of specification,[743] a syntactic usage which is not recognized in Old Irish,[744] though in the

[736] The combination of a preposition and a suffixed personal pronoun is called a "conjugated preposition" (e.g. by Thurneysen 272). It seems to me that "declined preposition" would be a better name.

[737] Thurneysen (505) places the form *don* as derived from *di* within parentheses.

[738] Note Thurneysen (279) to the effect that in the predicative construction we regularly have *do* (or *la*) with a suffixed pronoun (i.e. a "conjugated preposition"; cf. fn. 736) rather than a stressed pronoun. Cf. further fn. 777.

[739] See below, §§246–49.

[740] We have found both constructions in *koine* Greek in the *NT*, though the dative is much commoner than the genitive (see §185). In the corresponding translations, Latin uses the dative oftener than the genitive (§186), whereas Gothic uses the genitive only (§187); Old English, in rendering the Latin, substitutes a personal pronoun, in either genitive (regular in West Saxon) or dative (regular in Northumbrian), for the Latin dative relative (§199). On the apparent difference in meaning between the genitive and the dative, see fn. 25.

[741] E.g. recently by Humbach, *MSS* 5.91. On this cf. below, fn. 747.

[742] See above, §116.

[743] Or at least as an adverbial accusative. See above, §43.

[744] Neither of the two great Celticists, Thurneysen and Pedersen, makes any mention of such a construction in his grammar.

shape of the construction *homo Iulius nomen* this language does at least possess the stuff out of which the accusative of specification can be formed. But if the Sanskrit *nāma* is to be considered an accusative of specification, then why not the Old Irish *ainm*? On the other hand, if the Old Irish *ainm* is *not* to be considered an accusative of specification, then why the Sanskrit *nāma*?

232. An important difference from Sanskrit exhibited by Old Irish—which is at the same time a similarity to Hittite—is its use of the possessive (*a*),[745] so that the locution is not simply *homo Iulius nomen* but *homo Iulius suum nomen*,[746] as in *KUB* 24.8.1.9–10 *nu-kan se-ir* LU-*as Ap-pu* SUM-*an-se-it* '(there is) up there a man Appus his name' (cited above, §23).[747]

233. Examples from Old Irish[748] follow. *BDD* 1 (1.1) bui ri amra airegda for Erinn, Eochaid Feidleach a ainm 'there was a wonderful, illustrious king over Ireland, Eochaid Feidlech his name'. *LL* 1 (6.1) boi ri amra for Grecaib, Salemon a ainm 'there was a wonderful king over the Greeks, Solomon his name'. *ScM* 1 (1.1) boi ri amrae for Laignib, Mac Datho a ainm[749] 'there was a wonderful king over the Leinstermen, Mac Datho his name'. A similar formula is used at the first mention of the particular hero involved, though not necessarily at the very

---

[745] See §226, also fnn. 706 and 747.

[746] On the Hittite possessive, cf. above, §20 and fnn. 62 and 161; on my use of *suum* to represent it, fn. 63.

[747] Pokorny in 1927 and Schmidt in 1961 ignore the Hittite evidence. Pokorny (*ZCP* 16.390) declares that, though constructions like the Irish one with *ainm* are met with 'name' in other Indo–European languages, this happens "niemals mit dem Possessivum". He believes (391) that the Irish construction is non-Indo–European, and cites parallels from Old Egyptian, Coptic, Berber, and Arabic (this is in line with his "substratum" theory, enunciated in *ZCP* 16.395). To be sure, it has been suggested above (fn. 62) that the Hittite construction *may* be a borrowing from Akkadian; but any parallelism between Old Irish and the Hamitic–Semitic languages cited by Pokorny seems to me purely coincidental. Schmidt (*ZCP* 28.233) views the Celtic use of the possessive merely as a later modification and therefore "nicht grundsprachlich", in opposition to Pokorny's view (which he quotes, ib. fn. 1) that it is "unindogermanisch".

[748] Most of the documents here cited are thought to date back in their origin to the Old Irish period (i.e. before 900 A.D.), although we may know them only in their Middle Irish recensions. However, *Togail Troi* and the two Alexander documents (*Lebar Brecc* and the *Book of Ballymote*) are regularly classed as Middle Irish, and are thought to be no earlier than the fourteenth century; for their dates see respectively Stokes, *IT* 2.1.1–2, and K. Meyer, *IT* 2.2.1 and 94.

[749] This is directly followed by a passage involving a quite different use of *ainm*; see §§227 and 238.

outset of the saga (which deals with Patrick's journey to Armagh) in *Patrick* (228.5) bai alaili fer soimm airmitnech i suidiu, Dare a ainm, 'i' Dare macc Findchadai 'there was a certain rich, honorable man in that (place), Dare his name, namely Dare the son of Findchad'.

234. It may well be urged,[750] in line with Brugmann's theory,[751] that the formulaic *Eochaid Feidleach* (*Salemon, Mac Datho, Dare*) *a ainm* constitutes an interpolated nominal clause; but when *a ainm* is not used, the name is clearly in apposition with the preceding *ri* 'king' or *fer* 'man', and I think we may hold that this is still true when *a ainm* is added, itself, as I believe, in partitive apposition with *ri* or *fer*. Two passages without *ainm*, but in other ways parallel with the preceding ones, follow. *Em.* 1 (20.1–2) bai ri amrae aeregdae i nEmain Macha fecht n-aill, 'i' Conchobur man Fachtnai Fathaig 'there was a wonderful, illustrious king in Emain Macha once upon a time [literally, in another time], namely Conchobur son of Fachtnai Fathaig'. *Et.* 1 (117.1) bai ri amra aireagdai i n-airdrige for hErinn 'i' Eochuidh Aiream mac Finn 'there was a wonderful, illustrious king in the high-kingship over Ireland, namely Eochaid Airem, son of Finn'.

235. It is interesting to note in the three preceding examples[752] the presence of 'i', an abbreviation of the Latin *id est*, rendered in Irish by *ed-on*,[753] corresponding in force to our *namely*. In these three passages it is used before a word which is clearly an appositive: an additional appositive *macc* 'son' following the usual formula *Dare a ainm* in the first example; and, in the other two, the personal name itself, used, as already noted, without *ainm*. We also find 'i' before the full formula,

---

[750] As indeed it is by Pokorny (*Historical Reader* 37) on the second passage cited, although, oddly, he holds (as did Baudiš also, *ZCP* 9.322) that this (so-called) nominal sentence stands in apposition to *ri* (I do not see how one can have it both ways, appositive and clause!). Schmidt too (*ZCP* 28.230–31) takes the *ainm* locution as a clause, as already noted in fn. 714; but the supposed parallel that he adduces from Old English (230) is utterly valueless (see above, fn. 701).

[751] See above, §6

[752] Also in *ScM* 1, according to the reading of Windisch, *IT* 1.96, which runs 'i' Mac Datho a ainm. See below, fn. 769.

[753] See Thurneysen 25. Pokorny, *ZCP* 16.389, attributes this common usage to non-Indo–European inflection (cf. above, fn. 747); but it seems to me it might have been a natural native development from the very common use, referred to by Thurneysen (4), of "glosses in Latin MSS., i.e. marginal and interlinear explanations in Irish interspersed with Latin" (would any one call Thurneysen's employment here of "i.e." non-Indo–European?).

which may either follow the main clause or interrupt it. An example of
the first is *Mer. Uil.* 15 (7.206)[754] ar in rigan ˙i˙ Peneloipi a hainm 'said
the queen, Penelope her name'. An example of the second is *Tain* (*St.*
12.22–23) im-soi in t-arae, ˙i˙ Ibor a ainm-side,[755] in carpat 'the
charioteer, Ibor his name, turns the chariot'.[756] In these two passages
it seems more natural to conclude that we again have appositives than
to assume that we have clauses after ˙i˙, meaning 'said the queen,
namely, Penelope (was) her name' and 'the charioteer—namely, Ibor
(is) his name—turns the chariot'.

236. But it cannot be denied that any attempt to deal consistently
with these ˙i˙ locutions on a logical and grammatical basis is doomed to
failure, as is probably to be expected in the case of groups of words
which were in many instances (though not in all) later interpolations
by a second hand made without regard to the construction of the
original text.[757] Thus even if we think we have appositives in the two
examples just cited, where the *ainm* interpolation follows a nominative,
the situation is different in those instances in which it follows some
other case. For instance, the word denoting the possessors of the names
is in the genitive plural[758] in *Tain* (*St.* 15.10–11) dun tri macc Nechtan
Scene ˙i˙ Foill & Fannall & Tuachell a n-anman 'the fortress of the
three sons of Nechan Scene, namely Foill and Fannall and Tuachell
their names'. We may note in this connection that very soon after this
(17.5–6, 14–15, 22–23), we find the possessor of the name three times
in the accusative singular, foichle in fer 'observe the man' followed
shortly by the interpolation Foill a ainm, Fannall a ainm-side,[759]
Tuachell a ainm. Like these three instances, except that it includes ˙i˙

[754] So too perhaps in *ScM.* See fnn. 752 and 769.

[755] On *side*, see above, §226.

[756] It is practically impossible to maintain in English the Irish order—'vertit auriga—
Ibor suum nomen eius—currum'.

[757] Glosses are regularly introduced by ˙i˙. We have already noted two of these glosses,
Alex. 4 (§226) and 38 (§228). To these we may add a third, *Alex.* 5 Cleopra a hainmm.
To all these I shall return later (§241).

[758] Provided the (uninflected) proper nouns can be explained as genitives (cf. fn. 763),
we might be reminded of the Greek example (Plutarch, *Solon* 12.4) cited in §139; but,
whereas there we have late Greek, in which an accusative of specification *onoma* has
clearly been generated, here we have early Irish, in which *anman* cannot be explained as
an accusative of specification (cf. above, §231). For another example of the use of *ainm*
after a genitive, see below, §242.

[759] On *side* cf. fn. 755.

as the earlier passage (15.10–11) does and as they do not, is *Tain* (*YBL* 810–11) tanetat Cuchulaind cloich fair, co tanic a inchind for a chluasa ˙i˙ Ferteidhil a ainm[760] 'he threw a stone at him, so that his brain came out over his ears, namely Ferteidhil his name'.[761] It might be theoretically possible,[762] provided the uncertain proper names can be correspondingly explained,[763] to call *anman* in the first passage a genitive plural in apposition with *macc*, and *ainm* in each of the other passages an accusative singular in apposition with *fer*, or, in the last one, with the singular accusative masculine pronoun, combined with the preposition *for* 'on, against' (here translated 'at') to form *fair*. But this explanation, at least so far as the genitive goes, seems unlikely in the extreme,[764] in view of the usual run of the wording after ˙i˙; I think certainly *anman*, and probably *ainm*, should be viewed as nominative.

237. Nevertheless this does not absolutely compel us to give up the idea that they may be appositives of a sort. This is the only possible explanation for the ˙i˙ phrase in ben Mess Gegra, ˙i˙ ri Laigen,[765] 'the

[760] This passage does not belong here at all if Pokorny (*ZCP* 16.390) is right in his belief that *ainm* "eher ein späterer erklärender Zusatz ist, um durch die Satzform den absoluten Nonimativ des Eigennamens zu stützen". Pokorny's suggestion seems plausible, since Ferteidhil has already been mentioned, though, to be sure, he has been designated merely as Orlam's charioteer (*YBL* 777 and 786–87) with no indication of his name (we may compare the postponement of Hrunting's name in *Beowulf*; on this see §§216 and 221). On the other hand, if *a ainm* is a later interpolation, perhaps *Ferteidhil* is too; for if *Ferteidhil* alone belonged in the original, the stylistic effect must have been choppy in the extreme.

[761] That it is the target of the missile (Ferteidhil) and not the thrower (Cu Chulainn) who suffers this horrible fate is of course made clear by the context; but perhaps *Ferteidhil a ainm* was added, no matter by whom (cf. fn. 760), just to make it doubly clear.

[762] And more favorable to my view as to the origin of the construction!

[763] Proper names in the sagas are sometimes indeclinable. To be sure, this is true, particularly, as in the Greek, Latin, and Germanic versions of the Bible (cf. fn. 489), of names borrowed from Hebrew, but it is not confined to them (see Thurneysen 217), and cf. the uninflected form *Philip* in *Alex.* 5, quoted in §241 and commented on in fn. 774).

[764] Especially as regards the genitive, for which I know of no parallel in any language. That *ainm* after *fer* or *fair* may be an accusative seems less unlikely, if only because of its identity in form with the nominative (cf. fn. 714). We have noted examples with the accusative *Iulium* in both Indic (§§47 and 55) and Greek (§118). But I am not claiming any cogency for these possible parallels; Old Irish is a law unto itself!

[765] This is the version as given by Pokorny, *ZCP* 16.390. Stokes, *RC* 8.60, has only *ben Mess Gegra rig*—which he translates (ib. 61) "(I am) the wife of Mes-Gegra the king"—with the genitive *rig* as logic demands; this he tells us (47) is from the original MS of the *Book of Leinster*, an Irish codex of the middle of the twelfth century. However, in a footnote, 61 fn. 14, he quotes from the Harleian MS the version used by Pokorny, ˙i˙ ri Laigen.

wife of M. G., namely the king of Leinster' 'id est rex' (not 'regis').[766]
Here there can be no question of predication in the 'i' phrase, since
ainm is lacking;[767] the word for 'king' must be a quasi-appositive,
even though it is in the nominative instead of the genitive as logic and
grammar would demand.[768] This must come under the head of the
(rare) use of the nominative cited by Thurneysen (156) "in apposition
to a noun in another case". Note Thurneysen's example, *Thes.*
2.240.13–14 dutet iar sin dia chennadich, aicme becc i Cliu, Catrige a
ainmm, which is rendered by him (or at least by his translators Binchy
and Bergin) "he comes afterwards to his (own) district, a small tribe
in Cliu, Catrige (is) its name"[769] (I would, however, prefer to render
the last three words 'Catrige its name', taking *Catrige* as an appositive
to *aicme* 'tribe', not a subject). Since there is no possibility that in 'i'
ri Laigen or *aicme becc* we have an interpolated clause, I believe these two
passages furnish a strong argument against the assumption that this is
what we have in the passage in the *Tain*.

[766] *Tain* (*YBL* 810–11) (already cited above, §236) belongs here if Pokorny is right, as
he may be, in considering *a ainm* a later addition. See above, fn. 760.
[767] Cf. the similar comment on the two passages in §234.
[768] We have already noted something of the same sort in a late stage of Old Persian;
see above, §113 and fn. 293. And I think a similar development is in process of taking
place in English. Perhaps because English nouns have lost all case distinctions except that
between a general case (embracing what are usually viewed as nominative and objective
cases) and a genitive case, English pronouns, though most of them still retain formal
distinctions marking three separate cases (nominative, genitive, and objective), seem to be
in a state of confusion so far as nominative and objective cases go, which may be the
sign of a transition period leading to the loss of the objective. (Cf. the frequent use of
who for *whom* and—far more objectionable in my opinion—of *whom* for *who*.) Thus
there seems to be a strong tendency to employ a nominative pronoun as an appositive
not only for a general noun (no matter whether it functions as a subject or as an object),
but even for an objective pronoun, which I must admit I find disturbing. I have recently
noted two instances of this in novels by the modern writer, Mazo de la Roche: in
Return to Jalna 333 (Boston, 1946), "For an instant she loved him, he who so often had
been antagonistic to her"; in *Renny's Daughter* 281 (Boston, 1951), "What had come
over her—she who scorned a girl who cried". Also, I was startled to find in a classical
periodical of all places (*CJ* 61.206) a nominative pronoun in apposition with a noun
depending on a preposition: "with the goddess Calypso, she who covers or hides".
Perhaps we might say here that *Calypso* is used in a sort of double sense, to designate
both the person and the name (cf. the Vergilian passages cited above in §§151–55), and
that it is with the noun in the latter sense that *she* is in apposition, as a sort of English
nominativus tituli (cf. fn. 205); but in that case *she who covers or hides* should have been set
up in italics or within quotes.
[769] Schmidt's objection (*ZCP* 28.231) that this is "nicht zwingend" because *aicme
becc* can be attracted to the case of *Catrige a ainm* seems to me in its turn not compelling:
I think *Catrige a ainm* gets its case from *aicme becc*, not the other way around.

238. However, this does not mean that we are *never* to recognize the presence of a nominal clause involving *ainm* (cf. fn. 7). I think we certainly have one in a passage directly following the formulaic use of *ainm* that we noted above,[770] *ScM* 1 (1.1–2) boi cu occo; im diched in cu Laigniu huili: Aelbe ainm in chon 'there was a dog belonging to him; the dog used to protect all the Leinstermen; Ailbe (was) the dog's name'. Here the interpolation of the clause *im diched in cu Laigniu huili* 'the dog used to protect all the Leinstermen' renders an appositive 'his name Ailbe' much less natural;[771] and that a separate clause is what we have is made practically certain by the presence of the genitive *in chon*[772] 'the dog's' in place of the usual possessive *a* 'his'.

239. We also have a clause—this time verbal not nominal—in a passage of quite a different type, *Usn.* 5 (69.23–24) = *Uisl.* 5 (44.52–53) "fir" ar-se "ingen fil and, ocus bid Derdriu a hainm, ocus biaid olc impe" '"it is true," quoth he, "there is a girl in it, and Deirdre will be her name, and there will be evil concerning her"'. The fact that we do here find a verbal clause ('erit Iulia suum nomen') does not prove that in the typical examples we have a nominal clause.[773] The tone is quite different here, and the clause *ocus bid Derdriu a hainm* 'and Deirdre will be her name', looking to the future, is used as a parallel to the second clause, *ocus biaid olc impe* 'and there will be evil concerning her'.

240. The construction *Iulius suum nomen* continues in Middle Irish, as in *Alex.* 56 (65.743) dosfanic iar sin beist ingnad, Distrianus a hainm 'there came then after it a remarkable beast, Distrianus its name'.

241. It is possible to explain in the same way at least two of the three glosses in *Alex.* already noted in fn. 757. These are as follows: 5 (19.49–50) over the text a ingen-sum Philip 'Philip's daughter',[774]

---

[770] See above, §233; for the present passage, cf. §227 and fn. 749. I quote both passages as they are given by Thurneysen (*IS* 6.1.1–2). Windisch (*IT* 1.96.1–2) has a slightly different version; but the variations, except for the insertion of *i* (on which see fn. 752) are not significant for my purposes.

[771] This type of formula, as already noted (§224), appears regularly with the first mention of the owner of the name—'there was a dog'.

[772] This last clause was cited above (§227) to illustrate the use of the genitive with *ainm*.

[773] Cf. above, §226.

[774] The employment here of the possessive *a* in what Thurneysen (279) calls "proleptic use ... anticipating a following genitive" (in other words, the seemingly tautological combination of a possessive pronoun and a genitive noun, already commented on above in §227) seems particularly natural in this instance to point up the genitive case of the uninflected *Philip* (on indeclinable proper nouns see above, fn. 763). On the

the words ï Cleopra a hainmm 'Cleopatra her name'; 4 (19.44–46) over the text tri toisig 'three field-marshals' the words ï Parmenion & Amintai & Atalir a n-anmunda-side[775] 'Parmenion and Amyntas and Attalus their names'; 38 (50.510–11) over the text Alestris ï rigan na Cichloiscthi 'Alestris, namely queen of the Amazons' the words ainmm ele di ï Minotha 'another name to her, namely Minothaea'. But, since these are explanatory, more or less parenthetical, interpolations by another hand, perhaps it is better to explain them as independent clauses,[776] 'Cleopatra (was) her name'; 'Parmenion and Amyntas and Attalus (were) their names'; 'there (was) another name to her [i.e. she had another name], namely Minothaea'. The presence of di 'to her' in the third example[777] would certainly seem to favor the view that here at least we have a clause, not an appositive.

242. We also almost unquestionably have a clause in *Alex.* 32 (44.413–14) ros gab Alaxandir iarom rigi catrach Pers ar ecin, Persipolis tra a hainm-side[778] 'then after that Alexander by force took the kingship over [literally, of] a city of the Persians, therefore its name (was) Persepolis'. Here, since hainm follows a genitive (*catrach*),[779] unless we adopt the explanation offered in §237, it can hardly be an appositive. However, a clause is really more or less in order here, because of the presence of tra 'therefore', showing the result of the previous statement (the characterization of the city as belonging to the Persians).

243. Absolutely indubitable examples of clauses[780]—both nominal

---

"emphasizing particle" of the third person singular, *sum*, earlier *som* (Thurneysen 252), cf. above, §225, on the corresponding form *siu* of the second person singular.

[775] On *side*, cf. above, §226 and fn. 723.

[776] This, however, would have no bearing on the origin of the usual construction, particularly in view of the comparative lateness of the Alexander material (cf. fn. 748).

[777] To be sure, it might be argued that di 'to her' or possibly 'of her' (cf. §229) is simply a substitute for the usual a 'her' (possessive), and that therefore the construction with di is not different from that with a. However, di seems to me to involve an expression of predication: 'another name, Minothaea, (was) to her', *anglice* 'she had another name' (cf. fn. 738).

[778] On *side* cf. above, §226.

[779] As in *Tain* (*St.* 15.10–11), quoted above in §236.

[780] Obviously, nothing but a clause is possible when we have an introductory statement preceding a list in the form 'these are the names, A, B, and C'. (We have met a similar list in the *NT*, *Mt.* 10.2; see above, fn. 574 and §202.) As examples of this type (all verbal caluses) may be cited *Uisn.* 8 (122.8) is iadso anmanna na bfiled robatar ocond fleidsin ï Cathbad macc Congail 'these are the names of the poets who were at that banquet, namely Cathbad son of Congal' etc.; *Troi* 4 (9.209–10) it he anso a n-anmand

and verbal—are also to be found during this (comparatively late) period.⁷⁸¹ These, as we have already noted, occur in both the forms *nomen hominis (est) Iulius* and *nomen homini (est) Iulius*.⁷⁸²

244. As an example of *nomen hominis (est) Iulius* may be cited *Alex.* 60 (69.796–99) ⁷⁸³ ro chumdaig Alaxandir iarom da chathraig isin tir sin ˙i˙ Alaxandria Aporus & Alaxandria Buicefaile equi ˙i˙ Buicefalis ainmm in eich ro marbad fai-sium, o ra hainmniged in chathair sin 'Alexander then built two cities in that country, namely Alexandria apud Porum and Alexandria of the Horse Bucephalus, for [literally, namely] Bucephalus (was) the name of the horse who was killed under him, from which was named the above-mentioned city'. Here an interpolated clause is absolutely necessary: 'Alexandria of the Horse Bucephalus' is the author's name for the city which we call Bucephala, and he could not logically say 'Alexandria of the Horse, Bucephalus his name', for here *Buicefaile equi* (note the Latin form *equi*, not *eich*) is regarded as the name of the city, and does not refer to the horse. Accordingly he must add a little later the clause 'Bucephalus (was) the name of the horse' etc.

245. As an example of *nomen homini est Iulius* may be cited *Alex.* 33 (45.430–32) ⁷⁸⁴ tanic in cu aigthige cho Alaxandir, amal at-fet Prescen insin Pergiseis Prescen, & is don choin sin is ainmm Bemoth 'then came the fearful dog up to Alexander, as Priscian relates in the Periegesis of Priscian, and the name of [literally, to ⁷⁸⁵] that dog is Bemoth'. Here

---

na ndorus ˙i˙ Antenor 'these are the names of the gates, namely Antenora' etc.; and *Alex.* 8 (21–22.87–88) batar he anmandai na ceithre litre sin, Anataile 'these were the names of those four letters, Anatolian' etc.—each including an enumeration of the names. A passage of much the same sort is *Alex.* 26 (39.343–44) Protolomeus ainmm cech fir dib i n-diad araile ˙i˙ Protolomeus Fisicon 'Ptolemy (was) the name of each man of them following another [i.e. Ptolemy was the name of each of them in order], namely Ptolemy Physcon' etc. (All these examples were cited in part above, §227, to illustrate the use of the genitive with *ainm*.) The last example differs slightly from the others here listed in that it follows another passage about a name (of which it is explanatory), namely (342–43) hairdrig diarbo hainmm Protolomeus, listed below (§249).

⁷⁸¹ Cf. fn. 776.
⁷⁸² Corresponding to *hominis* we find the genitive; corresponding to *homini*, the preposition *do* plus the dative. These alternative manners of expression have already been discussed, with extracts from the passages here quoted in full, in §§227–28.
⁷⁸³ Already cited (in part) above (§227) to illustrate *nomen hominis*.
⁷⁸⁴ Already cited (in part) above (§228) as an example of the use of the preposition *do*.
⁷⁸⁵ On *don* as coming from *do* rather than from *di*, see above, §229 and fn. 737.

the interpolated clause 'as Priscian relates' etc. interrupts the construction and necessitates the introduction of a second clause after it. Were
the usual formula, which would be *Bemoth a ainm*, itself a clause, it
might have stood, introduced by *ocus* 'and'; but if, as I believe, it is an
appositive, it could hardly follow the interpolated clause, and I think
it is significant that it does not.[786]

246. As a parallel to the principal clause *nomen hominis (est) Iulius* or
nomen homini (est) Iulius, we find developing in early Middle Irish a
relative clause *cuius nomen (est) Iulius* or *cui nomen (est) Iulius*.[787] This
employs *dia*, which consists of the preposition *di* 'of' or *do* 'to'[788] plus
the invariable relative particle *a*.[789] Of course *dia* corresponds to *cuius*
if from *di* and to *cui* if from *do*.[790] Examples follow: *Alex.* 37 (48.486–
487) isin catraig Maicedondai dia[791] n-ainmm Diho 'in the Macedonian city whose name (is) Dium'; and 39 (51.524–25) in catraig dia
n-ainmm Nisam 'into the city whose name (is) Nyssa'.

247. We also find beside these nominal clauses verbal clauses in
which *dia* is combined with the conjunct form of the copula, third
person singular, either the present indicative -*id*, producing *dianid* (and
its variant *dianad*), or the imperfect indicative -*bo*, producing *diarbo*.[792]

---

[786] Cf. what was said above, §238, of *ScM* 1—a passage also, as it happens, about a dog.
But the present passage makes even clearer than did the earlier one that the usual formula
Iulius suum nomen (in both instances, as I believe, deliberately rejected) is an appositive
and not a clause, for there an appositive might have been considered possible, since *cu*
'dog' is the subject of the interpolated clause as well as of the first one, but here the
interpolated clause has a different subject, and an appositive after it would be awkward
and perhaps ambiguous.

[787] Cf. fn. 782. A clause of this type could evolve from such a clause as *Alex.* 5 Cleopra
a hainmm, or, still more readily, *Alex.* 38 ainmm ele di ˙i˙ Minotha, both quoted above
in §241. But in Old and Middle Irish, just as in Germanic (cf. above, fnn. 548 and 622),
relative clauses are far from well established; and Professor Meyer suggests to me that
this particular type, instead of being a native Irish development, probably began in
translations from Latin. (However, the original Latin clause does not necessarily in every
case show the same construction as the corresponding Irish one; see fn. 794.)

[788] Cf. above, §229. In this particular construction, it seems impossible to determine
which we have.

[789] Thurneysen 312.

[790] Again cf. §229.

[791] See fn. 793.

[792] This is probably a syncopated form of *dia-ro-bo*, the -*ro*-, which in Old Irish gave
perfective force to both the preterite (Thurneysen 341) and the imperfect (id. 342), here
serving simply to mark the preterite. (I owe this information to Professor Meyer; I was
completely baffled by the form.)

The difference between the two tenses is neatly brought out by *Alex.* 13 (26.154–55) cathraig diarbo ainmm Gordiana & dianad ainmm Saraifir indorsai 'the city whose name was Gordium and whose name is now Sardis'.

248. Some examples with *dianid (dianad)* follow: *Alex.* 9 (23.103) na hardchatrach dianad ainmm Effis 'of the chief city, whose name is Ephesus'; 8 (21.78–79) is in catraig Maicedondai dianad[793] ainmm Diho 'in the Macedonian city whose name is Dium'; 27 (39.347–48) icon chathraig dianid ainm Debritai 'by the city whose name is Debritae'; *BBal.* following 272b (101.8) abaind dianid ainm Baimar[794] 'a river whose name is Buemar'.

249. Some examples with *diarbo* follow: *Troi* 8 (15.415–16) fer diarbo ainm Alaxander 'a man whose name was Alexander'; *Alex.* 26 (39.342–43) hairdrig diarbo hainmm Protolomeus[795] 'high-kings whose name was Ptolemy'.

[793] Note *dianad* here instead of *dia* in the otherwise identical passage *Alex.* 37 (already quoted in §246).

[794] The Latin relative clause represented by this passage is, as Professor Meyer reminds me, (Pseudo-)Alexander, *Epistula ad Aristotelem* 12 prope fluvium qui dicebatur Buemar (Pfister 30). See fn. 787 (end).

[795] Already quoted in fn. 780.

B. BRITANNIC

250. Britannic does not provide so fertile a field as Gaelic for the study of naming constructions.[796] Some of the earliest material is as old as that of Gaelic, but is much less extensive;[797] and in general the remains are later. Moreover, this language-group has changed far more—I am tempted to say even more—than Gaelic at the earliest stage that we can reach,[798] notably in its complete loss of case inflection of nouns.[799]

251. I do not find traces of any elaborate formula such as was noted above[800] in Old and Middle Irish.[801] We do meet occasionally the construction noted in Old Irish, *Iulius (est) nomen hominis*,[802] or *Iulius (est) nomen suum*.[803] Examples follow.[804] W. *BDe.* 1.8 enw y mab oed

[796] I am myself sorely handicapped in dealing with Britannic, since my knowledge of it is even scantier than my knowledge, such as it is, of Gaelic; indeed, it is well-nigh nil. But Professor Meyer has once again (cf. fn. 703) very graciously provided me with a considerable collection of examples, and of these I have made a study and a selection. He drew his instances from Middle Welsh, Middle Cornish, and Middle Breton (which I abbreviate respectively W., C., and B.); as they are fairly similar so far as naming constructions go, I group them together instead of dealing with them separately as I did e.g. with Avestan and Old Persian. They seem to follow a fairly limited number of patterns, of which I have chosen some typical illustrations, and these I have done my best to organize and classify. I follow almost everywhere, with only a few clarifying modifications, the translations provided for me by Professor Meyer (either his own or those of other scholars), since I am scarcely competent to make new ones for myself.

[797] Thurneysen 2.

[798] Thurneysen 2.

[799] Pedersen, *KG* (2.72).

[800] In §§224 and 231.

[801] Elsewhere also, to a limited extent in Hittite (§23), Sanskrit (§44), and Greek (§117), and above all in Old Persian (§89).

[802] Since Britannic nouns have lost case distinctions, the genitive relation is simply suggested by the word order, the noun used like a genitive following the main noun (Pedersen, *KG* 2.82).

[803] See §226. In Old Irish the genitive of the pronoun is far commoner than that of the noun (see §225)—*Iulius est nomen suum* or, rather, in Celtic, *eius* (see fn. 706, also fnn. 712 and 746).

[804] The works on which Professor Meyer drew are the following. (1) For Welsh. *BDe.* = *Buchedd Dewi o Lawysgrif Llanstephan 27*, ed. by D. Simon Evans. *Branwen* = *Branwen Uerch Lyr*, ed. by Derick S. Thomson. *Martin* = *Buchedd Sant Martin*, ed. by Evan John Jones. *Pwyll* = *Pwyll Pendeuic Dyuet*, ed. by R. L. Thomson. *RBH* = *The Red Book of Hergest*, Part 2, *The Bruts*, ed. by John Rhys and J. Gwenogvryn Evans. (2) For

Sant 'the name of the son was Sant'. *BDe.* 3.4 enw y lleian oed Nonn
'the name of the nun was Nonna'. *Pwyll* 620–21 Pryderi uyd y enw
ef 'Pryderi will be his name'.[805] C. *BMer.* 831 Meryasek yv ov hanov
'Meriasek is my name'. *O* 678 Seth a vyt y evn hanow 'Seth will be
his just name'.[806] There is a Welsh example of the type *haec sunt
nomina hominum*:[807] *RBH* 2.64.29–30 sef oed enweu y verchet:
Goronilla, Ragaw, Cordeilla 'these are [literally, it is] the names of the
daughters: Gonoril, Regan, Cordelia'.

252. As a variant for *Iulius (est) nomen hominis*, we occasionally meet
the construction *homo (est) Iulius nomine*,[808] as in C *Pascon* 174 un den
a-s-dyerbynas, Symon o a'y ewn hanow 'a certain man met them, he
was Simon by his right name'. *Pascon* 234 un den da Cryst a-gara,

---

Cornish. *ACD* = *The Ancient Cornish Drama*, ed. and transl. by Edwin Norris. *BMer.* =
Beunans Meriasek: The Life of Saint Meriasek, ed. and transl. by Whitley Stokes. *O* =
Ordinale de Origine Mundi (*ACD* 1.1–219). *Pascon* = *Pascon agan Arluth*, ed. and transl. by
Whitley Stokes (*Transactions of the Philological Society for* 1860–61, Appendix 1–100).
R = *Ordinale de Resurrexione Domini Nostri Jhesu Christi* (*ACD* 2.1–200). (3) For Breton.
Barbe = *Le Mystère de Sainte Barbe*, ed. and transl. by Émile Ernault. *Nonne* = *Buez
santes Nonn*, *Vie de Sainte Nonne*, ed. and transl. by E. Ernault (*RC* 8.230–301, 406–91).
Patrice = *Buez Sant Patrice*, *La Vie de Saint Patrice*, ed. and transl. by Joseph Dunn.
References to *Pascon* and *Barbe* are to stanzas, not lines; references to *BDe*, *Martin*, and
RBH are to pages and lines. For additional details see the Bibliography.

[805] We may compare Hittite, *KUB* 24.8.3.10 (§24), and Greek, *Od.* 19.409 (§123),
although these differ from the Welsh passage in two ways: (1) they have datives, while
the Welsh passage has the genitive typical of Celtic; (2) they use imperatives, while the
Welsh passage has the indicative (the consuetudinal present used in a future sense). It
might also be theoretically possible (although the word order is certainly against it) to
explain the Welsh passage as meaning rather 'he his name [literally, he the name of him]
will be Pryderi', and to class it as an example of the ambiguous type, *Iulius nomen (suum)
est* (see fn. 17), comparing Hittite *KUB* 24.8.3.16 (§24), and, less closely, Greek *Od.*
7.53–54 (§117); but the parallelism of the other Britannic examples quoted in the above
paragraph doubtless rules out this explanation (cf. fn. 806). However, there is a passage
that might more easily be assigned to the type, *Martin* 9.3–4 ac ar hynny i doeth gwr
o'r dinas, Rusticus oedd i henw 'and thereupon there came a man from the city,
Rusticus was his name' or 'his name was Rusticus', which (except that the clause is
verbal, not nominal) is absolutely parallel in construction and order to the Old Irish
examples cited in §233, and accordingly might also be translated 'he was Rusticus his
name'.

[806] This Cornish example is a precise parallel to the Welsh example *Pwyll* 621, and
presents precisely the same problem. See fn. 805. Such a close parallel as *BMer.* 831
makes it particularly clear that this is *not* the ambiguous type.

[807] For Irish examples, see fn. 780.

[808] The expression of specification *nomine* is in these instances represented by the
preposition *a* 'by' plus *hanow*. For comparable instances of a prepositional phrase in
Germanic, see §197 on Old English, and fn. 617 on Icelandic.

Nycodemus y hanow is perhaps parallel (except that *Nycodemus* is subject of a nominal clause, not of a verbal clause as is *Symon*); the meaning then is 'a certain good man who loved Christ, (he was) Nicodemus by his name'. However, it may be that *Nycodemus* is not a subject at all, but an appositive to *den* 'man'; the construction then is simply *homo Iulius nomine*, and the meaning is 'a certain good man who loved Christ, Nicodemus by his name'.

253. We meet the familiar *hominem Iulium voco* and *homo Iulius vocatur* in Welsh and Cornish. For the active may be quoted the following. W. *Pwyll* 616 da yd enweist by uab Pryderi 'well hast thou named thy son Pryderi'. *RBH* 2.64.27 ac ae gelwis Kaer Lyr 'and he called it Kaer Lyr'. C. *O* 123 yt'hanwaf bugh ha tarow 'I name cow and bull'. For the passive may be quoted the following. W. *RBH* 2.64.28 ac yn Saesnec y gelwir Leissestyr 'and in English it is called Leicester'. *BDe.* 2.14–15 ac a elwir yr awr honn Eistedua Badric 'and it is called now the Seat of St. Patrick'. C. *O* 1 en Tas a nef y'm gylwyr 'the father of heaven I am called'.

254. The verbs in the foregoing, Welsh *gelwir* and its variant *elwir*,[809] and the allied Cornish *gylwyr*, are true passives. Much commoner than true passives are periphrases consisting of the verb 'be'[810] and the passive participle[811] used predicatively, corresponding to what in a language with case inflections we would call a predicate nominative. Examples follow. W.[812] *Pwyll* 190–91 ac y gelwit Pwyll Penn Annwuyn 'and he (was) called Pwyll Head of Annwn'. *BDe.* 10.7 a disgybyl y Dewi a elwit Eliud 'a disciple of David who (was) called Eliud'. C. *R* 197 Ennoc sur ythof hynwys 'Enoch surely I am named'. *BMer.* 1 me yw gylwys duk Bryten 'I am [apparently literally I is!] called Duke of Brittany'. *BMer.* 970 Meryasek ythyv gelwys 'Merya-

---

[809] In *elwir* the initial *g* has been lost as the result of lenition, although the word which caused the lenition—possibly the relative *a* 'which'—may have disappeared. (I owe this information to Professor Meyer.)

[810] Or, less commonly, no verb at all. In that case we of course have a nominal instead of a verbal clause. Examples are *Pwyll* 190–91 and *BDe.* 10.7.

[811] The participles commonly used are Welsh *gelwit* and *elwit* (on which cf. fn. 809), Cornish *gelwys* (*gylwys*) and *hynwys*, and Breton *hanuet*. In this usage, frequently *vocatus est* seems equivalent to *vocatur*, and *vocatus erat* to *vocabatur*, just as in later Latin (cf. Grandgent 51) and, so far as they use the tournure, the Romance Languages. (English usage varies, according to the verb employed and the context: thus as a rule *the book is read* corresponds to Latin *liber legitur*, but *the book is written* to Latin *liber scriptus est*.)

[812] On these two Welsh examples see fn. 810.

sek is he called'. *Pascon* 124 Barabas yth-o gelwys 'Barabbas was he
called'. *BMer.* 1072–73 carek Meryasek holma gelwys vyth wose helma
'the rock of Meryasek will this be called hereafter'. B. *Nonne* 74
Runniter aman off hanuet 'I am called Runniter'. *Patrice* 124 ezew bet
badeet a hanwet Patrice 'he was baptized and named Patrick'. *Barbe* 132
eux un den so hanuet plen Origenes 'there is a certain man who is
called surely Origen'.

255. I can also cite one Breton passage[813] exemplifying a peri-
phrasis of the passive participle used predicatively in combination not
with 'be' but with 'have',[814] in other words corresponding to what in
a language with case inflections would be called a predicate accusative.
This is *Barbe* 6 an guerches man ameux hanuet 'the maiden whom I
have named'.

256. Beside these predicative uses of the passive participle, I can also
cite instances in Cornish and Breton[815] of its attributive use. C. *BMer.*
2465 mytern Casvelyn gelwys 'the king called Casvelyn'. *R* 1471–72
mos a wren ny the'n castel Emavs gylwys 'we are going to the village
called Emmaus'. *BMer.* 511–12 me yv escop in Breten in conteth gelwys
Kernov 'I am bishop in Brittany in a county called Kernou'. *Pascon* 214
un burges, Iosep hynwys 'a certain burgess called Joseph'. B. *Nonne*
14–15 ez duy aman vnan an sent hanuet Deuy 'there will be born here
a saint named David'.

257. I find especially interesting the variants for the types *hominem
Iulium nominant* and *homo Iulius nominatur*, respectively the types
homini nomen Iulium indunt and *homini nomen Iulius inditur*.[816] Here the
verbs used are those with the meanings 'put, place', 'give', and
'make';[817] for the first we find Welsh *dodi* (which is particularly
common), for the second Welsh *rodi* (used interchangeably with *dodi*)

---

[813] The name is not given, the verb being used in the sense of 'mention' rather than
'entitle', so this is strictly not an example of a naming construction; but I none the less
include it because the locution seems to me an interesting one.

[814] See Pedersen, *KG* 2.165 and 409–10. The construction occurs commonly in
Hittite and occasionally in classical Latin, and so is doubtless Indo-European; but
Professor Meyer tells me that in Celtic it is met only in Breton, and so may be due there
to the influence of the French verbal system (in this respect French of course, like the
other Romance Languages, goes back to late Latin, on which see Grandgent 54–55).

[815] I have none in Welsh.

[816] See above, §14 and fn. 39. Like the genitive (on which see fn. 802), the dative is
replaced by a prepositional phrase, the preposition used in this type being *ar*.

[817] Cf. above, fn. 39, for instances of the similar use in other languages of verbs with
these meanings.

and the allied Cornish *ry*, for the third Breton *ober* (participle *gret*).[818] I can cite active examples from W. and C., passive ones from W. and B. They follow. W. *Pwyll* 620 Gwri Wallt Euryn a dodyssom ni arnaw ef 'Gwri Golden-Hair is the name that we gave him'. *Pwyll* 546 sef enw a dodet arnaw, Gwri Wallt Euryn 'the name that was given him was Gwri Golden-Hair'. *Branwen* 211 sef enw a dodet ar y mab, Guern uab Matholwch 'the name that [literally, it is the name that] was given to the son was Gwern son of Matholwch'. *BDe.* 3.5 a Dauyd a rodet yn enw arnaw 'and David was given to him as name'. C. *O* 135 y rof hynwyn the'n puskes 'I give names to the fishes'. *O* 120 ro thethe aga hynwyn 'give them their names'. B. *Patrice* 568 pe hano eta Autro a vo gret anezan? 'what name, sir, shall be given to him?'

258. There is one particularly interesting passage in Welsh which combines a number of different naming constructions,[819] *quid est nomen?, nomen quod ei indidimus est Iulius, Iulius erit nomen eius.* This is *Pwyll* 619–21: "Mae yr enu?" heb y Pendaran Dyuet. "Gwri Wallt Euryn a dodyssom ni arnaw ef."[820] "Pryderi," heb y Pendaran Dyuet, "uyd y enw ef."[821] '"What is the name?" asked Pendaran Dyfed. "Gwri Golden-Hair is the name that we gave him." "Pryderi," said Pendaran Dyfed, "will be his name."'

259. These examples have seemed to me of interest as providing parallels for usages in Old and Middle Irish and in other Indo–European languages as well, but they throw little or no light upon the original constructions.

[818] It is tempting to connect Welsh *dodi* etymologically, in view of its syntactic use in the naming construction (cf. fn. 39), with Indo–European *dhē*- 'place' or possibly with Indo–European *dō*- 'give'; but, as Buck reminds us (*Syn.* 832–33), it is "not included by Walde-P. or Stokes with either". Welsh *rodi* and Cornish *ry* can more plausibly be connected with Indo–European *dō*-, the *ro*- standing for (*p*)*ro-d*-; see Pedersen, *KG* 2.380 and 473, and Buck, *Syn.* 749. The forms in *gr*- of the Breton verb meaning 'make' (from which the infinitive *ober*, a derivative of Latin *opera*, is wholly distinct etymologically; cf. Pedersen, *KG* 2.411) represent the development *gn- gwn- gwr- gr-* (ib. 1.96 and 2.545–46), from the stem *gni*- 'produce' (ib. 2.544).

[819] Similar composite passages occur in Hittite, *KUB* 24.8.3.7–16 (see §27), and in Greek, Homer, *Od.* 19.403–9 (see §§123 and 124, and fn. 332), and Aristophanes, *Av.* 809–17 (see fn. 308).

[820] Already quoted in §257.

[821] Already quoted in §251. See also fn. 805.

VII. TOCHARIAN

260. The two related languages Tocharian A and B[822] (the latter better entitled Kuchean[823]) have words for 'name' exhibiting our stem and our construction. The word appears in A as *ñom* and in B as *ñem*. Pedersen (*Toch.* 40) unhesitatingly equates these with Sanskrit *nāma*, Latin, *nōmen*, etc.; the final nasal is regularly lost in Tocharian (ib.), so an original ending in *n* for the prototype of both forms is perfectly possible. But the fact that the word begins with the palatal (*ñ*) and not the dental (*n*) causes trouble. Pedersen (221–22) accounts for this by the assumption that the Tocharian words go back to an *e*-grade form not otherwise attested, **nem-*, since the *e* would have caused palatalization.[824] These words are what SSS (33) call neuters, which means they are masculine in the singular and feminine in the plural; and they behave as we would expect words derived from Indo–European neuters to do, having the same form in the nominative and the accusative (or "oblique" case).[825] In the nominative plural we have in A *ñomäntu*, which Professor Lane tells me is ambiguous as to origin; and in B *ñemna*, which Couvreur (*Toch.* 43 and 93) equates with Latin *nomina*.

261. There are numerous examples in Tocharian A and B (as published in SS and SS, *B*), from which Professor Lane has kindly made a selection for me. I choose two from each for inclusion here.[826]

[822] Since my knowledge of Tocharian is almost as limited as my knowledge of Avestan—which is practically non-existent—I have had to depend in this section mainly on information graciously supplied to me by Professor George S. Lane of the University of North Carolina.

[823] See Lane, *SKG* I fn. I.

[824] He takes cognizance (222 fn. I) of the fact that Cuny has a different explanation (cf. above, fn. 59). Pedersen's explanation is by no means completely satisfactory, since it posits a form for the existence of which there is, so far as I know, no other evidence whatsoever; but none the less it seems to me much more plausible than Cuny's.

[825] Cf. Pedersen, *Toch.* 44.

[826] As in Indo–Iranian I omit diacritics (including henceforth the one on the initial *n* in the word for 'name', which I of necessity employed in §260) except macrons.

262. From A. 18b2 Khadgavisānakalpā nom mskatar 'he (his) name is Khadgavisāna'. 73a5 sas tas lānt se maskit Mukaphalku nom 'this (is) here the son of the king, (his) name Prince Mukaphalgu'.

263. From B. 2b4 Jātisrone nem brāhmane 'a Brahman (his) name Jatisrona'. 19a3 sakkets soy sai ksa Hastake nem ostmem ltu 'there was a certain son of the Sakyas, (his) name Hastaka, gone out of the house'.

264. Since the words to which *nom* and *nem* relate are uniformly nominatives, and since *nom* and *nem* themselves may be either nominative or accusative, we have our familiar formula, *homo nomen Iulius*. Hence the Tocharian examples, though so much later than the Sanskrit ones that we examined above (§§44–47), still present the same state of affairs as they do. However, the Tocharian testimony is not necessarily of independent value, since the usage may be a borrowing from Sanskrit[827] and not a native inheritance at all.

[827] I make this statement on the authority of Professor Lane.

CONCLUSION

265. There seems to be no indication that in naming-constructions we have an accusative of specification inherited from Indo–European. What I believe was inherited was the very common use of the word for 'name' (*nomen*) in partitive apposition with the word denoting the owner of the name (*homo*).[828] From the nature of the case, when *homo* and *nomen* appeared in apposition, *homo* was usually in the nominative or accusative:[829] (*est*) *homo nomen Iulius*[830] or *hominem nomen Iulium nominant*.[831] But as a result of the shift from parataxis to hypotaxis which brought about the ultimate and almost total disappearance[832] of this primitive type of expression in favor of a more complex and sophisticated one, namely, a nominative or accusative with modifying genitive, *nomen* as an appositive which could be either nominative or accusative[833] might be wrongly interpreted as invariably accusative.

[828] See §10.

[829] When *homo* and *nomen* are in *different* cases, as in *homo Iulium* (or *Iulius*) *nomen habet*, *homini Iulius* (or *Iulio*) *nomen est*, and *homini Iulium* (or *Iulio*) *nomen indunt*, *nomen* is clearly either a subject or an object, and obviously no one would think of calling it an accusative of specification. (For these constructions see fn. 25 and §§14 and 17.)

[830] See §§6 and 7.

[831] See §13.

[832] Never completely total, of course. Instances of this type of expression are still met in the publications of the present day. I cite just two examples (italics mine). One is from the press, *New York Herald Tribune* (November 24, 1955), p. 1: "Senator Walter E. George, D., Ga., an influential *voice* in Congress, appealed today to both political parties." The other is from a recent novel, Angela Thirkell's *Enter Sir Robert* (New York, 1955), p. 80: "Sylvia was telling her father about her children, their *beauty*, *charm* and *intelligence*."

[833] Only in languages in which *nomen* had ceased to be neuter would this not be true. Neuter *n*-stems became masculine in West Germanic, Baltic, and Tocharian (see fn. 14), but none of these languages provides relevant evidence. Gothic and Old English apparently do not employ the word for 'name' either as an appositive as I believe many Indo–European languages originally did, or as an accusative of specification (see fn. 14 and §272). Lithuanian and Lettish do not use our stem for 'name' (see fn. 1), and Old Prussian has no apposite examples (see fn. 14). Tocharian masculines from Indo–European neuters keep the nominative and accusative alike (see fn. 14 and §260).

266. However, where this happened, I believe it was an independent development within each particular language.[834] The only indubitable proof that it did happen would be the appearance of the potentially nominative-accusative *nomen* beside a case of *homo* other than the nominative or accusative, and this so far as I know is never clearly exemplified except in Greek.

267. Certainly Hittite does not seem to have progressed beyond what I take to be the partitive apposition stage. In this language partitive apposition still abounds:[835] the language *can* say *hominis nomen*, and is very likely to do so if the structure of the sentence demands it; but when it does say *homo nomen* or *hominem nomen*, I see no reason for explaining the phrase in any way except as an instance of partitive apposition.[836]

268. In Sanskrit[837] all the examples known to me of *nāma* in the use here under consideration involve its combination with a nominative or an accusative.[838] In Avestan we perhaps find one passage containing an instance of *nama* with a genitive, but this is not only late but highly dubious.[839] In Old Persian too we find two examples with a genitive, but these again are very late, and furthermore are in badly written texts, in both of which nominative and genitive forms seem to be used almost indiscriminately;[840] and in an earlier period of Old Persian, there is the strongest reason to believe that *nāmă* was still a nominative, since it altered in gender to agree with nominative nouns.[841] Therefore in Old Persian, at least the development of 'name' into an accusative

---

[834] I believe this *may* have been true also of words of size, dimension, etc., which are used as 'name' is in both Avestan and Greek (see §12 and fn. 378).

[835] See §§20–21.

[836] See §§22–23.

[837] The employment in this language of *nāma* as an adverb may be thought to suggest that it was also an accusative denoting specification (see §43), but it certainly does not prove it (see fn. 156); and the seemingly tautological use of *nāma* with another case of the same word would in my opinion tend to disprove it (see §52).

[838] See §43.

[839] See §57.

[840] See §§113–14.

[841] See especially §§64 and 74–78. Because of this alteration in gender, I have regularly treated Old Persian *nāmă nāmā nāmă* as an adjective (on the form, see §87) modifying the word for *homo*, i.e. the noun designating the possessor of the name. But it might also be possible (as I did indeed suggest in §88) to treat it as a second noun in apposition with *homo*, and agreeing with it in gender as perhaps in Sanskrit the appositive *Iulius*, changed to *Iulium*, agrees in gender with the word for *homo*; see above, §51, on Thieme's explanation for the gender of *dhenu* in *RV* 6.66.1. As I said there, it seems to me to matter

of specification, whether or not it ultimately took place, had *not* taken place at the time of the earliest records.[842] If there was no accusative of specification meaning 'in name' for Old Persian to inherit, there was presumably none for Avestan to inherit, and the latter must have developed its accusative of specification independently if it really did develop it (which I doubt); and if there was no accusative of specification for these two Iranian languages to inherit, there was presumably none for Indic (i.e. Sanskrit) to inherit. And if there was none for Indo–Iranian to inherit, there was presumably none for Greek or any other Indo–European language to inherit.

269. Indeed, at the earliest stage of literary Greek that we possess at present—Homer[843]—there is no convincing evidence for an accusative of specification 'in name' any more than in Sanskrit.[844] For 'race' yes,[845] but for 'name' no.[846] But we can see in Homer the conditions that tend toward producing the development of the usage; and by the time of the Homeric Hymns this development has already taken place, at least so far as *epiklêsin* is concerned.[847] Herodotus contains sure examples of the accusative of specification with both *epiklêsin* and *epônymiên*,[848] and Xenophon some possible examples with *onoma* itself;[849] but a positive example with *onoma*, proved such by its combination with a genitive,[850] occurs for the first time, so far as I know, as late as Plutarch.[851] In view of the much greater difficulty of demonstrating the occurrence of the usage in a neuter word than in one of animate gender, I am ready to believe that what is true of its synonym

---

little whether we call the word agreeing in gender an adjective modifier or a substantive appositive; perhaps the second explanation is even more in line than the first with my treatment of *homo*, *nomen*, and *Iulius* as all in apposition with one another.

[842] Of course it might be argued that in Old Persian we have misinterpretation of an inherited accusative of specification as a nominative, but this seems much less likely than misinterpretation of an inherited nominative or accusative appositive as an accusative.

[843] Alas that the use of Linear B was—seemingly—limited to purely utilitarian purposes! Whether we shall ever obtain any specimens of pre-Homeric literature still remains on the knees of the gods.

[844] See §§116–17.

[845] See §132.

[846] And, as it happens, the same is true of Homer's imitator Vergil. See §160, also §270 and fn. 853.

[847] See §134.

[848] See §135.

[849] See §§137–38.

[850] See §268.

[851] See §139.

epiklêsin may also apply to *onoma*, and that where the latter word seems to be used as an accusative of specification in e.g. Herodotus or Xenophon, it really is so used, and is no longer an appositive. But *only* in Greek did anything so extensive evolve, and there is no evidence that it was inherited. If the Linear B material should reveal a clear instance of an accusative of specification,[852] I shall, or at least I may, have to revise my ideas on the subject. But unless and until that happens, I shall insist that the use of 'name' as an accusative of specification is purely a Greek construction well entitled *accusativus graecus*, and derived, like other instances of the Greek accusative,[853] from partitive apposition.

270. Latin seems not to have used *nomen* in this way at all, with the possible exception of three passages in the *Aeneid*,[854] which, if they do

[852] In answer to a query from me as to whether such a construction can be cited for Linear B, Professor Emmett L. Bennett of the Institute of Research in the Humanities, University of Wisconsin, very kindly provided me with two possible instances. These are *PY Ta* 641.1 ti-ri-po a-pu ke-ka-u-me-no ke-re-a₂ and *Ta* 708.1 to-no a-ja-me-no o-pi-ke-re-mi-ni-ja e-re-pa-te; with the latter we may compare the extremely similar *Ta* 714.1 to-no a-ja-me-no ku-wa-no pa-ra-ku-we-qe ku-ru-so-qe o-pi-ke-re-mi-ni-ja. These are translated by Ventris and Chadwick, *Doc.* 336, 344, and 344 respectively, as "one tripod cauldron, burnt away at the legs", "one chair inlaid with ivory on the back", and "one chair, inlaid with *kyanos* and silver and gold on the back". *Doc.* specifically explains ke-re-a₂ as "accusative of respect" (337), and in the vocabulary classes ke-re-a₂ (i.e. *skelea*) as "acc. plur. neuter" (396) and o-pi-ke-re-mi-ni-ja as "acc. plur. fem." (402). But both can just as well be nominatives: in neuter nouns the nominative and accusative are of course identical, and in feminine a-stems they are written alike, the final *a* representing both the nominative plural ending -ai and the accusative plural ending -ans (*Doc.* 83). They would then be in partitive apposition with the nominative nouns ti-ro-po 'tripod cauldron' in the first and with to-no 'chair' in the second and third; and the meaning would be literally "one tripod cauldron, (its) legs, burnt away" for the first and "one chair, (its) back, inlaid" for the other two. In that case Mycenaean Greek differs from Homeric Greek but resembles Hittite in its ability to place a body-part noun in partitive apposition with a nominative; see above, fn. 60.

[853] On this development in general, once more (cf. fn. 298) I refer to my article in *TAPA* 85.197-289, especially 254-89. I discuss there mainly the development, already complete in Homer, of the accusative of specification in words denoting parts of the body (see especially 219-39, 254-79, 282-86); but I also refer to the similar use of general words —mainly neuters—denoting size, length, width, shape, form, etc. (289). Since the words take the same construction in Avestan, it is possible that this particular construction is inherited; but whether it evolved in Indo-European or, as is also possible, independently in Avestan and Greek, I think it must be traced in its origin to partitive apposition.

[854] These are 3.613-14 and 12.514-15 (discussed in §148), in which the reading *nomine* is also met; and 3.692-94 (discussed in §156), in which *nomen* may be the direct object of *dixere* (also a Grecism) rather than an accusative of specification.

illustrate the construction, are certainly to be explained as Grecisms.[855]

271. Tocharian is at the same stage as Sanskrit, and perhaps the construction it did have was borrowed from Sanskrit.[856]

272. The evidence is against the existence of anything of the sort in Germanic, at least so far as Gothic and Old English go. In the one instance in *NT* Greek where Wulfila met a possible use of *onoma* (in the contracted form *tounoma*) as an accusative of specification,[857] he apparently did not recognize it as such; at all events he did not render it by an accusative of specification[858] (which he does sometimes use when he meets an accusative of specification referring to parts of the body[859]), or by a dative of specification (which is his normal construction for 'in name'[860]). Old English apparently uses neither an accusative nor a dative of specification for 'in name' when it encounters the ablative of specification *nomine* in the Vulgate, but renders it by a prepositional phrase, or substitutes a clause, either purely paratactic or quasi-relative.[861] This is particularly striking because it does use a dative to translate *nomine* as an ablative of source or of means.[862]

273. Old Irish[863] resembles Old Persian[864] in its very common use, when a person not previously mentioned is introduced in the course of a narrative, of a stock formula (*erat*) *homo Iulius nomen*[865]—or rather,

[855] Indeed, I believe this to be true of the accusative of specification in general as used in Latin, where it seems everywhere to have been a borrowing from Greek by artificially Hellenizing writers (I discuss this in *TAPA* 91.221–38). If I am right in my view that the native development in Greek of the accusative of specification, including the special type 'in name', has its origin in partitive apposition, its absence in Latin is a natural result of the comparative rarity in Latin of partitive apposition, especially in the accusative (I discuss this in *TAPA* 84.92–123; on the accusative in particular, see 102–3 and 102 fn. 52). On Vergil's possible use of 'name' as an accusative of specification, see above, §148.

[856] See §264.
[857] See §§182 and 190.
[858] See §§183 and 191.
[859] See fn. 477.
[860] See §181.
[861] See §197.
[862] See §193.

[863] All our evidence so far as Celtic goes must be sought in Gaelic. Brittanic is practically useless for the purpose, since it has lost all case distinctions (cf. §250). The remains of Gallic and our understanding of them are alike so scanty that consideration of them seems hopeless (cf. Pedersen, *KG* 1.3).

[864] See fn. 208.
[865] See §§224 and 233.

in the case of Old Irish,[866] (*erat*) *homo Iulius nomen suum*.[867] Here *nomen*, so far as I know, has never been explained as an accusative of specification—a construction which seems to be lacking in Old Irish.[868] It apparently is usually interpreted as subject or predicate nominative of an interpolated paratactic clause, and indeed there are instances where it must be such;[869] but in general it seems to me possible and even preferable to interpret it here as elsewhere as an appositive.[870]

274. To sum up then—wherever an Indo–European language[871] uses the construction *homo nomen Iulius* at all, the evidence seems to me to point to an inherited use of *nomen* as in partitive apposition with *homo* (or *hominem*) and not as an accusative of specification.

---

[866] As in that of Hittite; cf. §20.

[867] See §§226 and 232.

[868] See §231 and fn. 744.

[869] See §§238–39, 241–44.

[870] See §234.

[871] At least so far as those go which are dealt with in the present study. (On my use of the term "Indo–European", see fn. 1.)

INDEX OF PASSAGES CITED

The passages are grouped under languages, and the languages arranged in the order in which they are treated in the monograph: Hittite, Sanskrit, Avestan, Old Persian, Greek, Latin, Gothic, Old English, Gaelic, Welsh, Cornish, Breton, Tocharian, Old Church Slavonic, and Armenian. Within languages, works (or authors) are arranged alphabetically. The form of the reference is generally that used by Professor Hahn in the text or footnotes, but occasional cross-references and bibliographical notes have been added.

Numbers in straight type refer to the numbered paragraphs of the text, while numbers in italic type refer to footnotes.

HITTITE

The standard abbreviations for Hittite texts are conveniently interpreted in the front of J. Friedrich, *Hethitisches Elementarbuch* or *Hethitisches Wörterbuch*.

ABoT
  48: *70*
  48.5: *113, 121*
  48.6: *111*
  62.1.38: 33
Appus (see also KUB 24.8, Bo 2595, ABoT 48; see fn. 70)
  1.8–9: *69*
  1.29–30: *69*
Bilingue of Hattusilis I (see Sommer, *HAB*)
  2.24: *85*
  3.65: *59*
Bo
  2527.2.11–13: *60*
  2595: *70*
  2595.2.7: 33, *115*
  4473: *70*

4473.2.2: *132*
8143: *70*
8206: *70*
Ges.
  2 §53: *69*
Hatt.
  1.40: 33
  1.45: 33
  3.38–39: *119*
  3.78: *119*
  4.12: 33
  4.18: 33
  4.29–30: *119*
  4.61: *119*
Hukk.
  2.25: *71*
KBo
  2.5.3.54: *71*
  3.3.1.7–8: *85*
  3.4.1.23–24: *100*
  3.4.2.12: *100*
  4.6.1.15: *75*
  4.12.1.1: *132*
  4.12.1.4: *132*
  4.12.2.5: *132*
  5.6.3.22: *90*
  5.11.1.6–7: 20

6.2 §9: *64*, 67
6.3 §9: 21, *64*
6.3 §§11, 12, 13, 14: 21
6.3 §15: 21
6.3 §16: 21
6.4 §VIII: 21, *67*
6.4 §IX: 21
6.4 §§X, XI, XII, XIII: 21
6.4 §§XIV, XV: 21
6.5 §15: 21
6.29.1.1: *132*
6.29.1.16: *119*
6.29.1.35–36: *119*
6.29.2.20–23: *87*
6.29.2.25: 25, *91*
6.29.2.37–38: *119*
6.34.3.27–28: *90*
KUB
  1.1.1.1: *132*
  1.1.1.10: *132*
  1.1.1.14: *132*
  1.1.1.49: 33
  1.1.4.22: *132*
  1.1.4.81: *132*
  1.1.4.87: *132*
  1.4.1.41: 33

[Numbers in straight type refer to the numbered paragraphs of the text, while numbers in italic type refer to footnotes.]

[Numbers in straight type refer to the numbered paragraphs of the text, while numbers in italic refer to footnotes.]

[Numbers in straight type refer to the numbered paragraphs of the text, while numbers in italic type refer to footnotes.]

[Numbers in straight type refer to the numbered paragraphs of the text, while numbers in italic type refer to footnotes.]

As.
10: 142
652: *391*
780: *435*
Aul.
164: 143, *674*
829: *90*
Bacch.
704: 142
945: *399*
Capt.
69: 143, *674*
174–177: *390*
239–42: *390*
285: 142
288: 141, *390, 412*
398: *390*
498: *390*
573: *389*
585: *390*
590: *391*
631: *390*
726: *399*
820: *399*
878: *405*
983–84: 143, *397*
Cas.
695: *477*
Cist.
154: 142, *470*
465: *395*
773: 142
Curc.
76–77: 142
Men.
42–43: *399*
44: *391*
77: 143, *470*
263: 143, *470*
297: 142
298: *391*
383: *391*
511–12: *477*
1068: 142
1096: 142
1107: 142
1122: *391*

1122–23: 142
1126: 143, *399*
1131: 142
1135: *391*
Merc.
516: 142
517: *390*
Mil.
86: 142
435: *391*
436: 142, 144, *45, 500*
Most.
70: *395*
Pers.
623–24: 142
700–5: 142
Poen.
92: 142, 164
Pseud.
185: *391*
636–37: 144, *397*
637: *395*
653: 142
655: *395*
744: 142
977: 142
988–90: 142
Rud.
5: 142, *470*
32–33: 142
236: *391*
934: *399*
Stich.
174: 143
239: *395*
242: 141, *422*
Trin.
8: *399*
18: 142
18–20: 143
390–91: 142
391: *469, 470*
843: *399, 470*
889: 142
889–91: *395*
927: *391*

Truc.
12: 142, *12*
Propertius
1.18.31: *205, 461*
Suetonius
Nero
49.1: *43*
Terence
Phorm.
739: *435*
Velleius Paterculus
1.11.2: *467*
Vergil
Aen.
1.247: *467*
1.267–68: 150, *405*
1.267–71: *405*
1.275–76: *405*
1.286–88: 151, 155, *422*
1.288: 153, *405, 440*
1.292: *405*
1.530: 146, 156, *12, 405, 407, 408*
1.532–33: *407, 408*
1.573: *276*
2.89: 152, 159
2.392–93: *477*
3.18: *405, 408, 420, 430*
3.132–34: *405*
3.133: *422*
3.163: 146, 156, *12, 405*
3.210–11: 146, *12*
3.334: *405*
3.334–35: 146, *405, 407*
3.350: 146, 147, 163, *405, 411*
3.613–14: 148, *854*
3.614: *4*
3.692–94: 156, *854*
3.693: *4*
3.693–95: *12*
3.702: 146, *405, 407*
4.12: 158

[Numbers in straight type refer to the numbered paragraphs of the text, while numbers in italic type refer to footnotes.]

[Numbers in straight type refer to the numbered paragraphs of the text, while numbers in italic type refer to footnotes.]

Tain (St.) (Cont.)
  10.6–7: 225
  10.7–8: 225
  12.12–13: 225
  12.22: 226
  12.22–23: 235
  15.6–7: 227
  15.10–11: 236, *779*
  15.11: 226
  17.5–6: 236
  17.6: 226
  17.14–15: 236
  17.15: 226
  17.22–23: 236
  17.23: 226
Tain (YBL)
  777: *760*
  786–87: *760*
  810–11: 236, *766*
  811: 226
Thes.
  2.240.13–14: 237
Troi
  4 (9.209–10): 227, *780*
  8 (15.415–16): 249
Uisl.
  5 (44.52): 225
  5 (44.52–53): 239
Uisn.
  8 (122.8): 227, *780*
Usn.
  5 (69.23–24): 239
  5 (69.24): 225
Wb.
  5a.17: 225, *720*

WELSH

For abbreviations, see footnote 804.

BDe
  1.8: 251
  2.14–15: 253

3.4: 251
3.5: 257
10.7: 254, *810*
Branwen
  211: 257
Martin
  9.3–4: *805*
Pwyll
  190–91: 254, *810*
  546: 257
  616: 253
  619–21: 258
  620: 257
  620–21: 251
  621: *806*
RBH
  2.64.27: 253
  2.64.28: 253
  2.64.29–30: 251

CORNISH

For abbreviations, see footnote 804.

BMer
  1: 254
  511–12: 256
  831: 251, *806*
  970: 254
  1072–73: 254
  2465: 256
O
  1: 253
  120: 257
  123: 253
  135: 257
  678: 251
Pascon
  124: 254
  174: 252
  214: 256
  234: 252

R
  197: 254
  1471–72: 256

BRETON

For abbreviations, see footnote 804.

Barbe
  6: 255
  132: 254
Nonne
  14–15: 256
  74: 254
Patrice
  124: 254
  568: 257

TOCHARIAN A

SS
  18b2: 262
  73a5: 262

TOCHARIAN B

SS, B
  2b4: 263
  19a3: 263

OLD CHURCH SLAVONIC

Leskien 238 (Codex Suprasliensie): 7

ARMENIAN

Bible
Lk.
  1.5: 5